WAR AND SOCIETY IN
EARLY-MODERN EUROPE
1495–1715

WAR IN CONTEXT
Series editor: Jeremy Black

WAR AND SOCIETY IN EARLY-MODERN EUROPE, 1495–1715

Frank Tallett

London and New York

For Judy

First published 1992
by Routledge
11 New Fetter Lane, London EC4P 4EE

Simultaneously published in the USA and Canada
by Routledge
29 West 35th Street, New York, NY 10001

First published in paperback 1997

Reprinted 2001

Routledge is an imprint of the Taylor & francis Group

© 1992 Frank Tallett

Typeset in 10/12pt Bembo by
Ponting–Green Publishing Services, Chesham, Bucks
Printed in Great Britain by
T. J. International Ltd, Padstow, Cornwall

British Library Cataloguing in Publication Data
Tallett, Frank,
War and Society in early-modern Europe, 1495–1715. -
(War in context)
I. Title II. Series
940.2

Library of Congress Cataloguing in Publication Data
Tallett, Frank.
War and society in early modern Europe, 1495–1715 / Frank Tallett.
p.   cm. – (War in context)
Includes bibliographical references.
1. Europe–History, Military.   2. Europe–History–1492–1648.
3. Europe–History–1648–1715   I. Title.   II. Series.
D214.T35   1992
940.2–dc20   91-43901

ISBN 0–415–02476–5 (hbk)
ISBN 0–415–16073–1 (pbk)

CONTENTS

PREFACE

War has long been acknowledged as a central feature of the history of early-modern Europe. Yet, until quite recently, historical enquiry into the subject has been characterized by a predominant concern with battles, tactics and campaigns and a neglect of any consideration of the ways in which war impinged upon, and emerged out of, the institutional, social and economic structures of the period. This book, which grew out of a course taught in the University of Reading, is an attempt to situate war in its historical context. Though it deals with the technicalities of waging war and the ordinary soldier's experience of conflict, it does not seek to provide a conventional military history of the campaigns of the early-modern period. Instead, it seeks to address other issues: why wars were fought; how armies were raised; the motives which impelled men to volunteer; the realities of life for the common soldier; war's multifarious impact upon the economy and civilian society; the implications for the development of state institutions of the waging of war; and attitudes towards war. I have not attempted to cover naval affairs, although a discussion of such matters would have been germane to many of the themes covered in the book. To have done so would have meant extending still further a text which is already long. Nor have I sought to cover countries lying to the north and east of Germany. Not only do I lack the necessary linguistic skills to deal adequately with them, I am not wholly convinced that developments in, say, Russia and Poland can be meaningfully discussed in the contexts of trends and changes which were, in many respects, particular to western and central Europe.

Anyone who writes a work of synthesis acquires a mass of

debts, and I am grateful to the large number of scholars, many of whose names are cited in the notes and bibliography, on whose work I have drawn. However, I wish to acknowledge the particular debt I owe to the writings of Michael Roberts, Geoffrey Parker and John Hale. Their works first awakened my interest in war as a subject of academic enquiry and have subsequently provided a continuing source of ideas and information. My thanks are also due to Anne Curry and Stephen Taylor who read various parts of the text and saved me from a number of errors of fact and interpretation; I, of course, am responsible for the errors which remain. My thanks also go to Karin Mochan who assisted with the translation of Dutch and Scandinavian material; and to Carol Mackay, Elizabeth Berry and, above all, Gill Fearon, for tirelessly typing and re-typing drafts of the book.

F.T.
Reading 1991

MAPS

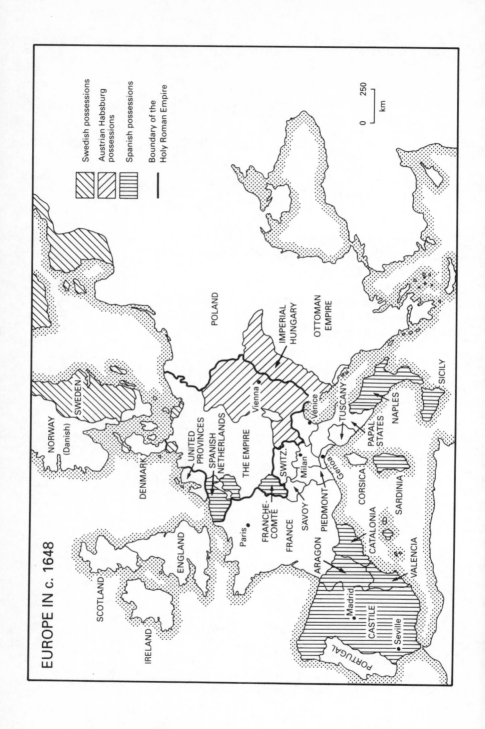

EUROPE IN c. 1648

Swedish possessions

Austrian Habsburg possessions

Spanish possessions

Boundary of the Holy Roman Empire

0   250
km

NORWAY (Danish)

SWEDEN

DENMARK

SCOTLAND

IRELAND

ENGLAND

UNITED PROVINCES

SPANISH NETHERLANDS

THE EMPIRE

POLAND

IMPERIAL HUNGARY

OTTOMAN EMPIRE

Vienna

SWITZ.

FRANCHE-COMTÉ

Paris

FRANCE

SAVOY

PIEDMONT

Milan

Genoa

Venice

TUSCANY

PAPAL STATES

NAPLES

SICILY

CORSICA

SARDINIA

ARAGON

CATALONIA

VALENCIA

CASTILE

Madrid

Seville

PORTUGAL

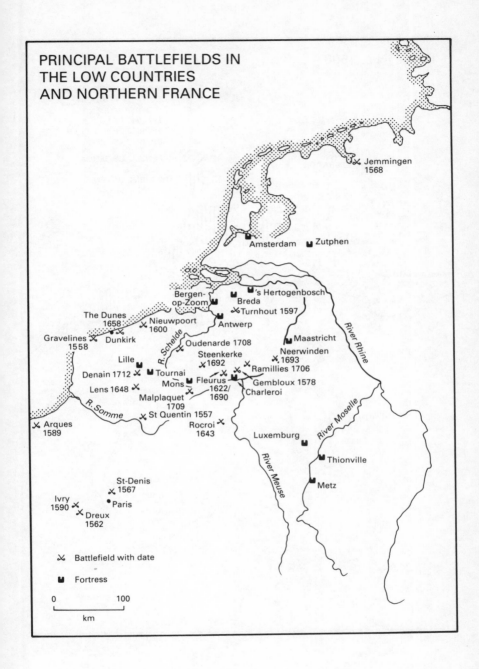

PRINCIPAL BATTLEFIELDS IN
THE LOW COUNTRIES
AND NORTHERN FRANCE

Jemmingen
1568

Amsterdam   Zutphen

Bergen-
op-Zoom   's Hertogenbosch
          Breda
The Dunes   Turnhout 1597
1658   Nieuwpoort   Antwerp
Gravelines   1600   Maastricht
1558   Dunkirk
          Oudenarde 1708
          Steenkerke   Neerwinden
Lille   1692   1693
Denain 1712   Tournai   Ramillies 1706
Lens 1648   Mons   Gembloux 1578
          Fleurus   Charleroi
Malplaquet   1622/
1709   1690
St Quentin 1557
Arques   Rocroi   Luxemburg
1589   1643
          Thionville

          Metz

St-Denis
1567
Ivry   Paris
1590   Dreux
1562

R. Schelde
R. Somme
River Rhine
River Moselle
River Meuse

✗   Battlefield with date

🏰   Fortress

0   100
⊢————————⊣
      km

ITALY IN c. 1500

1 MARQUISATE OF MONTFERRAT
2 MARQUISATE OF MANTUA
3 DUCHY OF FERRARA
4 DUCHY OF MODENA
5 REPUBLIC OF LUCCA
6 REPUBLIC OF FLORENCE
7 REPUBLIC OF SIENA

REPUBLIC OF GENOA

REPUBLIC OF VENICE

SWISS
CONFEDERATION

GRAUBÜNDEN

Valtelline

DUCHY OF
SAVOY

Milan

PIEDMONT
Turin

DUCHY
OF MILAN

2

Venice

MARQUISATE
OF SALUZZO

1

3

4

5

Florence

6

Siena

PAPAL
STATES

7

CORSICA
(Genoa)

Rome

KINGDOM
OF NAPLES
(Spain)

Naples

KINGDOM OF
SARDINIA
(Spain)

Palermo

KINGDOM OF
SICILY
(Spain)

0   150

km

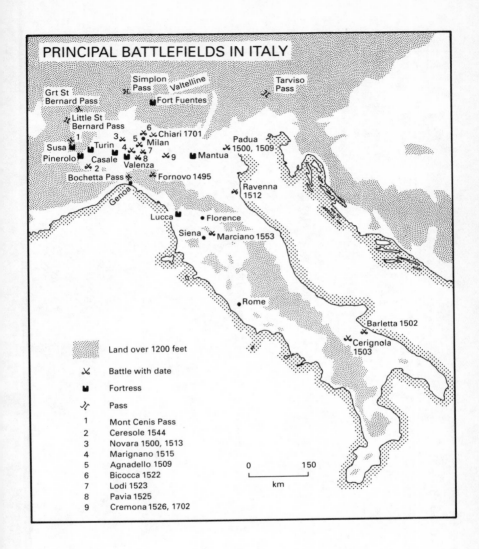

PRINCIPAL BATTLEFIELDS IN ITALY

Grt St Bernard Pass
Little St Bernard Pass
Simplon Pass
Valtelline
Fort Fuentes
Tarviso Pass
1
3
5
6
Chiari 1701
Milan
Padua 1500, 1509
Susa
Turin
4
7
Pinerolo
Casale
8
9
Mantua
Valenza
2
Bochetta Pass
Fornovo 1495
Ravenna 1512
Genoa
Lucca
Florence
Siena
Marciano 1553
Rome
Barletta 1502
Cerignola 1503

Land over 1200 feet

Battle with date

Fortress

Pass

1   Mont Cenis Pass
2   Ceresole 1544
3   Novara 1500, 1513
4   Marignano 1515
5   Agnadello 1509
6   Bicocca 1522
7   Lodi 1523
8   Pavia 1525
9   Cremona 1526, 1702

0   150
km

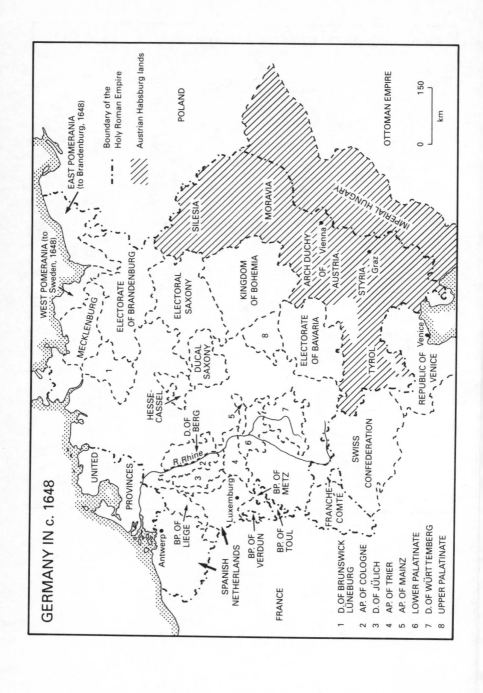

GERMANY IN c. 1648

Boundary of the
Holy Roman Empire

Austrian Habsburg lands

1 D. OF BRUNSWICK
    LÜNEBURG
2 AP. OF COLOGNE
3 D. OF JÜLICH
4 AP. OF TRIER
5 AP. OF MAINZ
6 LOWER PALATINATE
7 D. OF WÜRTTEMBERG
8 UPPER PALATINATE

EAST POMERANIA
(to Brandenburg, 1648)

WEST POMERANIA (to
Sweden, 1648)

POLAND

OTTOMAN EMPIRE

0   150
         km

MECKLENBURG

UNITED
PROVINCES

Antwerp

SPANISH
NETHERLANDS

FRANCE

BP. OF
LIEGE

Luxemburg

BP. OF
VERDUN

BP. OF
TOUL

BP. OF
METZ

R. Rhine

D. OF
BERG

HESSE-
CASSEL

ELECTORATE
OF BRANDENBURG

ELECTORAL
SAXONY

DUCAL
SAXONY

KINGDOM
OF BOHEMIA

SILESIA

MORAVIA

ELECTORATE
OF BAVARIA

ARCH DUCHY
OF
AUSTRIA

Vienna

STYRIA

Graz

IMPERIAL HUNGARY

TYROL

REPUBLIC OF
VENICE

Venice

FRANCHE-
COMTÉ

SWISS
CONFEDERATION

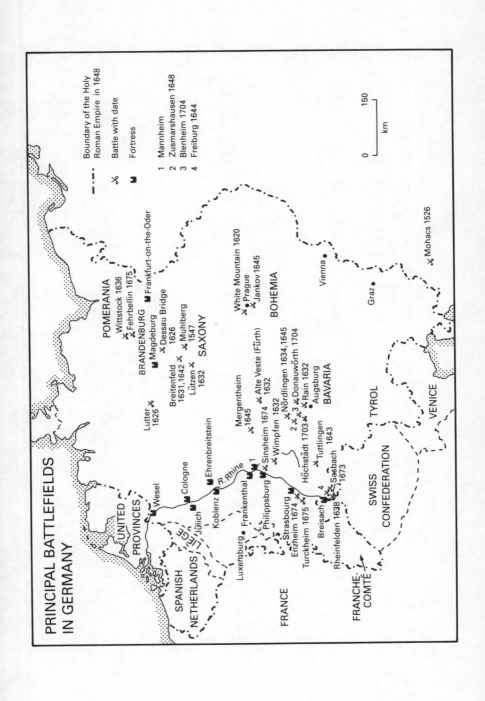

PRINCIPAL BATTLEFIELDS
IN GERMANY

- ·-·-· Boundary of the Holy
       Roman Empire in 1648
- ✗ Battle with date
- ▆ Fortress

1 Mannheim
2 Zusmarshausen 1648
3 Blenheim 1704
4 Freiburg 1644

0 ___ 150
    km

UNITED
PROVINCES

SPANISH
NETHERLANDS

FRANCE

FRANCHE-
COMTÉ

Wesel
Cologne
Ehrenbreitstein
Koblenz
R. Rhine
JÜLICH
Jülich
Luxemburg ● Frankenthal
1 ✗ Sinsheim 1674
Philippsburg ✗ Wimpfen 1632
Strasbourg
Enzheim 1674
Turckheim 1675 ✗
Höchstädt 1703 ✗
Breisach 1638
4
Sasbach
1673
Rheinfelden 1638

SWISS
CONFEDERATION

TYROL

VENICE

POMERANIA
Wittstock 1636
✗ Fehrbellin 1675
BRANDENBURG ▆ Frankfurt-on-the-Oder
Magdeburg ✗ Dessau Bridge
▆   1626
Breitenfeld ✗ Mühlberg
1631,1642 ✗   1547
Lützen   1632   SAXONY
1632

Lutter ✗
1626

Mergentheim
✗ 1645
Alte Veste (Fürth)
✗ 1632
2 ✗✗ 3 Nördlingen 1634,1645
✗ Donauwörth 1704
Rain 1632
Augsburg ●
✗ Tuttlingen   BAVARIA
1643

White Mountain 1620
✗ ● Prague
✗ Jankov 1645
BOHEMIA

Vienna ●

Graz ●

✗ Mohacs 1526

1

INTRODUCTION

REWRITING THE HISTORY OF WAR

The writing of military history has only just begun to escape from the unfortunate influence of its nineteenth- and early twentieth-century practitioners. For the most part these tended to be military men who wrote for other military men: either practising soldiers or teachers in the army staff colleges and training schools. The function of military history was seen as the provision of lessons and examples from the past of good generalship, strategy, tactical formations and the correct use of weapons. Military history was didactic, and since most nineteenth- and early twentieth-century soldiers saw the annihilation of the enemy's forces as the chief aim of all strategy, the history they wanted was chiefly one of battles: how they had been ordered, fought and won.

Academic historians for a long time hesitated to become involved in military history. They were not welcomed by practising soldiers, being regarded with deep suspicion as amateur dabblers; and the subject was not anyway regarded as a suitable one for members of the profession. On learning that Hans Delbrück was about to embark on a history of the art of war von Ranke opined that the subject was not worth the effort; and as late as 1939 Charles Oman, *doyen* of Anglo-Saxon military historians, felt obliged to include a justificatory chapter entitled 'A plea for military history' in his general work *On the Writing of History*. Moreover, even when they did belatedly enter the arena, academic historians did not markedly deviate from the battle- and campaign-oriented approach of their military predecessors. To be sure, Hans Delbrück did attempt to

1

relate military history to pertaining political forms and institutions, as the title of his monumental seven-volume *History of the Art of War in the Framework of Political History* suggests, arguing that in any period between the Persian Wars and Napoleon changes in one sphere produced alterations in the other.[1] And in the best Rankean tradition of scholarship, his work was characterized by a meticulous and critical approach to the sources (he showed, for example, that most accounts of battles vastly exaggerated the number of men involved), a characteristic the more especially laudable given the slapdash attitude of so many of his predecessors and contemporaries. Yet at no stage of his work did Delbrück provide a sustained analysis of the relationship between politics and war, and the uninformed reader might be forgiven for thinking that here was one more catalogue of campaigns through the ages.

Delbrück's influence was almost entirely confined to Germany, yet elsewhere academic historians displayed an approach to military history which was scarcely less narrow. In France, military writers remained obsessed with Napoleon, especially in the aftermath of the defeat by Prussia in 1870, when an analysis of his successful campaigns seemed to promise the lessons – in respect of generalship, strategy and tactics – which would avoid the repetition of a similar national disaster and possibly lay the basis for a restoration of France's military greatness. In England, the pattern for historical writing on military matters was established early on by the publication in 1851 of the amateur historian Sir Edward Creasy's influential *Fifteen Decisive Battles of the World*, and subsequently confirmed in the prolific writing of Sir Charles Oman, especially his seven-volume *History of the Peninsular War* (1902–30) on which subject he was an acknowledged expert, his *History of the Art of War in the Middle Ages* (1898, 1924) and the sequel, *A History of the Art of War in the Sixteenth Century* (1937). As he noted in the latter, his purpose was to depict the 'strategy, tactics and organisation of armies',[2] and these were illustrated by reference to a series of set-piece battles, which were loosely connected via a narrative framework dwelling on the political and diplomatic events of the period. In the hands of less competent practitioners than Oman this approach degenerated to become merely the chronicling of 'one damn battle after another', with interludes for the description of badges and buttons.

For all the very real worth of authors such as Oman this restricted, campaign- and battle-oriented approach does a disservice to the military history of the early-modern period (no less than to war in the Middle Ages, when, incidentally, knights were quite happy to get off their horses and fight on foot). It distorts our understanding of the nature of warfare which was not primarily characterized by pitched battles at all, but rather by sieges and what would now be called 'low-intensity operations': skirmishes, ambushes, raids, forays against civilians and prisoner-taking expeditions. Moreover, whole areas of enquiry which ought properly to be included in a study of warfare in the early-modern era, no less than in any other – the rank and file of an army, its supply, its camp-followers, relations with civilians, attitudes towards conflict for example – all go by default.

Set against this background the transformation which has taken place in the writing of military history in the last three decades or so can only be described as revolutionary. By taking advantage of the voluminous archive material which armies produced and by asking new questions of old material, historians have succeeded in elucidating a range of topics which were neglected by their predecessors. To be sure, much remains unclear. But we do now know a good deal more about the ordinary soldier for example: what impelled him to join up, what his conditions were like; about the 'tail' of an army: even the role of women in armies has been broached;[3] and thanks to the efforts of Jacquart, Gutmann and Friedrichs amongst others, we are better informed about the impact armies had on the economy and civilian life.[4] Even battle has been newly scrutinized, from the perspective of the ordinary soldier, in John Keegan's brilliantly evocative *The Face of Battle*, in which he seeks to demonstrate what it was actually like to participate in a set-piece engagement.[5] Indeed, what has not unfairly been termed the 'socialization' of military history has been carried so far that it is now near-impossible to produce a work on this topic without a reference to 'society' at some point in the title.[6]

The founding father of this new approach in France was André Corvisier, who, in 1964, produced a weighty study of his country's army in the late seventeenth and eighteenth centuries.[7] In the Anglo-Saxon world a shift in historians' perspective on military history was signalled in Michael Roberts's inaugural lecture to the University of Belfast in 1955: one of the few such occasions, surely, to produce a seminal piece of thinking.[8] In this he focused attention on the sixteenth and seventeenth centuries, and suggested that the years 1560–1660 in particular witnessed a military revolution. Changes in weaponry and tactical formations, he argued, lay at the heart of wider developments, which included an enormous growth in the size of armies, an increased impact of warfare on civilians and the emergence of more powerful states in the seventeenth and eighteenth centuries characterized by their burgeoning professional bureaucracies, their willingness to intervene in matters of finance and the economy and a disregard for existing social structures. Roberts's thesis has not gone unchallenged.[9] The profundity, nature, genesis and even the reality of the changes he outlined have all been questioned; but not the least of his contributions to scholarship has been to promote further research and thinking on a topic and a period which most historians – whether or not they accept the military revolution thesis in detail – would agree *did* witness profound changes in warfare and its wider importance.

SOLDIERS, SOLDIERS, SOLDIERS

One change in the sixteenth and seventeenth centuries to which Roberts pointed and on the reality of which there is general agreement was the dramatic increase in the number of men under arms. Indeed, this was such a marked feature of the period, and so heavy with consequences, that it demands at the outset some extended discussion and analysis.

The growth in numbers is difficult to quantify with any precision. A conventional way of measuring growth is to look at the major engagements during the period, since most contemporary early-modern accounts of battles give some indication of the size of the forces involved, albeit often exaggerated. An increase is indeed clearly discernible, apparently being most marked at the very end of the seventeenth and beginning of the eighteenth centuries (see Table 1). However, battle accounts do not provide a reliable indicator, not least of all since we now know that the extra men under arms were not necessarily put into field armies, but were to be found serving in garrisons, laying siege to cities and forts and occupying territory. A more reliable assessment of growth can be obtained by looking at the

Table 1   Numbers in battle

Date	Battle	Force	Number
1512	Ravenna	Spanish-Papal	15,500
1522	Bicocca	Imperialists	14,000
		French	23,000
1525	Pavia	Imperialists	20,000
		French	28,000
1544	Ceresole	Imperialists	13,000
		French	12,000
1562	Dreux	Huguenots	13,000
		Royalists	18,000
1590	Ivry	Henry IV	11,000
		Catholic League	16,000
1631	Breitenfeld I	Swedes/Saxons	41,000
		Imperialists	31,000
1632	Lützen	Swedes	19,000
		Imperialists	19,000
1634	Nördlingen	Swedes	23,000
		Imperialists	31,000
1644	Marston Moor	Royalists	15,000
1644	Freiburg	French	17,000
		Imperialists	17,000
1645	Jankov	Swedes	15,000
		Imperialists	15,000
1645	Naseby	Parliamentarians	12,000
		Royalists	9,000
1674	Enzheim	French	18,000
		Imperialists	32,000
1690	Fleurus	French	43,000
		Allies	37,000
1704	Blenheim	Allies	50,000
		French/Bavarians	54,000
1708	Oudenarde	Allies	76,000
		French/Bavarians/Spanish	80,000
1709	Malplaquet	Allies	105,000
		French/Bavarians	76,000

total numbers of men mobilized for a particular campaign or maintained permanently in a theatre of war. To establish this is an exercise fraught with difficulties, however, for all statistics produced by early-modern governments need to be treated with caution, most especially those connected with the military. Rulers and their ministers were incorrigible wishful thinkers: Philip IV, for example, claimed in 1625 to have 300,000 men under arms, whereas the real number was not much more than half this.[10] Generally, administrators simply did not know with any degree of accuracy how many men were actually serving. 'I am sure I may puzzle my brain to pieces, and not be able to make out such an account', was the frank and unusually honest response of one harassed official in the Secretary of State for War's office when pressed on the matter by Parliament in 1710.[11] In theory, records of musters should have provided administrators with accurate totals of men present, especially as musters were subject to increasing scrutiny by cost-conscious royal officials in the later seventeenth century, but in fact fraudulent captains continued by a variety to means to pad out the actual numbers in their units, the real size of which was continuously being reduced by sickness and the ceaseless flow of deserters. As a result, numbers fluctuated widely during a campaign, and 'paper' strengths were never attained, a state of

Table 2   Forces raised for a campaign or kept permanently in place

Year	Force/Campaign	Number
1494	Charles VIII's invasion of Italy	18,000
1499	Louis XII's invasion of Italy	23,000
1523	Henry VIII's invasion of France	20,000
1544	Henry VIII's invasion of France	40,000
1552	Imperialists in Metz campaign	45–50,000
1552	Effectives available to Charles V	150,000
1557	Spanish forces in Picardy campaign	43,000
1558	French troops in Picardy	48,000
1572	Spanish forces in Netherlands	61,000
1580	Philip II's annexation of Portugal	36,000
1598	Effectives available to Philip II	125,000
1607	Effectives available to Dutch States-General	54,000
1626	Spanish forces in Netherlands	48,000
1627	Effectives available to Wallenstein in Germany	90,000
1630	Effectives available to Wallenstein in Germany	120,000
1632	Swedish forces in Germany	105,000
1634	Total French effectives	48,000
1635	Total French effectives	70,000
1643	Effectives in Army of Flanders	70,000
1680s	Swedish peacetime forces	65,000
1691	Total French effectives	190,000
1708	Oudenarde campaign:	
	Allies	150,000
	French/Bavarian/Spanish	160,000
1710	Total French effectives	310,000

affairs which had perforce to be accepted by contemporary administrators. 'If you wish to have 50,000 men serving, you must raise 100,000,' was Richelieu's realistic advice to the king in his *Testament politique*, 'working on the assumption that a regiment of 20 companies which should include 2,000 men will in fact only have 1,000.'[12]

As a consequence, the figures in Table 2, which are culled from a number of sources and which I have sought to adjust up or (mainly) down in the interests of accuracy, must be regarded as very approximate. They nevertheless point clearly to a dramatic growth in the overall number of men under arms. Indeed, in two respects the figures may underplay the phenomenon. First, they do not fully reflect the growing permanence of armies. Governments throughout the period generally disbanded forces as soon as a campaign was over, either to save money or because they could not anyway be held together. Thus Louis XII's army of 23–29,000 men used to capture Milan in the summer of 1499 was dispersed back to France in November, a force of only 500 being retained to hold the city (a dubious economy since it was lost and had to be expensively re-taken); and following the seizure of Amiens from a Spanish garrison under Portocarrero in September 1597 Henry IV wrote to his sister Catherine, 'On Thursday evening I had 5,000 gentlemen [in the cavalry]: on Saturday at midday I have less than 500. Amongst the infantry the loss through disbanding is less, though still very great.'[13] But there was a tendency to retain a larger core of men in peacetime around which fresh forces could be assembled quickly in time of emergency. The Valois kings were first off the mark, Francis I building on schemes of his predecessors with a proposal in 1534 for the formation of seven permanent infantry *légions* comprising 42,000 men, a proposal which, however, was more successful on paper than in reality; it is doubtful if peacetime levels rose much above 10,000 at any time during the sixteenth century, and were down to 8,500 in 1598, having fallen below this during the chaos of the Religious Wars. Yet by 1626 Richelieu estimated peacetime requirements at 22,000, a figure which may actually have been attained. After the Peace of the Pyrenees (1659) the size of the army, which had expanded enormously during the Thirty Years War, was reduced to a strength of 55,000, being built up again during the Dutch and Devolution Wars, to be held at a peacetime level of

130,000 after the Treaty of Nijmegen in 1678, at about which level it hovered for the next one hundred years. By this stage certain regiments enjoyed a clearly established permanent existence safe from the threat of peacetime dissolution: the *Gardes Françaises, Maison du Roi, Gardes Suisses*, plus the six 'provincial' regiments of Picardy, Piedmont, Navarre, Champagne, Normandy and *La Marine*.[14] Similarly, the Spanish monarchy retained a nucleus of men in the Iberian peninsula after the conquest of Granada in 1492; and the subsequent acquisition of territory in Italy, notably Naples (1504) and Milan (1535) led to the permanent stationing of about 10,500 troops in the Italian dominions to guard against native rebellion and outside invasion. But its biggest force was the Army of Flanders, maintained in the Low Countries from 1569, which even during the Twelve Years Truce (1609–21) and after the Peace of the Pyrenees (1659) had a permanent core of 13–15,000 troops which could be expanded five- or sixfold in times of crisis.[15] Or again, Spain's occasional ally and competitor in the Mediterranean, Venice, had kept a permanent force of men since the first quarter of the fifteenth century, which by *c.* 1510 hovered around the 2,000 mark; it had more than doubled by the 1570s and stood at nearly 9,500 in 1615.[16]

Second, by the seventeenth century a number of small and medium sized states were supporting larger forces than ever before and doing so not just in time of war but also in time of peace. Whereas the sixteenth-century Vasa dynasty in Sweden had disposed of a handful of men, Charles XI maintained some 25,000 mercenaries, mainly in the Baltic provinces, in addition to yet larger numbers of native levies kept in the homeland. Within Germany, Brandenburg-Prussia was most notable for the expansion of its army: the Great Elector is generally regarded as having upwards of 30,000 troops at his death in 1688, a number which was to increase by one-third under his successor. But rulers in other German states, such as Hesse-Cassel, Württemberg, Saxony, Jülich and Berg, either because they wished to flex their muscles on the European scene or because they felt the need to look to their own defence once the protective umbrella provided by the Empire had been to some extent removed in the aftermath of the Peace of Westphalia, also sought to increase the size of their forces, though none of them matched Brandenburg-Prussia in this respect.[17]

Overall, we may posit a ten- or twelvefold increase in aggregate in the numbers of men under arms during the course of the sixteenth and seventeenth centuries. However, growth was not linear. The increase was marked in the first half of the sixteenth century, but reached a plateau around the 1550s. Charles V had a total of 148,000 men at his disposal, dispersed throughout his European and North African dominions in 1552; Henry II put together perhaps 40,000 for the attempt on Metz in 1552; whilst Philip II fielded 43,000 in July and August 1557 for his invasion of northern France, the largest single force thus far assembled by any monarch. Even England's military efforts reached a mid-century numerical climax in 1544 with Henry VIII's third French expeditionary force, numbering some 40,000. But these were levels which were unprecedented, and were not again attained until the seventeenth century.[18] Another round of expansion then took place, connected mainly with the Thirty Years War (1618–48), which raised numbers to a new peak. Spain, France, the Empire and Sweden were each, at one stage or another and on various fronts, supporting forces in excess of 100,000; and at the height of the fighting there were over one-quarter of a million men engaged in soldiering in Germany.[19] There followed a sharp reduction in numbers with the return to relative peace signalled by the treaties of Westphalia (1648), the Pyrenees (1659) and Oliva (1660), though peacetime forces nevertheless remained well above their pre-war levels. But this was short-lived, and the inflationary process received yet another sharp boost from the 1670s onwards, from which only Spain of the major powers was excluded (a sure sign of her decline), to peak at an all-time high around 1710, by which time there were some 860,000 serving soldiers in central and western Europe, compared to roughly 300,000 in 1609, with the figure rising to 1.3 million if forces in Poland, Russia and Turkey are added in.[20] Thereafter, numbers remained relatively stable throughout the eighteenth century, until the Revolutionary and Napoleonic Wars, which were marked by a further dramatic increase in army size.

Insignificant though these totals may be by twentieth-century standards, the multiplication of troops in the sixteenth and seventeenth centuries was wholly unprecedented, and marked a quantum leap forward in the number of men under arms. How is the phenomenon of growth in general, and how are the stages of growth in particular, to be explained?

Innovation in the technology of warfare undoubtedly played a part in the process. The development of more effective techniques of fortification between *c.* 1470 and 1520 rendered places defended in the 'new style' invulnerable to direct assault and meant that they could only be taken by being encircled and starved into surrender. Large numbers of men were required to enforce a blockade, and troops were also required in large quantities to garrison the growing number of sites which were defended by these 'new-style' fortifications. Also, changes in the types of hand weapons employed by soldiers engendered a shift in emphasis in early-modern armies away from the heavily armoured, laboriously trained cavalryman, who could be recruited only from the ranks of the nobility, to the more lightly armoured, easily equipped foot-soldier – the pikeman at first and then the newly proficient handgunner – who could be recruited from any section of society, and this may have removed one possible restraint on the growth in numbers. Moreover, the use of linear tactics, which evolved as the best means of utilizing the fire-power of the handgunners, gave advantages on the battlefield to those armies which could deploy the largest numbers of men. But on their own, these technological explanations for the prodigious increase in the number of men under arms are inadequate. Fundamentally it was a question of money and inter-state competition.

As contemporaries never tired of pointing out, *pecunia nervus belli*, and even infantrymen, who were relatively cheap to equip, nevertheless proved horrendously expensive when employed in large numbers. The initial expansion in the numbers of men under arms during the first half of the sixteenth century was only made possible by the fact that monarchs of the period were, in general, richer than their predecessors.[21] Their greater wealth derived in large part from what might be termed a 'revolution in monarchical finances' which occurred from *c.* 1450 on, and which involved the more effective exploitation by monarchs of their resources. For example, taxes which had hitherto been occasional – such as the *alcabala* and the *taille* – now became permanent, new imposts were introduced and the collection of taxes became more efficient. To be sure, not all monarchs were equally successful in the exploitation of their resources and it was the rulers of France and Spain who achieved the most conspicuous success in this respect and who, consequently, were the predominant military powers in Europe. One monarch in particular was fortunate: the Emperor Charles V. Partly by conquest and partly through a series of (for him) happy family marriages and deaths he came to rule a set of dominions which included Spain, parts of Italy, Sicily, Sardinia, the Low Countries, the Austrian patrimonial lands and the New World possessions, as well as being the elective Holy Roman Emperor, all of which gave him, potentially at least, access to resources greater than anything available to his contemporaries. He was able to field forces for service in the Mediterranean, Germany, France and against the Turks on Europe's eastern frontier. Rival rulers dared not allow their forces to be handicapped by being grossly outnumbered and what might loosely be termed an arms race developed, funded by increased monarchical wealth, with the Habsburgs leading the way closely pursued by France.

Yet one should not exaggerate. If rulers in the first half of the sixteenth century were richer than their predecessors they never succeeded in raising all the money they required; if the Habsburg power bloc appeared to give its rulers the key to mastery of Europe, nevertheless Charles, for all that he had extensive lands, also had extensive problems, and he was never successful in mobilizing sufficient resources to tackle them all successfully.[22] Armies might grow in size, but they were raised with difficulty; by about mid-century they had reached a numerical plateau, and there they stagnated for about half a century. In part this was because one of the major competitors in the race, France, was debilitated by internal civil war. But there were also indications that a sort of fiscal-administrative ceiling had been reached, as the institutional structures and fiscal resources available to monarchs proved inadequate to recruit, pay and supply forces of any greater size.

The next ratchet in the inflationary process came with the Thirty Years War. It might be supposed, and has indeed been argued, that this new round of expansion was only made possible by the existence of governments 'capable of organizing and controlling large forces'.[23] Yet this does not seem to have been the case. For all that the Habsburg war machine remained impressive in the 1630s and although many states had made improvements in their internal organization in the preceding decades, none of the rival states was really capable of raising on its own account all of the forces which it was to field during the extended conflict. This was only achieved by resort to large-scale military contractors, entrepreneurs who were prepared to substitute for the institutional structures and financial resources in which states were deficient by shouldering, in the short term, the administrative and fiscal burden of raising and supporting very large numbers of troops. Whole armies were supplied by these men to their employers on credit terms, the contractor subsequently being recompensed for his initial outlay by the profits of war and by deferred payments from the ruler's treasury. Even armies raised on this 'fight now pay later' basis stretched rulers' resources to breaking point, yet there was little alternative, for no state dared fall behind in this arms race since to do so would be to court military disaster: as one Spanish general commented in 1632, 'I have seen by experience in Germany that whoever has the larger army will win.'[24]

The final round in the inflationary cycle – and this time it was Louis XIV's France which led the way and the remaining states, sometimes in coalition, which endeavoured to keep up – was different. By this stage a number of states had become capable of mobilizing their financial and demographic resources to a hitherto unachieved degree in pursuit of ever larger armies. Not all states managed the trick, however: of the major powers Spain proved unable to compete during the second half of the seventeenth century, and the country which had for long set the pace in the expansion of troop levels now lagged far behind. Indeed, it seems clear that France too had overreached herself by the end of Louis XIV's reign. Both here and in other states another fiscal-administrative threshold had been reached, which would not be decisively broached until France's declaration of the *levée en masse* in 1793 and the development of a new kind of 'revolutionary' war.

There was no single reason for the dramatic expansion in the number of men under arms: it was a complex phenomenon which requires a complex explanation and we shall need to return to look in greater detail at aspects of the military, administrative and political factors involved, which have been sketched out in a necessarily rather brief and schematic form. What does seem clear, however, is that finance and inter-state rivalry had at least as much, and probably more, to do with the growth in troop levels than any purely technical changes connected with new weapons, fortifications or tactics.

But if the concept of an arms race explains the necessity for states to keep raising the size of their forces so as to match their opponents', it does not explain why they were needed: that is to say, the purpose to which they were put. An answer to that demands some consideration of why wars were fought.

WARS: WHEN, WHERE, WHY?

By any reckoning the early-modern period was a remarkably bellicose age. Even the rather artificial exercise of tabulating conflicts reveals as much. Between 1480 and 1700 England was involved in 29 wars, France in 34, Spain in 36 and the Empire in 25. In the century after 1610 Sweden and the Austrian Habsburgs were at war for two years in every three, Spain for three years in every four; indeed, in terms of its belligerency the seventeenth century was outstripped only by the twentieth.[25] Such figures gain added force when we consider that many of the conflicts were protracted, as their names imply (Eighty Years War, Thirty Years War), and involved continuous fighting: between April 1572 and April 1607, with a six-month ceasefire in 1577, and April 1621 to June 1647 in the case of the Eighty Years War, for example.[26]

The sixteenth century was ushered in by the Italian Wars. A series of campaigns waged between Charles VIII and Ferdinand and their successors in France and Spain for control of Naples and Milan, and which sucked in Venice, Genoa, Savoy, Piedmont and the papal states, blossomed into a broader rivalry between Habsburgs and Valois which helped to produce conflict north of the Alps. France was invaded – if that is not too strong a word – on three occasions by Henry VIII, and by the forces of Charles V and his son, Philip II; Luxembourg was overrun; 6,000 French troops even landed at Leith in Scotland in 1548; and in 1552–3 Henry II intervened in the Empire, in cooperation with a number of German princes, reversing the crushing military victory which Charles V had won over the Protestants in the earlier Schmalkaldic War of 1546–7. That this rivalry was not pursued more actively after the Peace of Cateau-Cambrésis (1559) was largely due to the Religious Wars which tore France apart between 1562 and 1598. Historians distinguish nine separate wars and peace agreements, but this is to impute a specious orderliness to a period in which fighting between rival factions, no less than outright brigandage, continued unabated regardless of the existence of truces and treaties. French internal weakness allowed Philip II an unaccustomed liberty in the conduct of foreign and domestic affairs. He was able to mount an effort against the Turks in the Mediterranean; suppress the revolt of the Moriscos in Granada (1568–70); successfully assert his claim to Portugal (1580); send an Armada against England; and, most importantly, to stage a huge military effort in the Netherlands, where he nevertheless struggled unsuccessfully to suppress a revolt – for the Dutch the Eighty Years War – which was not finally resolved until the formal recognition of the independence of the United Provinces in 1648.

During the sixteenth century the Baltic witnessed one war of major significance, the Seven Years War (1563–70), together with several localized conflicts. But these Baltic conflicts, and the Baltic states themselves, remained largely peripheral to the rest of Europe until they became involved in the general maelstrom known as the Thirty Years War. The term usually refers to the war fought in Germany (1618–48), but this involved a number of other overlapping conflicts. Only England's Civil War came to constitute a major exception to Gustavus Adolphus's observation that 'all the wars that are waged in Europe are commingled and become one', so that the Thirty Years War concerned virtually the whole of Europe.[27]

The second half of the seventeenth and the early-eighteenth centuries were dominated by the wars waged by and against the resurgent France of Louis XIV: the Devolution War (1667–8), the Dutch War (1672–9), the War of the League of Augsburg (1688–97) and the War of the Spanish Succession (1701–13). States involved in the last two conflicts numbered, in addition to France, the United Provinces, England, the Empire, Austria, Savoy, Brandenburg, Portugal, Bavaria and Spain. But it is worth noting that Franco–Spanish hostilities, opened in 1635, did not end until 1659, and there were significant conflicts in the north of Europe: between Denmark and Sweden in 1643–5 and again in 1657–60; the intermittent Scanian War of 1674–9; and, most important of all, the Great Northern War (1700–21) which involved a semi-concerted effort by Russia, Poland,

Denmark and Saxony to dismember Sweden's Baltic empire. And extending throughout the early-modern period were the hostilities with the Turks in the Mediterranean and on Europe's eastern frontier in Hungary, which were at their most pronounced in the decades before 1580, between 1593 and 1606, and in the 1680s and 1690s.

In addition to these major wars there were a host of smaller ones, though no less significant for the parties involved, ranging from England's intermittent and, ultimately, largely successful efforts to subdue her neighbours in Scotland and Ireland, to Venice's undeclared War of Gradisca (1615–17). If to this list of more-or-less well-defined conflicts are added such violent disorders as the persistent marauding of dukes Charles and William of Guelders in Holland and Brabant before 1543 and the feuding of Sicilian nobles which had to be resolved by regular peace treaties,[28] together with preparations for war which came to nothing, then it is easy to see how, as John Hale notes, there were few, if any, years where 'there was neither war nor occurrences that looked and felt remarkably like it'.[29]

Why so many wars? A tempting, and not wholly inaccurate, answer is religion, at least in the period prior to *c.* 1650, though after this date it ceased to play much part in the calculations of statesmen. The intensity which underlay religious antagonisms in the age of the Reformation and Counter-Reformation may be gauged from Philip II's heartfelt declaration to the pope that he preferred the loss of his lands and his life a hundred times over to being the ruler of heretics.[30] Yet, with the exception of the Anabaptist seizure of Münster and subsequent siege in 1534–5, and, just possibly, Charles V's war against the Protestant princes in 1546–7, it is hard to think of any conflict in which religion was the overriding, let alone the sole, motivating factor. Though religious and dynastic rivalries could become confused, rulers and statesmen were capable of disentangling them for the most part, and religion was just one of the factors of which they took account in the formulation of policy. Thus one of Philip II's aims in launching the Armada was the re-catholicization of England, but of greater weight was his wish to end the loss of prestige and profit engendered by English piracy and trade with the New World, and, above all, to bring the revolt in the Netherlands, which England was succouring, to a speedy conclusion; and he had spent the years before 1588 seeking to avoid war with Protestant England. Similarly, Gustavus Adolphus was sincere in his wish to save Protestantism by his intervention in Germany in 1630, but he was above all concerned with the wider question of Sweden's security. Even in the French Religious Wars, in which religious antagonisms above all might have seemed a cause of conflict, the advancement of the religious cause went hand-in-hand with the advancement of secular interests. The monk, Emeric Crucé, indeed insisted with some justice that the wars were undertaken 'for honour, for profit, to right some wrong, or just for practice. One could add for religion, except that experience has shown that this most often serves as a pretext.'[31]

Nevertheless, if religious antagonisms were not of overriding significance as a cause of war, their contribution to conflict was enormously significant in three other respects. First, whenever they were present the fighting was likely to be especially bitter. Second, short of outright victory for one or other of the sides, such conflicts were likely to be protracted since they were hard to resolve by the normal process of negotiation. Neither side would easily compromise on an issue as fundamental as toleration of heresy. Thus efforts to reach a negotiated settlement in the Netherlands in the 1570s consistently broke down over the issue of confessional pluralism: on the rights of the Church Philip II instructed his negotiators 'not to shift an inch', while his Calvinist opponents proved no less intransigent.[32] Third, the existence of rival religious parties within a state offered disaffected nobles the possibility of extending their power base, thus putting them in a position whereby they could offer a military challenge both to the Crown and to their rivals. Organizations such as the Huguenot party and the Catholic League in France, for example, provided the noble leadership with recruits for their armies, funds, and a means of rallying mass support both geographically and across a wide spectrum of social classes.[33]

If religion was one variable which went into the decision-making process – war or peace – at least before 1650, what were the others? It is worth reminding ourselves that in an age of dynastic rule, as this was, the king had sole, if not unlimited, authority in matters of war and peace, and the issues which weighed heavily in the decision were those of significance to the ruler. This meant that economic considerations came low on the agenda: trade was not the *métier* of kings. Colbert may have thought of war against the Dutch in terms of the establishment of French economic dominance in Europe, but there is little to suggest that his royal master viewed the matter in the same light, and he it was who directed foreign policy.[34] Kings were not, of course, wholly unmindful of economic matters: how could they be in a mercantilist age which stressed the need for the state to be economically self-sufficient and strong? One factor in Sweden's Baltic expansion from the time of Erik XIV onwards was the desire of her rulers to control as much of the lucrative trade of the area as possible. Yet here, as elsewhere, economic considerations reinforced a policy that was essentially decided on the basis of other priorities.[35] Only the Dutch and the English engaged each other in trade wars in the early-modern period, and in this, as in so much else, they were atypical.

Conversely, questions of honour and precedence were not without significance in an age of dynastic rule – Louis XIV threatened to occupy the papal enclave of Avignon after falling out with the Vatican over ambassadorial rights[36] – no less than personal rivalries, such as that which exacerbated tensions between Francis I and Charles V. But what mattered above all to rulers were their dynastic rights: only rarely would a ruler renounce his inherited rights, and almost all were prepared to go to war, certainly to defend territory which they held by right of inheritance, and also to gain territory to which they had a claim. Some inheritance claims were self-evidently justifiable: those made by Sigismund III and Philip II to the Swedish and Portugese thrones respectively, for instance. However, it is easy to be dismissive of others as mere pretexts for political adventurism and the acquisition of glory on the battlefield, something which kings certainly did crave. French claims to Naples and Milan, dormant for some time until asserted by Charles VIII and Louis XII, might be regarded in this way. So too Henry VIII's claim to the French throne, which 'justified' his three invasions, and Louis XIV's contrived claims to territory in the Netherlands and Germany which provided the legal underpinning for war in 1667 and 1689. Yet we should hesitate before jumping to a conclusion which may be anachronistic. The very tenacity with which the Valois rulers asserted their claims down to 1559, though their cause in Italy was effectively lost by 1530, is indicative of the importance which they attached to them. And Louis had an almost obsessive concern with dynastic rights, evidenced in the *Instructions* to his ambassadors, for example.[37]

However, it is possible to detect a significant shift of emphasis between the sixteenth and seventeenth centuries, though we should be careful not to exaggerate the extent of it nor to polarize matters unduly. In the sixteenth century it was rare to find any territorial aggrandizement not justified by some dynastic claim, however tenuous. Henry II's seizure of Metz, Toul and Verdun in 1552 affords one rare exception, and even in this case he agreed to hold the lands in trust, as it were, as 'imperial vicar'.[38] Moreover, the rights themselves were above all important, and rulers pursued them with a seemingly irrational disregard for where the lands lay and the practical difficulties that would be encountered in enforcing them. The outstanding example in this respect is that of Charles VIII, who took the risky option of marching the length of Italy in pursuit of its southernmost kingdom when there were more 'rational' targets – Calais, for example – closer to hand. It is also significant that Charles V seriously considered yielding to the claim of the Duke of Orleans, son of his rival Francis I, over Milan, though the duchy's importance as the 'gateway to Italy' was pointed out to him.[39] Ultimately Milan was not relinquished, yet there would have been no such havering on the part of subsequent rulers, certainly in the seventeenth century, with respect to such a crucial territory. Increasingly rulers came to adopt a more pragmatic approach towards the enforcement of their rights,[40] pursuing them only when the perceived value of the territory concerned appeared to justify this, rather than at any cost. Moreover, there appears to have been a somewhat greater preparedness to acquire, or at least to occupy militarily, territory to which there was no prior dynastic claim. Sweden, for example, simply took over German lands by right of conquest, and especially during Richelieu's ministry the French occupied numerous towns and fortresses under the dubious guise of 'protection'.[41] Put very simply, the focus of interest had shifted from rights to territory.[42]

How was the value of territory adjudged? Economic potential might be a consideration. But what was above all important was what might broadly be called its strategic value, defined in the broadest terms. Hence the propensity to acquire territories contiguous to the ruler's own, to round off boundaries and to render frontiers more secure: France's efforts to acquire Franche-Comté, Flanders, Alsace and Luxembourg, for example, Swedish attempts to consolidate its holdings in the Baltic, and Savoy's persistent efforts in 1613–16, 1628–31 and 1635–48 to acquire Italian territory to the south. Hence too the concern with territories and specific fortresses which controlled lines of communication, possible invasion routes into the state, or which gave access to future areas of advance. It was in this spirit that Richelieu advised Louis XIII in 1629: 'I believe we must fortify Metz and advance as far as Strasbourg, if possible, in order to acquire a gateway into Germany'[43] (there was a French claim to overlordship of Metz but none to Strasbourg, though this does not appear to have carried much weight with the Cardinal); and control of key forts such as Saluzzo, Casale, Pinerolo, Breisach and Ehrenbreitstein bulked large in the conduct of French foreign policy throughout the seventeenth century. It was in the context of protecting and strengthening communications with the Austrian Habsburgs and the Low Countries – the famed 'Spanish Road' – that Spain intervened in Jülich in 1613 and occupied the Rhine Palatinate in 1621, and sought to establish control of Alsace, Mantua, Montferrat and the Valtelline, for example. Conversely, it was in an attempt to disrupt these communications that the Dutch occupied Wesel and Cleves in the aftermath of the disputed succession (1609–14).

Territory, then, was a dominant concern in the figurings of rulers: whether it was the defence of land already held, the acquisition of more land for its own sake, or the acquisition of land of perceived 'vital interest'. Because there were so many conflicting dynastic claims to land in an early-modern Europe of intermarried ruling families, and because the acquisition of territory by one state was almost bound to be at the expense of another, war was always potentially possible, made the more likely if questions of religious rivalry, honour and precedence were involved, and because rulers so often felt the need to prove themselves on the battlefield. Not inevitable, of course, for rulers had a choice about initiating conflict, and not always on the same scale, for relations between states 'lay along a continuum ranging from all-out enmity to all-out friendship',[44] with varying gradations of neutrality and cold war in between. But in a Europe in which dynastic aggrandizement was regarded as the 'most fitting and most pleasing occupation of a king',[45] it was always highly likely.

Were dynastic rivalries governed by any 'balance of power' principle? The term was certainly in use, and had been since the Renaissance, though it was then used to refer exclusively to Italy.[46] Francis Bacon analysed the manoeuvrings of Henry VIII's foreign policy by reference to the concept[47] – though hardly accurately, since England was, for the most part, allied to the Habsburgs, the stronger power, and against France. By the seventeenth century there does seem to have been a growing awareness of the need for joint action to prevent the hegemony of any one power, whether it be Spain or, subsequently, France. In particular, Louis XIV's acceptance of the whole of the Spanish inheritance for his grandson meant an aggrandizement of the Bourbon dynasty which was not tolerable for the other states of Europe, and it was resisted by force. Yet though the balance of power formed part of the common vocabulary of discussions on inter-state relations by 1700, the concept remained pretty nebulous, never moving beyond the fairly obvious notion of preventing the dominance within Europe of a single power, to the more developed form which it would acquire only in the later-eighteenth and nineteenth centuries.

Dynastic aggrandizement above all fuelled wars in the early-modern period, then. But how effective was warfare as a means of achieving the objectives of rulers? To answer that, we need to know something about the conduct of war.

2

THE CHANGING ART OF WAR

PIKE AND SHOT

Medieval warfare had been conducted with a plethora of hand weapons, but the early-modern period witnessed a diminution and a standardization in their range. Regional variations still remained: the Scots clung to the use of the two-handed claymore until the eighteenth century, and the Irish persisted with the axe (McLaghlin M'Cabb claimed to have used one to kill eighty Spaniards shipwrecked from the Armada).[1] But European warfare was increasingly dominated by soldiers using the pike or a hand firearm.

The defensive capabilities of pikemen had been established since the early fourteenth century. Large, tightly packed bodies of pikemen, the butt of their weapons firmly grounded, the point projecting out at 45°, were virtually invulnerable to cavalry or infantry attack. The Swiss in the late fifteenth century first developed the offensive possibilities of this formation. Effective unit discipline, based upon constant practice and a strong communal organization, allowed them to manoeuvre with the cumbersome, 18-foot long *langspiesse* while retaining formation, and the devastating effectiveness of the Swiss 'steamroller' – the *gewalthaufen* – produced crushing victories over the Burgundians in 1476 and 1477. Swiss methods were widely copied, notably by the Spanish, Germans and Italians, though the length of the pike was shortened to around 13 feet, and by the first decade of the sixteenth century the pike reigned supreme as 'queen of the battlefield'.[2]

Like the pike, hand firearms had a long provenance, but only by the sixteenth century had they reached a point of technological development at which they were capable of affecting decisively the conduct of war. Easily the commonest type of arquebus (the generic term for all sixteenth-century hand fire-arms) was the matchlock. Over 4 feet long and weighing about 12 pounds, it was fired by pulling a trigger which lowered a piece of smouldering match into the powder in the priming pan. From the 1560s a heavier type of arquebus, the 6-foot long musket, weighing 20 pounds and requiring a metal support, came into vogue. Its weight restricted its use. Gervase Markham in his *Souldier's Accidence* (1625) reckoned that only 'the squarest and broadest [men] will be fit to carry musquets, and the least and nimblest may be turned to the harquebus'.[3] There was also a cost consideration: musketeers received higher rates of pay and allowances than other handgunners. Thus, despite its enthusiastic adoption by the Spanish in the 1550s, musketeers were still outnumbered by arquebusiers in the Army of Flanders fifty years later.[4] The musket nevertheless proved its worth, especially in sieges when it could be loaded with scattershot and propped on a wall or window opening; and its stopping power was greatly valued, for the 2-ounce ball it fired could kill a man in shot-proof armour at 100 paces, and bring down a horse.[5]

Operation of the matchlock required two hands, for the length of match projecting from the lock had to be continuously adjusted, and this rendered it unsuitable for mounted men. In this respect the wheel lock (so called because a pull on the trigger caused a serrated wheel powered by clockwork to revolve against a piece of iron pyrites, producing a shower of sparks which ignited the priming powder) was a great advance. It could be loaded, held ready for use and then fired with one hand. Although wheel locks were mass produced – several hundreds were made for the arsenal at Graz in the seventeenth century[6] – their high cost and fragility largely restricted their employment to the pistols and small carbines used by the cavalry. Cheaper than the wheel lock, and more efficient as a means of ignition than the matchlock, was the flintlock, de-veloped early in the seventeenth century. The priming powder here was ignited when a piece of flint, held in the jaws of the lock, fell onto a metal plate and (hopefully) produced a spark. Lighter and easier to reload than the matchlock, the flintlock was also more expensive, a key consideration for governments faced with re-equipping large numbers of men, and consequently it was not widely adopted until late in the seventeenth century: by the Dutch, Swedes, French and Danes in the 1690s, the Habsburgs and most German states by about 1710.[7]

As well as better means of ignition, other technical developments improved the performance of hand firearms. Stocks became curved rather than straight, and fitted against the shoulder, so improving accuracy and helping to absorb recoil. Loading times were lessened by the use of pre-packed cartridges containing measured amounts of powder, ball and the wadding needed to hold both in the barrel. By 1600 lead, easily cast and with good ballistic qualities, had become the standard metal for bullets. Yet the performance of hand firearms remained indifferent. The rate of misfire with an arquebus might be as high as 50 per cent; even with a flintlock it was one shot in five. A sixteenth-century musketeer would take several minutes to reload, and even a well-trained soldier in Marlborough's army would do well to fire twice per minute. By contrast, a long-bowman could loose twelve arrows in the same time.[8] François de la Noue hardly exaggerated when he claimed, in 1587, that pistols were accurate up to only three paces.[9] This was bettered by the arquebus of course, but even this, in the hands of a skilled operator, was accurate only up to 60 yards: no better than a crossbow. No wonder Robert Monro counselled that gunners should aim 'never higher or lower than levell with the enemies' middle'.[10]

Perhaps surprisingly then, the adoption of handguns was rapid and universal in the sixteenth century. By 1500 Venice had decided to re-equip all its crossbowmen with them; and by 1550 the arquebus had replaced the crossbow as the main missile weapon in all continental armies. Only England resisted the trend. As late as 1588 the fleet sent to confront the Armada carried 200 longbows and 600 sheaves of arrows, but this partly reflected the lack of available handguns, and by this stage only a handful of die-hards continued to oppose the use of the new weapons. Arquebusiers gradually edged out not just crossbowmen and archers, but halberdiers, billmen, specialist swordsmen and even cavalry. The adoption of firearms was due in part to the endless fascination of rulers with 'state-of-the-art' technology; in part to their superiority over bows in siege warfare; and also to an appreciation that they could be used by men with little training. 'Men shall never shoot [the longbow] well except

23

that they be brought up in it', noted Hugh Latimer in 1549[11] (and a strong man at that, for the bow had a pull of 80 pounds); less time was needed to train a crossbowman, but it was still considerable. On the other hand, a few days sufficed to produce a competent arquebusier. There was, too, a growing realization that handguns could wreak havoc on massed bodies of pikemen, the formation which for forty years had appeared near-invincible. The decade around 1520 was probably crucial.[12] At Marignano (1515), La Bicocca (1522) and Pavia (1525) pikemen proved vulnerable to gunfire, and thereafter no army could do without arquebusiers, both to protect its own pikemen and to threaten the enemy's. The proportion of handgunners to pikemen rose inexorably, increasing, in the case of the Spanish regular infantry, to one in three by the 1570s and almost parity by 1600, while the Dutch muster lists (unusually accurate records of their type) reveal that by the 1590s an infantry company of 135 men included 74 handgunners (44 arquebusiers and 30 musketeers) and only 45 pikemen.[13]

The introduction of firearms was to have profound implications for battlefield tactics, formations and the training of soldiers, but it took time for these to be fully worked out. Initially, arquebusiers were used as skirmishers, or slipped into the ranks of pikemen (often taking the place of halberdiers); or specialist units of arquebusiers and musketeers, firing scatter-shot, were attached to the corners of the pike phalanx. But the sixteenth century was essentially a period of experimentation, and nowhere was the potential of firepower fully realized.[14] The really crucial developments in this respect came in the 1590s and were associated with three members of the house of Nassau: William Louis, Count of Nassau and stadholder in Friesland; his brother John; and Maurice, son of William of Orange, who held various stadholderships and served as captain-general of the Dutch forces in Flanders and Brabant. The developments were broadly threefold.[15] Most importantly, William devised a technique which allowed a body of arquebusiers to subject the enemy to a continuous hail of shots: volley fire. In a letter to Maurice, dated December 1594, he indicated how handgunners could be arranged in six ranks. The first rank fired together, then retired to the rear (the counter-march) while the next rank in line fired, and so on. In practice, it initially required ten ranks to give the men who fired first time to reload before they had to fire again; nevertheless volley fire overcame a grave disadvantage of the arquebus, namely its slow rate of fire, which meant that a body of arquebusiers firing together might be able to get off only one round before the enemy was upon them. Second, William and Maurice followed upon what was increasingly the practice in the sixteenth century, and, while decreasing the depth of the unit, spread the men outwards in linear fashion. This allowed maximum firepower to be directed against the enemy and minimized the effects of any return fire. All this posed problems, however. Volley fire presupposed that the gunners were skilled in the use of their weapons, and capable of acting in unison. Moreover (though this was dimly perceived by the reformers, if at all), men in thin, linear formation lacked the psychological reassurance which comes from being part of a large tightly packed body. The feeling of group solidarity in a pike phalanx, for example, was considerable, and was undoubtedly a major factor in holding such formations together under attack – not to mention the fact that it was anyway difficult to run away if one was in the middle of such a formation, one reason why commanders tried to station experienced and courageous men on the exposed periphery. The answer to both problems was drill, so as to familiarize soldiers with their weapons and the counter-march and to inculcate that discipline and bond which develops between men who together perform the same movements repetitiously and over a prolonged period. Herein lay the third contribution of the Counts of Nassau. By 1597 definitive words of command had been laid down to govern each manoeuvre, and the Dutch army was kept busy marching, forming and reforming ranks and practising the handling of weapons. In 1607 a drill manual was produced under John's supervision, Jacob de Gheyn's *Wapenhandelinghe van Roers*, depicting the movements which pikemen and arquebusiers needed to master in order to use their weapons. Not all of this was entirely new, of course: sixteenth-century Swiss and Spanish pikemen marched to the sound of the drum for example.[16] What was original was that drill should be both standardized and part of a daily routine.

Quite why it was the Counts of Nassau who clearly formulated these ideas, rather than other military practitioners, is unclear. It was hardly the result of battlefield experience: Maurice fought only one major engagement, at Nieuwpoort, and that was in 1600 after the reforms had been initiated. One suggestion is that the reforms evolved from the efforts of John to turn the local *Landrettung*, or militia, composed of partially trained civilians, into a body capable of standing up to the roving bands of professional soldiers who plagued the country.[17] But this seems hardly likely, and of the three men John was least involved in initiating the reforms. Most probably, the ideas emerged as a particularly perceptive response to the debate which exercised all students of military affairs in the sixteenth century: how best to deploy the new weapons so as to make the most effective use of their potential. It is clear that the inspiration for the reforms derived from a reading of the classical authors, whose writings were studied not just by the three members of the House of Nassau but by many other professional soldiers and thinkers on war. The most important single influence on sixteenth-century students of warfare was Vegetius, whose *De Re Militari* was published in a revised form at Antwerp in 1585. Probably most important in the Dutch context, however, was the *Taktike Theoria* written by the fourth-century Greek, Aelian: many of the words of command in the Dutch army were translated directly from those in Aelian, who also suggested versions of the counter-march.[18] In addition to these writings, the three Dutch reformers are known to have consulted the Byzantine Emperor Leo IV's *Tactica*, together with the works of Caesar, Polybius and Agricola for example. The writings of many of these authors had of course been available in the Middle Ages: Vegetius in particular had been widely translated and his writings put into easily digestible form. But their status had undoubtedly been enhanced since then by the respect which the Renaissance encouraged for classical scholarship, and the advent of printing allowed their works to be more widely disseminated than previously. The basic principles which they preached, such as the need for drill, discipline, linear formations and the importance of infantry appeared to have a contemporary relevance and application in the circumstances of the sixteenth century, and these were also forcefully advocated in the classically-inspired *De Militia Romana* (1595–6) written by the influential Dutch political philosopher, Justus Lipsius.[19]

Interest in the 'Dutch drill' was enormous, initially from other nearby Protestant states such as Brunswick, Hesse-Cassel,

Brandenburg and the Palatinate; while in England John Cruso's *Militarie Instructions* (1632), John Bingham's *The Tactiks of Aelian* (1616) and Henry Hexham's *Principles of the Art Militarie* (1642) made lavish and glowing references to the Dutch model. But interest was by no means restricted to Protestant areas and authors: in France, for example, influential writers such as Louis de Montgommery and Jean de Billon acknowledged the debt they owed to the Dutch reforms.[20] Undoubtedly the Thirty Years War, in which the Swedes especially made great use of them, provided both a testing ground and a forcing house for the new ideas. Not all proved to be viable: Maurice's use of very small units in particular was found wanting. But the main lines of development were now clear. Armies in the seventeenth century increasingly adopted linear formations, though the older-style squares (albeit hollow rather than solid as in the early sixteenth century) were retained as a means of defence. For example at Rocroi in 1643 the Spanish infantry regrouped to form an enormous hollow rectangle which beat off three attacks by the whole French army; at Fleurus in 1690 the sixteen Dutch battalions formed a vast square; and Gaya's *L'Art de la guerre* of 1689 contained detailed instructions on how to adopt such configurations. Yet by this time such 360° formations were untypical.[21] Prior to the commencement of battle the army was generally drawn up in one continuous line, with one or more lines of reserve behind,[22] one consequence of linearity being that battlefields perforce became larger: at Malplaquet, for instance, the troops under Marshal Villars were stretched out on a front over 3 miles long.[23] Volley fire remained the norm and lines continued to decrease in depth. By the time of the Spanish Succession War improvements in weaponry enabled the British and Dutch to draw their men up in only three ranks, though French regulations continued to specify five.

Pikes played a steadily diminishing role. Robert Monro in 1637 continued to rate them highly for use in storming a breach; and on the battlefield they were still used in shock action, notably in the English Civil War and in the Thirty Years War. A letter in 1632 from Wallenstein to his colonels argued that in any infantry clash the pikemen decided the issue. But by this stage their battle-winning role had disappeared: indeed the point of Wallenstein's letter was to chide his officers for equipping their weakest, least trained men with the pike.[24] The function of the pikemen was now to defend the shot, especially from cavalry attack – a reversal of the sixteenth-century situation – and to this end they generally adopted a loose formation, with about a yard between pikemen, thus giving the gunners space to retreat to shelter. The tightly packed shoulder-to-shoulder configuration of the early-sixteenth-century Swiss pikemen was no longer used.[25] Indeed, as techniques of volley fire and the ability of infantry to defend itself from cavalry by moving from line to square improved in the second half of the century, handgunners had less need of the defensive umbrella provided by the pikes. The development of an effective bayonet in the 1690s removed this justification for their existence altogether. By then critics who argued that use of the pike entailed a waste of firepower had won the day. Pikemen declined in numbers from 1650 and largely disappeared altogether after about 1705. The handgun, not the pike, was now 'queen of the battlefield'.

The gradual abandonment of the pike as a weapon of offence, together with the introduction of hand firearms and their new associated tactical formations, undoubtedly strengthened the defensive superiority of the infantry. Some effort was made in the seventeenth century to endow the handgunners with an offensive capability. By reversing the order of the countermarch and getting each rank to advance before firing it was possible to use the manoeuvre in an attacking way. But this effort appears to have met with limited success at best: until at least the eighteenth century a salient characteristic of battles is the effectiveness of infantry acting in defence, and this was so whether they were acting against other infantry or against cavalry.

CAVALRY

The growth in numbers and importance initially of pikemen and subsequently of handgunners was matched by a corresponding decline of the mounted soldier. The proportion of cavalry to infantry decreased as armies grew in size, though in absolute terms the numbers of horsemen may have remained roughly stable in the two centuries after 1500. To be sure, there were marked variations over time and place which render generalizations dangerous. Thus the proportion of cavalry to foot in the Parliamentarian forces rose during the Civil War to about 1 : 2 by 1645; the Swedish field army in Germany in 1645 contained more horse than infantry; and the Army of Flanders reckoned to use fewer cavalry in the siege-dominated fighting in the Netherlands than when on campaign in France. It is none the less hard to resist the overall impression of a general decline in the proportion of horse in armies. In the reconquest of Granada, for example, the Spanish Crown consistently maintained about 10,000 cavalry from 1484 onwards, but increased the number of foot soldiers from 10,000 to 50,000 by 1491. It is true that a chronic shortage of horses in the peninsula may have restricted the number of cavalry, but a similar picture emerges in relation to France. In 1494 Charles VIII's army for the Italian expedition comprised (on paper at least) almost as many cavalry as footmen, yet at Pavia and for the Metz campaign of 1552 the horse accounted for only about one-fifth of the army. Even in the Venetian standing army, which for long cosseted the man-at-arms, numbers declined in the second half of the sixteenth century. Here, as elsewhere in Europe, the trend continued into the following century, perhaps to be halted but not reversed after about 1650. Wallenstein's army lists reveal that cavalry accounted for 27 per cent of his forces in 1625, 14 per cent in 1630 (though in absolute terms the number had risen from 16,600 to 21,000). The number of horsemen in Louis XIV's armies fluctuated widely but never seems to have risen above one man in four. At the major battles of Blenheim, Ramillies, Oudenarde and Malplaquet the total cavalry present comprised between one-quarter and one-third of the forces involved.[26]

The key reason for this decline had nothing to do with military utility, everything to do with economics: horsemen were ruinously expensive. The gear carried by a late-fifteenth-century knight cost as much as a small farm. Even the more lightly armoured cavalryman of the sixteenth and seventeenth centuries (helmet, shot-proof cuirass, heavy leather boots and carrying a sword, pistols or light carbine) was expensive. An English cavalry horse in the 1690s cost about £15; mounts for the Dutch army, because they were not easily available, cost even more. To be sure, many governments tried to insist on cavalrymen providing their own horses, but this was not always feasible: after 1590 the Army of Flanders was sent government-issue horses on credit as a matter of course. In any event, remounts were always reckoned the employer's responsibility. Given the dreadfully high wastage rate of horses on campaign (they succumbed to cold and damp as well as gunshots) this could be a heavy charge. Additionally, the cavalryman's pay was higher than an infantryman's to cover the extra cost of his equipment and feeding his mount. Estimates prepared by Bullion, the *surintendant de finances*, in 1632, put the unit cost of a cavalryman at over twice that of an infantryman (almost certainly an underestimate).[27] No wonder governments seeking to increase the size of armies looked first to the cheaper infantry.

Arguments of economy were compounded by a decline in the military effectiveness of the cavalry in face of the new weaponry. The horse was even more vulnerable to gunfire than its armoured rider: Blaise de Monluc had five horses killed under him in the 1521–2 campaigns; Piccolomini lost seven in a single day at Lützen (1632). Monluc described how he learned early in his career that a cavalry charge could be stopped by the controlled fire from even a small group of arquebusiers.[28] Yet in fact pikemen could pull off the same feat, for horses simply will not run into an apparently solid and immovable object but instead will shy away. Sir Roger Williams made the point obliquely in his *Discourse on Warre* (1590), and it was forcefully reiterated by Santa-Cruz in 1730.[29] The much vaunted 'shock' value of the cavalry charge was anyway near impossible to achieve in practice, since in any charge the swifter horses outran the slower, the less courageous riders held back, and the galloping horses fanned out. Montecuccoli accurately described the phenomenon:

> over a distance of 200 paces one sees this long rank [of horses] thin out and dissolve. Great breaches appear within it....On many occasions only twenty or twenty-five of a hundred horse actually charge. Then, when they have realized that they have no support or backing, after having fired a few pistol shots and after having delivered a few thrusts of their swords, they withdraw...by and large, they are unable to collide with great force.[30]

As a result, cavalry had little effect on bodies of pike or shot which stood firm and whose ranks were unbroken. This was proved time and time again: at Marignano, where the Swiss pikemen threw off successive charges by the French cavalry before succumbing to gunfire; at Pavia, where the French cavalry faltered before the Spanish infantry; at Breitenfeld, where Pappenheim's seven charges against Swedish pike and musket brigades were all repulsed. To be sure, if they could get amongst a body of infantry whose formation had been broken, or which was in flight, the cavalry, with its superior height, could wreak fearful carnage. At Breitenfeld, for example, Gustavus Adolphus's cavalry charges against the Imperialist infantry squares succeeded because gaps had been opened up in the latter by cannon fire; and at Ramillies the English cavalry turned the French retreat into a rout, the Scots Greys sabreing down two battalions of the *Régiment du Roi* as they flooded back to the baggage train. In an attempt to create gaps in the infantry ranks which could then be exploited the cavalry developed the *caracole*, an elaborate manoeuvre in which successive ranks of horsemen trotted forward, discharged their pistols, wheeled and retired. The tactic was for the most part a hopeless failure. The cavalry's pistols were out-distanced by the infantry's arquebuses; and the horsemen always faced a heavier volume of return fire from the massed ranks of the foot soldiers than they themselves could deliver. Unaided, the cavalry simply could not blast holes in infantry formations six or ten ranks deep, and in these circumstances the insistence of military 'reformers' such as Gustavus Adolphus and Oliver Cromwell that the cavalry should always charge to contact after firing seems to fly in the face of reality.[31]

Given all this, why did cavalry survive at all? It was certainly not without use. Horsemen were crucial for scouting, essential for foraging, and useful in the raids and skirmishes which comprised much of early-modern warfare. They might deliver the *coup de grâce* in a large-scale engagement as the enemy fled the field. On occasions dismounted cavalrymen were used when storming a breach in a fort's walls, for here their greater weight of armour gave them an advantage over the more lightly armed infantrymen. And the cavalry remained the most socially prestigious branch of the army. Although entry was no longer restricted to the nobility, it continued to attract 'more men of good background and thus of nobler spirit', as the Venetian Francesco Martinegro put it.[32] But the cavalry's days of battlefield dominance were over.

ARTILLERY AND FORTIFICATIONS

The defensive superiority of the infantry could not be overcome by cavalry acting alone. What was required in this respect was highly mobile field artillery, capable of moving rapidly about the battlefield in conjunction with the cavalry, and with the power to shatter infantry formations preparatory to a cavalry charge.[33] This, however, was not to become available until the eighteenth century. This is not to say that cannon played no part on the battlefield in the preceding two hundred years. The Swedes massed over seventy heavy guns at Breitenfeld (1631); at Ravenna (1512) and Marignano (1515) they were crucial in determining the outcome of the engagement; crucial too at Rocroi (1643) where two French cannons, together with massed infantry fire, finally broke open the Spanish defensive square. But it proved near impossible to relocate the heavy and unwieldy cannon on the battlefield. At Rocroi the French gunners toiled for hours to move their two pieces a few hundred yards to train them on the Spanish infantry, and at Ravenna and Marignano the guns were *in situ* when battle commenced and did not move during the course of it. Significantly, these two French victories were followed by a defeat at Pavia which pointed up the limits of battlefield artillery. Initially, cannon took a heavy toll of the advancing Habsburg forces, but, outflanked by arquebusiers, they could not be manoeuvred to return fire nor withdraw, and their capture precipitated a French defeat.[34] Static, unable to manoeuvre with the cavalry or infantry, cannon had a limited usefulness in battle.[35]

This is not to deny the improvements in manufacture and design which had transformed artillery since its appearance early in the fourteenth century.[36] Early versions were often of wrought-iron construction, strips of metal being hammer-welded together on a wooden former and bound by hoops shrunk on to them. Although stronger than often thought, wrought-iron guns could only be made as a tube, open at both ends, and hence had to be breech loading. The various arrangements to plug the breech were highly inefficient, limiting the charge which could be employed and proving dangerous to gunners and onlookers: James II of Scotland was mortally wounded in 1460 when a securing wedge was blown out. One-piece cast guns provided the answer. Initially these were of bronze, but, from the mid-seventeenth century, as better casting techniques eliminated the often fatal flaws in iron guns, and because they were one-third cheaper than their bronze equivalents, these came to predominate. Cast-iron guns were also lighter and stronger than bronze, and could therefore make full use of 'corned' gunpowder. This was powder which had been wetted, dried and ground into small pellets. Robert Norton in *The Gunner* (1628) reckoned it to be three times more powerful than powder grains.[37] The substitution of cast-iron shot for stone cannon balls gave better penetrative qualities and allowed the size and weight of cannon to be reduced. Rates of fire were improved. In a contest staged at Brescia in 1564 an Italian gunner, Giordano Orsini, managed 108 rounds in five hours from a 50-pounder cannon, i.e. 2.7 minutes per round.[38] This was under ideal circumstances, of course, and William Eldred's estimate in 1646 of eight shots per hour was probably nearer the norm, itself an improvement on sixteenth-century performance.[39] By about 1500 guns were mounted on carriages using trunnions – round projections – on each side of the barrel. This simple invention was a major advance. Situated level with the bottom of the bore they ensured downward pressure on the carriage during firing, helping to absorb recoil, and they allowed the barrel to be elevated or depressed easily, making aiming more accurate and rapid.

Yet, for all this, cannon remained unwieldy and cumbersome. A full cannon of the mid-sixteenth century weighed over 8,000 pounds; the ubiquitous half-cannon weighed some 4,500 pounds and needed a dozen horses to move it. By 1500 cannon were sufficiently mobile to keep up (just) with an army on the move (though Marlborough's famous march to the Danube was only accomplished by leaving much artillery behind). But hitching up draught animals and manoeuvring on a crowded battlefield was largely impracticable. (The much-vaunted 90-pound 'leather' gun, designed by Colonel Wurmbrandt and employed for its mobility by the Swedes in the Polish campaigns of the 1620s, proved to be insufficiently strong and was dropped.) Immobility – rather than inaccuracy and slow rate of fire – severely curtailed the utility of cannon on the battlefield throughout the early-modern period.

However, the static nature of cannon during an engagement was much less disadvantageous in a siege, and in this context the use of heavy artillery had a dramatic impact. The high, thin walls of medieval castles, designed to counter assaults with scaling ladders, were vulnerable to cannon fire: continually pounded at their base, the stone walls simply fractured and collapsed. Within a generation, heavy artillery rendered medieval fortress architecture obsolete.

Charles VIII's invasion of Italy in 1494 is usually adopted as the outstanding example of the effectiveness of siege cannon when used against old-style castles. It is true that his forty guns knocked down the walls of Monte San Giovanni in only eight hours – it had previously withstood a traditional siege lasting seven years – but after this the mere threat of his cannon was sufficient to induce most forts to surrender at word of his coming.[40] A more convincing demonstration of the power of artillery had come earlier, in the Spanish conquest of Granada between 1482 and 1492. The crucial factor had been the royal artillery train which, as a contemporary noted, caused castles to fall 'within a month, the least of which in the past could have held out a year, and which could not have been taken, except by hunger'.[41]

Charles VIII's invasion of Italy was nevertheless a watershed, for it prompted military architects, who had experimented in the later fifteenth century with fortress designs capable of countering the effects of gunfire, to redouble their efforts. And they produced the answer: a new type of fortification which became known from its place of birth as the *trace italienne*.[42] It comprised a number of different elements. Fortress walls were redesigned: stripped of crenellations and projections, which splintered dangerously, they were sloped backwards to present a glancing surface to artillery shot; they were constructed of earth and rubble and faced with brick (or even turf in the case of later Dutch models), the better to absorb the impact of shot; and they were made much lower and thicker than ever before. Fortress layout was altered to allow the defenders to subject the besiegers to the maximum amount of return fire. The crucial development here was the introduction of the angle bastion, a huge triangular-shaped projection, open to the sky in its fully developed form, which served as a gun platform, allowing counter-bombardment of the enemy guns.[43] A series of mutually supporting bastions added to the curtain wall at carefully measured intervals, with guns concealed in their sides, provided effective flanking fire, and ensured that there was no 'dead' ground in front of the fortress which was not swept by the defenders' guns. Attacking troops could thus not penetrate to the fort without passing through a barrage of fire. The firepower which could be delivered from a well-designed bastion was enormous: the one built on Rome's southern wall in the late 1530s accommodated sixteen heavy cannon, eight lighter cannon, and numerous anti-personnel weapons such as arquebuses, muskets and swivel-mounted guns firing scattershot. In addition, a wide ditch in front of the walls – sometimes filled with water – provided an additional obstacle to attacking infantry, and helped prevent the walls being mined. Further refinements were added in time. Designs by Antonio da Sangallo the Younger in the 1530s and 1540s included sophisticated forward chambers and shafts with listening devices to detect the approach of enemy mining operations. The area in front of the ditch – the *glacis* – was gently sloped and cleared to expose the besiegers to the full effects of the fort's guns. A complex pattern of outworks, consisting of pill boxes, redoubts, detached bastions and an infantry covered way, were added, all of which gave the fort tremendous defence in depth. The fullest flowering of the military architect's art came in the seventeenth century with master designers such as Vauban and Coehoorn, but the essential features of the new military architecture, established around 1500, remained unchanged.

The superiority of the *trace italienne* over older styles of fortification was quickly and universally accepted. Fourquevaux claimed in 1548 that any town fortified more than three decades previously was outmoded and unfit for service 'since the art of building proper ramparts has only recently been discovered'.[44] But the cost of constructing the new star-shaped fortifications *ab initio* was enormous; and even the modification of existing structures – a more common practice – strained the resources of even the richest princes. Consequently, the dissemination of the *trace italienne* from its birthplace was gradual, and it was adopted only when the imminence or actuality of large-scale, semi-permanent warfare made it a military necessity.[45] In the first half of the sixteenth century the Venetian Republic hired the brilliant Michele di Sanmicheli, to design new defences against the Turks and to secure the *Terraferma* by strengthening the fortresses at Padua, Chiusa, Legnano, Brescia and Bergamo for example. It was deployed rapidly throughout the Habsburg possessions in Italy and then in the Low Countries, initially by Charles V who spent lavishly on securing his borders with France, and subsequently by both the Spanish and the Dutch during the Revolt of the Netherlands. Indeed, the Revolt witnessed something of a frenzy of fortress building, so that by the end of the century few towns of any size in the Netherlands were without their defences. By contrast, the *trace italienne* was in only very limited use in the coastal areas of Spain and her North African possessions by the 1540s. In France, Francis I strengthened the defences of his southern frontier with Spain in the 1530s, but most effort and money went into the vulnerable and troubled northern and eastern borders where only 150 miles at most of easily traversable terrain separated his capital from Habsburg forces in the Netherlands and along the Meuse. In 1543 Girolamo Marini, 'reckoned the greatest man in Italy for besieging fortresses' according to Monluc,[46] was brought in, together with one hundred compatriots, to re-fortify Luxembourg. Existing fortresses at Mézières and Mauzon were strengthened and new ones built at Villefranche-sur-Meuse and Vitry-le-Francois. The Crown was unable to sustain this building programme during the anarchy of the Religious Wars and it did not recommence until the seventeenth century, reaching a peak during the bellicose reign of Louis XIV. A number of German towns updated their fortifications during the conflicts of the 1540s, but it was the threat of internal war early in the next century which stimulated both Catholic and Protestant princes to re-fortify: Dresden was rebuilt for the Duke of Saxony to a design by the topographer Wilhelm Dilich and a new fortress constructed at Mannheim for the Elector Palatine, for example, while the Duke of Bavaria spent over one million *thalers* on fortifications between 1598 and 1618.[47] In England, invasion scares produced a spate of fortification building at various times. Thus in 1539, after the declaration from Charles V and Francis I that they would co-operate in an attack upon Henry VIII, 1,400 men were set to work on the defences of the Downs, notably the castles of Deal, Walmer and Sandown; rebuilding of the fortifications at Berwick began at the end of Mary's reign, under the supervision of Sir Richard Lee, to protect against an attack by the pro-French Scottish government; and frantic efforts were made to update defences of towns in southern

England on the eve of the Armada. But, with the exception of Berwick, the work was much inferior to the best Italian practice, probably because Italian engineers, who were the experts employed throughout the continent, took no leading part in designing any of the fortresses.[48] And the new forts were restricted to the coast: few inland towns were protected by permanent fortifications of any strength. Even more than England, Ireland and Scotland remained isolated from large-scale warfare, and the *trace italienne* made little if any impact here. In 1643 Alexander Leslie, commanding the New Scots army in Ulster, found there was so little need for his siege train that he dispensed with most of it.[49]

Thus, by the early seventeenth century, the new-style fortifications had come to dominate northern Italy, northern and eastern France, the Low Countries and, to a lesser extent, Germany: those areas, in short, which witnessed most military activity and which would come to be known as 'the cockpit of Europe'.

Places fortified in the new style were invulnerable to assault by infantry alone, and difficult to capture even when the besieger was well equipped with siege artillery. The classic means of siegecraft was to dig a series of entrenchments around the fort (lines of circumvallation) with perhaps a second ring outside this (lines of contravallation), out of range of the fort's guns, to defend the besiegers against attack from a relieving force. A series of trenches, zigzag in form to prevent the defenders firing directly into them, was then dug towards the point of the wall chosen for the attack. A breach was opened in the wall using massed siege artillery or by mining. Rubble from the breached wall hopefully filled the ditch and provided a ramp over which the infantry, waiting in the approach trenches, could pass. Such methods were invariably costly in human lives, for the massed ranks of attacking infantry presented an easy target. Moreover, a massed infantry assault could not be certain of success. If the breach was not quickly made – and here the number and rate of fire of the siege guns was a crucial factor – the defenders might be able to construct a second line of earthwork defences, or retrenchment, behind the wall, as Monluc did, for example, when directing the defence of Siena in 1555, arranging also for the attackers who passed through the breach to be met by the fire from musketeers and arquebusiers as well as four or five heavy cannon, 'each loaded with great chains, nails and pieces of iron'.[50] Not surprisingly, commanders sought to avoid a direct assault if possible, preferring instead to blockade the fortress and starve it into surrender.

A blockade, however, required time and also prodigious numbers of men if it was to be successful, for the fortress had to be completely encircled by the attacking force and denied all contact with the outside world. In 1552 Charles V assembled a force of around 40,000 men to invest Metz whose perimeter defences measured some 8–9,000 paces, but even the siege of a minor fortress was costly in manpower. In 1637, for example, the encircling Spanish siege lines at Leucate stretched for 2,400 metres and were manned by 4,000 sappers and 13,000 regular troops.[51] In addition to the men enforcing the blockade it was common by the seventeenth century to employ a masking force, which patrolled the vicinity and gave the besiegers protection against a relief column coming to the aid of the defenders. In 1684 Louis XIV personally commanded just such a force, which numbered no less than 20,000, while the main French army besieged Luxembourg.[52]

Substantial numbers of troops were also required for garrison duties. In February 1585 Parma complained from the Netherlands of the numbers tied down in 'the defence of a frontier which runs from Gravelines to Luxembourg, and from there on to Groningen'.[53] Not all were stationed in the major fortified cities: many were to be found in supporting positions in the outlying towns and villages whose garrisons might number only a couple of dozen men. In an area such as the Netherlands, whose landscape was thickly dotted with the new-style fortifications and where war was mainly an affair of sieges, the proportion of troops swallowed up in garrison duties was extraordinarily high. In early 1626 the Army of Flanders employed 31,046 men in this way out of a total force of 48–55,000: 6,000 were in twenty strongholds in Flanders, nearly 4,000 in twenty-four strongpoints in Brabant, the remainder scattered throughout positions on the Maas, Lower Rhine and Ems, and the Dutch committed an equally high proportion of their army in the same way.[54]

Even in those areas of Europe which lacked the new-style fortifications large numbers of men were also to be found in garrisons, sheltering behind the relative safety of a town's medieval walls or moat, or the hastily improvised earthworks of a village. From this strongpoint the garrison could dominate the surrounding countryside and exploit its resources. Eustache Piémond, a notary from the Dauphiné, described in his diary the plethora of garrisons set up by the Huguenots in the Midi during the Religious Wars 'to eat up the people'. During the English Civil War both sides maintained substantial numbers of their troops in garrisons, ranging in size from the 3,000 Royalist troops who occupied Reading in the spring of 1644 – doubling the population of the borough – to the handful of men stationed at places such as Faringdon and Greenland House near Henley whence they could control the down-river trade to London.[55]

THE SPREAD OF KNOWLEDGE; SPECIALIZATION AND PROFESSIONALISM

Knowledge of the new weapons, drill, tactical formations, techniques of fortification and siegecraft, and other aspects of warfare, was widely disseminated and argued over in a military literature comprising pamphlets, leaflets, books, treatises, drill books and memoirs, which began to appear in increasing quantities from the early years of the sixteenth century, reaching a flood around the 1560s and continuing almost unabated through the seventeenth century.[56] Some of the authors were armchair theorists such as Sir Thomas Audley, or political philosophers of one sort or another, such as Seyssel, Machiavelli or Justus Lipsius, who combined, in varying degrees, discussion of military theory and practice with observations upon the political and social organization of states and the nature of government. But they included a steadily growing number of former, or practising, military men who used their experiences, often set out in more or less autobiographical form, as the basis for an evaluation of contemporary practices and a source for the formulation of universally applicable precepts on all aspects of the conduct of war. Amongst the best-known here were the Englishman Sir Roger Williams, the German von Schwendi, the Spanish diplomat and soldier Mendoza, the Danish captain Rantzau, the Frenchman Jean de Billon and the Italian Raimondo Montecuccoli. The sixteenth century especially was also marked by an enormous resurgence of interest in the military writings of the ancients. A listing of useful Greek and Roman authors drawn up in the Netherlands ran to over 2,000 folio pages,[57] and translations of classical authors' works appeared in unprecedented numbers, together with commentaries and glosses on their writings, generally designed to elucidate the key elements in classical warfare and demonstrate their applicability to the contemporary early-modern situation. All too often military writers without any practical background themselves (and occasionally even those who did have experience of campaigning) advanced, on the basis of their reading of the ancients, wholly impracticable techniques and formations – arrow-head, half-moon, wedge and double-winged shapes – which had a spurious geometrical plausibility on the pages of a book, but which were of no value on the battlefield.[58] But even experienced veterans, such as that no-nonsense soldier Roger Williams, who condemned these wilder flights of fancy which did not accord with experience, saluted the ancients, and cited classical precepts in support of their own opinions when it suited.

There was, too, a steady outpouring of a more narrowly technical literature: drill books, such as Gheyn's much-copied *Wapenhandelinghe* (1607), Callot's derivative *Exercises d'armes* (1635) and de Lostelneau's more comprehensive *Mareschal de bataille* (1647), demonstrated in numbered pictorial sequences the movements of body and weapon which the soldier had to master; the Brescian Niccolo Tartaglia was one of the first to suggest a mathematical means of calculating the trajectory of shot in his *Nova Scientia* (1537); while Luigi Collado provided the artilleryman with a practical manual giving ranges, weights of shot and powder, trajectories, allowances for windage, in his *Practica Manual de Artiglierra* (1586). Above all, there was an enormous literature on fortifications, how to build them and how to assault them, culminating in Vauban's *Traité de sièges et de l'attaque des places* (1704).

Only rarely were books meant to have a limited circulation amongst initiates, though this was true of Wallhausen's *Kriegs-kunst zu Fuss*, commissioned for use in a military school, and de Gheyn's *Wapenhandelinghe* for example. But pirated versions of both soon appeared, and a majority of authors hoped for a large market, the best books being widely copied and translated. Later versions of de Gheyn were designed in such a way that letterpress in Dutch, German, French, Danish and English could

40

be inserted, so assisting the manual's Europe-wide distribution. Different armies were at different times acknowledged to be the current leaders in particular aspects of the art of war. In an effort to cash in on the reputation of the Swedish forces a second edition of Monro's book, originally entitled *Monro, his Expedition with the Worthy Scots Regiment*, was brought out in 1644 with a revised title: *The Scotch military discipline learned from the valiant Swede*. What this did for sales is uncertain. What is clear, however, is that the dissemination of military literature helped to ensure that no one state retained a monopoly of military techniques or knowledge.

The same effect was also achieved through the constant interflow of personnel between armies. At one level, this might comprise young men of a certain social status who were sent to acquire some military knowledge as part of their general education, travelling to one of the 'Schooles of Warre' – the Low Countries, Germany, or the Austrian-Turkish frontier – where the art of war was practised in its most developed forms, and serving a spell in one of the armies; for whatever the claims made for the benefits to be obtained from reading military literature, it was accepted that book-learning on its own was no substitute for actual experience. Thus Abraham von Dohna, a member of an east Prussian noble family, together with his brothers and cousins, was sent to serve a turn in the Netherlands; so too was Frederick William, the future Great Elector, who was coached in the military sciences in Leyden in 1634 and in Frederick Henry's military camps. The latter, an acknowledged expert in the art of siegecraft, attracted a host of observers and volunteers to witness his attempts on 's-Hertogenbosch (1629) and Maastricht (1632).[59] Some of the young gentlemen, of less elevated rank than Frederick William, might hope for soldiering as a future career, in which case a period of military sightseeing would stand them in good stead: for as Hermann Kirchner asked, 'What captain of warre is to be appointed over an army, if not he that hath searched the manners of other people, & hath scene their skirmishes and exercises in military affairs?'[60] If successful the young aspirant joined that far larger body of professional soldiers (see below, page 143) constituted not just of officers but of rank-and-file troops as well, who looked to war as a full-time occupation, and who moved from one employer to another in the course of

41

a career in the profession of arms, in the process acquiring and helping to spread a knowledge of contemporary military practice.

The early-modern period also witnessed the establishment of the first military schools to train officers. By the turn of the sixteenth century military engineering was firmly established on the curriculum of a number of universities, court-based schools had been set up at Tübingen, Cassel and elsewhere, and the Venetian government sponsored academies founded between 1608 and 1610 in Padua, Udine, Treviso and Verona – though these were perceived largely as a solution to a law and order problem by keeping high-spirited young gentlemen out of trouble, rather than as a means of equipping them with any serious training for war. But the first military academy proper, aiming to provide more than just lessons in equestration and swordsmanship, was founded in 1617 at Siegen in Westphalia by John of Nassau, with Wallhausen as its first director. Others followed: in France (1629), Savoy (1677) and at Berlin (1717); artillery and engineering schools were set up in France (1679), Austria (1717) and Russia (1701–9); and cadet companies for officer training were maintained in France and Prussia.[61] We should not set much store by the practical contribution of these academies. The school at Siegen folded in 1623 having had only twenty-three students; the French *Académie des exercises militaires* was only slightly longer-lived and marginally less socially exclusive. Elsewhere only a tiny fraction of officers were channelled through these institutions. Nor did this matter very much, for most officers were able to acquire the expertise they needed through reading and practical experience. The truth was that war was steadily becoming more technical and complex, but things had not gone so far as to necessitate a formal military education for its practitioners. Nevertheless, the foundation of schools and cadet companies was a recognition of the way things were moving. It was no longer sufficient for an officer to be able to ride a horse, display personal valour and handle his personal weapons (indeed the latter qualification was of declining importance as officers engaged less and less in hand-to-hand combat and the range of offensive weapons they carried declined). Other qualities and skills were needed: some elementary knowledge of ballistics, cartography, military drawing, geometry and mathematics was required to design a set of earthworks, set out a series of entrenchments, lay a gun, mount a siege, read and draw a campaign map and deploy a given body of men into a particular formation; an ability to drill men on the parade ground, teach them the use of arms, and lead and inspire them in conflict was needed; so too was an understanding of the problems of feeding and transporting large bodies of men and their equipment. No wonder Thomas Audley advised Edward VI that the quality of English forces would never improve until captains were appointed for their 'worthynes' rather than out of 'favor'.[62]

Internally the structure of armies altered, albeit slowly and haphazardly, in response to the growing complexity of war and the introduction of new technology. The artillery began to emerge, alongside the cavalry and infantry, as a separate component of the army, with its personnel of skilled technicians: master-gunners, superintendents of artillery, wheelwrights, carriage makers, carpenters, gunpowder experts, metal founders. Under Philip II the artillery in Spain had its own system of justice under the Council of War, its own finances and its own hospital services. Similarly the artillery was treated as a distinct entity in the sixteenth-century French forces: expenses incurred during the 1537 Piedmont campaign were paid in a separate *tranche* via a treasurer of the artillery, for example, though full-time artillery regiments did not really emerge here, nor elsewhere, until the very end of the seventeenth century.[63] Military engineers remained as a sort of sub-branch of the artillery, their status within the army often uncertain, not least of all because civilians were frequently called in to serve, and there was no proper rank structure. But the number of officers and troopers employed in an 'engineering' capacity rose steadily, and by the late seventeenth century most armies had companies of miners, sappers and pioneers for use during sieges, and in the construction of bridges, roads and defences for military camps. By this stage too the number of provosts, marshals and others concerned with the enforcement of discipline had grown. Foraging was left less to the initiative of individual captains and placed under the overall control of quartermasters and their staff, who had some responsibility too for the transportation of baggage, equipment and stores, although the provision of carts, horses and drivers was still largely achieved by resort to civilians.[64] Nevertheless in this respect, as in others, a perceptible degree of specialization of functions had been reached during the course of the period 1495–1715.

THE EXPERIENCE OF CONFLICT: SIEGE AND BATTLE

The proliferation of gunpowder weapons, the adoption of new tactical formations, the use of new forms of siegecraft: all these developments affected the ordinary soldier's experience of conflict, whether battle or siege, making it very different by the late seventeenth century from what it had been two centuries earlier. It is difficult to seize hold of that experience, for the journals and diaries which might inform us in detail only begin to proliferate in the eighteenth and nineteenth centuries, and barely exist at all for the sixteenth century. It is nevertheless clear that the reality of conflict was a far cry from the glorious picture of charges, wheeling horses, bright armour and deeds of individual heroism beloved of battle painters and chroniclers. Laying siege to a fortress in early-modern Europe, for example, was an experience not dissimilar to that endured by soldiers in the First World War: damp trenches which threatened to cave in (Alba's German troops at Metz worked in 'mud up to their ears');[65] troops huddled together as they waited the moment of the assault, their heads down as they were subjected to a hail of shot from defenders' guns, including howitzers, which dropped shells vertically into the approach trenches; the use of explosive mines in the mining and counter-mining operations which became a standard part of siegecraft (one observer at Steenwijk in 1592 saw one of the bastions and its defenders blown up, 'the bodies of men...hovering piecemeal in the air, the torn and divided limbs yet retaining their decaying vigour and motion');[66] the bloody hand-to-hand fighting in the cramped trenches between besiegers and small sorties from the beleaguered garrison;[67] and the massed assault on the breach under a barrage of gunfire. Reminiscent, too, of the First World War were the long-range artillery duels between the fort and siege gunners in which the latter would probably come off worst, for they were obliged to remain standing and move round their weapons in order to service them, and thus presented relatively open targets despite the erection of protective screens of wood and earth-filled wicker baskets.

On the battlefield close-quarter fighting, the prime objective of the medieval knight, gradually gave way to longer-range musketry duels. In 1598 one English writer commented that 'it is rarely seen in our days that men come often to hand blows as in old times they did',[68] though some actions in the Civil War were still noted as being settled at push of pike. The transformation was certainly complete by 1700. In an analysis of 411 men, wounded survivors of the battle of Malplaquet, Corvisier found that only 2.2 per cent were victims of bayonet thrusts, necessarily inflicted at close quarters, but a majority had suffered gunshot wounds: 64.3 per cent from hand firearms, 13.7 per cent from cannon.[69] The noise of the firearms, together with the clouds of heavy dirty-white smoke from the only partly combustible gunpowder which they used, would have been an increasing feature of battles and sieges. In 1637 the Spanish besiegers of Leucate were hampered, when themselves attacked, by the smoke blown into their eyes by the north wind. The *Swedish Intelligencer*'s account of Alte Feste recorded that 'the cannons and muskets went off all day long incessantly: so that nothing was to be seen upon the mountain, but flame and smoke'. And Robert Monro recounted that at Breitenfeld he successfully led his musketeers against enemy cannon, but then 'the smoake being great, the dust being raised, we were as in a darke cloude not seeing the halfe of our actions, much lesse discerning, either the way of our enemies, or yet the rest of our briggads.'[70]

Monro's account highlights not only his narrow range of vision but the confusion he felt during the battle, for he lost touch with the progress of the engagement as a whole and was only able to maintain contact with his immediate comrades, in this instance by summoning them to him with a drum. Was this confusion and isolation a general feature of the soldier's battlefield experience? Probably. It resulted on occasions not from the blinding smoke of the guns but from the weather conditions. Lützen, for example, was fought in a fog, Narva in a snowstorm, and Poltava in mist and rain which prevented Charles XII's soldiers from seeing their Russian opponents until they collided. More generally it stemmed from the limited ability of commanders to exercise any sort of central direction over the conduct of an engagement once it had begun. Generals lacked a specialist staff of *aides-de-camp* and riders to transmit orders to their subordinates during the course of a battle; and those subordinates anyway regarded themselves as exercising a semi-independent command, and were not always disposed to accept or wait for orders. Marlborough was unusual in having reliable officers such as Parke, Bingham and Richards, and this helps to explain the greater tactical control he was able to exercise during an engagement, but most contemporaries were not so fortunate. As armies and battlefields grew in size, and as linear formations were adopted, it anyway became difficult for a single man to keep track of what was happening everywhere on the battlefield. By the seventeenth century commanders were, for the most part, obliged to content themselves with drawing up their forces before battle and issuing orders on what was to be done during the course of it, but without knowing whether those orders would turn out to be relevant or be obeyed. (One might question whether the propensity of military treatises to stress the key role played by the commander in setting out his troops before battle was not to compensate for, and gloss over, his limited ability to influence the outcome of the engagement thereafter.) Once the engagement began the general could, of course, personally command one part of the army; or he might dash about the battlefield, going to wherever the fight was hottest in the fashion of a mobile fire brigade,[71] hoping to rally or inspire his troops. Gustavus Adolphus met his end in this fashion at Lützen, shot down together with a couple of companions. But neither he nor any other commander could hope to synchronize operations on the battlefield. Particular decisions about whether a unit should advance, fire or retreat had of necessity to be devolved upon subordinate commanders at the head of the regiment or the brigade, and they based those decisions on what was happening in their immediate vicinity, rather than on any knowledge of the progress of the engagement as a whole. Even at this level of command the ability of officers to control their men was limited. Montecuccoli warned that moving men from one place to another easily resulted in 'tumult and confusion'.[72] Robert Monro did well to rally at least part of his brigade in the confused fighting over the guns at Breitenfeld, for, as Montecuccoli also noted, troops once committed to combat were not psychologically amenable to discipline.[73]

Small wonder then that the ordinary soldier's perception of battle would have been fragmentary and confused. He would have had little concept of acting as part of a well-ordered, articulated machine, wheeling, forming and reforming in response to some central direction, since for the most part armies simply did not function like that. What we may say is that for the ordinary soldier conflict was, above all, a test of his nerves, or what nowadays would be termed the 'will-to-combat'. It was a test which probably became more severe during the seventeenth century. The prelude to an engagement, as men huddled in the trenches or stood exposed in line, was always an ordeal, but one which was made worse by the increasingly common practice of preceding a battle by an extended cannonade.[74] The actual engagement itself was supremely a test of will. As we have seen, apart from the brief period of battle-winning dominance enjoyed by the Swiss pike phalanx in the late fifteenth and early sixteenth centuries, the introduction of new weapons and tactics on to the battlefield merely reinforced the defensive superiority of the infantry. As a result, battles tended to be attritional, each side skirmishing, charging, and firing with musket and cannon, until the nerve of one side gave way and it fled the field. This probably represented the most dangerous moment of an engagement, at least for the infantrymen; for, as Robert Monro pointed out, they were easily cut down in flight, and he advised that they stand firm and thus get quarter.[75]

The conduct of soldiers when confronted with the test of conflict was far from uniform. At Malplaquet the regiment of the *Maison du Roi* endured a six-hour cannonade unflinchingly, and Corvisier's analysis of the position of the wounds on 411 survivors suggests that the men maintained discipline to the last, an overwhelming majority having sustained injuries on the left side of the body when they were presumably facing the enemy, ready to fire or presenting their bayonets.[76] The Spanish *tercios* at Rocroi retained unbroken formation despite suffering enormous losses, and at Marignano the Swiss fought for twenty-eight hours without breaking order. On the other hand, the Saxon contingent at Breitenfeld disintegrated at the mere approach of Tilly's troops; and at Naseby the bulk of the Royalist troops fled without engaging the enemy, the crucial moment coming, according to Clarendon, when the king was prevented from leading a charge: 'upon this they all turned their horses and rode upon the spur, as if they were every man to shift for himself'.[77]

How are these differing reactions to be explained; and what made men prepared to fight at all? It is clear that not all did so willingly, and some had to be coerced. 'The men must be deprived of all hope and every means of saving themselves through flight. They must be forced to fight', wrote Montecuccoli, whose *Sulle Battaglie* contains some of the most perceptive insights into the nature of conflict from any seventeenth-century writer.[78] He suggested destroying roads and bridges in the army's rear, while officers, standing behind the squadrons, were to cut down those who fled or broke ranks. He also suggested the administration of intoxicants before battle, and these were certainly handed out on occasion, the English soldiers receiving an allowance of brandy before Malplaquet, for example, though how far this was done as a matter of course is unclear. The holding of some form of religious service, also counselled by Montecuccoli, was not unusual, especially in those armies which felt (or whose commanders felt) that they were engaged in a religious crusade of sorts. Prayers were offered in the Swedish army before battle during the Thirty Years War, for example, while soldiers in the Army of Flanders carried a plethora of religious artefacts – crosses, charms, *agnus dei* – about them as they engaged in fighting.[79] All this may have boosted the soldier's morale, persuading him that victory was divinely ordained and reconciling him to his personal fate in the conflict.

Most early-modern treatises and accounts of battle also point to the crucial importance of the pre-fight speech from the commander in raising the men's ardour for the engagement. The government newspaper, the *Mercure Française* stressed that before Rocroi, Enghien (later Prince de Condé), 'roused all the officers and men to eagerness for the battle with a speech whose eloquence was distinguished by martial ardour'.[80] Thomas Audley's 'Treatise on the Art of War', prepared for Edward VI, contained a prototype for the king to use as need arose (mercifully, given the quality of the speech, it never did).[81] While not denying its importance altogether, we may be sceptical of the value of the speech, not least of all because it would have been audible only to those in the speaker's immediate vicinity and would not have carried to an army of several thousands, even were it gathered in one place. In all probability military writers stressed the importance of the pre-battle speech partly because, in so doing, they were following the precedent set by the classical authors; partly because – like Audley – they were often dependent upon the patronage of kings and nobles, precisely the sort of people who commanded armies; and partly because this was yet another way of heightening the otherwise limited role played by the commander in guiding the engagement to a successful conclusion. Probably more important in boosting morale than any set-piece speech were the informal words of encouragement spoken by commanders if they were able, and inclined, to tour the battlefield before the engagement began, and by officers and seasoned veterans to their immediate comrades: but on this aspect of battle we have virtually no evidence.

We need have no doubt, however, about the key part played by booty and ransom in motivating the soldier. 'It is possible to make soldiers resolute by raising the hope of great reward and prizes if they succeed', wrote Montecuccoli, advising the general to point out to them that a victory enabled them 'to seize everything – men, women, gold, silver, the enemy's whole country'.[82] They hardly needed to be told this. The dead and wounded were routinely pillaged after an engagement. Monluc recalled the lucky escape of François de Bourbon, wounded thirteen times and left for dead at the battle of Pavia, who just managed to cry out as a Spanish soldier made to cut off his finger with a ring on it, and so was ransomed instead.[83] And it was widely recognized that the three days' uninterrupted pillage allowed to soldiers who took a city by storm were indispensable if the men were to be persuaded to mount the hazardous assault.[84] Indeed, Sydnam Poyntz even argued that in order to get the best out of the soldier it was necessary to keep him impoverished, for 'A rich souldier will never fight well.'[85]

Montecuccoli finally pointed towards one aspect of the will-to-combat which was probably most crucial of all, and which has been more fully investigated and confirmed by research into combat in the twentieth century: the value of comradeship. Troops who developed ties of loyalty to one another were likely to fight with great commitment and to make personal sacrifices, both in order to help their comrades and so as not to incur the group's contempt by acting in a cowardly manner. 'Troops who are known and familiar to each other are placed side by side,' wrote Montecuccoli,

This is because their proximity provides great strength in times of peril. One unit will generously bear the brunt of the struggle in order to rescue the other. For if it did not grasp the opportunity to earn merit *vis-à-vis* its neighbour, or if it were to abandon him through flight, the men would experience great remorse and shame.[86]

In the heterogeneous armies of early-modern Europe such ties of comradeship developed naturally amongst men from the same national background. The Army of Flanders was not alone in recognizing the military value (as well as the administrative convenience) of putting soldiers into national units, and had long adopted this as standard. But ties of comradeship grew up amongst soldiers of whatever nationality who served together over a long period of time, and it was amongst veterans that the will-to-combat was most developed. Such men, familiar with the handling of weapons, habituated to the rigours of war and enjoying a self-confidence born of sustained victories in conflict, always comprised an elite in any army, and were the troops that commanders and governments most wished to employ.[87] A force of veterans, all other things being equal, would always triumph over less experienced men. Where they were over-whelmed by superior numbers, or greater firepower, as were the Swiss at Marignano and the Spanish at Rocroi for example, they were prepared to fight to the bitter end. When veteran forces clashed in battle, as they did at Alte Feste, Lützen and Nörd-lingen, then the fight was bloody and prolonged.

CONSTRAINTS ON WAR: THE LIMITS OF THE POSSIBLE

The early-modern period thus witnessed important changes in the art of war, most of them brought about by the introduction of new technology. The increasing use of firearms had profound implications for battlefield tactics and the ordinary soldier's experience of conflict. The adoption of the *trace italienne* altered the pattern of siege warfare, and was one of the factors responsible for the increase in the number of men under arms. Largely in response to the new technology armies became more professional and specialized. Yet important though these changes were, they were not the whole story, and they should not blind us to the fact that in many ways European warfare was far from revolutionized in the two centuries after 1500.

In his *Arte della Guerra* (1521) Machiavelli had predicted major changes in the conduct of war. He correctly foresaw an increase in the size of armies. He also prophesied that these armies would fight short, well-planned campaigns, culminating in a single decisive battle which would shatter the enemy's will and bring the war to an end. In these respects he could hardly have been more wrong. With a few exceptions, such as the Schmalkaldic War of 1546–7, campaigns in the two centuries after Machiavelli wrote rarely proved decisive, and wars frequently dragged on for years until mutual exhaustion forced an inconclusive peace on the combatants. Far from being well-planned, campaigns were increasingly characterized by a paucity of strategic thinking. Pitched battles were certainly fought, often with great commitment and intensity, but generally only when they were unavoidable, and military activity chiefly consisted of set-piece sieges, assaults on small garrison towns and what the French Chancellor Antoine Duprat described as 'dribbling war':[88] actions by concentrations of troops sometimes numbered not even in hundreds but in dozens, who raided, ambushed, skirmished, seized prisoners, all the while seeking to destroy the enemy's economic resources by burning crops and villages while protecting their own.

One reason for Machiavelli's mistaken predictions lay in his failure to comprehend the effect which the adoption of the *trace italienne* would have upon the conduct of war. Blockading one of the new-style fortifications – the only certain means of reducing it – was a lengthy business. The siege of Haarlem lasted ten months, for example, and Ostend held out for over three years. Fourteen months were needed to capture La Rochelle in 1627–8, and it took Marlborough one hundred and thirty-one days to reduce Liège in 1702. Two years earlier the Swedes had successfully defended the great fortress at Riga from February to August against the army of Elector Augustus.[89] To be sure, such examples were exceptional, and by the seventeenth century the conduct of sieges generally followed an established pattern. Vauban claimed to be able to predict their course on a daily timetable, and allowed between forty and sixty days to bring one to a successful conclusion. Yet even a siege as brief as this would occupy much of the available campaigning season. Even the most vigorous commander would be left with little time for further actions before returning to winter quarters. Where the new-style fortifications proliferated, which, as we noted, tended to be the most fought-over areas of Europe, warfare was reduced to a seemingly interminable succession of sieges.

Was there no alternative to this pattern of warfare? A few contemporaries, as well as subsequent commentators, regarded the almost universal predilection of military commanders for sieges rather than the apparently more decisive and altogether briefer activity of a battle as a sign of mediocrity, and a perversion of what warfare ought really to be about.[90] Yet this was not really the case. In eschewing battle commanders were following medieval precedent and the injunctions offered by the much admired classical authors. Ravage the countryside, seize the strongpoints, advised the Roman author, Vegetius,[91] and this made sound common sense, for battles were risky and unpredictable. They might involve the death or capture of the commander, as happened in the case of Gaston de Foix at Ravenna (1512), Condé and Montmorency at Dreux (1562), Tilly at Rain (1632) and Turenne at Sasbach (1675). The loss was the more damaging if the general was also the monarch, as in the case of Francis I, captured at Pavia, or Gustavus Adolphus, killed at Lützen. The army itself might be destroyed: Marston Moor in July 1644 cost Charles I his northern army and the north of England; Naseby cost him his last field army and the war; while only 1,500 of the 20,000 men whom Charles XII led into battle were left after the disaster at Poltava in 1709. The outcome of a battle was always uncertain, even when the odds appeared to be firmly stacked in favour of one side. Thus, at Rheinfelden in 1638, Bernard of Saxe-Weimar's disordered army was caught by a superior Bavarian force while crossing the Rhine, but pulled off a victory in the ensuing conflict, capturing the opposing commander Von Werth. Even when victory was achieved in battle it was difficult to exploit, and the cost in human lives might be appalling. At Malplaquet the Allies lost 25,000 men, or 23 per cent of their force, an unacceptable casualty rate to governments who increasingly regarded their trained soldiers as valuable assets, not to be squandered lightly. To be sure, sieges bled armies of men – 15,000 at the Allied siege of Lille for example – but here the casualties were spread over four months, and this was more acceptable to governments and commanders reconciled to the ceaseless haemorrhaging from illness and desertion which afflicted armies at all times.[92] Moreover, few engagements, however decisive the outcome on the battlefield, broke the will of the army's political masters to carry on fighting, or rendered them incapable of doing so: Mühlberg and Naseby were two of the few exceptions which prove the rule.

In contrast to the hazards of battle, the outcome of a siege was predictable, for, providing it could be effectively blockaded and given enough time, even the strongest fortress could be starved into surrender. Moreover, a captured fortress was a tangible and valuable gain. It might be used as a bargaining counter at the conclusion of the war, and it was strategically significant, for the occupying garrison could control and exploit the surrounding countryside, an important consideration given that the aim of most wars was to seize or hold down territory. It is significant that even those generals who attached a high value to pitched battles actually fought relatively few. This was true of Turenne, for example, who advised the young Condé, 'Make few sieges, and fight plenty of battles; when you are master of the countryside the villages will give us the towns.' Marlborough, who had learned his craft under Turenne, reckoned a victory on the battlefield 'of far greater advantage to the common cause than the taking of twenty towns': yet he fought only four pitched battles as against thirty major sieges.[93]

Given all this, it might reasonably be asked why battles occurred at all? In the particular case of the English Civil War one can point to the amateurishness and inexperience of the leaders on both sides which led them to commit their forces in this way with relative frequency: there were twenty-four significant field engagements between Edgehill in 1642 and the surrender of Sir Jacob Astley at Stow-on-the-Wold in 1646. (The conventional view that strategy in the Civil War had to be battle-oriented because of the lack of new-style fortifications in England, which in turn meant that there could be few sieges, ignores the fact that the war witnessed numerous assaults on towns, though these were usually defended by old-fashioned or hastily improvised defence works.) More generally, however, battles in the sixteenth and seventeenth centuries either arose out of a siege, and were fought between a besieging army and a relief column – as at Ravenna (1512), Pavia (1525), St Quentin (1557), Nördlingen (1634), Breitenfeld II (1642), Rocroi (1643), and Vienna (1683), for example – or they were fought for logistic reasons, usually when an army was cut off from its supply area and gave battle rather than starve.

In fact logistics – what has been defined as 'the practical art of moving armies and keeping them supplied'[94] – was crucial, not just in bringing about a number of battles, but in determining the conduct of war as a whole. Like siegecraft, this was an aspect of war whose importance Machiavelli underrated. Significantly, he never commanded an army in the field. Had he done so he would have realized the extent to which considerations of provisioning and transport dominated the thinking of military leaders and shaped their actions. The problem was fundamentally one of numbers. An early-sixteenth-century army of 10,000 men was bigger than most towns of the period; and at over 40,000 Henry VIII's army of 1544 in northern France was two-thirds the size of London, and roughly equal to one of the great cities of Europe such as Antwerp, Rouen or Toulouse. In addition to the fighting soldiers all armies carried a tail of lackeys, clerks, wives and prostitutes who all had to be fed. Henry II's expedition into Germany in 1552 had a paper strength of 40,000, but the authorities in Lorraine were told to cater for twice this number and one estimate in 1648 put the Imperial-Bavarian army at 40,000, with a further 100,000 followers.[95] There were also animals to be fed: cavalry horses, pack mules, each carrying loads of between 200 and 400 lbs, and draught animals for hauling the baggage and supply carts. In 1621 Jacobi von Wallhausen suggested, as a rule of thumb, that one cart was needed for every ten fighting men, but this proportion was exceeded in many instances. In 1573 Don Lope de Acuña's tiny expeditionary force of twenty-five companies needed 140 baggage carts; and 2–2,500 wagons accompanied Spinola's 15,000 men in 1606, each cart requiring between two and four horses to pull it.[96] Yet more draught animals were needed to haul the cannon, powder, ball, match, ladles, measures and associated paraphenalia which made up the artillery train. When a siege was in prospect the amount of equipment, together with the number of carts and animals to transport it, rose accordingly. Three divisions of wheeled transport were needed to move the Royalist army's siege train in 1642, which included

500 shovels, 100 pickaxes, and 10 wheelbarrows; and sixteen thousand horses were needed to drag the 100 great siege guns, 60 mortars and 3,000 wagons brought by the Allies to the siege of Lille in 1708.[97]

The provisioning requirements of even a small force were enormous: when the army reached 60,000 they became staggering. To meet its ration allocation an army of this size required 45 tons of bread, over 40,000 gallons of beer and the meat from 2–300 cattle every day. Its animals consumed 90 tons of fodder (the equivalent of 400 acres of grazing) and each of its horses needed 6 gallons of water per day to remain healthy.[98] Towns and cities had established complex transport and marketing systems involving grain-dealers, millers and carters to supply their needs, and their provisioning zones reached many miles beyond the town's boundaries. Armies, though they were ambulant cities in terms of size, had nothing like this. How were they to be fed?

The normal expectation during most of the sixteenth century was that soldiers would purchase food out of their pay, either directly from local producers and suppliers, or from one of the dozens of sutlers who accompanied every army and acted as middle-men, buying from local farmers to resell to the troops at a profit.[99] This worked tolerably well when the troops occupied a town and could benefit from its established provisioning systems (though these would easily be overloaded if the number of soldiers was too great, of course), and not surprisingly, towns were valuable military objectives for this reason alone. But away from an urban setting it worked much less well, for the army rapidly exhausted the supplies in its immediate vicinity and more could not easily be brought in. The system anyway depended on the soldiers being regularly paid, which was generally not the case. As a result, armies frequently resorted to a system of more-or-less well regulated plunder to supply themselves. Either the soldiers took what they wanted by force, indiscriminately damaging crops and property in the process, an exercise euphemistically described as foraging; or supplies were requisitioned at prices set by the army; or the troops were billeted in local households which had to provide them with food and lodging against a promise of future payment. The system of regulated plunder was brought to its highest peak of development in the *kontributionssystem*, which emerged during the Thirty Years War as a response to the problem of feeding armies of hitherto unprecedented size from the limited resources of Germany.[100] Initially used in the 1620s by Mansfeld in Bohemia and by Spinola in the Palatinate, the system was subsequently fully exploited by Wallenstein and wholeheartedly adopted by Gustavus Adolphus. Territory occupied by their armies, be it enemy, friendly or neutral, was systematically milked of its resources. The local administration, where it continued to exist, was obliged to allocate and collect regular weekly or monthly contributions from the local population, in the form of money, foodstuffs, or whatever else was required, which were handed over to the occupying forces. Spinola used existing tax registers as the basis for assessing the level of contributions in the Palatinate. Demands for contributions were backed by the threat of force: failure to pay would result in the butchery of the recalcitrant population and the destruction of its property, though this of course was meant to be an expedient of last resort, since the whole purpose of the *kontributionssystem* was to preserve the productive capacity of the territory intact, while tapping it for the army's benefit. Ironically, the need to extract contributions under continuous military pressure served to increase the size of the armies still further: as Wallenstein noted, a force of 20,000 could not hold down sufficient territory to make it viable, whereas a force of 50,000 could sustain itself indefinitely.[101]

The *kontributionssystem*, like requisitioning and billeting, left the army dependent on locally available supplies. In an effort to lessen this dependence, armies on the march habitually took supply carts with them loaded with reserves of food. In 1544, for example, elaborate preparations were made to ensure that Henry VIII's army in France was as near self-sufficient as possible. Over 2,000 bakers, millers and other men connected with victualling accompanied the army, whose train 'was out of all reason, for besides the munitions and artillery there were mills, ovens, vessels for brewing ale...with a good deal of flour and malt, great herds of cows and bullocks, and flocks of sheep and wethers'.[102] But the animals and men added to the provisioning requirements of the force. And, as was always the case, even with such large victualling trains, the wagons were physically unable to transport more than a few days' worth of the supplies needed. Within a short time Henry's army was reduced to living off the countryside.

Because there were no easy or cheap answers to the problems of supplying armies, governments, at least in the sixteenth century, generally preferred to be as little involved as possible. But they did not always adopt a 'hands-off' approach. Where troops were stationed permanently in garrisons on home territory, or where they moved regularly along established military corridors, it made sense for the government to have some arrangements for providing them with food. One way of doing this, widely used until the 1570s, was for the Crown to use its medieval rights of purveyance to allow its officials to requisition food at fixed prices and arrange for this to be delivered to the army, or stockpiled in villages along its route; or, as was increasingly the case by the later sixteenth century, agreements were made with private merchants who contracted for the acquisition and supply of agreed quantities of food to the army.

Government involvement in the matter of supply did score some important successes. Most spectacularly, many thousands of Habsburg troops were moved rapidly and relatively safely after 1567 along the 'Spanish Road', the 700-mile transit route between Lombardy and the Netherlands, living off a chain of pre-stocked magazines. In 1551 French government *commissaires* set up similar supply dumps in the Maurienne valley, the military corridor leading into north Italy. And the Privy Council in England arranged the shipment of large amounts of foodstuffs to English troops 'overseas' – a neglected achievement in a state generally reckoned to be backward in military affairs in the sixteenth century. Thus, troops in Scotland were supplied with grain from East Anglia, dairy produce from Suffolk, and meat, brought 'on the hoof' from the Midlands. In the 1540s, Calais and Boulogne received flour from Hull and fish from Norfolk and Hampshire, and between 1598 and 1601 contracts worth over £10,000 were entered into with English merchants for provisioning the much increased numbers of troops maintained in Ireland.[103] The English government was unusual, however, in being able to transport most of these supplies by ship, the cheapest and easiest method of large-scale long-distance transport available in early-modern Europe. But neither England, nor any other sixteenth-century state, had either the administrative ability or the purse to arrange the vast numbers of carts, horses and drovers needed to move supplies in bulk long distances overland.[104] Thus, supplies brought to the army as a result of government initiative had, for the most part, to be obtained locally, and did not lessen the army's dependence on resources from its immediate surroundings. In any event, no state made arrangements for continuously supplying its forces when they operated on enemy territory: the army then was expected to obtain the bulk of its supplies from the local countryside as a matter of course. This had the advantage of shifting the burden of war on to the opponent. As Francis I told the English Ambassador in 1521: 'You see what charge I am at, and also how my [troops] eat up my subjects, wherefore I will march on straight and live upon my enemies' countries, as they have done on mine.'[105]

Francis was not the only ruler to allow the considerations of supply to affect his conduct of a campaign. Logistics shaped the conduct of war at all levels. The duration of the campaigning season – usually from March to October – was established by the availability of pasture and fodder for the horses and fresh food for the men. The need to spread the army out to forage for that food (always an ideal opportunity for would-be deserters to make a run for its unless the operation were properly handled), plus the need for the army to halt altogether every third or fourth day to rest and bake bread, dramatically reduced the speed at which it moved.[106] Mobility was further restricted by the ponderous accompanying train of wagons, horses and cannon – another reason for campaigning only in the spring and summer months when the roads were at their best.[107] Troops using the 'Spanish Road' were expected to average 12 miles per day, and one force managed an extraordinary average of 23 miles in 1578.[108] But outside of a well-established military corridor such as this, 8 miles per day would be good going, less if the roads were really poor or the weather bad. Even Marlborough's 250-mile march to the Danube in 1704, rightly acclaimed as a masterly piece of logistics management, averaged only 12–14 miles per day.[109] Generally, commanders who tried to force the pace for a sustained period paid a heavy price in men lost through illness and desertion: in 1626 Wallenstein covered the 373 miles from Zerbst to upper Hungary in twenty-two days, but at the cost of three-quarters of his force of 20,000 men. Of course, marching times could be improved if the artillery and reserve supplies were moved by ship, either by sea or along navigable rivers. The progress of troops down the 'Spanish Road' was greatly facilitated after 1621, for example, by the Spanish conquest of the Palatinate which gave them control of the Rhine; Christian IV's operations in Germany in 1625–6 centred upon the river systems of the Weser and the Elbe; and both Turkish and Imperialist forces depended heavily on supplies brought along the Danube and Tisza in the campaigns of the 1690s.[110] But waterways were not always available, and too heavy a reliance on them severely curtailed an army's area of operations. With mobility so restricted, and the campaigning season limited, it is not surprising that most campaigns were slow and indecisive, especially when, as we have seen, they were largely given over to the conduct of sieges.

Logistics determined not just when campaigns were fought, the pace of operations and what might be achieved, but how wars were conducted. A victory over an opponent in a pitched battle might result in the destruction of his army: but the same result could be achieved just as effectively, and with less risk to oneself, by depriving him of supplies. Much military activity was therefore aimed at the capture or destruction of an opponent's economic resources. The records of the *Chambres de comptes* in Lorraine, for example, list hundreds of mills and bakehouses destroyed as a result of military action in the 1620s and 1630s.[111] Monluc dwelt at length, and with pride, on a sortie he had led against windmills near the Imperial positions at Auriol. It was hardly epic stuff, but, as he pointed out, campaigns were won by the cumulative results of such actions.[112] Maurice of Nassau burned over two hundred villages in the course of his campaigns. He was outdone by Elizabeth's generals in Ireland who, in the 1590s, systematically ravaged territory so as to deny its use to the rebels, a policy which was ultimately successful but which left much of Ulster, Munster and Cork decimated, the crops burnt, the countryside uninhabited and the towns destroyed.[113]

A scorched-earth policy such as this might also be used to hamper an advancing army. The Count of Nassau, Charles V's general, in retreat from Mézières in 1521, left a trail of destruction behind him in hope of halting the pursuit by Francis I. The French king adopted a similar policy in Hainault in the autumn of the same year, engaging in 'the most piteous destruction of towns and spoiling of so fair a country as never have been seen among Christian men', as one contemporary noted.[114] In 1536 the Duke of Montmorency evacuated Aix and turned lower Provence into a wasteland: only the fruit trees were deliberately left standing in the hope of giving dysentery to the advancing army of Charles V. This pattern of ravaging the countryside in order to deny its resources to an opponent was repeated in the seventeenth century. Large tracts of Germany were laid waste in this way during the Thirty Years War; and the French commander Ville, who strongly advocated this method of waging war, put it into operation in Roussillon in 1639. After his victory at Sinsheim, Turenne devastated much of the Palatinate in order to deny its use to Montecuccoli; and in 1704 Marlborough ravaged much of Bavaria, his troops removing whatever crops, livestock and property they could carry before destroying what remained.[115] When it was properly carried out, ravaging the countryside in this way served a dual purpose: it starved the enemy, and it secured supplies for the army which performed the operation.

In addition to the fighting and foraging carried out by the field armies, much military activity concerned the garrison troops who, as we noted, formed a large proportion of the men under arms. Where both sides in a conflict maintained garrisons in neighbouring areas the resulting hostilities usually settled into a pattern of patrols and ambushes, skirmishes and raids into 'enemy' territory to capture prisoners, seize supplies and destroy crops and property, as each garrison sought to extend its control over the surrounding countryside and its resources, while denying these to the enemy. This was the reality of much of the fighting during the French Religious Wars, the Dutch Revolt and also the English Civil War, for example. As a well-known jingle from Somerset put it:

> I'ze had zix oxen tother day,
> and them the roundheads stole away,
> a mischief be their speed.
> I had zix horses left me whole,
> and them the cavaliers have stole,
> God zores they are both agreed.[116]

Yet important though garrisons were for defence and for holding down territory, wars could only be won by field armies which took the initiative. By the beginning of the seventeenth century, however, and certainly by the time of the Thirty Years War, the ability of commanders to seize the initiative was becoming severely circumscribed by the logistic problems of feeding armies of unprecedented size. Logistics, which had acted as a constraint on commanders in the sixteenth century, came to dominate their actions to the exclusion of almost all other considerations during the next century. Simply keeping the army in being became an end in itself. Strategy was increasingly divorced from the stated war aims of the combatants, and was reduced to a crude concern to occupy territory with as much supply potential as possible, or at least to deny it to the enemy.

Nothing illustrates the constraints imposed by logistics upon these mass armies better than the career of Gustavus Adolphus.[117] After landing in Pomerania in 1631 his growing forces exhausted the local resources, and the king sought to expand his contribution base, fighting the battle of Breitenfeld both in order to gain control of Saxony and at the same time deny this fertile area to Tilly. After Breitenfeld Adolphus chose not to advance against Vienna, the heart of his enemies' power, since this would have taken him through the harsh uplands of Bohemia, but instead moved into the Rhineland. The route offered easier going for his artillery, and the rich principalities of this most fertile area of Germany could be systematically exploited to feed his swollen army. He thus gave up the chance of a knockout blow against the Habsburgs, and, by occupying the Rhineland, he antagonized his chief ally, France. The logistic interests of his army took precedence over political considerations. The need to extend still further his contribution base drove the king along the Danube and into Bavaria in 1632. The second half of that year was dominated by a cat-and-mouse game played between Gustavus Adolphus and Wallenstein for control of the supply areas of Germany. Saxony was deliberately devastated by Wallenstein to deny its resources to the Swedes. Penned down for two months in front of Nuremberg, the king's army exhausted the local resources and its numbers dwindled by half. He was forced to retreat north-west, but Wallenstein, his army too exhausted to capitalize on this, made the mistake of dispersing his troops so as to avoid the supply difficulties which had decimated the Swedish army, and was surprised by Adolphus at Lützen. The Swedes claimed a victory in the battle, but their king lost his life.

The Swedish army at Lützen numbered some 19,000, although there were around ten times this number in Swedish employment at the time. Throughout the Thirty Years War it proved impossible for Gustavus, or any other commander, to concentrate on a single front the forces which were theoretically available. Too many troops, packed into a single theatre of operations, simply exhausted the area's supplies and risked starving to death. The *kontributionssystem* anyway demanded that the troops be widely dispersed in garrisons to supervise the collection of contributions. Thus, of the 180,000 men in Swedish pay in the autumn of 1632, over 60,000 were maintained in nearly one hundred separate garrison towns in north Germany, while a similar number fought as separate units elsewhere in the Empire. The same was true of the Imperialist forces: over 40,000 were permanently tied up in garrisons.[118] The result of this was that, despite the unprecedented numbers of men under arms, battles and operations were carried out by field armies scarcely bigger than those of the sixteenth century (see above, Table 1, p.5). Breitenfeld was wholly atypical in the large numbers involved: slightly over 40,000 Swedes against 31,000 Imperialists. For the most part it was rare for armies to number more than 20,000. The ability of states to raise troops had not been translated into an ability to concentrate them at a single point in order to secure an overwhelming and decisive victory over the enemy. Larger armies did not lead to shorter or more decisive wars.

Ultimately, the *kontributionssystem*, designed to feed these huge forces, proved a failure. The demands of the armies were crippling. The discipline in them, a prerequisite if the system was to work effectively, was too poor to prevent the unlicensed pillaging which quickly reduced the supply potential of an area to zero. This was true even in the Swedish army, generally reckoned to be one of the better controlled. As early as May 1631 an official wrote, 'The cavalry do as they list...they plunder the land to the very bones, provoking complaints and curses fit to make you shudder.'[119] By the 1640s this, plus the deliberate ravaging of territory to deny its resources to the enemy, had laid waste to whole areas of Germany. Field armies were reduced in size to 10–15,000 men, not because more could not be recruited but because more could not be fed; and the cavalry constituted a higher proportion than previously, simply because they were the most adept at foraging. French, Swedish and Imperial forces struggled for control of territory from which supplies could be extracted by force, as the war degenerated into a series of battles, raids and manoeuvres which had little to do with any overall strategy designed to secure the political objectives of their masters, everything to do with the survival of the armies themselves.[120] Strategy had become an appendage of logistics.

The Thirty Years War carried important lessons for the states which had raised the armies. One was that if they were to be effective instruments of state policy, armies had to be brought under state control. Equally clear was that a failure of supplies could easily destroy their efficiency as fighting machines. As Richelieu noted: 'History knows many more armies lost through lack of bread and the want of order than through the actions of their enemies.'[121] France's recent experience provided a host of examples: the army sent to Mainz in 1635 melted away because of supply difficulties; the mere news that a French regiment was to be moved across the Rhine into war-torn Germany was enough, the Cardinal claimed, to induce most of its men to desert; while a lack of food, munitions and money rendered the Duke of Rohan's campaigns in the Valtelline and Lombardy in 1635–7 largely nugatory.[122] If such collapses were to be averted in the future greater state intervention in army provisioning seemed unavoidable, and most governments moved in this direction during the later seventeenth century.

In many ways France led the way, notably under the guidance of two successive Secretaries of State for War: Michel Le Tellier (1643–66) and his son Louvois (1666–91).[123] Le Tellier designated a series of routes within France to which armies had to adhere when on the move, and supply dumps were set up on them by the local *intendants*, one marching day's distance apart, the intention being to avoid the indiscriminate plundering which resulted when unfed troops were moved across the country. Louvois oversaw the establishment of a series of magazines at strongpoints along the frontier: at Breisach in Alsace, Metz, Nancy and Thionville in Lorraine, Sedan and Rocroi in Champagne, and Pinerolo in north Italy, for example. Stocked with non-perishable foods (onions were a great favourite) each had the theoretical capacity to withstand a six-month siege. In addition, *magasins généraux* were set up near the frontier to supply the field army as it embarked on campaign, and a permanent pool of vehicles and military drivers was set up – the *équipage des vivres* – to supplement the locally requisitioned transport which was still commandeered to carry reserves of food with an army on the march. Some military supplies were purchased directly by government officials such as the *surintendants généraux des vivres*, established by Richelieu in 1627, the *commissaires des vivres*, or the *intendants d'armée* who, by the 1670s, were permanently attached to the armies. However, a lack of ready money meant that contracted victuallers remained the basis for gathering and delivering supplies. They were employed on a much increased scale by the Crown, but their activities were more closely supervised than in the past, especially by the *intendants d'armée*, who checked the quality, quantity and price of the supplies they delivered. Where France led, others followed. Much of the bread for the English forces in Flanders was supplied by large-scale contractors: Solomon and Moses Medina, Vanderkaa and the Dutchman Mynheer Hecop for example; and Salvador Segundez and the Gomez brothers supplied the Dutch and Portuguese forces in the Iberian peninsula.[124]

None of this was exactly new: Sully had designated a number of military corridors within France early in the seventeenth century; magazines had been used in the sixteenth century, and so too had bulk contractors. The later seventeenth century witnessed an intensification of government involvement in military provisioning, rather than any new initiatives. And arguably just as important were measures undertaken by armies themselves to improve their supply position. By 1700 most armies on campaign included a specialist staff whose primary function was to ensure the location and provision of foodstuffs. The English forces, for example, had quartermasters and their assistants attached to each regiment, headed by a quartermaster-general for the whole army, a post filled under Marlborough by the redoubtable Cadogan.[125] Improved discipline meant that the *kontributionssystem* could be made to work more effectively. And there were the glimmerings of a realization that by splitting an army on the march into several columns, and not concentrating it on to a single route, the troops could move more rapidly, subsist more easily and the countryside would suffer less damage. In 1675, for example, the 70-year-old

Derfflinger moved the Prussian army to confront the Swedes by dividing it into several units spread over a distance of nearly 80 miles, subsequently achieving a victory at the battle of Fehr-bellin.[126]

Armies were undoubtedly better supplied in the later seventeenth century than previously, as a result of initiatives such as these and the greater involvement of the state in military provisioning. Marshal Navailles was able to congratulate Louvois for securing 'all the necessary victuals, cannons and munitions' for the siege of Ghent in 1678; Villars wrote of the way he had arranged 'such a large force together with its supplies' for the siege of Mons in 1691;[127] and for the first time it became possible to concentrate bodies of troops one hundred thousand strong for a single field engagement. Yet fundamentally the conduct of war remained as shackled as ever by logistic constraints. Magazines might be well stocked, but it remained impossible to provide the immense numbers of wagons and horses needed to transport all but a fraction – 10 or 12 per cent – of the foodstuffs required by an army on the march. French armies operating inside their own country or close to its borders could be provisioned, but they, like all other armies, were obliged to live off the land when on campaign outside their frontiers, with all the restraints which this entailed. As Creveld notes 'it was the availability or otherwise of *local* supplies, much more than magazines or convoys, that determined the movements of Louvois' forces just as it had those of Gustavus Adolphus.'[128]

What conclusions can we then draw about the changing art of war in the early-modern period? The two centuries after c. 1500 undoubtedly witnessed significant changes in warfare, many of them related to, or deriving from, the introduction of new technology. There was a shift from weapons of cold steel to firearms; battlefield formations evolved from mass to line; in a way that had not previously been the case, the brute strength of the soldier counted for less than his proficiency at handling his weapons under orders; and armies evinced a tendency towards specialization and professionalism. Yet it is doubtful if all this amounted to a 'military revolution'.

For one thing, it is in many ways the continuity in the nature and practice of early-modern warfare when compared to that of the Middle Ages which is striking, rather than the differences. On the battlefield the defensive retained its traditional supremacy over the offensive: indeed, if anything, it was strengthened by the introduction of new weapons and tactics. Moreover, battles remained relatively infrequent events, and it was the siege which predominated. This was also the pattern of an earlier period. Dr Allmand has written of the Hundred Years War, for example, that it 'was not typified, and certainly not decided by the outcome of battles ... war was characterised more by sieges than by any other form of martial exercise';[129] and it is notable that Richard the Lionheart, the pre-eminent military figure of his age, in an adult life given over almost entirely to active campaigning, though he conducted innumerable sieges nevertheless fought only two or three set-piece battles.[130] To be sure, sieges perhaps lasted longer on average in the early-modern period – the nine-month siege of Rouen in 1418–19 was one of the most extended of the Hundred Years War, for example – and the total number of sieges (and battles) was greater than in the late Middle Ages, reflecting the greater incidence of warfare in the early-modern era, but none of this alters the fact that the siege remained the predominant set-piece engagement of the period 1495–1715. Moreover, even when they were fought the outcome of battles proved no more decisive in the sixteenth and seventeenth centuries than it had in the Hundred Years War: that is to say, it was almost never decisive at all. For all that Rocroi, Nördlingen, Jankov, Wittstock, Blenheim and Ramillies produced crushing victories for one of the sides, they did not end the conflict.

Additionally, logistics continued to exert a preponderant influence on the conduct of war. Vegetius' dictum that 'the main and principal point in war is to secure plenty of provisions for oneself, and to destroy the enemy by famine',[131] was accepted and acted upon by medieval and early-modern commanders alike. Ascanio Centorio might have been paraphrasing Vegetius when he wrote in 1567 that warfare was best conducted by laying waste the countryside and depending upon fear and starvation to achieve one's objectives.[132] As a consequence, most military activity was concerned, as in the Middle Ages, with foraging, raiding, destroying the enemy's economic resources, occupying territory with supply potential and besieging the strongpoints which allowed its control and denied its use to the enemy. Warfare remained attritional in nature, its aim being to wear down the enemy, rather than annihilate him with a single blow.

To be fair, that one aspect of early-modern warefare which markedly distinguished it from that in earlier periods – the vastly increased numbers of men with which it was waged, notably in the seventeenth century – has not yet been mentioned. But the purely military, as opposed to, say, the bureaucratic or fiscal implications of this, were hardly startling. Indeed, the greater numbers of men under arms served largely to intensify the logistic difficulties outlined above. Until the very end of our period it remained impossible to concentrate these men into large field armies on a single field of battle, and even then the occasions were very few, the armies were forced to disperse immediately afterwards, and the outcome of the battle was not anyway decisive. Michael Roberts has argued that having more men under arms opened up new strategic possibilities, allowing states to campaign more ambitiously, on several fronts, using several armies. Yet his vision of Gustavus Adolphus's plan to destroy the Habsburgs through the 'simultaneous and effectively co-ordinated operations of five or seven armies moving under the king's direction on an enormous curving front extending from the middle Oder to the Alpine passes', was less a 'strategic concept more complex, vaster, than any one commander had previously attempted', than a recognition by the king of a basic fact of military life: that if he did not spread his men out, but tried to group them together in the same theatre of war, they would all starve.[133] Increasingly throughout the seventeenth century, campaigns were planned and executed around the local availability of supplies, rather than as part of an overall strategy designed to secure the state's war aims. It is scarcely surprising that armies were drawn to, and military activity concentrated in, those areas of Europe which were agriculturally and commercially prosperous and which offered the best possibilities of subsistence: the Rhineland, Westphalia, Lombardy, the Spanish Netherlands and northern France.

In this respect, then, we may speak of 'limited' war by the close of our period: not limited in the sense that the war aims of the protagonists were restricted. On the contrary, these, as David Chandler points out, had never been more grandiose. In 1672 Louis XIV set out to dismember the United Provinces; the

War of the Spanish Succession concerned the readjustment of the whole balance of power within Europe and overseas.[134] But limited in the sense that, in practice, the armies proved unable to implement the grand aims and designs of their political masters. States were able to conjure up ever larger armies, but they failed to develop commensurate administrative mechanisms to supply and move them, and the armies thus remained prisoners of their antiquated logistic systems. As armies grew in size warfare became progressively protracted and indecisive: a far cry from the vision of Machiavelli in the early sixteenth century.

3

RECRUITMENT

THE METHODS

Armies were raised either through some form of voluntary enlistment, or by compulsion. In practice, although the seventeenth century witnessed an increasing resort to compulsion, a majority of soldiers generally joined as volunteers. Two different methods were used to recruit them: commission and contract. In the former the central government appointed a captain to raise a specified number of men from a given area within the state's sovereign territory. Under the second, the government negotiated with a military contractor for the delivery of an agreed number of troops, raised outside the state's territorial boundaries, at an agreed time and place, in return for the payment of a sum of money laid down in the contract. This system had evolved from that in use in fourteenth- and fifteenth-century Italy,[1] the chief difference being that by 1500 (and with the important exception of the Swiss) the contract was no longer made between a ruler and a company of soldiers, but between a ruler and an individual captain.

It was in sixteenth-century Spain that the commission system reached its most developed form.[2] Under Philip II, the Council of War, overseeing a system which remained essentially unchanged since the time of his father, fixed the numbers of men, established recruiting districts and appointed the captains. Local officials were ordered to assist by providing lodgings for the captain and his staff, a lock-up for the men (to prevent those who changed their minds about signing on subsequently from deserting), and money for their upkeep as they marched from the recruiting area to where they were mustered. By these means the Council looked to raise an average of 9,000 men per annum, with as many as 20,000 being recruited in occasional years.[3]

The advantages of the commission system were considerable and made it the ideal choice for any government wishing to raise men. It allowed flexibility in the choice of numbers raised, the timing and area of recruitment. Greater loyalty might be expected from the recruits, who would be subjects of the Crown, than was to be had from 'foreigners' – at least in theory. And the process established at the outset a bond between the captain and the men he had raised and whom he would subsequently command on campaign. Most importantly, it gave a substantial measure of government control over all aspects of the recruiting process. A state official verified the numbers of men mustered, thus preventing fraud by the captain, and checked their physical condition. In Castile a *comisario* organized routes, billets and provisions. In addition the captain and – in theory at least – the subordinate officers were named by the government. Yet the system was not without its disadvantages. It was relatively slow, the whole process from issue of the commission to final muster requiring a minimum of six weeks. Despite official vigilance, desertion *en route* to the muster point meant that the captain could not be sure of having a full complement when he arrived. The Spanish Council of War reckoned as a rule of thumb to lose one-seventh in this way, but it could be many more: half of Pero Méndez de Sotomayor's company of 425 had quit by the time he had travelled 10 leagues.[4] It was difficult to keep companies up to strength on active service unless the captain was detached from his command and returned home to find fresh volunteers, a cumbersome process and not generally feasible, especially when the service was overseas. With a minimum 'wastage' rate of 20–30 per cent per year, companies rapidly dwindled to a size where they were no longer viable. The system also required governments to provide money to pay for the purchase of flags, drums and other paraphernalia, together with, most important of all, the signing-on bounty, without all of which the recruiting captain was unlikely to have much success. To be sure, the sums involved were not necessarily large: each company cost the Spanish Crown around 500 *ducats* to raise in the second half of Philip II's reign, though admittedly the cost per man increased as the size of the company declined.[5] The real problem, however, was that this was money which had to be provided 'up front', and for governments always short of ready cash this was a major stumbling block. In practice, this frequently nullified one of the supposed advantages of commission recruiting, namely the government's unrestricted choice of captain, for ministers found that shortage of money obliged them to appoint men who would agree to finance the operation themselves, subsequently recouping their outlay plus a sizeable amount for interest from the state's coffers. Moreover, it was often found that only by delegating management of the recruiting process, including appointment of the captains, to an influential local figure with powers over clients, retainers, tenants and other dependants, could the required number of 'volunteers' be induced to come forward, a move which of course further eroded government control. Perhaps the major difficulty with commission recruiting for sixteenth-century states, however, was that if it was to work well it required that most unusual phenomenon: an extensive and reasonably efficient royal bureaucracy.

Some of these problems could be obviated by resort to the contract system.[6] To be sure, this too had its own disadvantages. Clauses in the contract might severely circumscribe the use to which the troops could be put. Thus, the 1589 treaty between the Grisons League and Venice forbade their use at sea, in assaults on Austrian territory and against fortresses.[7] The Swiss and *landsknechts* companies, with their well-developed corporate sense of identity, were notably assertive in defence of their own self-interests. The Swiss serving in Italy early in the sixteenth century, for example, developed a bad reputation for forcing battle against their employer's wishes in order to profit from the spoils (though forcing their commander, Lautrec, to fight at La Bicocca in 1522 proved counter-productive since they lost the battle):[8] or, conversely, of holding back when they were not paid. Moreover, contracting for troops was not cheap. Rates of pay were not always higher than average, but elite companies often demanded special bonus payments for winning or doing unpleasant work such as entrenching, and they insisted on a larger number of 'dead pays' than was usual. In addition, employers might feel it worthwhile paying well-established contractors pensions or a formally negotiated standby fee in peacetime to guarantee their service in times of emergency. Philip II disbursed over 50,000 florins to German captains each

71

year during the 1560s in this way; and in 1560 Venice signed an agreement with Melchior Lusi of Unterwalden giving him the considerable sum of 1,200 *ducats* per year in return for agreeing to ensure the availability of twelve Swiss captains and 3,600 men in case of need.[9] On top of this, there was a lump sum which had to be paid to the contractor when a contract was signed – unless of course he could be persuaded to fight on credit.

On the other hand, the use of military contractors offered substantial advantages. It allowed manpower resources outside the state's boundaries to be tapped. Troops could be raised speedily, perhaps within 2–4 weeks;[10] they usually came ready equipped; they were generally, in the sixteenth century at least, seasoned campaigners accustomed to military discipline and needing no training; and despite the strictures of Machiavelli and others, contract troops proved no less courageous or willing to give their lives in battle than men raised by other methods – indeed, the reverse often proved to be the case.[11]

Although two separate systems for voluntary recruiting existed – commission and contract – both shared a number of characteristics which makes it proper to regard them as variations of a single type. Both the commissioned captain and the contractor customarily commanded the companies they had raised on active service. More importantly, both were entrepreneurs who had made an investment in their company (often a considerable one in the case of the contractor) and looked to make a profit from it: by selling commissions, charging fees for promotion, by taking a percentage of the men's pay, fleecing them out of clothes and medical allowances, defrauding the government paymasters through false musters and accounting, as well as through the more legitimate means of booty, plunder and wages. Each regarded the company as a private or semi-private piece of property, nominally at the disposal of the state but only loosely under its control, and which, particularly in the case of the contractor, could be bought or sold, exchanged, or handed on to a legatee.[12] In short, armies were quasi-private institutions, and there was an important commercial aspect to the recruiting of troops, no less than to other aspects of war.

Both systems of recruiting, or some localized version of them, were in use during the sixteenth century. The Landgrave of Hesse was able to raise considerable forces for a time after 1550 employing only commissioned captains,[13] but of the major states only the Spanish monarchy had a sufficiently large pool of native subjects, an administration of the necessary size and sophistication, and the funds, to operate a fully-fledged system of commissioning as the predominant form of recruitment. And even here the commission system was restricted to those areas where royal authority was most extensive: Naples, Lombardy and Sicily, and, in the Iberian peninsula, Navarre, Aragon and Castile, the latter kingdom being the area where the system was most fully developed, and which provided the largest drafts of men and those reckoned to be of superior fighting quality. Moreover, by the end of the sixteenth century the system of recruitment was beginning to break down even in Castile, as a declining population, weakened by New World emigration, plague and the unremitting demands of the recruiting sergeant, had insufficient reserves of manpower to provide all the volunteers needed. One sign of this was the decline in the average size of the company into which new recruits were formed, and which comprised only 105 men in the first decade of the seventeenth century compared to 288 in the 1550s.[14] As a result the old system of recruiting by commissioned captains came to be virtually abandoned. Olivares had plans after 1632 to entrust the raising of troops internally to the nobility, while increasing numbers of mercenaries were hired abroad.

In the more autonomous regions of the Spanish monarchy – Catalonia, Galicia, Asturias, the Basque provinces and Portugal – acquired by Philip II in 1580 – manpower reserves were either untouched or tapped by using the services of the local nobility who took upon themselves the task of seeing that men were raised in return for payment or the hope of royal favour. Such men were not commissioned (though they might themselves commission captains to beat the recruiting drum), nor was their relation to the Crown a contractual one. They acted rather as voluntary agents, assisting the Crown, and because of this I. A. A. Thompson, whose research into Habsburg Spain has enormously enriched our understanding of the relationship between war and government, has called this a system of 'intermediary recruitment', which clearly had parallels elsewhere in Europe in the efforts of monarchs to persuade their nobilities to use their local influence to ensure that the demands of the recruiting sergeant were met.[15]

If Spain was the only major power in the sixteenth century to operate a fully-fledged system of recruiting by commissioned captains, the use of contractors was ubiquitous. It is true that in England Elizabeth, who had a profound contempt for professional soldiers and an aversion to spending money, used them in penny numbers and only in dire emergency, preferring to rely instead on a cobbled-together assortment of militia and pressed men. But her father had few such reservations and hired soldiers in substantial numbers for his campaigns in France and against Scotland; while under Edward VI the force commanded by Protector Somerset which defeated the Scots at Pinkie in 1547 included sizeable contingents of contracted men.[16]

Venice, on the other hand, used contractors to furnish the bulk of her forces in times of crisis or actual war. Some 24,225 troops, mainly infantry, were contracted for as part of the quota owed to the Holy League during the Turkish War of 1537–40 (though not all in fact turned up); and forty years later 62,000 new troops were raised, mainly by contract, and again to fight the Turks.[17]

The Danish kings too depended largely on contract soldiers, paid for with the revenues derived from the Sound Toll levies, and from 1572 the Dutch were substantial employers of contract men. France's forces always contained a substantial element of hired men in time of war: in 1515 Francis I contracted for 23,000 *landsknechts* alone, including the Guelders 'Black Band', proponents of the double-handed sword. And hired companies of Germans, Swiss, Italians and Scots were used by both sides during the Religious Wars – one estimate suggests that they comprised over 80 per cent of Henry of Anjou's army in 1569.[18]

Agreements with a contractor might be struck on a casual, one-off basis, but not infrequently the relationship between employer and contractor developed on a more permanent footing in the sixteenth century, especially as rulers sought to secure the exclusive services of particularly valued men. Venice, for example, had long-term arrangements with agents such as Count Giovanni of Corbavia and the Sanjaks of Bosnia for the supply of light cavalry. In 1521 a treaty was signed with the Graubünden, establishing a relationship which endured for 100 years. Venice also maintained agents in the Swiss cantons on a semi-permanent basis to negotiate the hire of these most sought-after troops, though negotiations were not infrequently blocked by Swiss treaty arrangments with other powers (one of the reasons why the Graubünden alliance was so useful was that the League, although lying within the Swiss cantons, did not form part of the Swiss confederation and was not bound by its treaty obligations). Francis I of France felt it worthwhile paying the Swiss a lump sum and an annual cash payment of 2,000 *francs* to each canton under the terms of the Perpetual Peace of Fribourg (1516) in order to secure their agreement not to fight against him in France or Milan and to open up the possibility of recruiting them for service in his own forces.[19]

A number of the sixteenth-century contractors operated on a substantial scale. Konrad Pennynck supplied Henry VIII with 3,000 *landsknechts* for example, and Hannibal von Ems's bill for troops supplied to Spain for coastal defence against the Turks and for service in the Netherlands in 1574 and 1578 came to well over 20,000 florins.[20] But the real heyday of the contractors came in the first half of the seventeenth century, and especially with the unparalleled opportunities presented by the Thirty Years War.

Although fought largely in a German theatre of war this conflict involved almost all the European states at one stage or another, and was waged using unprecedented numbers of men. Demand for the contractors' services had never been greater. Some of the states on the periphery of the actual fighting, such as the United Provinces and England, found it convenient to maintain an arm's length involvement by using contractors, thus avoiding the administrative burden and expense of recruiting soldiers themselves.[21] Of those countries directly concerned in the war, Denmark and Sweden, to say nothing of the German principalities, had limited native manpower resources, and could not hope to expand their armed forces to the unprecedented levels called for by the war except by resort to contractors. And none of them anyway had the administrative structures or the liquid cash necessary to do so. This was especially true of one of the major participants in the war, the Holy Roman Emperor, who, though he possessed sizeable potential resources in the form of his patrimonial lands, had few troops at his disposal at the outbreak of the conflict, and entirely lacked the bureaucratic machinery in his Austrian lands, still less within the Empire, rapidly to augment their numbers – all of which made him an ideal employer from the contractors' point of view.[22] Even France, a large and more administratively developed state, lacked the bureaucratic structures and the financial resources to mobilize effectively all the soldiers she needed after 1635. To be sure, as David Parrott has pointed out, the Crown 'played upon the enthusiasm for military office amongst the wealthy groups of French society' by encouraging native nobles and office-holders to raise regiments and contribute to the cost of their upkeep.[23] But such forces, their status-seeking officers frequently absent from duty, vastly under-resourced and ill-disciplined, performed disastrously on campaign; and the numbers raised in this way were anyway insufficient, and France too was obliged to depend upon the services of military contractors.

Contracting was a well-established practice within the Empire by 1600, providing a number of minor princes with their livelihood, and they were rapidly joined by captains from all over Europe attracted by the potential of the war. Redlich has estimated that there were about 1,500 contractors operating during the course of the conflict, some 300 in the early 1630s and never less than 100 each year during the remainder of the conflict.[24] Some operated on quite a small scale: in 1624, for example, the French government paid 710 crowns to a number of Graubünden colonels who each raised 100 men.[25] But other contractors – and these were the men who made possible the scale and duration of the war – operated at quite a different level, supplying not just companies of soldiers, but regiments and whole armies. Thus Count Ernst von Mansfeld provided Frederick of the Palatinate with a 32,000-man force; and in October 1635 Duke Bernard of Saxe-Weimar agreed to furnish the French crown with 18,000 soldiers. Standing head and shoulders above the rest, however, was the Bohemian Albrecht von Wallenstein, the Imperial commander from 1625 to 1630 and 1632 to 1634. Contracted initially to provide an army of 24,000, by 1630 he had nearly 151,000 men on his muster lists, grouped into forty regiments.[26] Major contractors like these not only recruited the soldiers, but also took responsibility for procuring their wages, clothing, arms and ammunition.

Although an employer would be expected to provide some cash 'up front' for the army – Saxe-Weimar's agreement with France was for 4 million *livres* annually – no state had the liquid resources necessary to support it fully. Contractors therefore offered armies on credit terms, and herein lay their crucial contribution to the war effort. They recouped their full costs through *kontributions* levied on the civilian population, the seizure of booty, the acquisition of land and property in conquered areas, as well as by the grants from their employers of cash sums, revenues from taxes, offices, lands and property. Wallenstein's personal loan of some six million *thalers* to the Imperial war effort between 1621 and 1628 was partially repaid by gifts of land in Bohemia and Mecklenburg, for example.[27]

To be sure, sixteenth-century contractors had been prepared to raise and supply troops, occasionally on credit; but never before had such a comprehensive package been offered to an employer, nor had operations of such scale and complexity been conducted. It was clearly impossible for a single contractor personally to recruit the thousands of men in an army, and hence a system of sub-contracting developed, in which a general contractor such as Tilly, Mansfeld or Wallenstein, made agreements for the supply of men with sub-commanders at regimental level, who in turn concluded contracts with captains, and so on down the line. Such were the profits to be made from the war that sub-contractors were prepared to pay for a commission in a well-established mercenary force: in 1627 Wallenstein was selling them 'for up to four regiments at a time to anyone offering his services'.[28] A contracted army thus represented an accumulation of venture capital on a vast scale.[29] To run the Imperial armies Wallenstein, in collaboration with the Dutch financier Hans de Witte, established a complex fiscal and commercial operation. Using a network of agents such as Walter de Hertoge and Abraham Blommaert, De Witte borrowed money at the great European financial centres of Linz, Frankfurt, Augsburg, Leipzig and Antwerp, which went towards recruiting expenses, the soldiers' wages and the purchase of equipment and provisions for the troops, much of the necessary clothing, beer, corn, horses, match, saltpetre and weaponry being supplied from Wallenstein's own enormous and ruthlessly exploited estates and factories in Bohemia and Mecklenburg. To service the web of debt and credit which all this involved, De Witte depended on payments from the Imperial Treasury – in 1626 Wallenstein wrote that he needed 'a couple of million in cash per year to keep the war going'[30] – revenues assigned from imperial taxes, and cash *kontributions* levied by the army commanders on friend and foe alike. As McNeill notes of the Wallenstein–De Witte operation, 'A more complete and grandiose merger of private commercial and military enterprise had never been seen before.'[31] In essence though, it was similar to operations run by other general contractors, being distinguished only by its size. Thus, the Berlin banking partnership of Weiler and Essenbrücher provided the money and credit facilities to support Hans von Arnim; the funds necessary for Bernard of Saxe-Weimar's intervention in the Upper Rhineland were found by the Lyons banker Bartholomew Herwarth, and he also had links with the financier Conrad Rehlinger; whilst the Frankfurt business founded by de Brier in 1620 flourished through its contacts with several of the major contractors so that it had capital assets alone of 517,000 *thalers* by 1636.[32]

The Thirty Years War could not, then, have been fought on such a scale had not military contractors supplied the administrative and credit facilities which governments lacked and which were necessary for assembling and sustaining large numbers of soldiers. Yet if the war demonstrated how far the contracting system might be developed, it also showed clearly the dangers inherent in it. Several of the great mercenary leaders, notably Wallenstein, manifested a dangerous independence of their employers. The Imperial commander-in-chief quartered his troops even in Habsburg and allied territories against the wishes of Vienna; he pursued independent negotiations with Saxony, Brandenburg and Sweden; and he conducted a military strategy often at odds with Imperial orders. Above all, this military adventurer, who by 1623 owned one-quarter of all land in Bohemia, had four palaces, kept a court of one thousand people at Prague, maintained a lifestyle of princely pomp and luxury, and whose lands the Emperor was obliged to elevate to the status of a duchy, appeared to be aiming for independent status within the Empire: he was, as one contemporary said, 'a subject become a soveraigne'. Fearful of his power, and suspecting him of open treason when in January 1634 he had his army officers swear an oath of personal loyalty, the Emperor connived at Wallenstein's assassination.[33] Saxe-Weimar was scarcely less troublesome to his French employers. 'An excellent commander, but so much for himself that no-one could make sure of him', was Richelieu's judgement on the man who refused to hand over the key fortress of Breisach and was determined to carve out an independent state for himself in Alsace.[34]

The armies themselves, consisting as they did of contractors and professional soldiers who lived on and for war, formed independent, self-conscious entities with their own corporate interests, not always amenable to control by their employers. Oxenstierna's sour comment, that he had been obliged to elevate the Swedish army to the level of a 'political estate' in his dealings with it over pay for the men and settlements for the contracting colonels and captains, was not wide of the mark.[35] The army had its own representative at the Peace Congress in 1648; and the subsequent demobilization of all the forces was protracted and exceedingly costly, requiring the holding of a separate Executive Congress in Nuremberg which operated always under the threat that the armies would re-start the war unless they received satisfaction.[36] Moreover, if the contracting system had proved capable of raising large numbers of men and sustaining them, it had only been possible through the most frightful destruction of people and property and the emptying of state coffers; and the contracting generals had not liberated themselves from the restraints of living off the land, nor had they led their armies to convincing victories.

The experience of the Thirty Years War thus convinced governments on the grounds of prudence, economy and military efficiency, of the need to restrict the autonomy of the military contractor, and to a large extent they achieved this during the second half of the seventeenth century, undoubtedly helped by the decline in the numbers of men under arms and reduced demand for the contractor's services in the aftermath of the war. To be sure, contracting was never fully eliminated. Christoph von Galen, bishop of Münster, was an active contractor, raising substantial forces for France, Spain, Denmark and the Empire between 1665 and 1678; and he was but one of a number of minor German princes including the rulers of Baden-Durlach, Wolfenbüttel, Württemberg and Hesse-Cassel who, finding it impossible to sustain large armies out of their resources, were prepared to hire regiments out to an employer in return for a cash payment and an agreement to provide for the men.[37] But these regiments were absorbed into the employer's own army, perhaps officered by his men and certainly commanded by his generals. The Great Elector used contractors to find men for his army, but recruitment was done in the Elector's name, and the recruits swore loyalty to him not the *condottieri*.[38] Elsewhere, greater use was made of commissioned captains, who were natives of the state. And governments increasingly took upon themselves functions which contractors had appropriated during the Thirty Years War – the supply of food, clothing, weapons and ammunition, and the payment of troops' wages. Yet it surely overstates the case to argue, as Otto Hintze has done, that 'Everywhere the system of condotta faded into the discipline of the royal army. The colonels ceased being military entrepreneurs and became servants of the state.'[39] The heyday of the great military contractor was over, but military entrepreneurship was not. Colonels and captains continued to regard their units as pieces of semi-private property; they expected those units to provide an economic return and officers still retained enormous control over the provision of goods and services to their men.[40] The age of the royal army might have come one step nearer by 1715, but it had not yet arrived.

The diminution in the number of men under arms in the immediate aftermath of the Thirty Years War proved to be a temporary phenomenon, and, with France leading the way, armies inflated to reach unprecedented size during the Spanish Succession War. States proved able to raise them, as they had not during the Thirty Years War, without recourse to general contractors. How was it done?

One way, as we have noted, was to lease regiments from a friendly power, and a number of governments secured semi-permanent links with other states to ensure the availability of troops: England with Hanover, and Venice with Cologne, for example. Another was to establish recruiting personnel in territories where the local government did not monopolize the market, as the rulers of Prussia did in the Duke of Mecklenburg's lands for example. However, this became harder to do as many states which were traditional recruiting areas forbade foreign recruiting agents, generally in order to secure the supply of men for their own standing army, part of which might then be leased out for a subsidy.[41] Although foreign nationals continued to form an important proportion of a state's armed forces, rulers were perforce obliged to look more closely at the native population as a source of recruits.

To some degree this source was tapped by an increased use of commissioned captains, a system now rendered more efficient than in the sixteenth century by the increased financial and administrative resources with which states were able to back it up. Yet it nevertheless proved difficult to find an adequate supply of volunteers by the closing decades of the seventeenth century. In 1694, for example, Alexander Stanhope, English Ambassador to Spain, reported that 'in four months they have not, with all their diligence, been able to get 1,000 men, though they are beating the drums every day', and such difficulties were far from confined to Spain.[42] The problem was one both of demand and supply. Demand for soldiers was running at an all-time high – there were perhaps two and a half times as many serving soldiers in 1710 as at the height of the Thirty Years War – yet the number of potential recruits had not risen accordingly. The strong demographic surge of the sixteenth century, which saw a doubling of the population in some areas (Castile went from 3 to 6 million between 1530 and 1594) and brought about a 50 per cent increase in the European population as a whole, was choked off in the early decades of the following century, which was marked by demographic stagnation, and even, in some areas, an actual fall. In these circumstances genuine volunteers became harder to find, and there was an increasing resort to trickery and underhand measures to obtain men. George Farquhar, himself a serving officer in 1704–5, brilliantly satirized these in *The Recruiting Officer*, in which Sergeant Kite (who listed the ability to lie, bully, swear, drink and pimp as the key qualifications of the recruiting sergeant)[43] intoxicated potential recruits and later claimed they had taken the king's shilling, and pretended to be a fortune teller in order to trick simple country fellows to join up. In Austria, captains pretended to be recruiting for the cavalry which offered higher pay and conditions, when they were actually after musketeers. Louvois acknowledged that such methods were reprehensible, but had to be tolerated: 'When the king lacks men for his army, that is not the moment to enquire whether they have been legally enlisted', he wrote in 1673 during the Dutch War.[44]

There was also an increasing resort to impressment as a means of filling the ranks. Not that there was anything new about impressment in itself. Sixteenth-century governments had been fully prepared to take certain categories of men – vagabonds and criminals – into service against their will. Orders from the Privy Council to the Lords Lieutenant in 1626 to press 'unnecessary persons that now want employment and live lewdly or unprofitably' had been prefigured in Elizabethan poor law legislation: between 1585 and 1602, the regime's most active military period, an average of 5–6,000 men per annum may have been found in this way, the actual business of rounding up the vagabonds being devolved upon the JPs, bailiffs and constables in the parishes. But the use of impressment grew considerably during the later seventeenth and early eighteenth centuries. Records of bounty payments made during the Spanish Succession War show, for example, that of 1,750 men handed over by the JPs in 1705 only 257 had come forward voluntarily; while 5,825 of the 6,912 recruits they produced in the winter of 1709 were pressed men. Nor was England alone in the increasing resort to impressment. An edict of November 1693 formalized a system in Brandenburg-Prussia whereby the central government fixed the numbers of recruits to be raised by each province, the local authorities meeting part of their quota by rounding up the useless persons. 'La presse' was also much in evidence during Louis XIV's wars; and by 1700 Frenchmen condemned to the galleys might be transferred straight into the army, though Protestants remained specifically excluded from this dubious benefit.[45]

Yet if governments were ready to resort to the use of impressment on an increasing scale, they nevertheless jibbed at imposing outright conscription. A number did consider it. The Spanish government threatened to call up one in five of all eligible males for the defence of Catalonia; a bill was introduced in the House of Commons early in the eighteenth century allowing a limited measure of conscription but subsequently abandoned 'lest it prejudice chances at the election'; and a fully-fledged scheme involving the peasantry was presented to the Great Elector by his adviser Bertram von Phul, though this too was rejected.[46] But only Sweden, with its tiny population and grandiose foreign adventures, actually introduced anything like a genuine system of conscription. Its origins went back to the Diet of Vasteras in 1544 when Gustavus Vasa had inaugurated a native militia. Service was soon made obligatory and not restricted to local defence. During Gustavus Adolphus's reign (1611–32) the system was further developed. He established the eligibility of all able-bodied males between 18 and 40 (the upper age limit was subsequently abolished) to serve for thirty years. Lists of eligible males were drawn up annually by the local pastors and churchwardens and used by the conscription commissioners to divide the men into *roter* or groups, each *roter* having to provide and equip one soldier, the size of the *roter* (generally between 10 and 20) being fixed according to the number of recruits needed in a given year. In this way almost 50,000 men were recruited between 1626 and 1630: 8,000 in 1626, 13,500 in 1627, 11,000 in 1628, 8,000 in 1629 and 9,000 in 1630. Subsequent modifications in 1642 and 1682 made farm-holdings rather than individuals the basis of the *roter*, and the demand for men under Charles XII (1697–1718) led to levies being taken more than once per year.[47]

Yet this was far from conscription in the modern sense of the term. It was not universal, whole sections of society being exempt: nobles and clerics, together with their peasants; workers in industries vital to the state; those with sons already serving; only sons of widows; plus, more surprisingly, apprentices in the royal gardens, church organists and employees of the inns connected with the postal service. Indeed, it is unrealistic to expect any early-modern state to have gone further and introduced universal conscription, not least of all because this would have transgressed one of the fundamental features of *ancien régime* society which all governments believed it their duty to maintain: the inequality of men before the law.

Yet if no other state went as far as Sweden in using conscription, a number did attempt to capitalize, as Gustavus Vasa had done, on the long-established principle that all adult males did have some duty, however vaguely defined, to serve under arms in defence of their homeland. This principle was expressed in the oft-reiterated (and as oft-disobeyed) injunctions to all males to keep and maintain arms; and also in the obligation to serve in one of the militias occasionally assembled for defence of the locality, be it town, village or parish, against outside attack. In practice the obligation to militia service tended to be honoured more in the breach than the observance. In the cities of the Low Countries during the sixteenth century, militias were reduced to rounding up ne'er-do-wells and drunks, and the better-off citizens found ways of escaping their tour of duty. Similarly, legislation from the German Diet in 1485, 1555 and 1654, urging burghers to organize in defence of their cities, proved of little practical effect. Some efforts were made by governments to breathe life into these local defence forces. Venice, for example, reactivated the militia for the defence of the *Terraferma* in 1528, officially enrolling 20,000 men. Two Militia Acts passed in Mary's reign aimed at ensuring the mustering of able-bodied men aged between 16 and 60, and subsequent Elizabethan legislation focused upon their training. In Spain military reformers floated plans for a national militia in 1558 and 1578, although it was not until 1590 that these eventuated in a general directive from Philip II, and even this bore no fruit until the 1620s. Denmark established compulsory militia service in 1614, and during the instability attaching to the implementation of the Reformation and the crisis years preceding and during the Thirty Years War, a number of states in the Holy Roman Empire, including the Palatinate, Bavaria, Ansbach, Hesse and Neuberg, reorganized their militias.[48]

The results of these efforts were uniformly disappointing. Militias manifested an invincible reluctance to train or to serve outside their own locality. It was perhaps just as well that Elizabeth's boast in 1580 that no king ever had a finer force with which to resist invasion was not put to the test, for the military performance of these part-time forces when confronted with professional soldiers was disastrous, as the Thirty Years War was to prove. As a consequence, princely interest in them declined for a time. However, it was revived at the end of the seventeenth century as genuine volunteers became harder to find, and some rulers began to explore the possibility of using the subject's obligation to perform militia service as a means of increasing the number of recruits into the regular army. In practice this could best be achieved by insisting that eligible men served in the militia, and then incorporating them directly into the regular army in time of war: in other words, compulsory military service by the back door. A number of states set up schemes along these lines: the bishopric of Münster in the 1670s, Piedmont in 1690, Denmark in 1710, Saxony in 1702 and Brandenburg-Prussia in 1701.[49] Easily the most extensive and successful, however, was that adopted in France. Established initially as an auxiliary to the regular army by Louvois in 1688, the *milice royale* was suppressed in 1697 and then reformed at the commencement of the Spanish Succession War, each parish having to provide one recruit on average, who was obliged to serve between three and six years. In this way some 260,000 men were raised between 1701 and 1713, which represents 46 per cent of all native French recruits.[50]

Yet only a few states looked to use the militia as a source of recruits, and here resistance to militia service was strong. In France, for example, the approach of the recruiting officials was a signal for young men to flee to the woods, to marry or to engage themselves as servants to the local *curé* (both married men and clerical servants were exempt from the initial recruiting draft) and there was in addition much outright physical resistance as well.[51] Moreover, militiamen, although they were useful for garrisoning forts and guarding prisoners, thus freeing regular soldiers for use in the field, were not rated highly as soldiers themselves. Volunteers remained the preferred option as recruits.

THE MEN

Writing in 1600, Thomas Wilson described those who 'went to the warres' as 'the common people...of the basest and most unexperienced sort'.[52] Lord Herbert of Cherbury spoke of the men who went on the expedition to the *Ile de Ré* as 'the mere scumme of our provinces';[53] and his words were echoed 150 years later by the war minister in France who insisted that 'As things are, the army must inevitably consist of the scum of the people, and of all those for whom society has no use.'[54] Such comments tell us more about the attitude of the authors towards soldiers than about the social origins of the recruits. Not until the advent of detailed record keeping in the eighteenth century is it possible to respond with precision to the question: 'Who joined the armies?' Nevertheless, sufficient evidence is available for the sixteenth and seventeenth centuries to enable us to establish the broad outlines of an answer for that period.

In a pioneering study, based on the lists of ex-soldiers admitted to the *Invalides* between 1670 and 1691, Robert Chaboche suggested that the average recruit was likely to be a young man. The median age on enlistment was 24, and over 60 per cent of the recruits were between 20 and 30 when they joined up, with a considerable proportion (24.3 per cent) aged below 20.[55] Much the same picture is revealed in Parker's study of the Army of Flanders. Men between 20 and 40 formed the overwhelming majority of those who enlisted, and of these the largest age-group was made up of men in their twenties.[56] The Swedish army of 1718, often believed to have been composed of old men and boys, in fact turns out to have had a similar age structure: only 6 per cent of those in it were over 40, and 17.7 per cent were less than 21. In one regiment, for which particularly good records exist, only seventy-three men were aged over 55, thirty-three between 15 and 17.[57] During the Thirty Years War the average age of native recruits from the Swedish homeland was undoubtedly lower. The insatiable demands which this war imposed on Sweden's limited manpower resources could only be satisfied by conscripting an increasing number of men in their early to mid teens. The records of the parish of Bygdeå, for example, show that by 1639 all but two of the conscripts were under 18, and the cohort's average age was only 15.[58] Examples of such extreme youthfulness remain confined to the Swedish experience. Nevertheless, literary evidence from autobiographies and memoirs confirms the impression of the recruit as a young man in his late teens or early twenties. James Turner, who left a detailed and vivid account of military life in the seventeenth century, joined up at 17; Sydnam Poyntz was a similar age; and Thomas Raymond was 23 when he first 'trail'd a pike' in Sir Philip Pakenham's company in 1633.[59]

Chaboche's study also suggested that although over half the native French soldiers were or had been married at some time during their army career, the majority had enlisted as single men. Amongst foreigners serving with the French army, the proportion was even higher: 58.8 per cent were single when they enlisted and never married subsequently.[60] Was this pattern repeated in other armies in the seventeenth century and earlier? The answer is almost certainly yes. Captain Antonio Flores, recruiting for Philip II, referred to the 'unemployed, single-men, upon whom the service of Your Majesty's standards depends'.[61] And we know that commanders discouraged the recruiting of married men, who burdened the army with their wives and families, and were believed to be less willing than unattached males to hazard their lives in battle. In 1586, for example, the Earl of Leicester urged Walsingham to ensure that no married men be included in the fresh drafts sent to reinforce his army in the Netherlands.[62]

In *A Pathway to Military Practice* (1587) Barnaby Riche

commented sourly on the social origins of recruits in Elizabethan England: 'When service happeneth we disburthen the
prisons of thieves, wee robbe the tavernes and alehouses of
tosspottes and ruffines, we scoure bothe towne and countrie of
rogges and vagabons.'[63] How accurate was this assessment?
Criminals certainly were drafted by governments. The Privy
Council released men from Newgate jail to help the besieged
English troops at Le Havre; and in 1633 two counterfeiters
were released from the Fleet prison on condition that they
signed on with a contractor recruiting men for overseas service
and never returned to England (an unlikely eventuality since the
recruits were destined for Russia).[64] Genoa pardoned Corsican
bandits who enlisted; and after 1569 a number of bandit gangs
in Catalonia were given amnesties by the Spanish Crown in
return for agreeing to serve a period with the royal armies.[65]
Yet, in truth, it was rare to find prisons being emptied to
provide men for the army. As Justus Lipsius noted in his
Politicorum (1589), hardened criminals were unable and unwilling to accept the discipline of army life and therefore made bad
soldiers. Only Gustavus Adolphus specifically forbade their
recruitment, but governments generally drafted them only in
small numbers and as a last resort.[66]

There is more justification for Riche's assertion that recruits
were, if not 'rogues', then 'vagabonds'. The well-to-do were
exempt from impressment and militia service – wholly so in the
case of the former, largely so in the case of the latter.[67]
Occasionally they fell foul of the recruiting sergeant, but they
were able to escape service with relative ease, by buying themselves out or finding a substitute. As Thomas Wilson noted in
respect of the 'richer sort of yeomen and their sons': 'the captain
will sometymes press them to the end to gett a bribe to release
them'.[68] The real target of impressment and militia legislation
were the masterless and unemployed – hence the joke in
Farquhar's *Recruiting Officer*, when sergeant Kite claimed to be
able to impress a coal miner since, working underground, he
had 'no visible means of a livelihood'. In enlisting such men
officials hoped not merely to find recruits for the army, but also
to rid the body politic of undesirable elements. Thus the 2,000
Irish taken in 1545 to fight in Scotland were drawn 'out of the
most wild and savage sort of them there, whose absence should
rather do good than hurt'.[69] Yet, as with the criminal element,

it would be easy to exaggerate the numbers involved. Most commanders would have agreed with the experienced Sir John Norreys when he warned Elizabeth that, like criminals, vagabonds were of dubious military value. While they were useful to make up the numbers, no commander wished to see his army flooded with such men, and in 1596 the local authorities in England were ordered (for a time at least) to cease impressment of them.[70] In any event, whilst the dragnet of impressment may have trawled in the work-shy and the destitute, a majority of men entering the army did so as volunteers, and they were not drawn from the ranks of the down-and-outs and the professional beggars. Rather, they came from those in the labour market, albeit often at the bottom end of it: minor artisans and petty shopkeepers, journeymen and wage labourers; and, from the countryside, the smallholders, subsistence farmers, ousted tenants and casual labourers. A few of those admitted to the *Invalides* in 1677 said that they had 'known no other way of life than war'. But most of the entrants had been employed before joining the army: as leather workers, carders and dyers, gilders, instrument makers, vineyard workers, agricultural labourers. There was even one innkeeper and six surgeons amongst the cohort.[71] Though they may have been at the lower levels of society, such men were emphatically not at the bottom of the social heap. What they frequently had in common was the lack of many, or indeed any, independent resources to fall back on, and this rendered them vulnerable to shifts in economic fortune, such as a subsistence crisis which pushed up the price of food, an industrial slump which caused workers to be laid off, a grasping landlord who lifted up the farmer's rent beyond a level which he could afford, or a failure of the corn or grape harvest which reduced the need for casual labourers.

Where, geographically, did the recruits come from? An answer to that question demands a response at a number of levels.

Virtually all armies in the sixteenth and seventeenth centuries were mongrel forces in the sense that they were made up, in varying proportions, of native and foreign troops. For example, Spaniards formed only a proportion of the men serving in the Army of Flanders, which rarely rose above 20 per cent and might fall as low as 7 per cent. To be sure, many of the other recruits, such as the Walloons and Italians, were technically subjects of the king, but the Army treated them as 'foreigners', putting them into distinct national units, in the same way that it treated the English, Scottish, Irish and German recruits for example. Henry VIII used very few foreign troops in England or against Scotland until 1545, but they comprised between one-quarter and one-third of the forces involved in his campaigns in France in 1513, 1523 and 1544.[72] It is of course difficult to be certain of the precise number of foreign troops serving in a given army since no government kept exact records (though the Spanish government in the sixteenth century was better than most). Foreign recruits were not always placed in separate regiments but often intermingled indiscriminately with native recruits. This was particularly the case with regiments brought together by a military contractor. Thus the records of one Bavarian regiment raised in 1644 listed no less than seventeen national groupings. Even supposedly national regiments contained outsiders: in 1613 it was discovered that over one-quarter of the Spanish light cavalry in the Army of Flanders were not Spaniards at all, but Walloons, who had presumably insinuated themselves to take advantage of the higher rates of pay and better conditions given to the Spanish.[73]

It is however clear that the number of foreigners fluctuated according to circumstances, generally reaching a peak in time of emergency or actual conflict, when demand for men was at its height, and when troops had to be raised quickly. This was the pattern in the Venetian forces during the sixteenth century, for example, and most spectacularly true in the case of the Swedish army at the start of its involvement in the Thirty Years War. A preponderance of the troops taken by Gustavus Adolphus into Germany in 1630 were native Swedes and Finns, but the urgency of expanding the size of the army meant that two years later they comprised only some 12 per cent of his forces.[74] It also appears that, having peaked during the Thirty Years War, foreigners formed a slightly decreasing proportion of armies during the later seventeenth and early eighteenth century. For example, during the Thirty Years War about one-quarter, and perhaps as much as one-third, of the French forces were raised abroad. Amongst the infantry the proportion fell to 12.7 per cent in 1671 (a time of peace), and although it rose again to 27.4 per cent in 1674 at the height of the Dutch War, it fell to just below 20 per cent during the final stages of the conflict. By 1690 the figure stood at just below 18 per cent.[75] However, what this reflected was an increasing use of native recruits, rather than a decreasing use of foreign ones. Thus, the number of foreigners employed in the French army during the Dutch War (1672–9) actually rose in absolute terms, although as a proportion of the total it fell. The fact was that states could assemble the armies of unprecedented size which were used in the later seventeenth and early eighteenth centuries only by tapping more effectively their reserves of native manpower.

A roll-call of any army reveals the widespread provenance of recruits in the early-modern period. Michel l'Hôpital referred to the royal forces in the third of the French Religious Wars as 'an army made up of bits and pieces' comprising as it did Germans, Italians, Spaniards, Walloons, Flemings, Albanians, Greeks and even some Slavs. The Welshman Elis Gruffudd did not hesitate to list his own countrymen amongst the 'many depraved, brutish soldiers from all nations under the sun' assembled for the siege of Boulogne: 'Welsh, English, Cornish, Irish, Manx, Scots, Spaniards, Gascons, Portingals, Italians, Arbannoises, Greeks, Turks, Tartars, Almains, Germans, Burgundians, Flemings, who had come there...to have a good time under the king of England, who by nature was too hospitable to foreigners.' In the Bavarian contract regiment of 1644 there were, together with the usual Germans, French and Italians, 26 Greeks, 54 Poles, 5 Hungarians and even 14 Turks. The States-General of the United Provinces employed Scots, English, and French brigades in the sixteenth and seventeenth centuries; and in 1661 the French Crown had twelve foreign regiments: two Scotch, four Irish, one Swiss, one Catalan, four German, and one raised in the bishopric of Liège.[76]

More positively, one can proffer two further generalizations about the geographical provenance of recruits. First, a disproportionate number came from the marginal regions of Europe: usually upland areas, characterized by poor soils, a harsh climate and an over-supply of population. The Swiss cantons are an obvious example. So too is Ireland, and the highlands of Scotland. Here, a propensity for cattle-raiding and domestic feuding imbued the inhabitants with an aptitude and a taste for arms which would stand them in good stead as mercenary soldiers. A complaint in 1606 noted 'That everie man that plesis wearis gunis, pistolis, rydis with jacks, spears, knopsknais, without controlment.'[77] In the *généralité* of Montpellier it was the unforgiving upland areas of the Cévennes, the Vivarais, the Gévaudan and the Velay, rather than the more fertile plains, which provided soldiers for the armies of Louis XIII and Louis XIV.[78]

Second, and sometimes cutting across this first generalization, a large number of recruits were drawn from the war zones themselves, at least in the seventeenth century. Thus, a disproportionate number of native French recruits came from the frontier provinces of the north and the north-east – Picardy, Champagne, and Franche-Comté after its incorporation into the French Crown in 1678 for example – all areas which witnessed considerable military activity and which had large garrison forces billeted on them. Similarly, the armies involved in the Thirty Years War picked up a large number of men from within Germany, increasingly so as the war continued and the devastation spread. Wallenstein's army lists reveal that in 1625, 61 per cent of his troops were of German origin; this had jumped to 79 per cent by 1627; and reached 87 per cent by 1630.[79]

A third generalization needs to be more cautiously offered. Traditionally, the bulk of the recruits are held to have derived from the towns, and there is indeed some evidence which supports this view. Chaboche's study found that of the native French soldiers 52 per cent were from the towns, 48 per cent from the countryside, though in the frontier provinces the proportions were reversed and here men of rural origins predominated: 63.4 per cent in Picardy, 61 per cent in Champagne, 56.8 per cent in Burgundy.[80] These figures gain added force given that less than 15 per cent of the French population would have been urban-based in the seventeenth century. A similar pattern emerges in relation to the English Civil War. Of 102 Parliamentary soldiers originating in the West Country 68 (67 per cent) were from the towns. A larger sample of 815 Royalist soldiers from Dorset reveals that 353 (43 per cent) were from the country, 462 (57 per cent) from the towns.[81]

Yet the generalization would not hold good for all armies. The system of conscription in seventeenth-century Sweden bore most heavily on the countryside, and meant that those recruited were overwhelmingly peasants.[82] Moreover, we should be sceptical about muster lists which record the recruit as coming from a town. When confronted with that ubiquitously posed question 'Place of origin?', a recruit was most likely to give the name of the nearest recognizable large town, rather than the (outlandish) name of some out-of-the-way village; and even if it were proferred a hard-pressed clerk would be unlikely to be able to spell it, and would therefore substitute the name of an adjacent and familiar town. Most likely of all, the clerk would record the name of the place in which the recruit was signed up; and this, most probably, would have been a town, for it was there, in the larger centres of population, that recruiting agents concentrated their activities. It is surely not accidental that most contemporary early-modern paintings and engravings, such as those by Jacques Callot, depict the recruiting sergeant in an urban setting. The man signing on in a town may well have been a countryman, who, hearing that a recruiting agent had set up his quarters there, made a special journey to the town in order to enlist. Or he may have been part of that growing number of rural inhabitants who, especially in the sixteenth century, found that there was no work for them in the countryside, and consequently drifted into the town in search of casual labour, poor relief, or in the expectation of making a living by engaging in peripheral crime. But at all events the recruit had his origins in the countryside, not the town.

The literary evidence on the subject is at best ambiguous. Thomas Wilson, for example, wrote that recruits in England comprised poor 'copyholders and cottagers...workeing by the day for meat and drinke and some small wages; thes last are they which are thrust out to service in weare', although he subsequently noted that they included 'artificers' (artisans and apprentices), many of whom might reasonably be expected to be urban-based. Barnaby Riche on the other hand wrote of scouring 'both town and country' for men.[83] In short then, whilst we can say that most recruits would have signed on in a town, it is unclear that a majority had been born there rather than in the countryside.

In the end it perhaps did not matter much. For army life had a way of shaping men who were drawn into it. And the motives which impelled men into the army were much the same whether they were rural labourers or urban artisans.

THE MOTIVES

Leaving aside those who were forcibly conscripted into the army, what impelled the volunteers – the majority – to join up?

For many, the answer was simple: hardship. As we noted earlier, recruits tended to be drawn from the most economically vulnerable sections of society: the wage labourer who, because of the overcrowded state of the labour market could command at best a minimum subsistence allowance, capable of supporting himself, a wife and perhaps one child (and then only if his wife worked as well); those thrown out of work in time of recession; the underemployed; the dispossessed cottagers and tenants from the countryside. For all of these the army offered the prospect of employment, and food. The twenty or so men from Myddle, Marton and Newton who joined the Civil War armies – thirteen of them never to return – included one who was maintained by the parish, a father and three sons so poor they lived in a cave, a homeless tailor and the son of a hanged thief.[84] As the impoverished recruit created by the playwright Calderón de la Barca so aptly put it:

> Only great need drives me to the war,
> I'd never go had I money in store.[85]

Sometimes war itself was the source of people's misfortune. Fighting in Germany in the 1620s disrupted the salt trade in the Salzkammergut, throwing out of work the salt-workers, together with the boatmen, the lock-attendants and porters who transported the salt down the Rivers Traun and Danube, many of whom subsequently joined the army to save themselves from poverty. Food shortages and high prices in 1707 led the whole of the orchestra at the Marseilles Opera House to volunteer, 'since they were dying of hunger'. In many respects the sixteenth-century French definition of a mercenary caught the situation well: 'a man forced to risk death in order to live'.[86]

To be sure, not all those who were needy or unemployed looked towards the army, otherwise there would have been no need for compulsion. There were ties of family, friends and community which held them back; and plenty of broken, limb-less, ex-soldiers eking out a living on the streets to remind would-be recruits of the hazards of military life. One Lord Lieutenant, explaining the failure of a recruiting campaign in England in 1625, wrote that 'our people do apprehend too much the hardships and miseries of the soldiers in these times'.[87] Yet need drove sufficient numbers of men into the armies to render the resort to compulsion on a large scale unnecessary.

If most joined the army to escape from hunger, others saw it as a means of evading other problems of civilian life: a pregnant girl, the threat of prosecution, imprisonment for debts (the signing-on fee might be used settle up with the creditors). The army also offered a refuge from religious persecution. As one of the troopers in Schiller's *Wallenstein's Camp* remarks:

> No questions are asked of confessions or creeds,
> There's only one difference that anyone heeds:
> Do you belong to the army or no?[88]

A newspaper suggested in 1633 that thousands of Protestants from Upper and Lower Austria had joined Wallenstein's army (notoriously lax in matters of religion) to escape forcible re-catholicization; while French Protestants in the aftermath of the revocation of the Edict of Nantes fled into the service of the Great Elector's army, or sought refuge in Louis XIV's armies, with the ironic result that by 1690 the state which had just proscribed Protestantism was defended by an army in which, when the foreign regiments are taken into account, more than one soldier in ten was a non-catholic.[89]

Relief from the problems of civilian life apart, what, more positively, did the recruit hope to gain from the army? The pay was hardly attractive, and its value was anyway whittled away by inflation, especially in the sixteenth century when prices may well have risen sixfold on average. The basic pay of the Spanish foot-soldier remained unchanged between 1534 and 1634. The pay of the infantrymen in Venetian service was fixed at 3 *ducats* per month in 1509 and stayed there for the next ninety years. Thomas Wilson put the average soldier's pay at 12 pence in 1600, but in fact most continued to receive the 8 pence per day settled by the government in the 1550s; whilst the pay of the soldier in Dutch service was unaltered at between 11 and 14 *guilders* per month throughout the seventeenth century. In any event, soldier's pay was set so low as to make it competitive only with the most menial civilian occupations. The average daily wage of a labourer in New Castile was about 83 *maravedis* in the 1580s: the common soldier received 34. The infantryman in Venetian service in 1616 earned only just over half the average daily wage of a building labourer.[90]

To be sure, things were not quite as grim as these figures might suggest. Many soldiers received additional sums for one reason or another. The Spanish front-line soldier was paid an extra 11 *maravedis*; and in 1527 handgunners in the French army stationed in Italy received 20 *sols* per month in addition to the basic wage of 6 *livres* to compensate for the greater cost of equipment and the difficulty of hauling it about, and an allowance was made for bonus pay to be handed out by the captain.[91] Moreover, the Spanish government revised the value of the money of account used to calculate its troops' pay upwards during the sixteenth century. This alleviated, though it did not eradicate, some of the worst effects of inflation. The Venetian government varied the number of days in its 'month', and, particularly when recruits were in short supply, found it necessary to pay by the calendar month rather than the 'month' of 38 or 45 days. The Dutch pay 'month' was reduced in similar fashion from 46 to 42 days in 1576.[92]

Yet the fact remains that the soldier's pay was uncompetitive, and in terms of wages he was close to the bottom of the social heap. Moreover, if, unlike his civilian counterpart, the soldier did not have to pay taxes, seigneurial dues or the church tithe, there were stoppages on his wage to pay for his food, armour, clothing and weapons. These might account for one-quarter of his pay.[93] In any event, the wages were more often than not in arrears, and sometimes never paid at all.

A far more important factor in enticing men into volunteering than pay, which was low and hard to collect, was the initial signing-on fee, or bounty. Here was cash in hand. Although the Mutiny Act of 1707 in England set the sum at £5, the actual amount offered varied thereafter, as it had done in the preceding two hundred years.[94] It fluctuated seasonally, generally being highest in the summer, when there was a plentiful demand for agricultural labour and food prices were lowest, and when recruits were consequently hard to attract. Conversely, it was lowest in the winter when outdoor labourers were laid off and food prices rose. Hence the enthusiasm of captains for recruiting at this time of year: not only was it cheaper, but, as Marlborough noted, 'in this winter, in all probability, [my officers] may get more men in a day than in a week hereafter'.[95]

In periods of extreme dearth the bounty fell away altogether: men in France offered themselves for service without any fee at all in the crisis years of 1709–10. On the other hand, competition between recruiting officers could push up the bounty.

Thus, in 1634, the agents of Horn and Bernard of Saxe-Weimar, recruiting in Lower Saxony, sought to outbid each other, offering up to 30 *thalers* for a horseman, 9 *thalers* for a foot soldier.[96] Not surprisingly, there were those who played the system, signing on for the bounty and deserting immediately afterwards, subsequently repeating the procedure with another company. The *curé* of Rumegies in Flanders recorded the activities of one such *billardeur* as they became known, a parishioner, who pulled off the trick with Spanish and French forces on at least five occasions.[97]

The bounty was paid (in theory) but once: the opportunity for the acquisition of wealth through booty or ransoms remained throughout a soldier's career. 'Do you think we are in the King's service for the four ducats a month we earn?', Henry VIII's Spanish captains asked their general. 'Not so my lord: on the contrary we serve with the hope of taking prisoners and getting their ransom.' The Balkan levies of Emperor Ferdinand II had emblazoned on their banners a wolf's head, with the accompanying inscription 'I crave for booty'.[98] Although in the later seventeenth century attempts were made to restrict indiscriminate plunder, there were always pickings to be had: from the dead and wounded after a battle; from the peasantry; and, especially, from the sack of a town. The pickings were not, of course, equally plentiful everywhere in Europe, and it was easiest to recruit when the company was bound for a prosperous region. Estevanillo Gonzales, who wrote a semi-fictional account of his life, stated that he deserted when he heard that his company had been drafted to Flanders 'where they make the very dogs work', but enlisted with a regiment bound for north Italy 'for fear of losing time or a good opportunity'.[99]

The truth was, of course, that, whatever their expectations, few soldiers were permanently enriched through plunder. Although the more sophisticated of them might use letters of credit as a means of transferring specie to safety behind the lines – as the heroine of Grimmelshausen's novel *Mother Courage* did after the battle of Lutter[100] – booty in kind was not easily transportable. Any gained (and the pickings were frequently less than imagined) was quickly lost again: to the 'fences' who accompanied all armies and took it off the soldier's hands at knock-down prices; in settlement of the debts that all soldiers acquired; through gambling; and not least of all by theft, for soldiers seem to have had little compunction about stealing from members of their own army. Thus the Parliamentarian Nehemiah Wharton told of being set upon by soldiers of Colonel Foynes's troop of horse, 'who pillaged me of all' – including a 'scarlet coate lined with plush, and several excellente bookes' – 'and robbed mee of my very sword'. (Wharton subsequently gained a partial revenge when his company 'searched every horseman of that troop to the skin, and took from them a fat buck and a venison pasty, but lost my own goods.')[101] To be sure, there were soldiers who emerged enriched from their career in the army. Sebastian Schertlin amassed sufficient booty in Italy in the 1520s to enable him subsequently to purchase an estate worth 17,000 florins. Gaspard de Saulx-Tavannes reportedly made 60,000 *livres* from the sack of Mâcon; and if the boastful Sydnam Poyntz is to be believed he had accumulated £2–3,000 near to the close of his time in Germany. But such men comprised the fortunate few. As the French monk Emeric Crucé shrewdly observed in 1623: 'for every two soldiers who are enriched through war you will find another fifty who get nothing out of it but blows and incurable illnesses.' Nevertheless the significance of those two men in bringing new recruits to the colours should not be underestimated. Returning home, their pockets full of gold, their exploits exaggerated a hundredfold in the telling, they kept alive the notion that there was profit to be had from war. The crafty recruiting captain would hold them up as models, telling, as did Gonzales, 'a thousand lyes' in order to persuade naïve fellows that by joining the army they too could become rich.[102]

For some it was not so much the prospect of enrichment as a taste for adventure – that 'restless desire' which imbued James Turner – together with the chance to slough off the humdrum tedium of the work-a-day world, which led them into the army. No wonder so many runaway apprentices figure in the recruiting lists. 'To bee bound an apprentice, that life I deemed little better than a dog's life and base', wrote Sydnam Poyntz,[103] whose craving for adventure was satisfied on the battlefields of Germany and England as well as in a Turkish harem during a period of captivity (though his master's wife claimed he had run away to escape prosecution for pilfering: but there was probably truth in both explanations).

Did such men also see the army as offering a chance for social mobility and career advancement which was denied them in civilian life? Probably. As the sergeant-major in Schiller's play put it to a young recruit:

> The whole wide world is yours my son,
> But nothing ventured, nothing won,
> These foolish townsfolk will always drag
> Round and round on the spot like the tanner's nag;
> Only the soldier can prove his worth,
> For war is the password now on earth.

And Thomas Wilson applied the same reasoning, albeit to a different social group, the younger sons of the gentry, when he wrote that by application to arms 'many times we become my master elder brother's master, or at least their betters in honour and reputation'.[104] Leaving aside the nobility and sons of gentry, how realistic were the expectations of low-born men for social and career advancement? Certainly it was possible for such men to move upwards socially, either being ennobled for military service, or, having acquired wealth in war, to acquire the trappings of the more elevated social classes (horses, carriages, house and, pre-eminently, lands) and even to marry nobly. Monluc gave credence to these possibilities by claiming that he had seen 'sons of poor ploughmen obtain wealth, honour and reputation through war';[105] and there are examples to be cited in support of his generalization. Sebastian Vogesberger, originally a baker, made a fortune supplying *landsknechts* to Francis I and married nobly; Georg Derfflinger (1606–95), a peasant's son from Upper Austria, served in the Swedish cavalry, became a field-marshal of Brandenburg, acquired large estates in Germany, and also married a noblewoman; Peter Melander (1585–1648), also of peasant origins, rose to become commander-in-chief of the Imperial forces, wealthy enough to buy lands from the Count of Nassau which entitled him to a seat in the German Diet, and married his only daughter to a prince of Nassau-Dillenberg. De Haes, son of a bricklayer from Ypres, was ennobled for military services to Ferdinand II, the Holy Roman Emperor; the Spaniard Julian Romero was knighted after the battle of Pinkie in 1547; eight common soldiers were knighted after Lützen in 1632; and between 1642 and 1660 Charles I and Charles II awarded 236 titles in return for military service, including 45 baronetcies and 164 knighthoods (though, to be fair, not all of these went to the low-born).[106] But we should pause before arriving at too certain a conclusion. Monluc's claim was made in the context of a propaganda piece designed to 'sell' the army. The examples which back him up are to be found in penny numbers, and stand out by reason of their very atypicality, and moreover, derive mainly from the period of the Thirty Years War which does appear to have offered enhanced opportunities for men of humble origin with talent, luck (or both) to rise. Equally, ennoblement for military service was relatively unusual, the record of the two Stuarts hardly appearing generous in this respect when compared to that of James I who knighted 906 men in the first four months of his reign, including 46 on one morning before breakfast, or that of Charles I himself between 1625 and 1642 who had awarded about 600 knighthoods for non-military reasons.[107] To be sure, there were possibilities of social advancement via the army, but a far more certain route, and one which did not offer the same risks of death or injury, was to acquire wealth through trade and then to purchase one of the patents of nobility or ennobling offices which monarchs freely offered for cash. Early-modern armies were no social escalators.

In the same way, it is possible to identify individuals who progressed from the ranks to officer level, occasionally to hold high command. Many, such as Erik Dahlberg who began as an NCO and ended as Director of Fortifications, or Rutger von Ascheberg who attained field-marshal rank having entered as a common trooper, come from the Swedish army, probably because it was more prepared than most to recognize and reward talent, and also due to the very high casualty levels sustained by the army at all levels, which left the way open for promotions from the ranks. For rather different reasons there were enhanced promotion opportunities in the English Civil War armies. Initially officered not by professional soldiers but by members of gentry families, there was scope by mid-1643 for the promotion of socially inferior rankers who had gained some experience of war, to replace the gentry officers who had frequently proved unwilling to command forces away from their own county. In this way Sigismund Beeton, son of a Midlands shoemaker, rose to become a colonel, Thomas Jennings, a Warwickshire cow-gelder, to be a major in the Royalist forces, and doubtless similar cases could be added from the Parliamentary armies.[108] Yet, as with ennoblement for military service, the examples are rare. Far more telling are the researches of Chaboche and Corvisier on the French army, which reveal that a substantial proportion of recruits remained as privates, even after many years service, and only a very few would have advanced beyond the rank of sergeant.[109] There is little here to confirm the naïve belief of one enlistee that he was 'within one step of being adjutant and but two removes from a captain'.[110]

The truth was that, although armies were beginning to evolve a clearer rank structure by the late seventeenth century – colonel, lieutenant-colonel, major, captain, lieutenant, ensign – there was no career structure to go with it. Appointments at officer level went generally to the nobility, those with influence at court and with cash getting the top jobs, the lesser nobility pre-empting the lower-level posts, and there remained a general reluctance to promote non-nobles. The situation was graphically described in Grimmelshausen's novel *Simplicissimus*, where the hero depicted the army as a tree, with the officers perched on the higher branches and the rankers down below. The latter could not climb up since 'the trunk was made greasy with oil and a curious soap of ill-will, so that nobody, unless he were of noble birth, could climb higher, in spite of his courage, skill and knowledge'.[111] Even in the relatively egalitarian Swedish army 80 per cent of the officer class came from the lesser and middle nobility, although here, as in armies generally, their dominance was not so pronounced in the least socially prestigious branches such as the artillery and engineering.[112] Thus, although hopes of social and career advancement may have lured some men into joining the army, in the same way that expectations of enrichment through plunder and booty prompted others, those who had their hopes realized were few in number; but they were nevertheless important, serving in turn as exemplars of the legend that the army was a pathway to advancement, and thus helping to draw in other recruits.

At one level, the motives which impelled the nobility to join armies were quite different from those which applied to non-nobles. Medieval notions, which identified fighting with the nobility, still retained much vigour amongst both members and non-members of the second estate; and the nobility could still justify its privileged status by reference to its military functions without any trace of irony, even though it had long ceased to comprise the main or even the predominant element within armies. Though in 1515 Claude de Seyssel was novel in his analysis of society in describing as a separate estate those traders and merchants who monopolized finance and commerce, his attribution to the nobility of the defence of the king and the realm was entirely traditional; and so too was the declaration of the Estates General one hundred years later that 'the nobility is the one among [the estates] to which has been committed the possession and handling of arms for the defence and protection of the kingdom.'[113] Not of course that *all* nobles saw it as their duty to fight: indeed there is ample evidence that a declining proportion (of an admittedly expanding class) actually did so, as alternative career opportunities opened up in royal and regional bureaucracies, estate management and diplomacy, as warfare became steadily less 'chivalric' and less of a lark, as the attractions of a settled prosperous peaceful existence grew, and as the military ethos itself began gradually to fade. About 75 per cent of the English peerage participated in the wars of the 1540s, but by 1576 only 25 per cent had seen any action, the proportion declining still further in the seventeenth century so that on the eve of the Civil War four out of five aristocrats had no military experience whatsoever. One study suggests that in any given year between 1552 and 1639 only 10 per cent of the nobility in the *élection* of Bayeux were in regular military service.[114] Nor was the nobility the only group in society in which the military calling was a tradition, maintained by successive generations. This was also true of non-noble Corsican families who provided sons for the Venetian armies throughout the sixteenth century, for example, and there was also a pronounced tendency for military dynasties to develop in later seventeenth-century Sweden. Here, men who served in the army were provided with a cottage which they had to relinquish at the age of 40, a severe penalty for those with no independent economic resources to fall back on. If, however the soldier's son was accepted into the army, the father kept the cottage until his death. Given this incentive, the very large number of instances in which army service was continued from one generation to the next is not surprising.[115] Yet if the nobility was being demilitarized (and this was an uneven development both chronologically and geographically across Europe), and if other non-noble groups evinced signs of a military tradition, it nevertheless remained the only social class to which a military function was formally accorded, and a sufficient number of nobles continued to present themselves for service to fill all the top commands and a majority of the lesser officer posts, of whom at least some (and the number should not be underplayed) did so because, quite simply, 'noblesse oblige'.

They did so knowing that there might be few financial rewards: quite the contrary, indeed, if the command they occupied was a top one. The Earl of Essex may have injected £28,500 of his own money into campaigning, spending £14,000 on the Rouen campaign alone; while Spinola secured his high command by using the immense family wealth to underwrite part of the costs of the Army of Flanders. At a less elevated level, nobles in Louis XIII's France were prepared to raise regiments for the Crown and serve in them (at least part-time) though they knew full well that these units would not survive disbandment above one season and they would be out of pocket at the end of the day, simply because even a whiff of military service would stand them in good stead with their peers. But perhaps the military calling in its purest form was to be discerned amongst the 'gentlemen-rankers', those of gentle birth who were prepared to serve in the ranks for nothing, or for only a modest amount of pay. About 224 such *aventureros* (unpaid aristocrats) with retinues of around 450, plus 220–30 *entre-tenidos* (mainly lesser nobles who received some support from the king), most of them Spanish but including Portuguese and Italians, turned up unasked-for in the spring of 1588 to offer their services in the great naval enterprise against England.[116]

And yet...we should not delude ourselves. The hope of economic gain was not absent from the minds of most nobles who took up the military calling. Monluc, like la Noue, might condemn those who fought *only* for money, rather than for honour, but if there was profit to be had from war, then so be it. He coupled the two things neatly together when he boasted of his children's vocation (despite having three of his sons killed in the wars):

> Their desire is rather to gain goods and honours [than to stay at home] and in the winning of them to hazard their persons and lives, and even serve the Turk rather than remain idle. If they did otherwise, I should not look upon them as mine.[117]

It is no accident that the best officers were generally to be found from the ranks of the lesser nobility, whose lack of economic resources tied them most closely to the military profession. It was a diminished family patrimony after all which had led Monluc to seek his fortune in the profession of arms in 1520; it was the impoverished *junkers* of Brandenburg-Prussia who formed the backbone of its army from the early eighteenth century on. In their hope for profit and advancement the motives of the nobility were not essentially different from those which drew non-nobles into the army.

And what, finally, of those higher ideals: defence of 'la patrie' or religion. These do figure amongst the plethora of motives which caused men to take up arms. Corvisier cites some evidence of the former from the last years of Louis XIV's reign when the realm was under threat;[118] and there are signs of the latter in the civil and religious wars of the early-modern period. The pastor, Pierre Viret, could write of the internal wars in France in the sixteenth century that, 'This war is not like other wars, for even the poorest man has an interest in it since we are fighting for freedom of conscience.'[119] But while admitting that such motives existed, we should not set much store by them as general explanations. A concept of the nation was barely beginning even to be formed in early-modern Europe. Men's loyalties were at a more local level: to their village, town or region. When contemporary Frenchmen used the word nation, for example, they meant by it the population of a province, not that of France as a whole. As to religion, Montaigne as usual had the right of it when he wrote in reference to the French wars, 'Let us confess the truth...that those who take up arms out of pure zeal for religion could hardly make up one complete company of *gens d'armes*.'[120] Even chancellor l'Hôpital (who would have been included in that single company) had to admit that there were many on both sides in the conflict who used religion as a cloak.[121] Moreover, the readiness of large numbers of men in the English Civil War to change sides in the aftermath of a battle surely argues against any overwhelming commitment on their part to a cause. The unflattering, but substantially accurate, description of Alexander Leslie as 'one who because he could not live well there [Scotland] took upon him a trade of killing men abroad, and now is returned for Christ's cause to kill men at home', could surely be extended to many others in that conflict.[122]

Overall, the veteran Venetian general, Giulio Savorgnan, came closest to summing up the motives for enlistment:

> To escape from being craftsmen, working in a shop; to avoid a criminal sentence; to see new things; to pursue honour (but these last are very few). The rest join in the hope of having enough to live on and a bit over for shoes and some other trifle to make life supportable.[123]

How far life in the armies was supportable remains to be seen.

4

LIFE AND DEATH IN THE ARMIES

MORTALITY AND MEDICINE

The soldier's profession, by definition, is, and always has been, a hazardous one: but exactly how risky was it in the early-modern period? It is impossible to give a precise answer, since the numbers of dead and wounded either went unrecorded or were subject to inaccurate reporting. Yet even allowing a generous margin for statistical error it is clear that the risks of military life were frighteningly high. Between May 1572 and April 1574, 396 of the 2,415 men in the *tercio* of Naples, stationed in the Low Countries, died from one cause or another, equivalent to an annual death-rate of 8.2 per cent. Losses in Count Sulz's regiment were even higher: 731 men were reported dead in the twenty-one months between August 1593 and May 1595. This represented just over 32 per cent of the unit's original strength, and was equivalent to an annual death-rate of 18.4 per cent. Landier has calculated that on average one-quarter of the soldiers in the French armies died each year, a total of 600,000 men in the period 1635–59. Another, albeit rough estimate, suggests that during the seventeenth century as a whole 2,300,000 soldiers died whilst serving with the armies, that is to say between 20 and 25 per cent of all those who carried arms. By comparison, the overall crude death-rate amongst the civilian population in the seventeenth century was about 3–4 per cent per annum. The rate for men in their late 'teens and twenties, who furnished the bulk of recruits for the armies, was even lower, since mortality was concentrated amongst the very young and the old. Death-rates of 20 per cent were attained only in times of epidemic and widespread harvest failure.[1]

What were the major causes of death amongst the military? 'Sickness and mortality [i.e. death from contagious disease] does consume more than the sword', wrote a well-informed correspondent of Sir Robert Cecil in 1600, and it is now a historical commonplace that the numbers killed in battle formed only a small proportion of the total dead.[2] Jacques Dupâquier suggests that the figure may be as low as one in ten, and that for every soldier who died in action three would die of wounds or accident, and six would succumb to disease.[3] However, estimates of this level may understate the numbers who actually died in conflict. Some engagements involved very heavy loss of life. After the battle of Marignano, gravediggers claimed to have buried 16,500 bodies, a figure which, given the heavy casualties known to have been sustained by the Swiss, may not be fantastic.[4] James Turner was horrified at the slaughter near Hammelln in June 1633. 'This was a battell wherein so much blood was shed, as was enough to flesh such novices as I was', he commented.[5] Des Bournays, who commanded a company at the battle of Malplaquet, subsequently wrote, 'I have never seen so many dead in so small a space...piled two and three high.'[6] The *Gardes du corps* lost one-third of its strength, and the two battalions of Provence were both reduced from about 1,000 men to less than 500. Malplaquet was unusual in one respect, in that the victors suffered even greater casualties than the vanquished. It is estimated that generally in the seventeenth century the winning side would lose 15 per cent of its men, the loser 30 per cent dead and 20 per cent prisoners.[7]

If losses in battle were high, those sustained in sieges might be even higher, especially if the fortress had to be taken by assault. In this case the victors might expect to lose 20 per cent of their force, the vanquished 50 per cent. Three hundred men in Robert Monro's regiment were killed during the siege of the castle of Bredenberg, for example, and over half the regiment was subsequently lost during the successful defence of Stralsund, with a further 300 wounded. There were so many dead after the sack of Frankfurt in 1631 that peasants brought in to bury them could not cope and 'in th'end they were cast by heapes in great ditches, above a hundred in every grave.'[8]

Heavy though these losses were, battle and sieges took their toll at intervals: deaths from illness were ceaseless. With their dense concentrations of personnel, and their insanitary camps,

106

billets and hospitals, armies offered ideal conditions for the transmission of crowd diseases, such as typhus, smallpox and the bubonic plague, together with those diseases associated with poor hygiene, such as typhoid and dysentery.[9] To be sure, there was some realization of the need to take preventive measures against the spread of disease. Hans Conrad von Lavater's *Kriegs-Büchlen* of 1651 advised wearing clothes without fur or seams, so as to inhibit the vermin which spread epidemics.[10] And all military regulations contained clauses relating to hygiene. Under Leicester's code, for example, rubbish was to be buried, animals slaughtered away from the camp, and imprisonment was ordered for any soldier who should 'trouble or defile the waters adioyning', or who should 'ease himselfe or defile the campe or Toune of Garrison save in such places as is appointed for that purpose'.[11] But such rules, all too often ignored, proved largely ineffective in preventing the spread of disease. Thus, one-third of the Marquis of Hamilton's force were dead within a month of arriving in Pomerania in 1631 following the outbreak of a contagion – possibly dysentery; whilst of the 215 men recruited from the parish of Bygdeå in Sweden who died in military operations in Germany between 1620 and 1640, no less than 196 perished from illness while serving in garrisons around the Baltic.[12]

The death toll from disease was doubtless so high because many sufferers were weakened by the undernourishment and privation characteristic of military life. In addition, recruits were frequently in poor physical condition when they were enlisted, and hence were ill-prepared to cope with the physical strains of army life. The Venetian Senate in 1571 expressed its concern at the number of 'abject and useless men' being enlisted.[13] Governments, it is true, did attempt to exclude such men from the recruiter's net. The Privy Council, for example, stressed that only men 'of able bodies and years meet for the employment' should be taken on the Rouen expedition.[14] And minimum heights were established which recruits had to attain: 5 feet 1 inch in Charles XII's army; 5 feet 2 inches for the French infantryman, 5 feet 4 inches for the cavalryman, and a bare 5 feet for the militiaman; 5 feet 5 inches under the 1708 Recruiting Act in England.[15] But all the evidence suggests that such restrictions proved of little avail. Shakespeare may have exaggerated for comic effect when he had an observer accuse

Falstaff of recruiting his company by stripping the gibbets of corpses, but he had a point, for every army drafted in its full complement of under-sized, weak, sick and deformed men, wholly unsuited to withstand the rigours of army life.[16] Altogether then, it is hardly surprising that disease claimed so many victims in early-modern armies.

For the most part the illnesses which afflicted the soldier were common to civilians as well. But a few conditions were specific to the military. Foot-rot for example – the same 'trench foot' with which the infantryman of the First World War was familiar – afflicted the ill-shod early-modern soldier. The clergyman, George Story, recorded that in Ireland in 1689 'there were some [soldiers] that had their toes, and some their whole feet fell off as the surgeons were dressing them'.[17] In these cases the peripheral circulation appears to have been so badly affected as to have resulted in gangrene. Soldiers also exhibited symptoms of psychiatric breakdown, known later as 'shell-shock', which was brought about by prolonged and unrelieved exposure to the stresses of active service. Such soldiers in the Army of Flanders were referred to as having *el mal de corazón* (heart trouble).[18]

Early-modern medical science had few effective answers to the problems of disease. In the seventeenth century the Faculty of Medicine at Wittenberg still gave as its official treatment for bubonic plague the application of grated radish to the feet; wealthy patients were also to swallow emeralds, sapphires and pearls prepared with hartshorn, whilst the poor imbibed a mixture of vinegar and sour sorrel-water.[19] However, if medicine could do little about the hazards posed by microbes, some progress was made in surgical techniques and the treatment of wounds. The increasing use of gunpowder weapons routinely presented surgeons with injuries more horrific than anything previously encountered. A contemporary at the siege of Maastricht recorded the 'pitiful sight' presented by those men wounded by artillery and handguns: 'Some lacked a leg, others an arm. Here there was a soldier whose guts were pouring from his body, and over there lay a man who had half his face torn away.'[20] Surgeons initially premised their treatment of gunshot wounds on the belief that they were burnt and poisoned by gunpowder carried into the body by the bullet. Brunschwig's *Buch der Wund-Artzney* (1497) therefore advocated drawing a silken cord through the wound to remove the powder and poison. The standard treatment, however, given in John of Vigo's influential *Practica copiosa in arte chirurgica* (1514 with forty subsequent editions) was to cauterize the wound with boiling oil, sealing any severed arteries by the application of a red hot iron. Such methods, unsurprisingly, frequently did more harm than good. A major advance in this respect was made by the Frenchman, Ambroise Paré (1510–90), a country barber's apprentice and later physician to Henry IV, who served in over forty campaigns, and who may be regarded as one of the founding fathers of modern military medicine. After an assault on the fortress of Villane in 1536 he had insufficient oil to treat all the wounded. The following day he observed that patients who had not received the standard treatment were in better condition than those that had. Thereafter, he advocated the use of soothing linaments and bandages in place of boiling oil, and additionally advised removing dead tissue and foreign matter from the wound since this, he observed, gave rise to infection. Paré was not the only surgeon to be working towards more humane and effective treatment of gunshot wounds in the sixteenth century. Bartholomeo Maggi at Bologna, Felix Wurtz of Zurich, Léonard Botal in Paris, and the Englishman Thomas Gale, who served with the Spanish forces for a time in the 1540s and 1550s (the diversity of their geographical origins attests to the widespread interest of surgeons in the problem), all published works urging similar treatment to Paré's. But it was Paré's writings, widely circulated in translation, which were the most influential.[21]

The sixteenth century also witnessed the introduction of better techniques of amputation. Blood loss was controlled by use of the ligature, a practice used and strongly advocated by Paré, and also by the tourniquet, which to a limited extent helped to anaesthetize the limb. William Clowes, a gifted English military surgeon, reckoned to remove a leg with the loss of only 4 ounces of blood.[22] Covering the stump of the amputated limb with a flap of skin and muscle, a technique advocated in Hans von Gersdorff's *Feldbuch der Wundarznei* (Strasbourg, 1517) helped to prevent infection, whilst the risks of gangrene were lessened by amputating well above the wound. In a pre-anaesthetic era little could be done to minimize the pain of an operation, except to administer alcohol and perform it as rapidly as possible.[23]

What, then, were the wounded soldier's chances of survival?

Much depended on how and where on the body the injury had been inflicted. Cuts and puncture wounds from sword and pike might heal themselves, provided they were cleaned and bandaged and no damage had been sustained by internal organs. Gunshot wounds were more problematic. A hit by a cannon ball was usually, but not invariably, fatal: of 411 wounded survivors of the battle of Malplaquet 13.7 per cent had been injured by heavy artillery.[24] The much lighter balls delivered by hand firearms could nevertheless shatter bone and tissue and cause internal haemorrhaging, as well as carrying pieces of cloth and dirt into the wound which set up infection. Surgeons were unable to deal effectively with either of these conditions, and hence a wound of this type in the trunk of the body was likely to prove fatal. In 1536 at Milan, Paré witnessed an old soldier slit the throats of three such hopelessly injured men in an act of rough mercy.[25] On the other hand, gunshot wounds in the arm or leg might be dealt with by amputation. To judge by the large numbers of limbless ex-soldiers, graphically illustrated in the drawings of artists such as Jacques Callot, who survived to beg on the streets, the operation could be surprisingly effective.

Chances of survival were also linked to the availability and quality of medical care offered to the injured soldier, and in these respects the situation, notably in the sixteenth century, was far from satisfactory. Although great noblemen were habitually attended by their personal barber-surgeon when on campaign, few surgeons were available to the common soldier. Only three were recorded in the list of payments made in the last quarter of 1537 by Francis I to troops involved in the Piedmontese campaign for example, and frequently there were no more than two with Elizabeth's forces in Ireland in the 1590s.[26] As a consequence, injured men looked to women camp-followers, or to the medical quacks who trailed after all armies, for assistance. Even when they were available the surgeons were frequently men of limited abilities, for the profession, with its irregular employment and low levels of pay – sixteenth-century English surgeons received little more than a trumpeter, for example – attracted few men of the calibre of Paré or Clowes. The latter, who served with Leicester's expeditionary force to the Netherlands, later complained in his *Prooved Practice for all Young Chirurgians* (1588) that bad surgeons had killed more men than the enemy; whilst a contemporary at the battle of

Montreuil (1544) described the 'great rabblement there that took upon them to be surgeons. Some were sow-gelders, some were horse-gelders, with tinkers and cobblers.'[27] Most treatment was carried out on the battlefield, or in churches, barns and houses hurriedly converted into makeshift hospitals. Little or no provision was made for evacuating the wounded. Nothing came of Thomas Digges's call to the government in England to create a permanent pool of carriages and drivers to serve as ambulances, and wounded men were perforce obliged to rely upon their comrades, wives, or camp-followers to move them.[28]

However, if there was no response to Digges's appeal to have transport facilities made available, in other respects governments did, from the late sixteenth century onwards, set out to improve and extend medical facilities. They acted not from altruistic motives, but out of a pragmatic concern to improve military efficiency. As countless examples showed, disease could decimate an army and ruin it as a fighting machine. It was particularly important to avoid the unnecessary loss, through illness or wounds, of veteran soldiers whose value had been proved in every theatre of war. As Mazarin noted, 'money is nowhere better spent than on hospitals to treat sick soldiers, for one of these men cured is worth ten new recruits'. Moreover, provision for the sick improved the morale of the troops and encouraged fresh volunteers to come forward. 'Nothing produces a better effect in armies than taking care of the wounded', opined the Cardinal;[29] whilst Nicholas Weston in 1598 argued in favour of the establishment of a military hospital at Dublin on the grounds that it would render soldiers who currently perished 'fit to serve her Majesty again, whereby others also would be encouraged more willingly to adventure their lives in Her Highness's service'.[30] There was also a cost consideration. Governments were unprepared to squander the financial investment they had made in training and equipping soldiers by allowing them to die needlessly.

It was Philip II's Spain which led the way with respect to the provision of medical services, as in most other military matters in the sixteenth century. Troops serving in Italy and the Low Countries were treated free of charge: by contrast soldiers in other armies had to pay for their medicines. Field hospitals were routinely set up for the Army of Flanders and civil facilities requisitioned as occasion demanded, and in 1585 Europe's first permanent military hospital was established at Malines. By 1637 it had 330 beds (the men, as was normal, were expected to share) and its budget between 1614 and 1629 ran to over 1 million *ducats*.[31] Other states belatedly followed the Spanish example. In France, the *code Michau* of 1629 stipulated that each regiment and garrison should have its own infirmary and surgeon, and that field hospitals should follow an army on campaign. There was increased government expenditure on drugs and surgeons' salaries from the 1630s, and in January 1708 a royal edict augmented considerably the number of surgeons serving in the forces and ordered the establishment of fifty new hospitals, mostly on the northern frontier, with an inspectorate to supervise them.[32] In England the Cromwellian and Restoration regimes sought to enhance the status of military medicine by appointing highly regarded civilians to the posts of physician-general, surgeon-general and apothecary-general.[33] Most impressive of all were the initiatives taken to improve the quality of military doctors in Brandenburg-Prussia. In 1713 an Anatomical Theatre was founded at Berlin to train army surgeons, and a decree eleven years later obliged candidates for the College of Surgery and Medicine to serve a probationary period as regimental surgeon.[34] To be sure, the implementation of these measures was neither rapid nor universal. Although permanent military hospitals were established at Calais, Pinerolo and Brouage during Louis XIII's reign, many of the provisions of the *code Michau* remained a dead letter for several decades, for example. Of the larger states Austria was especially slow to act. Although paying lip-service to the need to improve medical services the *Generalkriegskommissariat* in practice tried to limit expenditure on these to 40–70,000 *gulden* per year, with the result that they remained woefully inadequate – a mere two carts sufficed to transport the medical supplies for the whole of Prince Eugene's army in 1701.[35] Yet despite such shortcomings the seventeenth century did witness a limited improvement in medical provision for the soldier, and in this respect his lot had been improved.

THE NECESSITIES OF LIFE

If the soldier was constantly at hazard from sickness and disease, he also had more mundane concerns: the availability of fuel to keep warm, a roof over his head, food to eat, clothes for his back and money in his pocket. Any number of examples might be cited to demonstrate that all too frequently the early-modern soldier had few or none of these things. Thus Lord Conway in 1642 wrote of his troops in Ireland that 'every one is sicke, [they have] few clothes, little money, ille meate, worse drink'.[36] The problem stemmed partly from the expectation that the soldier would purchase such necessities out of his pay. Yet this was simply not possible, for, as we have seen, wages were abysmally low, and often proved inadequate to cover expenses. This was more especially the case since the presence of troops in a locality had an inflationary effect on prices, particularly of foodstuffs, putting them way above what the soldier could afford. By the end of the siege of Rouen in 1592 the men in Essex's army were expected to live on wages of 8d per day, when the price of a halfpenny loaf had rocketed to 12d, beer to 18d a pot, wine to 2s, and a pound of cheese to 12d.[37] In any event, governments paid wages infrequently or not at all. Thus, the 15,000 or so Swiss in French service received no regular pay between 1639 and 1648, and were sustained on the personal credit of their officers and by pillage; whilst the English Parliament, generally reckoned to have been a better paymaster than the King in the Civil War, nevertheless owed an accumulated £2 million in wage arrears to its serving soldiers by 1647. Garrison troops often seem to have come off worst. By 1644 Parliament had largely ceased payment to these troops altogether, and the same was true in the Iberian peninsula, where none of the frontier garrisons received wages in 1588 for example. By February 1592 soldiers in the fortresses of Pamplona had been unpaid for five years.[38] The wage claims of these troops were ignored because governments assumed that in the relatively settled life of a garrison town the soldiers would make ends meet by taking part-time civilian jobs; they might be billeted on the local population; and they were usually not elite troops whose loyalty it was crucial to maintain. There may have been something to all this, but it did not necessarily prevent the soldiers suffering. In 1574 it was reliably confirmed that a soldier in the fortress of Salces had died of starvation. Vauban noted in the 1670s that many garrison troops were in a pitiable condition, and there was at least one report of garrison troops dying of starvation in the electorate of Brandenburg in the same period.[39]

Low, or non-existent, pay was only part of the problem, however. Soldiers also suffered at the hands of corrupt officers. As proprietors of their companies and regiments, officers looked to make a profit from war, not least of all by defrauding both their men and the government. And they were in a good position to do so, for the soldiers, until the later seventeenth century at least, had little or no direct contact with the government for which they fought or with its officials, but instead received wages, food, clothing, medicine and equipment via the captains, even if these things were ultimately provided or paid for by the state. The system was wide open to abuse. Captains withheld pay; they docked the soldier's wages for goods and services which he never received; or they provided sub-standard goods which were charged at high prices. In addition, they defrauded the common soldier out of his share of ransom and booty; and they fined him arbitrarily for offences against the military code. Impoverished troopers were obliged to turn to their officers for credit, which was provided on extortionate terms. Captains appropriated for themselves the best food and quarters, 'for it is a custom of ancient standing that the soldier must have the worst', as Gonzales sarcastically observed in a passage which satirized the abuses and peculations of the officers.[40] Captains cheated not only their men but also the government, usually by falsifying the muster records. Servants, lackeys and peasants were brought in to be counted at musters, artificially inflating the number of men in the company and the amount of money the captain could claim for wages. Subsequently, these *passe-volants* were dismissed with a token payment, the captain pocketing the funds he received for these non-existent soldiers. Alternatively, men who were unfit for service, or who had been killed, had their names retained on the muster list. Although by custom a captain would be given a certain number of 'dead-pays', the amounts involved frequently became excessive.

Of course, not all officers should be tarred with the same brush. There were some who showed a genuine concern for their men's welfare. Money from 'dead-pays' did not always go into the captain's pocket, but might be put towards the purchase of clothing and food for the men. There are numerous instances of officers – Parma and Spinola are two of the best-known and highest-ranking – using their personal fortunes and credit to sustain their men. Yet so long as war remained a business, and the administration of armies was so decentralized, the temptation for captains to make profits at the expense of their men was enormous, and, for many, irresistible.

One consequence of the failure to provide for the troops' needs was a breakdown in discipline and order. When troops ran out of money or could not get their credit extended the sutlers accompanying the army were often the first to suffer. Unpopular anyway because of their assumed practice of hoarding goods and selling only at inflated prices, they were now attacked, their carts and tents plundered and their wares either stolen or sold cheaply, the soldiers delighting in the opportunity to settle old scores. 'The vivandiers being look'd upon as Thieves, that convey away all the money of the Army, the men had no more Pity on them than if they had been lineally descended from Nero', wrote Gonzales, after leading an attack on one group of sutlers.[41] Disorder was not just confined to the camp. There were heated exchanges and brawls with innkeepers, shop-owners and householders over unpaid bills, credit reneged on and goods stolen. Most serious of all, the lack of pay could lead to uncontrolled plundering of civilians and their property. The sack of Rome in 1527 by Charles V's unpaid mercenaries, and of Antwerp by units of the Army of Flanders in 1576, are merely the two best-known instances of an occurrence which was all too frequent. Such uncontrolled looting invariably resulted in a total breakdown of discipline, well illustrated by Robert Monro's graphic description of the sack of Frankfurt-on-the-Oder in 1631:

> All men were carelesse of their dueties, were too carefull in making of booty, that I never did see Officers lesse obeyed, and respected than here for a time...and well I know that some Regiments had no man with their colours, till the fury was past...such disorder was amongst us all occasioned by covetousnesse.[42]

Less spectacular, but even more debilitating for the army, was the pillaging of villages, farms, crops and orchards by soldiers on the march, which might devastate the theatre of war to such a degree that the army could no longer subsist. As Matthew Sutcliffe rightly observed, such unregulated plundering 'hath been the ruine of many armies'.[43] Nor were soldiers overly concerned with whether their victims were friend, foe or neutral.

The four regiments of regular French troops in Languedoc in 1634 ravaged the territory they were supposed to protect when they went unpaid.[44]

The hardships of military life elicited two further responses from soldiers. One was desertion. In 1622 conditions in the trenches at the siege of Bergen-op-Zoom were so appalling that over 2,500 of the besiegers actually fled into the town pleading for help, one Italian with pardonable hyperbole claiming to have escaped 'from Hell'.[45] Desertion posed a more serious threat to an army's strength than losses incurred in battle or through disease, and, if unchecked, could cripple the effectiveness of a unit as a fighting force. Commanders routinely expected to lose 10 or even 20 per cent of their men annually in this way, but wastage rates could be far higher. Thus 223 of the 565 new recruits assembled at Lisbon castle in October 1581 fled within three weeks of being mustered; by the end of 1609, 500 of the 600 men newly raised for the Navarre garrison had deserted; and more than one man in three deserted from the army of Saxony between 1717 and 1728.[46] Not surprisingly, the phenomenon was most marked amongst the lowest paid troops. Handing out occasional double pays and bonuses could help staunch the flow, but this had its own dangers, for desertions increased after a large pay-out or following a windfall of plunder, as men quit the army to enjoy their gains, though some subsequently rejoined once they had worked their way through the cash.[47]

Although deserters sometimes slipped away in groups, desertion was essentially an individual reaction to hardship. The final response involved collective action: mutiny. This was usually the resort of professional, long-service soldiers, with a sense of corporate solidarity, usually, though not invariably, serving away from home, who were confident of their indispensability to the war-effort. The mutinies which occurred in units of the Army of Flanders have been most studied. There were over forty-five between 1572 and 1607, at least twenty-one of them after 1596, some lasting for over a year. They were organized with great sophistication, the mutineers electing their own leaders, negotiating with the government, generally maintaining good order, and levying taxes and contributions on the local population to sustain themselves.[48] But mutiny was a chronic malady which afflicted or threatened all armies in the early-modern period. Major instances occurred amongst Spanish soldiers serving in Naples in 1501; amongst English troops at Tournai in 1515, those serving in the Low Countries in the 1580s, and in the Civil War armies. In the autumn of 1578 forces in the pay of the States-General, subsequently known as the Malcontents, followed the example of their Spanish opponents and seized the town of Memen, holding it against payment of their arrears. There were widespread mutinies amongst Habsburg forces during the Thirty Years War.

Always at the top of the mutineers' list of demands was pay, but they also wanted better food, clothing and medical facilities, an end to bullying and arbitrary punishments by officers and a guaranteed amnesty for all who had taken part in the revolt. Where the mutiny was on a wide scale, governments were obliged to concede these demands, either wholly or in part, for a major revolt could have devastating consequences, not just bringing a campaign to a juddering halt, as happened in 1647 when Turenne's proposed advance into Flanders had to be aborted because of a mutiny by his German cavalry, but on occasions paralysing the whole war-effort and entailing far-reaching political consequences. Thus the mutiny of Spanish troops in the Low Countries in 1576 not only allowed the Dutch to recapture much of Zeeland, but the behaviour of the troops, in particular the sack of Antwerp in November, brought both loyal and rebel provinces together in an alliance against Philip II, the Pacification of Ghent. Similarly, Sweden was forced into an unwanted dependence on France in 1641 in order to obtain the subsidies which alone could induce her armies, disabled by mutiny, back into action.[49]

Mutiny was the most spectacular response of soldiers to hardship. But whatever form the response took – mutiny, brawls with civilians, disorder in the camp, rioting, wanton plundering and desertion – the effect was always to subvert military efficiency. In the same way that a concern to maintain the military effectiveness of their armies had led governments to improve medical facilities, so it induced them in the seventeenth century to improve the welfare of their soldiers more generally. As Richelieu noted in his *Testament politique*, 'If one has a special care for the soldiers, if they are provided with bread throughout the year, six pay days and clothing...then I dare to say that the infantry of the kingdom will be well disciplined in

the future.' Le Tellier subsequently made the point more con-
cisely: 'To secure the livelihood of the soldier is to secure victory
for the king.'[50] It needs to be stressed that a pragmatic concern
with military efficiency, not an altruistic concern with the
soldier, lay behind these remarks. Nevertheless, the tone of the
comments contrasts markedly with that revealed in the remarks
made by Charles V at the siege of Metz in 1552, and illustrates
the extent to which government attitudes towards the welfare of
soldiers had altered in the succeeding century. When told that
the men in his camp who were dying were not gentlemen and
men of note but poor soldiers, the Emperor declared that

> it was no matter if they died, comparing them to cater-
> pillars, grubs and insects which eat buds and other fruits
> of the earth, and said that if they were men of means they
> would not be in his camp for the 6 *livres* a month which he
> paid them.[51]

There was little that cash-starved governments could do
about paying wages in full – only the United Provinces came
near to achieving this.[52] But it was increasingly recognized that
it was preferable to pay the soldier something on a routine
basis, even if not the full amount, rather than allow him to go
for long periods without any pay. With these small sums he
could sustain his credit with victuallers and tradesmen: hence
Le Tellier's order in 1660 that soldiers' wages be paid regularly.
Additionally, attempts were made to protect soldiers from
rapacious captains, and ensure that they actually received their
pay. Civilian officials, such as the *intendants d'armée* in France,
supervised musters and, in some instances, actually handed the
money over to the men. In Italy muster-masters noted names,
complexion and hair colour of soldiers to prevent the use of
passe-volants. Not that there was anything particularly original
in having government paymasters supervise the captains. The
intendants d'armée, who included this as one of their myriad
functions, and who were permanently attached to the French
armies by the 1670s, were the heirs to the *controlleurs* and
commissaires used by Francis I; in the early sixteenth century
paymasters employed by the Venetian Senate had kept registers
detailing the distinguishing marks of soldiers; and the Dutch in
the 1590s had even employed undercover agents to ferret out
abuses in the pay system.[53] What was different by the second

half of the seventeenth century was the greater number of officials employed, and the regularity and efficiency with which they carried out their functions.

Of course, in establishing closer supervision of the arrangements for pay, governments were not simply seeking to protect the interests of the soldiers, but also their own, for they were robbed blind at every turn by the swindling captains. The same admixture of motives led to efforts to supply, directly and in kind, some of the items which previously the soldier would have been expected to obtain himself, or which came to him via the captain.[54] Large-scale contractors hired by the government supplied the goods, and the troops' wages were docked accordingly. The most important item provided was bread. For a time after 1601 a single contractor, the *proveedor de viveres*, victualled the whole Army of Flanders, and between April 1678 and February 1679 contractors supplied on average a staggering 39,000 loaves, each between 1 and 3 lbs weight, to the Army every day.[55] After bread the next most important item of government supply was clothing. In Sweden there were plans in 1626–7 for the establishment of a central depot to provide clothes, which came in two standard sizes: two-thirds were large and one-third small, though in practice the government seems to have contented itself with issuing cloth to its troops and leaving them to make it up. Le Tellier in 1647 specified three sizes for government-issue clothes: one-quarter small, one-quarter large, and half regular. Louvois subsequently confirmed the War Ministry's concern with the soldier's dress when he wrote, in 1664: 'It is not sufficient to have a lot of men; they must also be well turned out and dressed.' In 1708 a clothing Board was established in England, consisting of senior army officers whose function was to scrutinize contracts, examine the clothes, and approve patterns. Weapons, armour, ball and shot were also supplied by governments to their troops, usually on credit, Spain taking the initiative in this respect at the end of the sixteenth century, other states subsequently following suit.[56]

Regular government contracts for large quantities of clothing, boots, powder, horns, cartridge belts and bandoliers, and increasingly detailed specifications concerning cut, colour and pattern of the soldier's clothes, led inevitably to an increased standardization of dress amongst soldiers and, slowly and falteringly, to the development of uniforms. By the end of Charles II's reign it was normal to specify red as the colour of the soldiers' coats, whilst in 1707 the Austrian War Council ordered that all infantrymen should wear clothes of light grey, the colour which had increasingly been associated with the Imperial forces from the time of the Thirty Years War.[57] The process was most clearly discernible in France, which set the fashion for the rest of Europe in military dress. Under Louvois, blue was stipulated for men in the French Guards and Royal Regiments, red for the Swiss Guards, and grey for the remaining infantry regiments. Epaulettes were introduced, not initially as a sign of rank but to protect the uniform from wear and enable the musket to be shouldered more easily. Hitherto, only elite troops, such as royal guards, had worn anything resembling a uniform, ordinary soldiers being identified as belonging to the same side by markings or badges – a cross, an armband or a sash, for example – or by sporting tokens such as a piece of fern or heather in the cap. In 1637 Halluin's Spaniards at Leucate wore their shirts outside their doublet and hose in order to recognize each other.[58]

It is unclear how far governments in their drive towards standardization of clothing were influenced by, or even recognized, some of the purely military as opposed to the economic benefits of putting men into uniform – that it helped distinguish one unit from another on a smoke-covered battlefield; that it helped promote an *esprit de corps* and raise group morale; that it made individuals more amenable to discipline – though all of these things were true. The sixteenth-century view, that a soldier's martial ardour would actually be diminished if he were denied scope for the free expression of his sartorial preferences and extravagances, took a long while to fade. The military were specifically excluded from the Spanish sumptuary laws of 1623 and later, for example, for precisely this reason.[59] In any event, no unit of soldiers, kitted out in uniform at the start of a campaign, retained the same appearance for very long. Socks, shoes and coats wore out rapidly, and men re-clothed themselves with odds and ends picked up from civilians, stolen from comrades or plundered from the dead and wounded. New recruits, deserters and enemy captives joined up in whatever clothes they possessed. In England the Clothing Board issued articles on a two-year cycle, and any soldier joining up in the 'second' year would not anyway receive a complete issue of clothes.

As well as bread and clothing, governments provided other services for their troops. Louis XIV's soldiers were offered tobacco at subsidized rates (it was believed to have prophylactic properties against plague).[60] There were also some moves towards the provision of accommodation. One of the earliest examples of this was the construction of a barracks for the 600-strong garrison at Messina in Sicily following a major mutiny in 1538. Stone and timber barracks, holding up to eight men, the soldiers sleeping two to a bed, were built for the Army of Flanders at 's-Hertogenbosch (1609), Dunkirk (1611), Maastricht and Damme (1616); and still larger buildings erected in the major cities of the Netherlands, such as Ghent, Antwerp and Cambrai. In England, accommodation at Berwick-on-Tweed was expanded between 1717 and 1721 to cope with 600 men, and £25,000 was allocated for barracks in Ireland and £9,300 for the same purpose to Scotland: in both instances it was desirable to separate the soldiers from a hostile native population. In France, an old building in the Rue du Bac in Paris was pressed into service as a barracks, and in 1690 the municipality was ordered to build accommodation sufficient to hold all troops in the city. The construction of barracks in towns on military routes inside France was ordered in 1719, with the result that twenty years later they existed in around 300 urban centres. However, the provision of barracks was slow and regionally patchy. Little was done in this respect in Prussia until Frederick II's reign, or until after 1748 in the Austrian lands, and they were not widespread even in France or England until the later eighteenth century. Moreover, when on campaign soldiers continued to be lodged in houses and barns, or they camped out in fields and hedgerows, like Nehemiah Wharton and his companions who lay out overnight, 'our beds, the earth; our canopy, the clouds'.[61]

Undoubtedly there was some improvement in the lot of the common soldier over the course of the early-modern period, largely as a result of greater state intervention in the management of armies. It is arguable that by the later seventeenth century he had more dependable wages, was better fed, clothed, had access to improved medical facilities, and was less likely to be swindled by his captain than his sixteenth-century predecessor. Significantly the mutinies which had crippled the Army of Flanders died out after 1607 as measures designed to improve the soldier's welfare gradually took effect. Nevertheless, the extent of the improvement should not be exaggerated. Not all of the initiatives adopted by states proved to be in the soldier's interest. This was notably the case with the provision of barracks, which were all too often damp, airless and insanitary. Lord Paston's regiment spent eighteen months in Portsmouth barracks in 1704–5 and, as a result of 'the sickness of the place, want of firing, and the badness of the barracks', was reduced by death and desertion to half its original strength.

Moreover, the creaky mechanisms of state control and intervention, designed to guarantee the soldier his pay and provide his basic foodstuffs and clothing, were built up *ad hoc*, and frequently broke down. Contracting services remained inefficient and corrupt, and food and equipment were often insufficient in quantity and inferior in quality. The outfit of British troops serving in Flanders was reported as 'shoes bad, clothing miserable, and arms defective'.[62] Six hundred muskets supplied to the French soldiers at Audenarde in 1667 blew up when fired, presumably with disastrous results for their users.[63] State supervision of captains and colonels was far from effective, and they continued to find myriad ways of cheating their own men and the government. It is a telling comment on the inadequacies of government in even a relatively centralized state such as France that Louvois recommended employing as captains men with private means who could afford to support their companies independent of state assistance. Austria, Spain, and many of the German states proved even less able, or willing, to assist their soldiers. In 1699 the colonel of a Bavarian regiment reported that thirty of his men were confined to bed for lack of clothing; and Prince Eugene wrote from Italy in 1705 of his 'half-starved and naked men, without a penny, without tents, without bread, without baggage, without artillery...I hear nothing but complaints and talk of want and misery'.[64]

DISCIPLINE AND RELIGION

If the living conditions of the soldier were only marginally improved by the end of the seventeenth century, in one important respect his situation deteriorated as he was subjected to closer control and regulation than hitherto. For commanders and governments did not seek to improve the efficiency of their armies merely through the implementation of military welfare policies, but also through the introduction of tighter discipline. Indeed, the two things were seen as mutually dependent. As Everhard van Reyd noted, 'One could not hang those whom one did not pay.'[65] Rules governing the soldier's behaviour were enumerated in Articles of War published by the general at the commencement of a major campaign. These were rarely drawn up *de novo*, commanders instead making use of existing examples and amending them as circumstances and their own prejudices dictated. Some codes proved especially influential, notably the one published in 1526 by Ferdinand, King of Bohemia and Hungary, and Maurice of Nassau's *Artikelbrief* of 1590 which served as a model for the Articles evolved by Gustavus Adolphus between 1617 and 1630, these subsequently forming the basis for the codes in Leslie's Scottish army of 1644, the New Model Army and the forces of the Great Elector.[66] The death penalty was prescribed for a wide variety of offences (it was mentioned in no less than 41 of the 60 ordinances comprising the English Articles of 1627)[67] including desertion, mutiny, disobedience, breaking ranks, sleeping on watch, abandoning the colours, unlicensed plundering and rape of civilians. Death was usually by hanging, though convention dictated that officers should be shot or beheaded, and there were variants for those who committed offences deemed to be particularly heinous: the Swedish code of 1683 allowed for soldiers who stopped to loot rather than pursue a defeated enemy to be clubbed to death.[68] The codes allowed for a wide degree of discretion, however, and, especially when the offence was a corporate one, commanders, loath to have their forces decimated by wholesale executions, singled out a few individuals for exemplary punishment, the remainder being pardoned or given lesser sentences. One of a range of physical punishments might be substituted for hanging, including whipping, running the gauntlet, the strappado, and riding the horse (the offender here was made to sit for hours on two boards nailed together in a vee shape with his legs weighted down). Lesser crimes, such as gambling, excessive drinking, failure to observe sanitary regulations and pawning equipment could also incur corporal punishment, particularly for repeated offences, but might be dealt with by way of fines, stoppages, demotion or imprisonment. Sometimes public humiliation was deemed sufficient. Certain offenders in the New Model Army, for example, were made to wear a placard around their neck giving details of their crime.[69] Executions and corporal punishments were invariably carried out in front of the assembled regiment, publicity being a *sine qua non* of military justice which was premised, like civilian justice, on a belief in the deterrent effect which exemplary punishments imposed on the few would have on the many.

The basic substance of the codes differed little over the course of two centuries. They all covered the fundamental military duties of obeying orders, not breaking ranks, following and guarding the colours; they sought to preserve order in the camp and on the march by regulating the numbers and activities of sutlers, prostitutes and other camp-followers, and by restraining drinking and gambling amongst the soldiers; they looked to maintain basic levels of hygiene; they said something about the moral behaviour of the soldier; and they regulated his conduct with civilians and their property. There was, however, a tendency for the codes to become increasingly elaborate, and for the offences to be ever more closely defined. Henry VIII's 1513 code, for example, was a disordered ragbag by comparison with Leicester's more structured set of rules drawn up in 1585; and neither had anything as specific as Eugene's stipulation in 1710, designed to prevent desertion, that men 'found 100 paces from the army on the march and 1,000 paces from the camp' be hung without favour or clemency.[70] Maurice of Nassau's *Artikelbrief*, drawn up in response to the disorders in the Dutch army in the 1580s, had no less than six separate articles dealing with the offence of mutiny alone, and by the early eighteenth century the Austrian War Council was issuing annual disciplinary codes for its forces. It had already become common practice by the mid-sixteenth century for printed copies of the code to be circulated to the officers; and the articles were read out to the men when they mustered, a laborious process which might take up to an hour. Gustavus Adolphus nevertheless ordered that this practice be continued at least once a month in order that no one might claim ignorance of them; and it was normal by the mid-seventeenth century to have new recruits swear an oath of obedience to the regulations. The *ad hoc* military codes also began to be incorporated into state legislation. Lazarus von Schwendi's articles of war were adopted by the Diet of the Holy Roman Empire in 1570 for example, and in 1590 the States-General of the United Provinces issued Maurice's *Artikelbrief* as the 'Laws and Ordinances for Martial Discipline'.[71] The Swedish Articles of War were revised by a committee of experts in the 1680s and published by the *Riksdag*; while the various Mutiny Acts passed by the English Parliament after 1689 helped to regularize existing codes of conduct. Separate pieces of state legislation also sought to correct military abuses: series of *plakkaten* issued in the Netherlands between 1590 and 1648 imposed severe sanctions on soldiers who deserted or who harassed civilians, for instance.[72]

Not only was the soldier being hedged about with an increasingly complex and detailed set of regulations by the late seventeenth century, but, just as importantly, the enforcement of discipline had become more efficient. Officers specifically charged with maintaining discipline proliferated in every army, under a variety of names – provosts, advocates, *barrachels*, *écoulètes* – and there was a corresponding growth in the size of their accompanying staffs. Military courts began to be held on a routine basis. In William Waller's army, for example, a 'Councell of Warre' sat every Monday, Wednesday and Friday between 8 a.m. and 12 noon for the administration of justice, frequently presided over by the general himself.[73]

Commanders in the second half of the seventeenth century were particularly concerned to enforce the regulations concerning plundering. Of course, they did not seek to abolish this altogether. How could they, when soldiers on campaign lived off the countryside by plunder, and when troops could only be brought to assault a fortress or fight a battle through the lure of booty? Rather, they attempted to curtail the indiscriminate pillaging which had proved so damaging to armies in the past, leading as it did to a collapse of discipline and order and the economic exhaustion of the theatre of war, and to substitute a regulated form of plunder, which harmed the enemy, which avoided damage to home territory, and which left the economic infrastructure of an area intact whilst extracting sufficient resources from it to allow the army to subsist. Thus, in 1707, Marshal Villars, on the point of leading his army into the Empire, reminded his troops of the facts of military life:

> We can no longer depend on our magazines. If you burn, if
> you drive out the population, you will starve. I order you
> therefore, in your own interests, to be reasonable...but if
> this not enough to convince you, the very greatest severity
> will be used against breaches of discipline.[74]

The restrictions on indiscriminate plunder meant that war did
not offer the same potentiality for profit to the late-seventeenth-
century soldier as it had to his sixteenth-century predecessor.

In addition to the discipline imposed under the military
code, soldiers were subject to informal punishment: the casual
blows and beatings administered by officers without formal
charges being brought. Quite how much of this went on is
unclear, and it probably varied from army to army. It was
likely to have been negligible in the self-governing, egalitarian
Swiss units of the early sixteenth century, but appears to have
been widespread in the Army of Flanders. A specific demand of
the mutineers in 1574 was that no man should be given
corporal punishment without due trial; and it was common for
mutineers in the Army to seek to change their unit so as to
escape persecution from tyrannous officers and NCOs.[75] It is
possible that the evolution of more closely defined offences and
punishments on the one hand, and of military courts and a
staff with the specific function of enforcing discipline on the
other, helped to protect the soldier from such informal punishments. Certainly in Brandenburg the establishment by the
Great Elector of a new military code in 1656, backed by
formal courts martial (he insisted on confirming personally the
sentence of the court) was accompanied by efforts to end the
beating of soldiers by their officers. However, this last reform
did not long survive the Elector's death in 1688, and elsewhere
the trend seems to have been to confirm the traditional informal
disciplinary powers of officers. Thus, the court martial records
of both Waller's army and Monck's army quartered in Dundee
reveal several instances of men being given severe sentences
(one pikeman received sixty lashes) for 'resisting an officer in
the giving of correction'.[76]

Without exception, Articles of War had something to say
about the religious duties of the soldier. Blasphemy frequently
headed the list of military offences (though it came well down

the scale of penalties); and, particularly in armies led by a notably devout commander, attendance at weekly or even daily prayers might be made an obligation, though one which was frequently honoured more in the breach than the observance, especially by the later seventeenth century. Yet even generals who doubted the spiritual efficacy of religious services nevertheless retained them as an aid in the maintenance of discipline and order, and, as we noted earlier, as a means of raising morale prior to an engagement. Chaplains who preached the 'wrong' message thus got short shrift. One *aumonier*, whose sermon was becoming over long and theological, was interrupted by his lieutenant-colonel: 'Soldiers, what monsieur the Abbé is saying is that there is no salvation for cowards. Long live the king.'[77] The seasoned campaigner, Sancho de Londoño, rated the morale boosting and disciplinary value of religion so highly that he urged the appointment of a bishop to each army. Nobody went as far as this, but only the Dutch made no provision at all for chaplains to accompany their forces.[78]

In practice, however, both the numbers and quality of chaplains tended to be low, like military surgeons, and for the same reasons: irregular employment, poor pay and low status. To be sure, the Jesuits and Recollects showed some propensity to serve in the armies of Spain and France and proved an exception to this general rule, and, in addition, some of the nursing orders provided staffing for military hospitals, though their role was limited to the care of the sick. But the Counter-Reformation Church, which spawned a number of new or revamped orders dedicated to the spiritual and practical needs of particular groups in society – fallen women, orphans, the destitute, Protestants and *nouveaux-convertis*, for example – produced no order to cater specifically for serving soldiers. Was this a reflection of the low status of the military profession, or an indication that, morally, soldiers were thought to be hopelessly unregenerate? It was certainly the case that military men were noted for their profanity and irreligion. Claude de Seyssel, for example, wrote that it was habitual, particularly amongst infantrymen, to 'blaspheme the names of God, the Virgin Mary, and the saints'.[79] There were exceptions to this general rule. The first Huguenot armies in the French Religious Wars and some of the Parliamentary forces in the English Civil War were noted for their piety, and so was the 'Catholic' Army of

Flanders, though it should be noted that religious observance in the latter was closely attuned to the particular needs of soldiers: it consisted above all in the carrying of religious charms to protect the wearer from injury, and in the testamentary disposition of wealth on alms, charity and other good works to help secure entry to heaven. Yet amongst many armies even this rather mechanistic, death-bed type of piety was absent, and, especially by the later seventeenth century, soldiers were remarkable for the lack of any religious sensibility at all.[80] The poor quality of military chaplains may offer a partial explanation for this irreligion. But in fact the army milieu as a whole tended to be dechristianizing. Habits of religious conformity, which had been developed in a civilian world characterized by its regular round of Sunday observances, feasts, patron saints' days and rites of passage, were soon lost in a military environment with its irregular and unsettled timetable. Most armies contained men of various religious faiths, all obliged to serve together, and an enforced mutual tolerance easily degenerated into religious indifference. Moreover, the ethos of soldiering encouraged an affected disregard for established norms of religious behaviour. As Seyssel noted, blasphemy was so common amongst military men because 'the soldiers would not be reckoned men of courage and valiant hearts unless they do it'.[81]

PRISONERS

Whatever the strength of their religious beliefs, only those soldiers committed to a suicidal fight to the last man in defence of their honour – the Swiss at Marignano, the Spanish at Rocroi, Newcastle's Whitecoats at Marston Moor for example – preferred death to surrender. In general, combatants who proferred their surrender, by throwing down their arms, would not be massacred: though that said, there were exceptions. The garrison of a town which unreasonably held out beyond the time when relief might arrive, for example, or which had taken a particularly heavy toll of the besiegers, might be put to the sword when the town was taken. The mood of the attackers, rather than any formal surrender terms, was crucial here, and the longer the siege dragged on the worse that mood was likely to be. The Spanish soldiers who had lost over 2,000 comrades in bloody assaults on the walls of Maastricht during its 111-day siege in 1579, exacted a fearful revenge on the defenders when it was stormed, for example.[82] Soldiers also became carried away in the heat of battle and killed unnecessarily. 'The soldiers got worked up to such a pitch that they spared no one, and butchered all who fell into their hands', wrote Prince Eugene of an engagement in 1697.[83] It was also significant in this instance that the enemy were Turks. Warfare in eastern Europe, where the opponents were considered to be less than human, was always characterized by great savagery. The same was true of Ireland. Soldiers of the Scottish Covenanting Army shot prisoners they had taken in a skirmish in Kirwarlin Wood; and during a minor engagement in 1690, English soldiers 'killed thirty-nine, and took four, whom they hanged without further ceremony', as George Story laconically noted.[84] Such measures were justified on the grounds that the Irish would not fight fairly, but resorted to guerrilla warfare instead. Even in the rest of western Europe prisoners who embarrassed their captors, because they could not be fed, for example, or who were taken in such large numbers as to pose a security risk, might be killed. On one notorious occasion during the Thirty Years War the Marquis de Sourdis hanged some 200 prisoners for this reason; and it may explain the execution of hundreds of German mercenaries by the Swiss after the battle of Novara in 1513.[85]

Yet there were powerful reasons for not acting routinely in this way. It was generally held to be against the laws of war, and it was certainly against the self-interest of the mercenary soldier who, victor one day, might shortly be on the losing side. Thomas Audley ended his Treatise by 'wishing all good souldiers to be no more blooddie than the Law of Armes doth require, for then no doubte thei shall have long countynaunce in the warres with good successe'.[86] Of course, not all soldiers could be assumed to be familiar with the rules of war, as one Royalist officer found in 1642, when seized by townsmen from Bradford newly drafted into the Parliamentary army. 'He cried out for quarter and they poor men, not knowing the meaning of it said – "aye, they would quarter him," and so killed him.'[87] But few people, even civilians, would have been as ignorant as these. Victorious commanders anyway had an interest in preventing wanton killing as far as possible, since they could make good the losses on their side by inducing prisoners to enter their service, veterans being especially welcome. Prisoners often had little compunction in swopping sides. When Charles I took Banbury in 1642 the whole garrison re-enlisted with him, for example, and 'many thousands' were said to have enlisted with the Royalists after the surrender of the Parliamentary infantry at Lostwithiel in 1644.[88] Above all, there was a pecuniary advantage to the taking of prisoners, for they might be worth ransoming. Officers would probably be in a position to pay a ransom out of their own resources, though it might take some time to raise. Even the impoverished common soldiers had some economic worth, for their captain, anxious not to lose their services, might be prepared to buy them back; or they might be exchanged on a one-for-one basis for prisoners of equal value taken by the enemy.

Although prisoners remained the personal property of their captor, negotiations for their ransoming or exchange were conducted in the sixteenth century by the officers of the army, who claimed a share of any ransom. Under the disciplinary code for Henry VIII's 1513 expedition to France privates paid one-third of the profits from a prisoner to their captain, who in turn paid one-third to the king, the high marshal of the army keeping a daily record of all prisoners taken to ensure that none of the interested parties lost out.[89] Disposal of prisoners was yet another area of military life over which governments in the seventeenth century increasingly extended their authority, however, asserting that the prisoner was the property of the state, which should handle negotiations for his release and take the lion's share of any proceeds. The result, of course, was that the common soldier lost out financially, just at the time when the potential profit from plunder was also decreasing. Yet there was some logic to the governments' position. With the demise of personal, hand-to-hand combat, most prisoners were taken in group surrenders and it was difficult to assign responsibility for their capture to any one individual. And as armies grew in size, so too did the numbers of prisoners, rendering unworkable the old system whereby captains negotiated their release. A number of bilateral agreements for the ransoming or exchange of prisoners were made between states. As early as 1599 an exchange agreement was negotiated between Spain and the States-General of the United Provinces, and others followed in 1602, 1622, 1623 and 1638. Similar ones were made between

Spain and France in 1639, 1643 and 1648 (after 1645 a Spanish commissioner was resident in France to oversee the interests of captives), between Sweden and the Empire in 1642, Denmark and Sweden in 1653 and between France and the United Provinces in 1673. Government involvement did not necessarily lessen the amount of time prisoners spent in captivity. Although they were generally exchanged or ransomed quite quickly, political considerations or wrangles over payment could delay their release. Gustavus Horn, son-in-law of the Swedish chancellor, was held by Maximilian of Bavaria for eight years after his capture at Nördlingen for example; and one group of 155 Frenchmen exchanged for Spanish prisoners in 1644 had been held for five years and ten months.[90]

THE COMPENSATIONS OF SOLDIERING: WOMEN; COMRADES; AN UNCERTAIN HIGH-LIFE

A review of the conditions of life for the early-modern soldier thus presents a bleak picture. Despite some minimal improvements in respect of pay, clothing, access to medical services and freedom from dependence on corrupt captains, he remained frighteningly vulnerable to sickness, injury and death, and a prey to hardships of all kinds. Moreover, in important respects, the soldier's position had deteriorated as opportunities for enrichment through plunder and ransoming of prisoners were curbed, and as he was subjected to harsher and more effective discipline.

However, we should be careful not to exaggerate the case, for the picture was not wholly bleak, and military life did have its compensations. A traditional perk of the soldier was the relatively easy availability of recreational sex. Women were to be found with all armies. 'I know not whether they list them, or what they do with them,' commented Bullock on the English armies of the later seventeenth century in Farquhar's *Recruiting Officer*, 'but I'm sure they carry as many women as men with them out of the country.'[91] Exact figures on the number of women are hard to come by, but they were certainly numerous. Using data derived from billeting records of the Flanders Army, Parker has suggested that on occasions they accounted for 28 per cent of troop strength, almost certainly a minimum, whilst

Langer cites the example of 368 cavalrymen camped at Langenau in 1630 accompanied by 66 women and 78 girls. Of these female camp-followers some were certainly prostitutes, though exactly what proportion is impossible to say, especially since contemporaries, such as the sour Welshman Elis Gruffudd who complained in 1544 of the 'numbers of shameless prostitutes [who] came at every tide from England' to join Henry VIII's forces in France, indiscriminately applied the label 'whore' to all women camp-followers.[92]

It has been argued that the later seventeenth century witnessed an attempt to deny the soldier this traditional perk by restricting the numbers of female camp-followers or banning them altogether. Thus in March 1687 a French ordinance ordering prostitutes found within 2 leagues of a military camp to have their nose and ears slit, and which had hitherto been applied only to the area around Versailles, was extended to the rest of France. Other regulations passed at about the same time sought to limit the number of wives with armies by discouraging marriages: officers who wed without permission were cashiered, whilst privates were denied promotion. Similarly, in Brandenburg-Prussia whores were banned from camps and garrisons by the Articles of War of 1656, a punitive fee was charged for marriage licences (6 *thalers* in Prussia), and in 1681 an edict restricted the number of married men per company to between thirty and forty. This was generous by English standards, where six was the norm by the early eighteenth century. However, such draconian regulations were far from novel, and did not of themselves indicate a new and more disapproving attitude towards the presence of female camp-followers. Slitting the nose was after all a traditional punishment for prostitutes, used by the Venetian commander, Alviano, in 1514, for example. English Articles of War from the sixteenth century were, if anything, even more barbaric, stipulating branding on the cheek for any 'common woman' coming within 3 miles of a camp (fifteenth-century versions spoke of breaking the arm), whilst the Dutch regulations of 1590 prescribed severe flogging for a second offence of prostitution. More importantly, there is little to suggest that regulations forbidding women were being enforced with any greater vigour in 1700 than they had been one or two hundred years previously. Thus the 261-man garrison at Spandau in Prussia had with it 171 wives and 295 children late in the seventeenth century; while the Münster garrison of Coesfeld comprised 918 soldiers, with 335 wives and 373 children.[93]

This is not of course to imply that commanders were at any time unaware of the problems which stemmed from having prostitutes in particular, and female camp-followers in general, with the armies. The former posed a health hazard through the spread of venereal disease – syphilis was rife in all armies – and were a threat to discipline if allowed to ply their trade in the camp unchecked. The latter added to the number of mouths to be fed and bodies to be lodged; they encumbered the baggage train and hampered the army's mobility; they produced children who had to be supported; and although Raimondo Monte-cuccoli argued that married men fought more vigorously so as not to dishonour themselves in front of their wives, the generally accepted view was that, having more to lose than their single colleagues, they were less likely to hazard themselves in action.[94] Yet at the same time commanders acknowledged that it was both undesirable and impossible to ban women from armies altogether. Undesirable because they undertook a range of vital, if often thankless tasks, in default of which armies would scarcely have been able to function. They served as sutlers, dealing in food, drink, tobacco, pipes, firewood and second-hand clothing; they laundered and mended clothes, cleaned latrines, and cooked; they tended the sick and infirm, bandaged the wounded on the battlefield and in the siege lines, and carried them to the rear; wives foraged for their husbands and not infrequently supplemented their meagre pay by working them-selves. And it was not just on the pages of Grimmelshausen's *Mother Courage* and More's *Utopia* that they were to be found wielding a sword and pike. The bishop of Albi, administering the last rites to the dying at Leucate in 1637 came across several women in uniform who had been cut down, and who had sold their lives bravely. 'They were the real men', he was told by Castilian soldiers, 'since those who had fled, including certain officers, had conducted themselves like women.'[95] It was also essential to have a certain number of prostitutes with the army 'to avoid worse disorders' with civilians, as Londoño explained in his *Discours* of 1589, 'for in no state is it as necessary to allow them as in this one of free, strong and vigorous men, who might otherwise commit crimes against the local people, molesting their daughters, sisters and wives'.[96] It was anyway impractical to rid the army of prostitutes altogether. They could circumvent the regulations forbidding their presence by becoming the 'wife' of a trooper; and in any event many must have been like Mother Courage, part-time whores, for whom prostitution was not a way of life but an occasional expedient, resorted to from time to time in intervals of need, whilst also serving as launderess, cook, maid and husband's helpmate.

Recognizing the inevitability and also the utility of having women in their armies, commanders in practice sought only to limit their numbers and control their activities, rather than ban them altogether, using the draconian punishments available to them in the Articles of War as a fall-back position. By the mid-sixteenth century the regimental *Hurenweibel*, or whore-sergeant, had become an established feature of German armies, as well as many others, his function, as defined by Leonhard Fronsperger's *Kriegszbuch* of 1598, being the supervision of women, boys and lackeys of the baggage train, who were to be kept busy 'running, pouring out, fetching food and drink, knowing how to behave mostly with regard to the needs of others, and taking it in turn to do what is necessary according to orders.'[97] Frequently ill-treated, their contribution to the functioning of the military largely unacknowledged, women nevertheless remained throughout the early-modern period as much part of the armies as men.

If the presence of wives and whores in an army, providing familial support and the opportunity for sexual *divertissements*, helped to make the hardships of the soldier's existence more bearable, a second compensation of the military life was the comradeship which it offered. To be sure, there was often much that was callous in soldiers' treatment of each other. George Story recounted one incident in which a Dane serving in Ireland, seeing that a fellow soldier was ill and near to death, shot him 'and took away his musket without any further ceremony'.[98] And we should beware of imagining that all those below officer level formed an egalitarian, undifferentiated group, united by ties of common fellowship. The society of soldiers was as riven with hierarchies and petty jealousies as any other. Cavalrymen believed themselves to be superior to the foot-soldiers; musketeers to pikemen; gunners felt themselves to be a cut above the rest because of their greater technical expertise, a superior status which was given concrete expression in Imperial armies by a patent from Charles V allowing them higher rations, priority in the allocation of plunder, and the right to keep wives and children with them rather than have them carried in the baggage train.[99] The *rötmeisters* or *appointés*, men of proven skill and experience who were positioned at key points in the line to steady the rest of the men and give a lead in drill and manoeuvring, formed an elite amongst the rank and file, rewarded with bonus pays and extra rations. Nevertheless, such divisions did not prevent the emergence of ties of comradeship amongst soldiers. In his *Discours* la Noue noted the 'general friendship' which existed amongst men of the same regiment, but he singled out for particular attention the comradeship which developed amongst groups of soldiers, numbering anything between two and ten, serving in the same company. These comrades occupied the same billets, perhaps even the same bed; they shared expenses of food, clothing and a servant's wages, thus living more economically than any one of them could do on his own; they ate and conversed together in the evenings; offered mutual assistance to one of their number who fell sick; marched and stood together in battle. So pervasive were these informal 'societies of friends' that la Noue likened any long-serving soldier who failed to form such a comradeship to a horse in harness which would not pull with the others.[100]

La Noue observed these comradeships to be particularly prevalent amongst Spanish forces of the sixteenth century, but in fact they existed in all armies at all times. De Vigenère and Fourquevaux, for example, referred to them in the French armies, the latter calling them *chambrées* because the men shared a room; whilst Robert Monro's account of his time with the Swedish armies of the Thirty Years War gives an indication of the more general ties of fellowship which grew out of the shared hardships and misfortune, as well as the shared pleasures, of a manly life. When seven of the companies which had served with his regiment were ordered to a separate destination, 'we severed not without teares, both of officers and souldiers'; and he applauded the several instances he had witnessed in which soldiers hazarded their own lives to rescue wounded comrades, advancing as a general principle of the soldier's existence that, 'We must not preferre the safety of our own bodies to the publique weal of our Comrades.'[101]

The army thus offered the possibility of close personal ties of comradeship which not only might not be so easily established in the civilian world, but which also enabled the soldier to cope with the intrinsic misfortunes and hardships of military life more effectively than if he had faced them alone. In these respects the soldier's existence was less bleak than might be imagined. Moreover, in any assessment of the military life we should guard against viewing it as one of unremitting hardship. Robert Monro gave his readers a salutary reminder in this respect, when describing his regiment's advance on to Frankfurt-am-Main:

> This march being profitable as it was pleasant to the eye, we see that souldiers have not always so hard a life as the common opinion is; for sometimes as they have abundance, so they have variety of pleasure in marching softly without feare or danger, through fertill soyles and pleasant countries, their marches being more like to a kingly progresse than to warres, being in a fat land as this was, abounding in all things except peace.[102]

Even Nehemiah Wharton, whose letters written in 1642 from the Earl of Essex's army to his former employer contain a veritable litany of complaints about the foul weather, shortage of plunder, lack of food and drink, poor quarters and surliness of the locals, the crudity of some fellow soldiers 'whose society, blessed be God, I hate and avoide', and of marches conducted 'up to the ancles in thick clay', nevertheless had to admit that there were bright spots. In Buckinghamshire 'which is the sweetest county that ever I saw, and as is the countrey so also is the people', he was well entertained; Coventry 'gave good quarter, both for horse and foote'; and he became positively ecstatic about Worcestershire, 'a pleasaunt, fruitfull, and rich countrey, aboundinge in corne, woods, pastures, hills, and valleyes, every hedge and heigh way beset with fruits', and especially about the abundance of perry, a drink made from pears, which, though dear, was better than anything to be had in London.[103]

Clearly then, there were good times and bad in the soldier's existence. Ultimately, however, a full appreciation of that existence is not to be gained by drawing up a balance sheet of its pleasures and pains, but through a recognition of its quintessential capriciousness. Times of feast gave way to times of famine with unexpected and bewildering rapidity. Plunder accumulated in battle or the sack of a town could be as quickly lost to thieves, enemy forces or on the turn of a card; cosy billets might have to be evacuated at a moment's notice as soldiers were turned out to make room for officers or to set off on a march; peasants, terrorized by soldiers, could subsequently band together to wreak a frightful revenge on any of their tormentors found wandering away from the army; long periods of boredom and inactivity were punctuated by the uncertain interludes of high drama provided by a battle, siege, raid on an enemy camp or foraging expedition; and although Daniel Lupton exaggerated when he claimed that soldiers 'are alwayes next dore to death',[104] there is no doubt that death, injury and sickness were their frequent companions. 'A soldier's life is an odd, unaccountable way of living', wrote Lieutenant-Colonel Blackader in 1705. 'One day too much heat, another too cold. A bad irregular way of living.'[105] Grimmelshausen, who was well acquainted with the ups and downs of military life, having spent fourteen years with the armies after being carried off by Croat soldiers as a boy in 1635, serving first as a musketeer and finally as a regimental clerk, expressed something of the soldiers' turn and turn about lifestyle through his best-known character, Simplicissimus: 'Murdering and being murdered, slaying and being slain, hunting and being hunted, robbing and being robbed; in short, hunting and hurting and being hunted and injured in their turn: this was the soldier's existence.'[106] Indeed, it was precisely because he was constantly at the mercy of circumstances beyond his control, enjoying an uncertain existence which entailed great dangers on the one hand coupled with the possibility of enrichment and high living for the quick-witted on the other, that the soldier's experience was such a pervasive theme of the picaresque novel, a genre which reached its peak of popularity in the early-modern period, and in which the fickleness of fate is a constantly reiterated theme. It was not just in Grimmelshausen's novels that the hero (or heroine) spent either all or a substantial period of their lives with the armies, but also in Mateo Aleman's *Guzman de Alfarache*, Quevedo's *La Vida del Buscón*, Le Sage's *Gil Blas*, and Defoe's *Moll Flanders*, for example.

Living in such a capricious world it is scarcely surprising that many soldiers evinced an attachment to superstitious practices, and magic potions and charms believed to give protection from accidental injury and death. Hucksters trailed round the military camps offering soldiers invulnerability by making their armour bullet proof.[107] Whatever the benefits derived from such practices (and they perhaps had a morale-boosting function), it was undoubtedly the veterans who coped best with the hazards of military life and exploited its potential to the full. They were most adept at finding the best billets when less experienced men were left to sleep in the hedgerows, and at bullying their hosts into providing extra food, blankets, candles and money; they were most proficient at organizing what the Germans called the *auf partei gehein*, raids by small groups on undefended peasant households which offered booty with little risk; they knew best how to pawn armour and equipment without being caught; how to avoid the wrath of an officer; they were alive to the possibilities of danger which threatened in the siege lines, in battle, or on a raid; most important of all they had had the opportunity to form those comradeships which helped insulate the individual soldier from the hazards of military life. The point was well made by James Turner. As a raw recruit in Germany in 1633–4 he 'suffered exceedingly great want of both meate and clothes, being necessitated to ly constantly in the fields with little or no shelter, to march allways a foot and drinke water.... *Dulce bellum inexpertis*' (a phrase he borrowed from Erasmus). Subsequently however, though many of his less experienced comrades remained in great need, he had

> learned so much cunning, and become so vigilant to lay hold on opportunities that I wanted for nothing, horses, clothes, meate nor moneys; and made so good use of what I had learned, that the whole time I served in Germanie, I suffered no such miserie as I had done the first yeare and a halfe that I came to it.[108]

THE EX-SOLDIER: MILITARIZATION AND THE CIVILIAN WORLD

If the common soldier enjoyed only a precarious existence inside the army, the same was often true when he left it. Much depended, of course, on the circumstances under which he left the army. The prospects for the maimed soldier were particularly bleak. The fortunate few, whose injuries were not so severe as to be disabling, might be employed on garrison duties. Prince Eugene urged that each garrison in Austrian service should include a company of invalids, who would thus be maintained in employment and would free able-bodied soldiers for active service. Others might be found a place in one of the few hospitals, funded by private charity, catering specifically for maimed ex-soldiers and -sailors. These existed at Dover, Hythe, Southampton and Hull in England in the early sixteenth century, though, like the house founded at Buckingham in 1559 with places for thirty-nine men, they dealt only in penny numbers. In Catholic countries the disabled ex-soldier might look to the Church for assistance, perhaps being taken into a religious house as a lay brother. He was indeed encouraged to do this by the government, which thus avoided any direct responsibility for his welfare, though some state funds might be provided for his upkeep. The General Assembly of the clergy complained incessantly to the French Crown about the numbers of men it was being forced to subsidize in this way, and of the disruptive effect their presence had on the life of the monastery.[109]

Complaints such as these which reached a crescendo around 1650, and, more importantly, the growing numbers of mutilated ex-soldiers resulting from the mass armies and extended conflicts of the seventeenth century, who overwhelmed the existing facilities, crowded the streets, and added to the general problem of pauperism and lawlessness, did prompt governments, both Catholic and Protestant, to found state-sponsored hospitals for the maimed and indigent veterans. One of the earliest was the 'Garrison of our Lady of Hal' for the Spanish army in the Netherlands. Another was at Vadstena in Sweden, set up by Gustavus Adolphus in the old convent of St Bridget, and reorganized and endowed with considerable state funds in 1646–7, whilst in France both Henry IV and Richelieu planned retreats for crippled ex-soldiers. Building actually began at the Bicêtre in 1633–4, only to be abandoned for lack of funds, and it was left to Louis XIV to found the *Hôtel des Invalides* in 1670. The best-known institution of its type, the *Invalides* probably inspired the foundation of a number of other hospitals elsewhere, including Chelsea, which offered accommodation for

472 'aged, maimed and infirm land soldiers', with approximately the same number attached as out-pensioners. In Piedmont a hospital of similar size was established in 1710. There was no equivalent institution in Brandenburg-Prussia, though from 1705 the state administered a fund for disabled soldiers, the *Invalidenkasse*. In Bavaria from 1680 some crippled soldiers were offered employment in the state textile factory, whilst the Dutch States-General paid some disabled soldiers a pension.[110]

Many of these initiatives were actually less generous than might at first appear. For example, whilst the initial cost of founding a hospital might be borne by the government, subsequent expenses were funded through compulsory deductions taken from the pay of serving soldiers, and in the case of the *Invalides* the *oblats* formerly paid to religious houses were diverted to its upkeep. The hospitals thus represented a reallocation of existing funds, rather than the injection of much new money. Moreover, institutional relief for maimed ex-soldiers remained grossly inadequate throughout the early-modern period. Only a small proportion of those eligible could be found places in a backwater garrison, or in one of the state or privately run hospitals, and the majority always ended up as beggars on the streets.

The prospects for the able-bodied soldier who was demobilized were not of course so grim. At least he had the use of his hands to earn a living, and he might be fortunate enough to leave the army with accumulated plunder and his arrears of pay settled either substantially or in full. This was the case with the 5,334 veterans of the Army of Flanders who in 1577 shared between them back-pay of 1,234,293 florins, and whose baggage and plunder on the return trip to Lombardy weighed 2,600 tons. In the 1590s some individuals in the Army received arrears totalling well over 2,000 florins each, transforming them overnight into men of substance; whilst the Swedish forces at the close of the Thirty Years War were apportioned a total indemnity of 5 million *thalers*, although admittedly this was not all paid in cash and was unequally divided.[111]

All too often, however, matters did not work out as favourably as this. At the end of the campaign soldiers were frequently disbanded far from home and with little or nothing of the pay owed to them by the government, whose chief concern was to be rid of its troops as cheaply and quickly as possible. English soldiers demobilized in France used up the small monies they received on the journey home, and were reported by magistrates at Rye where they landed in 1590 to be 'in most miserable sort...some wounded, some their toes and feet rotting off, some lame, the skin and flesh of their feet torn away with continual marching', and all without money or clothes.[112] Such men quickly joined the ranks of the destitute. Yet even ex-soldiers who were not in such desperate straits as these poor wretches often found the transition to civilian life and work difficult, not to say unwelcome. Governments did, it is true, legislate in an effort to facilitate their return to civilian employment, allowing ex-soldiers to resume their former trade without hindrance from local guilds, for example, giving them a limited exemption from distraint of stock and tools, and obliging former employers to re-hire them. But such legislation proved largely ineffectual. It was difficult to enforce, and the inelastic labour market of early-modern Europe was anyway incapable of absorbing large numbers of men suddenly thrown on to it. In any event, a return to artisanal activity had little appeal for those soldiers who had joined the army precisely to escape the humdrum tedium of the work-a-day world, whilst other ex-soldiers had never learned a trade and were in the position of Anthoine Bloquier who declared frankly in 1677 that 'he knew no other trade but war'.[113]

How far did army life serve to 'militarize' those men who experienced it, with the consequence that they found it difficult subsequently to re-integrate into the civilian world? Some of the specifically military conditioning factors which are frequently mentioned in this context – uniforms, barracks and drill – were, if of growing significance by the later seventeenth century, nevertheless still of limited importance. Uniforms, as we have seen, barely existed by 1700, barracks accommodation was far from generalized, and training was hardly extensive. Moreover, serving soldiers were certainly not isolated from contact with civilians. Not only were they frequently billeted in their houses but large numbers of civilians moved with the armies, providing support services as servants, grooms, carpenters, drivers, pawnbrokers, sutlers, butchers, laundresses, wives and prostitutes. Additionally, soldiering would usually, but did not necessarily, imply a cessation of civilian employment. Troops in backwater garrisons in particular frequently continued to pursue a secondary trade, both to overcome the boredom of such postings, and, more importantly, to eke out their pay. So extensive was the practice of retaining civilian employment in Brandenburg-Prussia – it was actively encouraged by the authorities who were thus able to reduce the already meagre pay of the troops still further – that Frederick William I claimed that the proceeds of the excise tax fell by one-third when his army was on the march and his soldiers had to relinquish their jobs.[114] Even when in action soldiers were not segregated from civilians. Peasants laboured to dig the trenches and throw up the ramparts which were manned by soldiers during a siege; townsmen (and women) were obliged to stand shoulder to shoulder with the garrison in defence of their town, or, at the least, endure the hardships of disease and starvation along with them. Only in battle was there a distancing between the two, though even here women came on to the battlefield to serve as nurses, and civilian spectators in search of the vicarious thrill of violence stationed themselves at a safe distance to watch the proceedings.[115]

Yet if there was little of the physical separation between soldier and civilian which was to form such a feature of military life in the nineteenth century, on joining the colours the early-modern recruit nevertheless entered a society which was markedly different to the civilian one. In a section of his *Handbüchlein* (1631) dealing with the privileges of the soldier Johann Newmayr von Ramsla listed some of the key differences: the military man was entitled to carry and use arms; he was not subject to royal, seigneurial or church taxes, nor did he pay customs dues; and he was governed by a separate legal code, with its distinctive offences and punishments.[116] Such legal and fiscal distinctions aside, there existed above all what John Hale has called a 'mental frontier between the man of war and the man of peace'.[117] It was underpinned by a hard-drinking, womanizing, blaspheming military culture in which manual labour was despised (hence the reluctance, often refusal, of soldiers to dig fieldworks or to drive carts), civilians existed to be bullied and exploited, and which contrasted the soldier's long periods of do-nothing cockaigne idleness with the tedious round of the labouring masses. It was reflected in the colourful, plumed, slashed-sleeved, convention-defying clothes which soldiers flaunted (though a hard campaign would reduce these to tatters), and in the *argot* or jargon which they adopted, composed partly of technical terms (battles, ravelins, demi-lunes, howitzer, hussar) and also of exotic curses and patter, though it is doubtful if this ever amounted, as has been suggested, to a separate *patois*, comprehensible only amongst the community of military men.[118] The words in this *argot* were of Czech, Hungarian, Turkish and Greek, as well as of German, French, Dutch and Swedish origin, and indicate something of the internationalism of the professional soldier which, together with ties of loyalty to comrades and company, replaced the local ties of town and village. This internationalism, which led men to serve willingly in the armies of states other than their own, can most easily be illustrated by reference to the officer class, where it is possible to follow the careers of individuals in detail. Sir Roger Williams, for example, served in the Dutch army (1572–3), the Spanish (1574–5) and the Anglo-Dutch forces (1578–87). Frederick von Schomberg held commissions with the French, Portuguese, Prussian, Dutch and English forces. Marlborough learned his trade in the French armies led by Turenne, who had not cavilled at acquiring a knowledge of siegecraft from the acknowledged master, the Calvinist Dutchman Frederick Henry. Yet the common soldiers, even if individual careers remain largely inaccessible to the historian, were no less part of this international fraternity of violence, and proved no less ready to join foreign armies than their officers. La Noue might deplore their willingness 'to serve no matter whom and no matter what cause so long as they find good and fat rewards', and James Turner echo his concern during the Thirty Years War, pointing to the 'dangerous maxim' followed by military men (himself included) 'which was, that so we serve our master honestlie, it is no matter what master we serve', but both acknowledged it to be an ineluctable fact of military life.[119]

Quite how far a recruit would be affected by contact with the society of soldiers, how far in short he would be 'militarized', depended crucially upon two factors. The first was the type of forces with whom he served. By definition the military culture which has been described above was most strongly evidenced by long-service, professional, combat-oriented troops who made war a way of life. Included here would be the Swiss mercenary pikemen, German *landsknechts*, the *reiters*, the Castilian infantrymen and Albanian light cavalry, all those soldiers in short to whom la Noue's paraphrase of a contemporary jingle could be applied:

> War is my country,
> My armour is my house,
> And in every season
> Fighting is my life.[120]

All commanders endeavoured to include at least some of these professionals in their forces, but the proportion varied considerably both from army to army and over time. There were relatively few in the English Civil War armies: Newman found only 273 soldiers of fortune in the Royalist field command, and although figures cannot be established with such certainty for the Parliamentarian forces, there were probably not many more there.[121] This resulted not just from the scarcity of native military experience in England before 1642, but also from the greater prospects for steady employment and enrichment which professionals found in the concurrent German theatre of war.[122] On the other hand, more were to be found in the armies of both sides at the outbreak of the French Religious Wars, as experienced soldiers, newly returned to France following the cessation of fighting in Italy, looked for fresh employment, and their numbers swelled as the conflict continued and offered sustainable opportunities to the free-lance mercenaries.[123] Where armies fought in a permanent or semi-permanent theatre of war then the proportion of veterans could rise very high. This was the case with the Army of Flanders, for example, and with the Swedish forces of the Thirty Years War which had developed such a strong sense of corporate identity and self-interest by the 1640s that Baner referred to them as 'this widespread state'.[124] Clearly, all other things being equal, a new recruit was more likely to be 'militarized' by service in one of the latter armies than in one of the former.

A second, and more important factor, was the length of time a man spent under arms. It is impossible to suggest a figure for the 'average' period of service. The Dutch in the late sixteenth century and the English at the end of the seventeenth experimented with fixed-term engagements of between one and three years, but this was highly unusual. Recruits generally made an open-ended commitment when they signed on, agreeing to serve until disbandment at the end of the campaign, or the war, whenever that might be. A more positive generalization which may be proferred is that new recruits went on to serve either for a very short period or for a much more substantial one. Those men who were recruited against their will, or who found army life uncongenial, deserted as soon as they could, within days or weeks of joining, whilst those who remained, perhaps becoming addicted to the life, stayed on sometimes for many years (though not necessarily in continuous service with the same army of course). Jean Jarlier and Louis Chambordon, for example, had clocked up nearly six decades of military service between them when they were admitted to the *Invalides* (a minimum of ten years service was required for entry) and they were far from unusual.[125] By 1715 the average length of service of those admitted to the hospital was 24 years and 9 months.[126] How long a period in the company of soldiers was needed for a recruit to be imbued with, and transformed by, their military culture? There can clearly be no precise or single answer to this, not least of all because individual temperaments and responses to army life varied. But Saulx-Tavannes urged as a rule of thumb that it took a year to make a soldier (he was here thinking of the time necessary to inculcate habits of military lifestyle, thought and discipline rather than the much shorter period necessary to train him in the use of arms).[127] Not surprisingly, then, it tended to be the long-service soldier who assimilated least easily back into civilian society.

The ease with which the army was demobilized in England following the Restoration in 1660 was therefore remarkable, since by that stage it contained large numbers of men with many years' military experience. It is explicable partly by the substantial arrears paid to the men, which cost the government and taxpayer dear, but which saved them from penury, and which they might use to set themselves up in business or resume a trade. 'Of all the old Army now you cannot see a man begging about the street', noted Pepys in 1663. 'You shall see this captain turned a shoemaker, the lieutenant a baker; this, a brewer; that, a haberdasher; this common soldier, a porter; and every man in his apron and frock.'[128] Explicable, too, by the existence of a small royal army which offered some chance of continued military employment to the most experienced. The instance nevertheless remains unusual. Generally, as soldiers were turned off at the end of a campaign many resorted to begging or crime (or a mixture of the two), driven to this by destitution, by their disdain for the constraints of civilian society, or because they had a taste for criminality which army life had done nothing to assuage and everything to promote. Thomas More was but one of a host of writers who bewailed the propensity of disbanded soldiers, habituated to violence and living off civilians, and with no trade save that of war, to resort to brigandage: 'Robbers do not make the least active soldiers, nor do soldiers make the most listless robbers; so well do these two pursuits agree.'[129] Numerous examples proved him right. Many 'great outrages and insolences' were committed in London and southern towns by gangs of soldiers demobilized after the Counter-Armada of 1589; and in the summer of that year several hundred men returned from the Portuguese expedition threatened to loot St Bartholomew's Fair, for which seven were subsequently executed. In the Spain of Philip II the petty thefts, assaults, rapes and murders committed by ex-soldiers were a consantly reiterated theme in the complaints of municipalities to higher authority, the scale of the outrages no doubt exaggerated for effect, but real none the less. In the eastern provinces of Austria, where troops were regularly disbanded at the close of each year's campaign against the Turks, these *gartbrüder* posed a major threat to law and order throughout the autumn and winter. Much the same was true of Lorraine in the late 1630s, where groups of deserters and demobilizees entrenched themselves so firmly in the countryside, preying upon isolated villages, farms and travellers, that regular units of the army had to be employed to dislodge them from their fortified sites.[130]

The threat to law and order posed by ex-soldiers was serious enough, though governments exaggerated it by conflating it with the growing and endemic problem of vagrancy (brought about chiefly by demographic increase), and by overstating the participation of ex-soldiers in riots and rebellions. Rulers responded by seeking to ensure the rapid dispersal of demobilized troops. Elizabethan legislation passed in the 1590s, when the problem was particularly acute, ordered former soldiers to return directly to their home or face imprisonment. French ordinances passed in 1518, 1521, 1523, 1525 and 1537 imposed the death penalty for the same offence, whilst a further edict following the Peace of Vervins in 1598 forbade them to carry

firearms and ordered provincial governors to enforce the existing legislation.[131] The States-General exported its problem,
disbanding 6,000 of the troops used in the siege of 'sHertogen-
bosch in 1629 in the neighbouring, neutral territories of Mark,
Cleves and Ravensburg, whilst Brandenburg and neighbouring
states took collective action in the 1570s against the bands of
unemployed *landsknechts* who infested the area.[132] Already
grave in the sixteenth century, the problem of the ex-soldier
grew with the mass armies of the following century. In 1644,
1655, 1657 and 1660 major police operations were mounted in
and around Paris to round up vagabonds in general and ex-
soldiers in particular. The more sturdy of the latter were sent to
man garrisons, the remainder incarcerated, along with other
paupers and vagrants, in the *hôpitaux-généraux*. By the second
half of Louis's reign troublesome ex-soldiers would find themselves placed in a more specialized institution, the *Invalides*, for
in France, as in the rest of Europe, the military hospital was
conceived and run not just as a place of refuge for the sick, but
as a place of confinement for the control of the able-bodied.
Indeed, it is a trenchant comment on the severity of the regime
in the *Invalides* that large numbers of the inmates left, either to
return home or even to rejoin the army.[133]

5

THE IMPACT OF WAR

THE LOCAL EFFECTS

War is quite rightly seen as one of the major scourges of early-modern society, but any precise assessment of its impact is difficult, not just because much of the necessary data – mortality levels, numbers of troops, figures on economic output, and so on – is either non-existent, or unreliable, but also because no two wars were alike. Extended conflicts, civil wars, the skirmishing, raiding and prisoner-taking of the *guerre de châteaux* and wars embittered by religious hatred, were all likely to produce their own characteristic effects which to some degree preclude generalization. Most striking, of course, is the direct impact of war on civilians caused by the presence in the immediate locality of an army, a raiding party or a garrison, though even in this respect it is often easier to describe than to analyse. Marching troops, moving heedlessly through fields and orchards, trampled crops underfoot and destroyed hedges and fences, and in addition to this 'accidental' damage civilians suffered losses as a result of theft, requisitioning and the deliberate destruction of property and livestock in pursuit of a scorched-earth policy. Even well-organized billeting of troops in households took a heavy toll of a community's resources; as James Turner noted, this

> proves oft the destruction of a country: for though no exorbitancy be committed...yet when an army cannot be quarter'd but close and near together, to prevent infalls, onslaughts and surprisal of an enemy, it is an easie matter to imagin what a heavy burthen these places bear.[1]

148

Mazarin opined that, 'having soldiers billeted for three days is more onerous for a man than the *taille*'.[2] When soldiers were uncontrolled the impact was much more severe. Alexandre Dubois, the *curé* of Rumegies, not far from Tournai, described in his journal the horrors suffered in June 1709 when the village was briefly occupied by Dutch troops : 'God! What an experience! Could the last judgement be more terrible? Lord, when I want to have an idea of what the last coming will be like, this is how I picture it.' For a while *curé* and parishioners, together with their goods and animals, retreated to the *presbytère* and church, but after they were driven out, several men killed, women raped and animals stolen, the villagers fled, returning only when the troops had left, to find that the village had been thoroughly pillaged. 'We found only the walls were left. Not a door, not a window, not a pane of glass, not a piece of metal, and, what is worse, not a single bundle of straw.'[3]

Yet while acknowledging the frightfulness of war, we need to recognize that its effects were differential. This was true geographically, for not all regions of Europe suffered equally from the incursions of armies. Logistic imperatives meant that, in the seventeenth century especially, armies headed time and again for those relatively prosperous areas where they could most easily subsist: the Low Countries, the Rhineland, Westphalia and northern Italy for example. And the political ambitions of rulers, and consequently the campaigning of their armies, tended consistently to be focused upon a limited number of regions: parts of Italy, the Low Countries and northern France in the sixteenth century, the southern Netherlands, Lombardy and the Rhineland in the seventeenth century, and the Ottoman–Habsburg frontier region throughout the period. Large areas of Europe thus never, or only rarely, saw an army, whereas others played host to them time and again, and suffered accordingly. The illegitimate son of James II, the future Duke of Berwick, described Hungary in 1686 as 'the miserablest country in the world, for it is plundered every day or else by the Christians or by the Turks or sometimes by both'.[4]

Even within a single conflict there might be enormous regional variations in the direct impact of the war. During the English Civil War the field armies of both sides never penetrated into Kent, which thus remained relatively immune from the direct effects of the fighting; and during the Thirty Years War 'war zones' such as Pomerania, Mecklenburg and Württemberg suffered a disproportionate amount of damage, rendering generalizations about the overall impact of the conflict on Germany largely meaningless.[5]

Arguably, most damage was sustained not by those regions under the direct control of a single army but by those areas, such as Hungary, which formed frontier-zones within which rival forces competed for control of the food supplies, roads and strongpoints. Berkshire, for example, suffered in this way after 1642, both from the operations of the field armies which moved back and forth across it, and from the activities of the rival Parliamentarian and Royalist garrisons stationed at places such as Wallingford, Reading and Abingdon. As a result of damage to property, loss of livestock, the heavy contributions of money (between November 1642 and June 1644 the Royalists alone extracted some £65,000) and forced loans, Berkshire had slipped in the league table of wealthiest counties, as measured by tax assessments, from fifth place in the 1630s to twenty-first by 1649. In a similar way, but on a smaller scale, the country around Metz, Thionville and les Marangeois was devastated in the 1550s by raiding parties from rival French and Imperial garrisons, which carried off corn and cattle, destroyed bridges and roads, terrified peasants, and reduced commerce to a standstill. Or again, in 1677 the town of Châtelet, in the region around Charleroi disputed by French and Spanish forces, received a demand for the payment of 1,000 *écus* from the Spanish commander, the same sum it had only a short time previously paid to the French. The money was handed over, but by way of reprisal the French destroyed the bridge over the Sambre, a severe blow to the town's commerce.[6]

The various 'military corridors' which criss-crossed Europe, those more-or-less well-defined routes regularly used to move troops from established recruiting areas to base of operations to war zone, also suffered disproportionately from the attentions of the military. The best-known was the 'Spanish Road', connecting north Italy and the Low Countries, but there were many others: especially important for French forces during the Italian wars was the route through the Dauphiné and the alpine passes;[7] large numbers of troops passed through Languedoc in the 1630s and 1640s on their way to and from the Spanish frontier; and ducal Lorraine was a crossroads for armies of every state. Although efforts might be made to establish supplies at various points along these routes before the troops' arrival, the passage of large numbers of men invariably engendered local shortages of foodstuffs and a degree of antagonism with the population over billeting, petty thefts and damage, unpaid bills and worse. Louvois advised officials to vary the routes used by troops on the move inside France, but in practice the limited number of suitable roads and bridges tended to funnel them consistently through the same areas.[8]

There is also a town–country dichotomy to be discerned in the geographical effects of war, although in this respect the impact was different rather than necessarily unequal. With their walls, fortifications and urban militias, the larger towns at least could resist attacks by small raiding parties, and by payment of a lump sum they might buy off an assault from a larger force, whereas the countryside was more routinely vulnerable both to small bands of marauders and to occupation by larger armies and the devastation they brought. But the damage inflicted on a town when it underwent a siege, if more occasional, was also more intense and concentrated. Not only did it undergo bombardment and risk pillage once it was stormed, but its defending garrison cut down trees, destroyed houses and razed suburbs to clear lines of fire. Salignac claimed that at Metz churches had wooden pillars substituted for their stone ones to make demolition easier, and at Gloucester 240 houses were cleared in 1643 to assist in the city's defence.[9] At Colchester 200 were demolished in the suburbs, and perhaps a fifth of all buildings at Worcester were destroyed, while it was noted of the town of Banbury that there was 'scarce the one halfe standing to gaze on the ruines of the other', following repeated sieges of the castle.[10] Fires were especially devastating in the heavily built up, highly combustible towns, and easily broke out as a result of bombardment or during the sack of a town. Fleurus was severely damaged in this way in 1684, and a letter from the inhabitants of Marcinelle the following year claimed that about one-third of the houses there had been burnt or otherwise ruined by the soldiers.[11] A town's occupation by large numbers of rowdy soldiers, with their often carelessly stored stocks of powder and match, also considerably increased the accidental risk of fires breaking out. The blaze at Oxford in 1644, probably begun by a soldier roasting a pig, destroyed around 300 houses and caused damage later put at over £43,000; while the discharge of a musket by one of Prince Maurice's quarrelling soldiers at Beaminster led to a fire which left the town 'the pittifullest spectacle that man can behold'.[12] Yet recovery from the physical damage done by war could be surprisingly – almost embarrassingly – swift, presumably because the widespread use of construction materials such as timber and thatch, rather than brick and stone, while rendering buildings vulnerable to fire, also meant that they could be reconstructed relatively quickly and cheaply. Shortly after the siege of Vienna in 1683, for example, Frederick Corner reported to the Venetian Senate that 'It is marvellous to see how the suburbs which surround the capital, as well as the neighbouring countryside, which was burnt by the Barbarians, have been completely rebuilt in a short space of time.'[13]

It was during a siege that civilians – both countrymen and urban inhabitants – were most likely to be caught up in the actual fighting between the armies. Vauban advised that masons, carpenters and other craftsmen be smuggled into the besieged city for a few days, for example, to glean information on its defences. Spying for an army in this way was clearly not without risks : the unfortunate peasant who in 1643 showed besiegers how to force their way into the castle of Freusburg in Trier was subsequently hanged.[14] More generally, peasants were drafted in large numbers to labour at earthworks, dig ditches and tear down fortifications: one estimate suggests that 12,000 were brought in to construct the 9 miles of trenches around Lille in 1708, and Louis XIV claimed that 20,000 worked on the siegeworks at Maastricht in 1713, though this figure, like the 7,000 reported for Ghent in 1678 and 20,000 for Mons in 1691, appears to contain a substantial element of exaggeration.[15] Trench-digging was dangerous enough, but a town's inhabitants were often pushed yet more firmly into the front line, since they might be obliged by the garrison physically to assist with its defence even when this meant exposure to cannon and mortar fire. Nor were women, who enjoyed non-combatant status in the laws of war, always exempted. It was perhaps to be expected that the wives of the tiny Spanish garrison at Estagel should assist their husbands during the siege by Schomberg's French troops in 1639, but at the siege of Marseilles in 1524 the commander, Lorenzo Orsini da Ceri, set all the women of the town, including nobles and bourgeois, to work at constructing an enormous defensive ditch. At Pavia in the same year the town's women toiled to repair broken ramparts, shift rubble and transport powder and shot, taking their share of casualties along with the men; so too at Siena, during the eighteen-month siege in 1552–3, and at Leucate in 1637.[16]

Even if they were not exposed directly to the besiegers' fire directed at the ramparts (and a great deal of shot also fell, either by design or accident, on the town's interior: Vauban's injunction only to aim at 'military targets' was whistling in the wind), the inhabitants necessarily had to endure the rigours of starvation along with the garrison. On entering Paris after the four-month siege of 1590, which had claimed 13,000 victims, Villeroy was moved by the misery of those left alive: 'They were not able to look at us, nor we at them, without sighing.'[17] It is true that garrison commanders frequently expelled 'superfluous persons', who consumed food but could not contribute to a city's defence, before the siege began, as did the Duke of Guise at Metz, though he was careful to retain civilians thought to be of value: masons, carpenters, barbers (for medical care) and even priests, to absolve the dying and boost morale (so much for clerical immunity). But it was in the besiegers' interest to keep as many 'useless mouths' from escaping as possible so as to increase pressure on the fort's food stocks: hence the vigour with which Louis XIII's forces drove back into La Rochelle the poor wretches who every night tried to escape through the besiegers' lines.[18] In this way, too, the theoretical distinction between the soldier and the civilian non-combatant was blurred by the practices of war.

The civilians trapped by a besieging army, and obliged to endure the rigours of a siege, often included, in addition to the town's peacetime inhabitants, numbers of peasants who had fled from an approaching army in the hope of finding safety behind the city's walls. These movements of the rural population townwards, especially frequent and large-scale occurrences during the Thirty Years War, might well engender no small degree of friction between townsmen and peasants. On the one hand, town councils felt a responsibility to take them in, especially if they came from villages owned by the town or under its jurisdiction, but they also feared the disorder that might result from an influx of unemployed and penniless refugees, and recognized the burden they would place on the city's resources and welfare systems; and they were aware too that fleeing peasants might bring disease with them, perhaps contracted by contact with the armies. Rural refugees thus met with an uncertain welcome. For a time villagers seeking asylum in Bar-le-Duc were sustained by a special tax levied on the citizens, the *taille des pauvres*, but after a while they were put to unpaid work on the roads, and a special force armed with halberds, the *chasse coquins*, was stationed to keep out undesirables. In 1630 Châtel-sur-Moselle refused to accept refugees because of the risk of disease, and at Metz they were allowed in only after swearing an oath that they had not come from an infected area. At Toul they were kept outside the city walls. 'It was a terrible thing to see and hear the cries of the peasants lying in the ditches around the town, begging for bread,' wrote Demange Bussy who witnessed their plight.[19] For their part, refugees who did secure admission to a town often felt themselves exploited. In the 1640s the town of Luneburg imposed taxes on them to meet army demands for *kontributions*; villagers from Swabia and Bavaria, who had fled to Augsburg, complained of the exorbitant prices they were charged by bakers (they were subsequently expelled by the town council); an influx of refugees also pushed up house rents in the town, leading to accusations by the villagers that they were being overcharged; while the *Wetterfelder Chronik* reported that at Frankfurt, 'it can scarcely be described how hard (the peasants) had to work for the tavern-keepers, merchants, tradesmen and others'.[20] In this way, the mutual antagonism between town and country, which was anyway a feature of social relations in early-modern Europe, was reinforced by the dislocation caused by war.

Town–country hostility was heightened still further by changes in the patterns of landownership brought about by the impact of war, and which generally worked to the detriment of the peasant and to the advantage of the townsman. The purchase of rural property by wealthy urbanites, for reasons of prestige or for economic gain, was not of course unusual in the early-modern period, especially around the larger cities, but war could provide enhanced opportunities for urban acquisition of land, as Cabourdin's study of the *Toulois* and county of Vaudémont in Lorraine between 1550 and 1635 shows. The impact of war here was particularly severe in the last two decades of the sixteenth century after Duke Charles III threw in his lot with the Catholic League. Soldiers were constant visitors, consuming bread, wine and meat, driving off cattle, extracting money, and leaving behind them 'a land stripped of foodstuffs and of the means to produce them'.[21] Peasants were obliged to borrow, both to pay the soldiers and to replace seed, livestock and tools which were stolen or destroyed, and to pay the higher wartime taxes, but after the soldiers left profits were often insufficient to repay the loan, and foreclosure and the sale of peasant lands ensued. The chief beneficiaries of this included the wealthier peasants, the *coqs du village*, but more especially the well-off urban officials, notables and merchants of Toul and Vézileze, such as César Daulnay, who, in a single day in April 1579, bought up 37 *jours* of land at Lagney and 3 at Lucey, most of which he rented back to its thirty-four former owners. The same picture of war-induced rural indebtedness leading to the loss of peasant land and its accumulation in the hands of a more restricted number of owners, and notably urban land-lords, is revealed with yet greater clarity in Jacquart's study of the Ile-de-France from the time of the Religious Wars down to the Fronde. Here it was not just individual peasants who fell into debt, but whole communities, resulting in the sale of the village's common lands, a loss which affected in particular the rural subsistence producer who depended on access to such lands to maintain his economic viability. A similar pattern of communal pauperization, resulting in the sale of common lands, is also to be perceived in many of the villages around Charleroi, an area regularly visited by armies during the seventeenth century.[22]

In parts of eastern Germany, too, the Thirty Years War brought about a deterioration in peasant landownership, though in this instance it was the landowning local nobility rather than townsmen who benefited, by reclaiming or buying up the holdings left vacant as peasants fled to escape the marauding armies, and by taking advantage of the economic impoverish-ment of those who remained, and using them to farm their large estates through what was effectively serf labour.[23] But we should be wary of assuming that war, even when it was prolonged, invariably resulted in a deterioration of peasant landownership and independence. This was not the case, in the seventeenth century at least, in the region of the Lower Meuse – roughly the area between Liège and Maastricht – studied by Gutmann. It was true that peasants here were obliged to borrow heavily, mainly from townsmen, and that these debts were often not paid off for a decade or more. But although the economic resources of the countryside were thereby drained off by the urban merchants and moneylenders, such men showed little inclination to buy out small peasant tenements, for there were better investment opportunities elsewhere, although they were prepared to purchase large farms belonging to the impoverished rural nobility, who, in this instance, were the chief victims of war-induced indebtedness. Moreover, the prosperity of the area, and in particular the abundance of alternative employment opportunities in rural industries such as textiles, mines and the river trades, allowed the rural smallholders to earn sufficient extra money eventually to pay off wartime debt, or at least to cover the interest payments without losing their land.[24]

Gutmann's study not only demonstrates that war's impact was geographically far from uniform, but that the individual character of a region was important in determining the precise effects wartime conditions would have. The prosperity and diversified economy of the Lower Meuse helped its population to emerge relatively unscathed from military occupation. In addition, a variety of mechanisms emerged here, and in other regions, which cushioned war's impact. Around Liège, for instance, a system was developed so that the costs of housing and feeding soldiers fell not on the individual householder but on the whole community; indeed, the burden might be spread over several communities, and in the last resort the estates of Liège might provide aid for oppressed villages, raising the necessary cash from taxes levied throughout the principality. In the north Italian provinces of Lodi and Como rental agreements between tenant farmers and landlords contained clauses which provided for a reduction in rents during a period of hostilities, and for the landlord to help with free repairs, cash advances and supply of seed in the post-war period. Similar tenancy agreements were made in parts of the Low Countries, though in Flanders, at least, such contracts appear to have been restricted to the larger tenant farmers, one reason why the smaller and middle sized tenants were less successful here in weathering wartime crises. Or again, in many parts of Germany during the

Thirty Years War peasants formed mutual self-help groups, such as the *Gemeinschaftliche Sache* set up at Erling in 1627: some peasants ploughed their own and their neighbour's fields, using the few horses which had not been stolen, while the rest stood guard over the crops and the workers. Warning systems were developed, sometimes quite sophisticated ones using bonfires, semaphore and spies, to give notice of the soldiers' approach, so that villagers had time to evacuate their homes, taking with them their livestock and goods. 'None of your subjects are here,' a Franconian official told his prince in 1645, 'they have all gone to Nuremberg, Schwabach and Lichtenau with every bit of their possessions, down to goods scarcely worth a *kreuzer*.'[25] By such means a locality might ameliorate quite considerably the impact of war.

Civilians were, however, less successful at preventing altogether the incursions of soldiers into their locality, though this was attempted more frequently than is often allowed for. During the Thirty Years War in particular peasants banded together to resist the soldiers. A report of 1620, for example, spoke of 400 of Mansfeld's men being killed by armed villagers. Peasants in the Sinngund district of Franconia, operating in well-armed and disciplined groups, successfully resisted Imperial troops for a time in 1626; and particularly large uprisings – some reports speak of several thousand participants – took place in the Harz area in the late 1620s, in Bavaria in 1633–4, along the upper Rhine and areas in the Black Forest and also in Styria in 1635.[26] A tradition of peasant association in Germany, stretching back to at least the early sixteenth-century *Bundschuh*, may help to account for the uniquely large-scale, highly organized and widespread nature of peasant resistance during the Thirty Years War.[27] But active civilian resistance to soldiers was by no means confined to Germany. In 1580 a peasant force several thousand strong, and fighting under a banner bearing a broken eggshell and a sword, succeeded in driving the troops of the States-General out of the province of Overijssel for a time; and in Flanders and Brabant there were attempts to form peasant militias, based on the *Huisliedengilde* or rural shooting associations, to provide some protection from freebooters, mutineers and deserters.[28] Nor were peasants the only social group involved in resistance, for all land and property owners were potentially at risk from an occupying army. The nobility of the *bailliages* of Nemour and Château-Landon condemned the indiscipline of the royal forces during the Fronde, and in the areas of the Beauce and the Vexin in 1652 they sought to raise private militias physically to oppose them. In the same year the inhabitants of the *faubourgs* of St Marcel and St Jacques in Paris put chains across the streets in an effort to prevent the billeting of soldiers; while three years earlier rioters had taken to the streets in Grenoble to achieve a similar objective.[29] In England the Civil War witnessed the development of large-scale militant neutralist movements, some gentry-led and some being spontaneous uprisings of villagers, the so-called clubmen. In both instances the aim was to oblige the king and Parliament to make peace, and, more importantly, by raising local forces to be in a position to prevent the soldiers of both sides from penetrating into the local area and damaging it. 'If you offer to plunder or take our cattle, Be assured we will bid you battle', proclaimed the banners of the clubmen.[30]

Although occasional, short-term successes were achieved by these civilian forces, in England and elsewhere, in the long run they proved unable to resist the incursions of the armies and no match for trained and well-armed soldiers, especially when they confronted them in open battle. However, small bands of soldiers, stragglers and deserters were vulnerable to the peasants' revenge. Even *curé* Dubois seemed to find a certain satisfaction in the fact that seventeen Spanish soldiers had been chased by villagers from the fields near to Rumegies, one being killed and seven taken prisoner; while the peasants of Provence in 1707 became notorious for the cruelty with which they treated Piedmontese soldiers who became separated from the army. These sorts of attacks often served, however, only to engender counter-atrocities.[31]

As this discussion of the regionally varied impact of war has implied, warfare was not only geographically but socially differential. The Florentine, Rinaldo degli Albizzi, made the point when he claimed that the best hope of the *popolo minuto* lay in war, for then the town and region was full of soldiers whose spending power brought an unaccustomed prosperity to artisans and craftsmen, while the rich, oppressors of the poor in time of peace, had their wealth plundered by the soldiery. 'Your ruin', he reportedly told the Florentine magnates, 'turns to their benefit and exaltation.'[32] Albizzi was certainly right to point to the varied impact which war had on different social classes, though whether matters worked out in practice quite as he suggested is dubious, for, in general, it seems to have been the better-off sections of society which coped best with wartime conditions, as Friedrichs has clearly established in another urban setting, Nördlingen. This moderately prosperous city, of some 9–11,000 inhabitants, was directly affected by the Thirty Years War right from the outset. It was faced with constant demands for food, money, and *kontributions* from the numerous troops of every army who passed through it, and from the sizeable garrison of Imperial, Swedish and Bavarian soldiers which it housed in turn; and in 1634 it underwent a destructive siege coupled with a deadly outbreak of the plague. As a result of these experiences the total wealth of the community declined, but the burden of military taxation and economic hardship fell disproportionately upon the middle and lower levels of society. Craftsmen and artisans found their earnings and valuables were carried off by the soldiers, whereas the rich proved better able to defend their fortunes. The wealthiest 2 per cent of the population increased their share of the community's wealth from 25.6 to 40.2 per cent between 1579 and 1646, most of this increase coming during the second half of the Thirty Years War, the conflict thus serving to reinforce, in a quite dramatic fashion, a pre-existing trend. This trend was briefly reversed during the two decades of relative peace which followed the Peace of Westphalia, but the renewed arrival of warfare from the 1670s against the Turks and the French once again hit the poor harder than the rich. Before 1702, when the battle of Blenheim was staged near to Nördlingen, the city experienced little conflict, although troops were regularly quartered there. This time the burden came in the form of higher taxes imposed by the Empire and the Swabian League.[33] Only future case studies will reveal whether Friedrich's conclusions for Nördlingen have a wider applicability to other cities during the Thirty Years War and outside Germany, but this seems not improbable.

It was certainly the case that the better-off sections of society were best placed to cope with the local inflation of prices which was invariably brought about by the sudden influx into a region of a large number of soldiers, who demanded food and other supplies, and who created further shortages, and hence raised prices, by the wanton damage they did, and by the interruption their presence caused to agriculture and trade. Pierre Vuarin noted in his diary that the presence of soldiers had pushed the price of corn in parts of Lorraine from 6 *francs* in 1632 to 16 *francs* by the end of 1635, and by 1638 it was selling for 37 *francs* around Metz.[34] Scarcity prices of this order simply could not be met by the poor, those on fixed wages and the small-holders who produced barely enough even in good times to feed themselves and their families. Those who were surplus pro-ducers, on the other hand, weathered the storm much better. Indeed, for those with something to sell the presence of an army might present an opportunity for huge, short-term profits, as Albizzi suggested. *Curé* Dubois wrote of 1693 that

> This year has sounded the death-knell of almost all the husbandmen who had no grain at all to sell; but it has worked to the enrichment of the great lords who, for the most part, still had grain from previous years, and who have made enormous sums.[35]

The ability to cash in like this depended, of course, on the good behaviour of the army: but when the troops were well disciplined and pay was available (and the two were inseparable), and when the army was not living off *kontributions* or deliberately stripping the country, then those able to meet the surge in demand could do well. The Dutch army under Prince Maurice was noted for its regular pay and discipline and such were the profits to be made from its presence that Dutch towns actually applied for troops to be quartered in them – a far cry indeed from their reaction to the billeting of Spanish soldiers a few decades earlier.[36] Although the French forces of the 1630s and 1640s were not in general remarkable for their good order, it was the case that Richelieu, who made a deliberate effort to woo the inhabitants of Alsace over to French rule by ensuring that troops who 'liberated' the area from the Swedes were well paid and disciplined, was asked by the local towns that these 'profitable' forces be maintained there. So lucrative was the market provided by the well-run army of the Marquis de Feuquières, encamped around Thionville in 1638, that Jean Bouchez, no friend of soldiers in general, nevertheless described it as 'the finest fair in the whole of France'.[37]

This regional and social texturing, which was a marked

feature of war's impact, is also to be discerned in its demo-graphic effects. Writing in 1946 Jean Meuvret acknowledged that these were profound, but argued that given the current state of research they remained too complex for analysis.[38] Since then a number of local case studies have been completed which have furthered our understanding, but much research remains to be done, and generalizations outside regional limits must perforce be advanced with caution. What does seem clear is that earlier historians, accepting uncritically the accounts by sixteenth- and seventeenth-century contemporaries of massive loss of life, overdramatized war's impact. Earlier estimates for the demographic effects of the Thirty Years War in particular, which presented it as a total catastrophe for Germany, have had to be scaled down, and an overall loss of population (which was probably in decline anyway before 1618) of the order of 15–20 per cent from some 20 million to 16–17 million by the war's end may be posited. Regional variations, however, were enor-mous: while Lower Saxony lost less than 10 per cent of its population some villages in Württemberg had only 40 per cent of their pre-war population by 1648.[39] Yet even revised esti-mates of this level testify to the severity of war's impact.

Other areas, too, suffered severe losses of population in times of war. During the French Religious Wars Rouen's population fell by more than one quarter, and Lyons too underwent a sharp decline from a mid-century peak of 60–70,000; while perhaps a fifth of the population of the Paris basin was lost in the two decades after 1630.[40] In much of Brabant, Flanders and Hainault the heavy and continuous fighting of the years 1581–92 reduced the population to 25–50 per cent of its pre-1573 level; and some of the rural areas around Courtrai and Ypres were practically deserted by the end of the 1580s. At Turnhout the population declined from 7,000 to 3,000 between 1565 and 1590; at Herentals the number of families was reduced from 720 to 203 over a similar period; while in Louvain the number of inhabited houses approximately halved between 1526 and 1600.[41] How-ever, population losses of this order resulted not so much from civilian mortality as from emigration, as peasants and towns-men moved to more tranquil areas to escape the fighting. One region's loss could thus prove to be another region's gain, especially if war refugees brought professional skills and wealth with them. Middleburg acquired 1,174 men together with their families, mainly from the southern Netherlands, between 1580 and 1591, all of whom could afford to purchase citizenship, and Leyden and Haarlem gained substantial numbers too. Towns further afield benefited from the population displacement engendered by the Dutch Revolt: Frankfurt and Cologne for example, and Hamburg, which had a colony of some 1,000 Dutch emigrants by 1600. Here, thirty-two of the largest accounts in the *Girobank*, founded in 1619, were held by men with Flemish names.[42]

Severe though these war-induced population losses were, they were often made good remarkably quickly, as some of the area's displaced inhabitants moved back, and as a result of immigration by newcomers in the post-war period. Rouen's population had been restored by 1600 to a level only slightly below that of the pre-civil war era, and many of the towns in the southern Netherlands which suffered in the 1580s had substantially rebuilt their populations within a decade, for example. But recovery was not invariably rapid nor universal. Although Swiss, Savoyards, Tyroleans and Auvergnois immigrants helped to repopulate villages in the *Xaintois* region of Lorraine, and were crucial in almost doubling the size of Nancy from a post-war low of 1,327 in 1649 to 2,460 in 1672, in other parts of the duchy villages remained deserted or were rebuilt only by the early eighteenth century. Nördlingen's population, too, had not grown sufficiently by the 1690s to achieve a return to pre-war levels, and elsewhere in Germany losses resulting from the Thirty Years War had only been replaced by 1700.[43] Such variations in the rate of demographic recovery clearly have much to do with differences in levels of population-loss as between one area and another, but this cannot be a complete explanation since levels of cut-back were similar in the southern Netherlands in the 1580s and in parts of Germany during the Thirty Years War, for instance, though rates of recovery were not. Probably a more important factor was the attractiveness of a given region to immigrants, who, presuming that they were allowed to settle – and in the case of Nördlingen settlement was curtailed by the urban authorities – were drawn in greatest numbers to those areas which promised prosperity, stability, freedom from oppression, and in whose future they had confidence.[44]

To insist upon the importance of emigration in bringing

about population loss is not, of course, to argue that civilian mortality was negligible, as the 13,000 who died during the four-month blockade of Paris by Henry IV testify. But it is clear that relatively few civilians lost their lives as a direct result of military action. To be sure, examples of soldiers wantonly killing civilians can easily be found: the inhabitants of Manetz burned alive in the church where they sheltered by soldiers of the Anglo-Dutch army in 1712; the inhabitants of Charmes, including women and children, slain by French troops in 1635; and although Jean Delhotel, *curé* of Avioth in Montmédy, doubtless exaggerated when he wrote of Croat soldiers killing and wounding on a wide scale in 1636, his account had some basis in fact.[45] Yet, generally, soldiers in the countryside were more interested in finding plunder and food than in killing villagers merely for the sake of it, although strong-arm measures might well be employed to force them to reveal the whereabouts of valuables, real or imagined. Civilians trapped inside a besieged city ran a greater risk of suffering a violent death, both from the shot which fell indiscriminately on them and the garrison, and especially during the sack which almost invariably followed the forcible storming of a city, when soldiers made no effort to differentiate between the garrison and the civilian population. But if the latter eventuality were avoided then surprisingly few civilians might figure as direct casualties of the fighting. Thus, only some 7 of the 72 people from the parishes of Saint-Lô and Saint-Martin-sur-Renelle buried during Rouen's five-month siege in 1591–2 appear to have been killed in this way: 6 were soldiers, the other a 'povre' shot while 'alant faucher'.[46] The majority of the civilians who perished at Rouen, like the 13,000 who died during Henry IV's siege of Paris, fell victim not to swords, pikes, musket balls or cannon shot, but to war-induced shortages and disease.

Apart from the obvious case of a siege, it is easy to see how war produced localized famines. Agricultural production was disrupted as armies drove off livestock, requisitioned horses and carts, stole or destroyed tools, and as peasants fled or were taken off to labour at siegeworks or were pressed into service as guides (for even when maps became available they generally contained insufficient local topographical detail to allow units to find their own way across country). Armies quickly consumed local food stocks, and even ate up the seed corn on which the following year's harvest depended, so ensuring that the effect of their passage through an area was felt even after they had departed. Hence the concern of the petitioners of Newton-ards in Ireland over the activities of the New Scots Army: 'The whole armie for these seven weekes bypast has beene eating the meal out of our mouthes, and now they are fallen upon that that should sowe the ground.'[47] Hence too the concern of *curé* Dubois, noted earlier, about the loss of the village's straw, for this meant that the animals could not be fed over the winter and carried the implication of shortages in the following year. Although Dubois claimed that some of his parishioners sub-sequently died for lack of food, it is unlikely that many civilians actually perished of starvation except in the particular circum-stance of a siege. However, undernourishment probably did render them fatally vulnerable to the epidemic diseases which armies carried, and which they passed on to the civilians with whom they came into contact. Contemporaries frequently bes-towed upon an epidemic the name of the army which had been its progenitor – hence the so-called 'Hungarian' and 'Swedish' plagues (probably typhus epidemics in fact) which were spread by the military in Lorraine in 1635 and 1637.[48] Those most likely to fall fatal victims to these soldier-spread diseases, and to illness in general, were pre-eminently the young and the very old.[49]

As well as acting as vectors for diseases such as smallpox, typhus and influenza, armies were also believed, until quite recently, to have been important in the spread of bubonic plague. However, this now seems less certain, though the precise relationship between plague and armies – if any – remains unclear. Bubonic plague was certainly a frequent visitor to army camps and war zones, though the notion that the infected rats and the fleas which transmitted the disease to humans travelled with the army's baggage has been sub-stantially discounted.[50] This uncertainty over the link between warfare and plague, which was the single most important 'killing' disease in early-modern Europe, renders suspect some of the figures on wartime levels of mortality contained in studies which assume a causal link between the two phenomena.

Also difficult to quantify with precision are the long-term effects of prolonged warfare upon a region's population, al-though it seems undeniable that these could be considerable.

Whereas a subsistence crisis brought about by harvest failure lasted only two or perhaps three years, and self-generating epidemics generally only as long, war could linger on over many years or even decades, bringing a continual trail of shortages, disease and death in its wake. Prolonged warfare also affected a community's powers of regeneration. The general instability caused by war seems to have led couples to delay marriage and put off starting a family until the return of more secure times, or at least until the woman had accumulated a sufficient dowry and the man the necessary means to support a viable household, a process which was necessarily more difficult and protracted during periods of economic hardship and uncertainty engendered by war. Also, war-related shortages of food probably weakened women's physical capacity to bear children, and brought about an increase in the number of miscarriages.[51] In these ways, prolonged exposure to warfare could affect a region's long-term demographic development, by curbing its population growth.

Ultimately, of course, much of the distress caused by warfare was intangible and cannot be quantified at all, though it was none the less real for all that. Warfare shattered the routines of everyday life. The diary of the shoemaker, Hans Heberle, reveals that he fled from his native village to shelter in the neighbouring city of Ulm on innumerable occasions during the Thirty Years War, while villagers in the county of Laubach were uprooted eighteen times in the years after 1634.[52] One estimate suggests that around 175,000 inhabitants in the southern Netherlands had to leave their houses between 1540 and 1630.[53] At Rumegies the rhythms of the day ceased to be punctuated by the tolling of the church bells after two were badly damaged and three dismantled by passing troops in 1709, and one of the first actions of the parishioners when peace came four years later was to have the bells recast and rehung in an attempt to reassert the return to normality. In contrast to previous decades nothing was spent on repairing or beautifying the church during the war of the League of Augsburg for fear that the effort would be wasted, though this did have the unlooked-for benefit that the churchwarden's funds had accumulated an unaccustomed reserve of 300 florins by 1698.[54] At least at Rumegies the *curé* remained in his parish and continued to proffer religious services. A petition to the king in 1650 from the diocese of Laon claimed that the severity of war damage was such that many of the parish clergy were no longer able to subsist and had been obliged to withdraw, twenty having resigned in the previous three months, leaving parishioners bereft of any form of religious or pastoral care.[55]

War also brought with it a discomforting intrusiveness. For the widow of Pierre Paul of Sains, it was less the physical damage done by the thirty soldiers billeted on her in 1648 which rankled, so much as the violation of her domestic sphere by men who 'lived in such disorder that, having made themselves masters of the house, fetched what they wanted from the wine cellar'.[56] There was intrusion too from assessors and collectors of taxes who redoubled their efforts in times of war, from militia recruiters, and from the saltpetremen who were licensed by governments to extract this constituent of gunpowder from lime, ashes and soil which had been soaked in human or animal excrement. An official investigation into their activities in England in 1630 found that:

> there was no part of the commission that the saltpetremen had not abused. As in digging in all places without distinction, as in parlours, bedchambers, threshing and malting floors, yea God's own house they have not forsworn: so they respect not times, digging in the breeding times in dove houses and working sometimes a month together whereby the flights of doves are destroyed, and, without respect to harvest time, in barns and malting houses when green malt is upon the floor, and in bedchambers, placing their tubs by the bedsides of the old and sick and even of women in childbirth and persons on their death beds.[57]

Contemporaries in the early-modern period were also concerned that warfare would destroy the underpinnings of society, by eroding the traditional familial order and the established social hierarchy, for example, and by corrupting moral values. 'Between father and son there is no longer any respect,' wrote the merchant André Ruiz, in part of a letter which described the frightening sense of insecurity which prevailed in the besieged town of Nantes in 1589. 'Nobody can leave his house, or send a letter from one place to another, which leaves us all in confusion. Nobody knows how he should speak, who is a friend or an enemy.'[58] In England, during the 1640s, there were worrying signs that women were using the opportunity of the Civil War to slough off traditional male dominance: they drafted petitions, formed fund-raising committees, issued pamphlets calling for equality of education and job opportunities and organized the military defence of their homes. And, inevitably, there were claims from both Royalist and Parliamentarian propagandists that women hustled their husbands into the armies in order to make cuckolds of them in their absence.[59] Other established patterns of social deference and order also appeared to be under threat. The local Justice of the Peace and owner of Easthampstead Park in Berkshire, William Trumble, was horrified by the lack of respect shown him by the Parliamentarian soldiers who occupied his estate, and elsewhere, too, aristocratic parks were invaded, enclosing landlords had hedges and fences torn down, while the landowning Wheate family were not alone in their complaint that tenants 'use their landlord how they list for their rents, taking this to be a time of liberty'.[60] When Bellièvre complained to his master Henry III in 1580 that 'the license of war has given an opening to the compete dissolution and corruption of morals', he was thinking primarily of the corruption which years of civil war had engendered amongst the royal administration, but declining moral standards amongst civilians continuously exposed to the pernicious example of a licentious and brutal soldiery was also a recurrent theme in *curé* Dubois's journal. The carrying of arms was become commonplace, he complained, people even bringing them into church, and as men also become more quarrelsome so arguments were increasingly settled by resort to violence.[61]

To be sure, we need to take these complaints with a substantial pinch of salt. Hyperbole, after all, was a stock-in-trade of most social commentators; and laments about the lack of respect children had for their parents, wives for their husbands and servants for their masters are common enough in all periods – and not just in times of warfare – while the theme of moral decline is one on which commentators love to linger. In so far as it is possible to subject any of these claims to the burden of proof, there is little that can be found to substantiate them. It is clear that war did not leave families untouched: it left orphans in its wake for example. So considerable were the numbers of orphans and foundlings at Antwerp by 1586 that the town council ordered every dyer to take one into his service; and the authorities in seventeenth-century Württemberg encountered problems when distant relatives refused to accept responsibility for them.[62] But there is little hard evidence to suggest that patriarchal authority over wives and children was undermined by war; indeed, one recent study has argued that the family unit emerged strengthened from the experience of the English Civil War.[63] Equally, although the social elites were always quick to point to – and unite against – anything which smacked of social revolution, it is very hard to detect any long-term war-induced changes in patterns of deference. However, we should not dismiss these concerns out of hand, for fears about war's threat to the social order, if they were unrealized, were nevertheless real enough and must be numbered amongst war's effects.

FINANCING WARS: WINNERS AND LOSERS

In 1586 Elizabeth complained to Leicester that his expedition in the Netherlands had become 'a sieve, that spends as it receives'.[64] Every ruler would have agreed that war swallowed up seemingly endless sums of money. One important element in the overall cost of warfare was the construction of the new-style fortifications. Earthen ramparts could be thrown up relatively quickly and cheaply: la Noue estimated that the cost of fortifying Ghent would have risen tenfold had the defences been done in masonry, for example.[65] But temporary earth and timber fortifications were simply not an option for cities and states that needed permanent defences; and permanent defences cost dear. Even when building costs were pared by having the heavy labouring done by criminals and galley slaves, as in the case of Florence, the Papal states and the Knights of Malta, unpaid peasants in the case of the Danish kings, or underpaid peasants in the case of the Venetian fort at Canea on Crete, raw materials were required on a prodigious scale:[66] 60,000 bricks were used in the four new bastions added to Alkmaar in the summer of 1573; 30 million were used for building the Antwerp citadel between 1568 and 1571; while the reconstruction of Longwy by Louis XIV involved the erection of 120,000 cubic metres of masonry.[67] There were also transport costs to be added on, and the wages of surveyors, engineers and skilled workmen who were used in considerable numbers. It was estimated in 1647, for example, that the addition of new crown-works to the defences of Milan would require the services of not less than three hundred master masons, all working at the same time.[68] And because the most effective forts were built to take advantage of rivers, marshy ground and rocky outcrops, construction was often technically difficult and hence more expensive. A major construction project could thus prove horrendously expensive. Modernizing Berwick-upon-Tweed between 1558 and 1570 cost Elizabeth I £130,000, equivalent to half the Crown's total revenue for a single year; excavating and building the nearly 170,000 cubic metres of the citadel at Antwerp cost 400,000 *ducats*; and the planned re-fortification of Rome early in the sixteenth century, originally costed at half a million *ducats*, had to be curtailed when the bill for a single Sangallo-designed double bastion and short length of wall came to over 40,000. No wonder that even Louis XIV, who was prepared to spend prodigiously on fortifications, was moved to ask Vauban if he had not built the walls at Besançon in gold, so expensive was the citadel.[69]

In addition to the initial building costs a fortress had to be stocked with a plethora of weapons. The latter were crucial, for a fort's effectiveness depended upon the weight of counter-fire it could deliver. The important fortress-city of Bergen-op-Zoom had 140 guns of various sizes in 1622, while Dresden, fortified in the 'Dutch' style in the seventeenth century, had 500 cannon and 1,000 hand weapons stockpiled in the five floors of its arsenal, all of which represented an enormous capital investment. Quite how much can be judged from the account presented in the 1640s by Leonhard Loewe, a Nuremberg cannon-founder, to the Duke of Weimar for two half-cannon-royal : 638 florins for raw materials, 2,005 florins for foundry workers' and tradesmens' wages. On top of this there were charges for ancillary equipment: 100 iron cannon-balls, 40 hundredweight of powder, 25 hundredweight of slow-match, gun carriage, hoisting-crane and so on.[70] By contrast, the running costs of a fortress – keeping it in repair, paying and provisioning its garrison – whilst not negligible, were relatively light.

Heavy though these fortress costs were, they were nevertheless exceeded by the expense involved in maintaining an army. A late sixteenth-century Spanish estimate put the cost of maintaining a single *tercio* of 5,000 men for a campaign season at 1,200,000 *ducats*:[71] a whole army was even more costly. What made armies so expensive? In part, it was a result of the large capital costs involved, especially those associated with the artillery. To some extent these might be offset by stripping forts of their guns to make up an artillery train, but carriages, carts, drivers, mules and horses all had to be found. If the artillery became involved in a lengthy siege quite surprising amounts of ammunition were used up. At the 55-day siege of Boulogne in 1544 the English fired off some 100,000 rounds of heavy shot, exhausting their supplies of powder, the French defenders nearly half as much again; and Bertrand de Salignac reported that up to 1,000 rounds were fired per day at the defenders of Metz in 1552.[72] Georg Schreiber estimated in the seventeenth century that it cost 5 *thalers* in materials each time a cannon was fired, which was about equal to the cost of a pike and represented roughly one month's pay for an infantryman.[73] A full-scale siege was certainly the most expensive endeavour undertaken by an army, for not only were there unavoidable expenses of powder and shot, but the numbers of men had to be kept up to strength if the blockade were to be maintained; provisions had to be transported in, since the besieging army rapidly exhausted local supplies; and there might be the extra cost of a 'masking' force to protect the besiegers. In view of this, estimates that the siege of La Rochelle cost 40 million *livres* – not far short of an average year's revenue for the French Crown – may not be unrealistic.[74] Well might the Duke of Parma prophesy that the 'heavy and endless costs' involved in retaking towns fortified by Prince Maurice would hobble efforts to reconquer the Netherlands.[75]

Other capital costs were incurred in equipping soldiers with the pikes, muskets, rests, powder flasks, bandoliers, scouring rods, gauntlets, flags, drums and other paraphernalia demanded by early-modern warfare. Additionally, allowance had to be made for provisioning and transporting the men. The cost of the latter was by no means negligible, especially when ships had to be hired and victualled and sailors' wages paid, as Elizabeth found when arranging for Essex's army to be shipped to France.[76] The saving was considerable when a force moved under its own muscle power and could live off the land.

But the greatest single expense in maintaining an army was pay. In the accounts of the Danish military treasurer, Aksel

Arenfeld, for the years 1626 and 1627, it represented 82 per cent and 69 per cent of expenditure respectively (though as some supplies had been obtained on credit from merchants who were yet to be paid the real proportion would have been slightly lower).[77] As a proportion of a regiment's total costs pay probably declined during the course of the seventeenth century, as governments came to supply more of the soldier's needs in kind, deducting the cost of his food, clothes and weapons from his pay. But the overall expense to an employer of maintaining a regiment did not of course decline.

Admittedly, some of these were 'theoretical' charges. Armies could extract supplies from conquered territory; no regiment ever went out fully equipped, nor were soldiers ever paid on time or in full; and merchants could be found to supply goods on credit. But although this might lessen the drain on the exchequer, or at least delay the day of reckoning, substantial sums still had to be found. Nor were the expenses of an army evenly spread. The 'start-up' costs of raising a force at the beginning of a campaign – bounty payments, coat-and-conduct money, equipment, captains' expenses, down payment to a contractor – were especially high. Christian IV of Denmark reckoned in 1625 that the cost of an English contingent of 5,000 men would be 100,000 *rigsdaler* in the first month, and half that in each succeeding month.[78] A second peak in the fiscal graph came with autumn disbandment, and there was another sharp jump connected with spring recruitment. It is small wonder that rulers, who were incapable of amassing the cash sums needed to meet these fiscal high points out of their relatively inflexible tax revenues, preferred instead to spread the financial burden by borrowing, or to use contract troops provided on credit.

Given the relative cheapness of forts compared to armies, why did states not adopt the apparently cost-effective option of making an initial heavy investment in forts, which could subsequently be maintained and garrisoned cheaply, rather than bear the heavy recurrent cost of maintaining armies? To a degree some states did attempt this: Venice and Siena in the sixteenth century, and the Swedes in the later seventeenth century for example. So too did Denmark, which spent some 662,000 *daler* between 1596 and 1621 on a network of fortifications designed to protect the frontier with Sweden and maintain her dominance of the Baltic. But the two – forts and armies – were not genuine alternatives. States with long frontiers required numerous fortified sites and garrisons which raised the aggregate costs, as the Swedes discovered under Charles XI when attempting to provide for the defence of their Baltic provinces. And when attacked a state required not just defensive sites but a field army as well, as the Dutch found. Although they spent heavily on fortifications after 1596, they were obliged to spend yet more heavily on their field forces.[79] In any event, lack of an army condemned a monarch to an inactive foreign policy, hardly tolerable for the ruler of a substantial state.

Warfare was always expensive, but the costs of waging war spiralled inexorably during the early-modern period, a fact not lost on contemporaries. In 1596 Esteban de Ibarra, one of Philip II's ministers in the Netherlands, wrote to his royal master:

> If comparison be made between the present cost to His Majesty of the troops who served in his armies and navies, and the cost of those of the Emperor Charles V, it will be found that, for an equal number of men, three times as much money is necessary today as used to be spent then.[80]

Rising costs were partly due to inflation: prices went up between three- and fivefold between 1500 and 1630. But the 'real' costs of waging war were rising too. One reason was the increased capital expenditure which early-modern warfare required, on forts, artillery, wadding, match, shovels, carriages, muskets, pikes and so on. Moreover, a growing proportion of this, plus costs of clothing, provisioning and transport, fell on the state's exchequer by the seventeenth century, rather than on the individual soldier or his captain. But mainly costs rose because, quite simply, more of everything, be it men or equipment, was needed, and needed for longer, as the scale and duration of warfare increased.

How did governments find the resources needed to meet these escalating military costs? It should be said at the outset that in many instances rulers and their ministers had little clear idea of how the money would be forthcoming for a particular campaign: they simply assumed it would be. 'I am so willing to confess my ignorance of finance...that the only advice I can give you is to use those methods which you find most useful to the king's service,' was Richelieu's reply when pressed by Bullion, the appropriately named *surintendant de finance*, on the difficulties of finding sufficient cash to fight the war in Germany.[81] While it would not be true to say that cost considerations played no part in policy making – the Spanish bureaucracy regularly monitored military expenditure, for example, and a plan was prepared for the Armada which included a cost estimate; whilst a *Staten van Oorlog*, or war budget, listing company strengths, expenditures and the contributions required from the various provinces, was prepared annually for approval by the Dutch States-General[82] – in general, policies were decided first, and funds allocated afterwards. Affairs of state took precedence over sordid questions of cash. Yet in the longer term rulers and their servants had to find means of boosting income, and this was achieved in a number of ways.

The wealth of the Church proved a tempting and time-honoured target. Ecclesiastical lands were expropriated in England under Henry VIII, and also in Sweden under Gustavus Vasa, where this took place as part of the introduction of a Protestant Reformation. Arguably, however, Catholic rulers were more adept at exploiting Church resources over the long term, the Spanish monarchs proving particularly successful in this respect. Using the threat from the Moors they obtained concessions from the papacy allowing them to exact levies on Church property and appropriate tithes, and they controlled ecclesiastical patronage, including that in the military orders, with the result that during the course of the sixteenth century ecclesiastical revenues provided a larger and more regular income for the Crown than the treasure of the Indies.[83] Their success contrasted with the relative failure of the French monarchs who, although they obtained considerable sums from the Church, notably in the form of a 'free gift' made every five or six years, nevertheless were obliged to allow the establishment of an institution, the *Assemblée générale du clergé*, which acted as the spokesman for the corporate interests of the Church, and which proved a remarkably efficient defender of ecclesiastical immunities and wealth against royal encroachment.

Aside from the Church, revenue-raising commonly involved a

resort to a host of *ad hoc* expedients. Crown lands were sold in Denmark and Sweden during the seventeenth century, and elsewhere royal monopolies were granted, for cash, on items as various as soap, sugar, currants, silk and playing cards. Extra revenues were generated by a more efficient exploitation of the ruler's patrimonial lands, or by converting feudal rights, such as royal control of wardships, into a source of cash income. Venice ran a state lottery after 1509, and in 1562 the Italian financier, Thomas Baroncelli, organized a lottery in the Low Countries on behalf of Philip II and the regent, Margaret of Parma, in which the local towns and villages were obliged to participate, the proceeds being used for the soldiers' pay.[84] And because mints were state-controlled, there was always a strong temptation to make money by manipulating the currency. The change-over to a copper coinage brought annual profits to the Spanish treasury of 2.6 million *ducats* between 1621 and 1626,[85] for instance, and even Pontchartrain, Louis XIV's gifted *contrôleur général*, was reduced to debasing the currency.

Such windfall profits aside, however, the commonest means of generating extra income was to use the tax system. A number of new taxes were introduced, such as the *millones* in Spain, a sales tax designed to help with the Armada expenses, a tax on livestock in Sweden in 1620, and the 'dancing' impost imposed in the Austrian patrimonial lands whereby taverns paid one florin per fiddler. Such levies tended to be variants of already existing taxes, however, and generally no radical innovations were made in the tax system, rulers concentrating instead on raising rates of tax, extending their incidence, and transforming occasionally levied imposts into regular taxes.[86] More importantly, they sought to 'stretch' tax revenues and other regular forms of income, such as the Sound Toll dues levied by the Danish kings on ships passing into the Baltic, by borrowing. At the simplest level this was done by farming out the collection of taxes to private individuals in return for an immediate lump-sum payment; in a more complex financial operation annuities assigned on royal revenues were sold; and regular forms of income were pledged as security for loans. There was of course nothing new about governments' use of credit: the medieval papacy had proved itself the most adept player at this game.[87] But the scale of borrowing after 1500 was novel. The Spanish Habsburgs led the way in the sixteenth century. Charles V borrowed nearly 29 million *ducats* from German, Portuguese, Flemish, Spanish and Genoese bankers at the fairs of Medina del Campo between 1520 and 1556, and almost one-quarter as much from the Antwerp money market, the scale of his borrowing increasing during the course of his reign. The arrival of large quantities of silver from the New World during the 1580s and 1590s – over 50 million *ducats* between 1573 and 1598 – allowed Philip II to increase royal borrowing still further, so that the total debt of nearly 30 million inherited in 1556 had risen to 60 million by 1575, and reached a staggering 100 million or thereabouts by 1598.[88] The sixteenth-century Spanish Habsburgs may have been the biggest borrowers, but every other ruler made use of credit. The sale of expropriated Church lands paid for only about one-third of Henry VIII's wars against France and Scotland in the 1540s – they cost well over £2 million, or about ten times the Crown's normal revenues – and part of the deficit was covered by sizeable loans from German and Flemish bankers.[89] Elizabeth too had to 'borrowe much money',[90] mainly from the London money market, to cover the cost of the Armada defences, involvement in the Netherlands and the Irish wars. Francis I raised loans with the bankers of Lyons – he owed nearly 7 million *livres* at his death – but very considerable borrowing was avoided until the second half of the sixteenth century, the extent of it subsequently increasing dramatically under Louis XIII and XIV. The Danish royal debt jumped too in the seventeenth century, from 1.4 million *rigsdaler* in 1629 to some 5.75 million in 1650.[91] The history of war is also the history of debt.

Besides the use of credit, a second revenue-raising expedient which had its origins in the late Middle Ages (again with the papacy as its leading exponent) and which was enormously developed from 1500 onwards, was the sale of public office in the judicial, financial and administrative services.[92] In this instance, France led the way. By the end of Francis I's reign a bureau had been established to regularize the trade, and 'paper' offices, to which no functions were attached, were being created by the Crown merely for sale; and it became possible after 1604 for a holder to ensure the heritability of his office by payment of an annual cash sum, the *paulette*. Office, in short had become private property. By the 1630s the sale of office accounted for about one-quarter of total royal revenues, and although this proportion dropped from 1642 as the market became saturated, the practice reached a peak during the crisis years of Louis XIV's reign.[93] Men were induced to buy partly because office was generally a sound investment, but mainly because office-holding was socially prestigious: indeed, some offices immediately ennobled the holder, while others would do so if retained in the same family for three generations.

Sale of office was not confined to France, though it was at its most extensive there, and also in Spain, where local government posts were sold under Philip II and posts in central government under his successors. It was practised in Denmark under Christian IV, Sweden during Queen Christina's reign and also in Venice, especially after 1510, to help finance the war of the League of Cambrai.[94] It was little used in England, but a related expedient which was adopted by the Stuart kings, as well as by other rulers, was the sale of honours. James I invented the baronetcy, selling it for a cash payment and a commitment to maintain thirty soldiers in Ireland for three years. Francis I was relatively modest in his use of ennobling patents, issuing no more than 183 during the course of his reign to assist the 'excessive and extreme expenditure that we are constrained to make for the maintenance and governance of the great forces which we have mustered on land and sea' (1544); but Louis XIV issued no less than 1,000 blank *lettres de noblesse* during the war of the League of Augsburg (though probably only 600 were ever sold).[95] In Spain membership of the knightly orders was for sale by the 1620s; sale of honours took off with a vengeance in some of the German states after 1600; and even in republican Venice nobility could be purchased for 100,000 *ducats* in the seventeenth century.[96] Only in the United Provinces, with its powerful urban bourgeoisie and relatively small and weak nobility, was there no inflation of honours.

Of course, not all the money raised by governments was spent on war: there were the expenses of the court, entertainments, administration and building to be met, plus the pensions and gratuities paid to great magnates and their clients. Nor should we imagine that if there had been no rising military costs, rulers would not have sought to augment their revenues. Nevertheless it is clear that the bulk of government expenditure was on warfare: either directly, via payment of troops' wages, costs of fortress building and so on, or indirectly, via interest payments on debts contracted largely to meet these immediate expenses. Thomas Wilson was right when he noted that 'the greatest and archpoint of expence [is] of warr in defending the realme and offendinge the enemyes of the same'.[97] The exact proportion clearly varied from one country to another and cannot anyway be established with certainty, not least of all because no state kept anything resembling a modern budget, and large sums were raised and disbursed without passing through a central exchequer. But, very approximately, something under one-half of a state's revenues were devoted to military expenditure in peacetime, about three-quarters in time of war. Thus, in England under Elizabeth, James and Charles I, military expenses represented some 40–50 per cent of expenditure in peace; the proportion rose to 75 per cent in the war years of 1598–1603 and after 1688, and reached 92 per cent during one period of the Protectorate. Debt service alone accounted for over 50 per cent of the Spanish Crown's theoretical income in the 1590s and 1620s, and this, plus direct costs of defence, swallowed up over 75 per cent in the mid-1570s. Louis XIV spent a broadly similar proportion of his revenues on war, the army absorbing some 65 per cent of expenditure and the navy 9 per cent during the war of 1689–97, for example, while some four-fifths of total government revenue was spent on the military in Brandenburg-Prussia under the Great Elector.[98]

It is also clear that warfare was the most important stimulus in the drive to raise extra revenues. The chronological 'fit' between wartime financial crises and the implementation of often frenetic revenue-raising expedients is too close to support any other interpretation. A graph of French royal income and expenses between *c*.1550 and 1750, for example, shows that ordinary revenues were only rarely sufficient to cover expenditure even in time of peace, and in wartime the overspending rocketed.[99] The Crown sought to meet this deficit through loans, sales of office, higher levies on the Church and increased taxation. And a similar pattern appears to have pertained elsewhere, though our knowledge of royal finances, which is incomplete for France, is even sketchier for other countries. In Spain the Crown's debts grew particularly in those periods when the Habsburg–Valois struggle was most intense; in Denmark there was a similar correlation between the growth of debt and the costs of war and rearmament between 1621 and

1650; in England the financial strains of war in the 1540s resulted in higher taxes, currency debasement and sale of land at knock-down prices.[100] Although tax levels generally rose during periods of warfare, sometimes quite markedly, as in the case of the *taille* and *gabelle* during Richelieu's ministry in France, nevertheless tax revenues were both inadequate and too inflexible to sustain the high and immediate costs of war, and governments sought to meet these by resort to the extraordinary measures we have looked at: chiefly the sale of office, honours and land, and the use of loans. No less than 89.6 per cent of French war finances were from these sources in 1635.[101] Although tax levels might drop at the conclusion of a conflict, they nevertheless tended to remain above pre-war levels, since extra revenues were needed to pay off the 'hang-over' costs of war, in particular the interest payment on debts.

What then were the social implications of this enormous growth in government fiscality? Generalizations must be advanced with caution, partly because, as we have seen, methods of revenue-raising varied from country to country, and also because they varied within a given country over the course of time. Everywhere, however, taxes were raised to pay for the state's bellicosity, and in general it would be fair to conclude that the overwhelming burden of these higher taxes fell on the third estate.[102] Although the privileged orders – the nobility and the Church, where it remained an independent corporation in Catholic countries – paid more than is often suggested since they were nowhere wholly immune, nevertheless they were able to evade the main thrust of taxation. The principal exception to this would be England, where the nobility enjoyed no legal exemption from taxation, although even here aristocrats succeeded in avoiding their full share of the subsidy which supposedly involved an assessment of each man's income and possessions. Of course, the burden of taxation did not fall equitably on all sections of the third estate. For example, whole provinces in France, and kingdoms in Spain, enjoyed exemption from some taxes, or a reduced payment of others. Broadly however, the countryside tended to be more heavily taxed than the towns, many of which had secured a partial tax immunity, though this urban–country dichotomy was not so pronounced in England and the United Provinces as elsewhere, and did not apply in Brandenburg-Prussia in the later seventeenth century, where the towns paid an excise tax, the peasants a land tax. The destitute, of course, paid nothing in taxes (though Wolsey's taxation was meant to include those with as little as £1 wages a year). However, the trend, especially marked in the seventeenth century, towards the imposition of indirect taxes, which were generally easier to collect and brought in quicker returns than direct taxes, but which tended to be regressive in their effects, may have shifted the tax burden on to the poorer elements in society and allowed the well-to-do to escape relatively lightly.

The burden of rising taxes accounts for many of the uprisings which litter the sixteenth and seventeenth centuries. The case of France has been especially well studied.[103] In 1548 there were major revolts in the Saintonge, Angoumois and Guyenne against royal efforts to extend the *gabelle*; between 1578 and 1595 there were revolts in Provence, Brittany, Périgord, Normandy and the Limousin, culminating in the movement of the *Croquants*, involving many thousands of peasants. Fiscal revolts were endemic between 1620 and 1650: Aix (1630), Languedoc (1632), the western provinces (1635), Saintonge and Angoumois, spreading into Poitou and the Limousin (1636), the Norman *Nu-Pieds* (1639), to cite only the most serious. And they did not end with Louis XIV's reign. There were uprisings of peasants and artisans around Bayonne in 1664; the revolt of the Vivarais involved a 5,000-strong peasant army; and although the Breton uprising of 1675 proved to be the last major open revolt of the reign, discontent and localized resistance to payment of taxes continued to bubble away. In all there were well over 1,000 major or minor disturbances during the seventeenth century, the overwhelming majority of them anti-fiscal.[104] Disturbances were by no means confined to France. In the Spanish monarchy the revolt of the Communeros (1520–2), Catalonia (1640), Naples and Palermo (1647) were inspired initially by the financial demands of the Crown. Revolts against the imposition of the *millones*, begun under Philip II, continued into the following century: a correspondent from Motril in 1683 wrote of 'continued riots every day and armed men in the streets'.[105]

To be certain, high taxation was not necessarily the only factor in these revolts, though for the urban working classes and the peasantry who participated in them it was the chief consideration.[106] Nor was the percentage of total income taken in tax especially high. To establish an average tax burden would require a multitude of regional instances, and is anyway impossible given the present state of research. But, by way of example, Ladurie suggests that in Languedoc government taxes in the late sixteenth century accounted for about 6 per cent of gross agricultural income and by 1650 the figure stood at 12 per cent, having doubled during Richelieu's ministry, while Vauban in 1700 calculated that 12–13 per cent of a country labourer's income went in royal taxes. In 1594 a contemporary document judged that farm labourers in the countryside around Pavia paid 10–15 per cent of their total earnings in direct taxation, and Dominguez Ortiz suggests a similar percentage for the Castilian peasant around 1650. Such levels do not appear exorbitant to the hardened twentieth-century taxpayer. But it should be remembered that there might be seigneurial and Church taxes on top of these. Also, royal taxes were inflating most; they represented no less than 47 per cent of the peasant's total tax burden in New Castile by the end of the sixteenth century, and were rising. And they had to be paid in cash, an onerous condition in an economy short of specie, which might necessitate the enforced sale by a peasant of valuable livestock, grain or equipment, thus reducing his future earning potential.[107] Moreover, the bulk of the tax-paying population lived at, or close to, subsistence level, with no slack in their economy to allow them to adjust to a sharp increase in royal impositions, especially when this was coupled with a harvest failure or drop in wages. At such times oppressive taxes became unsupportable.

It is true, too, that the geography of tax revolt did not always coincide with the areas of highest taxation. Thus, in 1640 revolt took place in Catalonia but not the more heavily burdened Castile; similarly in France, revolts in both the sixteenth and seventeenth centuries tended to cluster in the relatively lightly taxed peripheral provinces; the much higher levels of taxation which pertained in England after the Civil War were paid without any of the outcry which had greeted Charles I's efforts to raise relatively modest sums; and hostility to taxes was greater in France than in England during the eighteenth century though from c.1700 onwards the latter country was the more heavily taxed.[108] Differences in the response to taxation are not simply to be explained by reference to the degree of governmental control over a region, though this was clearly an important factor, but a more crucial point was how taxes were perceived. If they were seen as being manifestly unfair in both their incidence and collection (as was the case in France); or unfair in the sense that they were imposed in violation of local privilege (the case with Catalonia, and the Netherlands in the early 1570s); or unfair in the sense of being levied for improper purposes (much as the Aragonese saw taxes levied on them under Philip II to be spent on 'foreign' wars in the Netherlands), then hostility to taxation might boil over into open revolt.[109] Plainly then, there was no simple correlation between taxation and revolt, but it is nevertheless clear that lying behind many of the disturbances which afflicted early-modern Europe were the state's incessant demands for higher revenues.

Anti-fiscal protests were by no means always unsuccessful. The *Pitauts* achieved the abolition of the salt tax in 1550; the 1632 uprising in Languedoc secured the withdrawal of the *édit des élus*; and, in what was perhaps the most outstanding government climb-down of all, Henry VIII led the retreat on the imposition of the Amicable Grant in 1526 after a virtually nationwide tax strike.[110] Nor should we forget that there was much passive and low-level resistance to the payment of taxes which never escalated to the level of outright revolt.[111] Nevertheless, as the case of the Amicable Grant suggests, it was generally only when the elites in society backed popular resistance that much was achieved; popular revolt on its own did little to halt the escalation of taxes.

However, if the urban working classes and the peasantry above all suffered from the growth in government fiscality, some elements in society were able to take advantage of the unprecedented opportunities offered by governments' financial needs. At one end of the scale were the great financiers. Merchant bankers such as Ludovico Nicola and the Affaitati family of Cremona, the Malvenda of Burgos, the Fuggers of Augsburg and the Antwerp financier Gaspar Schetz provided rulers with loans on a quite extraordinary scale.[112] Individual and also groups of financiers bought the right to collect royal taxes in return for a straight cash payment to the Crown, which thereby anticipated future tax revenues and received a much-needed sum of cash in hand for immediate use. In a variant of this standard form of tax farming the Dutch Spierinck brothers organized the levying of tolls on shipping entering Swedish-controlled ports in the Baltic in the 1620s and 1630s, retaining a 5 per cent cut of the amount collected.[113] The financiers were not just needed for the cash they could raise. Armies operating outside their state's boundaries had to be paid, but the movement of large quantities of specie was both dangerous and difficult – 1 million *livres* in silver coin weighed over 9 tons, and a single shipment of 125,000 *livres* under Henry II cost 6,750 *livres* in transport and security expenses, for example[114] – and hence recourse was had to the credit transfer services of international bankers. Herwarth, for example, handled many of the payments to the French armies in Germany in the 1630s; and a cartel led by Samuel Bernard transferred 4–5 million *livres* every month to Louis XIV's forces in Italy, Germany and the Netherlands between 1704 and 1708.[115] Moreover, since many early-modern bankers were *hommes d'affaires* with wide commercial as well as strictly financial interests, their fiscal dealings with the state frequently spilled over into complex commodity deals for the supply of armies. In Sweden, for example, the armaments dealer and financier, Louis de Geer, had secured a monopoly of the state's arms production by 1627, and his commercial interests extended to virtually every sphere of the country's economic life, while the wealthy *Liègois*, Jean Curtius, supplied arms and gunpowder to the Army of Flanders, and in 1613 arranged to establish an ironworks near Santander to cast cannon and shot in return for a fifteen-year exclusive patent on the use of his machinery.[116]

Activities such as these increasingly blurred the line between public and private finance, a distinction which was further eroded as financiers came to occupy posts in the official fiscal apparatus, either through purchase or by appointment. This process was most marked in France, reaching a high point under Colbert, himself a financier's son and protegé of the most successful financier of all, Mazarin, but elsewhere, too, financiers entrenched themselves at the very heart of the state's finances. In the United Provinces a surprisingly large number of private *solliciteurs-militair* advanced money at regular intervals to the captains in the army, enabling them to pay their men, and were reimbursed with interest by the captains out of funds provided by the government. In this way the soldiers received regular pay, the government received credit, and the *solliciteurs* made a profit. In Spain arrangements were made from the 1560s onwards with prominent financiers who simultaneously held positions as paymasters of the royal forces and in the administration, culminating in the appointment in 1598 of Juan Pascual to 'all the paymasterships in Spain', so that for a while this single individual monopolized domestic military financing from the collection of taxes to their disbursment.[117]

Naturally the great financiers have received most attention from historians. But we should not underestimate the numbers of people involved in the burgeoning machine of royal finance and taxation. Initially the financiers of the early sixteenth century lent to the state out of their personal fortunes, but, while this never ceased to be the case, they increasingly came to invest funds lodged with them by clients and dependants.[118] Moreover, from about 1540 money for government use was raised from the wider public through the sale of state bonds (*juros* in Spain, *renten* in the Netherlands, *rentes* in France) and through loans raised via intermediary institutions which themselves had investors, such as the great municipalities, the Church, the provincial estates and the growing number of deposit-taking banks – the Venetian *Banco del Giro* and the Milanese *Banco di Sant' Ambrogio*, for example.[119] The English ambassador, Sir William Temple, estimated that there were 65,500 *rentiers* who had invested in government annuities in the Netherlands by the mid-seventeenth century,[120] and investing in this way went well down the social scale. Thus we find that the subscribers to a 60,000 *livres* loan raised by the estates of Languedoc in 1674 included two widows, a baker from Montpellier, a professor and a convent in Pézenas; whilst amongst the many smaller investors in Venetian government bonds was Annelio Stichiano, a runaway monk, who had investments worth 48 *ducats* per year when he was arrested in 1549.[121]

As well as these *rentiers*, large numbers of men – and the two groups frequently overlapped – acquired places in the government's fiscal apparatus as receivers of taxes, collectors, assessors, and treasurers. And to these should be added the growing body of contractors who helped to supply the armies. A whole class of *munitionnaires* developed in France and elsewhere during the course of the seventeenth century: the powder and saltpetre contractor Berthelot, the victualler Jacquier, the weapons supplier Dalliez de la Tour, the Monnerot, Pâris and Gruin brothers and Claude de Boislève were simply amongst the biggest and hence best known of a much larger group.[122]

Involvement in state finance was not, of course, without risk. As Pierre Goubert has written of France, with only some exaggeration, 'Almost all the financial history of the Ancien Régime can be summed up in the formula: how not to pay one's debts.'[123] It was not just in this country that monarchs repudiated their obligations. Philip II's technical declaration of bankruptcy in 1557 and its sequel in 1560 while rates of interest were renegotiated with lenders, brought down a large number of financiers, in Antwerp especially. Further bankruptcies followed in 1575, 1596, 1607, 1627 and 1647. The declaration in 1627 effectively sounded the death knell for the Genoese bankers and their investors at Piacenza (known as the Besançon fair) which since 1579 had raised between 5 and 10 million *ducats* annually, mainly for the pay of the Flanders Army.[124] The Fugger news letters reported with monotonous regularity the failure of banking houses which over-extended their involvement in monarchical finance. In France especially the Crown not only demonstrated bad faith towards its creditors, but financiers ran the additional risk of legal prosecution. *Chambres de justice* were established periodically to investigate their misdeeds and impose substantial fines on them, or even condemn a few individuals to death, in effect a crude method whereby some of the Crown's debts might be written off.[125] Additionally, office-holders here, and elsewhere, might be subject to forced loans and their stipends withheld.

Yet the drama which attaches to the failure of many great financiers – Semblançay's execution, de Witte's suicide, Fouquet's arrest and trial – can lead one to exaggerate the dangers. The Spanish and French governments were notably poor credit risks. But investors with the sixteenth-century Venetian or the later seventeenth-century English government, or the financiers of the Kiel money market who received a steady 5–8 per cent on their loans to Denmark before 1627, were much more secure. So solid was Dutch credit that when the government began in 1655 to pay off part of the principal of the public debt the investors, according to Sir William Temple, 'receive it with Tears, not knowing how to dispose of it to Interest, with such Safety and Ease'.[126] Especially high risks were partly offset by high interest rates: Charles V borrowed at rates which averaged around 17 per cent between 1520 and 1532, but which touched 49 per cent between 1552 and 1556, and the French Crown paid an average rate of 24 per cent on its tax contracts in the 1630s. Risks were offset still further as financiers demanded and obtained solid collateral for their loans. Thus the Genoese acquired land, rents, the right to buy the wool clip in Castile and the administration of the salt-pans in Andalusia; and the Fuggers held important mining and trading concessions in Germany and the Iberian peninsula which allowed them to ride out the bankruptcy of 1557, though they largely abandoned royal finance after this date.[127] Moreover, attempts to prosecute financiers were far from thoroughgoing. Royal dependence on them was such that the Crown dared not alienate them by pressing matters too far, and so deeply had they penetrated into royal finance and taxation by the seventeenth century that it was wholly unrealistic to think of doing without them. Antoine Feydeau, the biggest revenue farmer in France, was specifically exempted from investigation by the *chambre* in 1624–5, and the *chambre* of 1661 merely confirmed the influence of those men favoured by Colbert.[128] Similarly, the Crown dared not press its demands on the *officiers* too far for fear of alienating altogether its own bureaucracy. Crown, money-lenders and officials were bound together in a nexus of mutual dependence and self-interest.

The biggest profits went to the great financiers. Genoese bankers, including the Spinola, Centurione and Fiesco families, who until 1627 handled the transfer of funds to the Netherlands, did so at a cost to the Spanish Crown of up to 30 per cent, besides being able to profit from playing the exchange rates as money was converted from one currency to another. The coinage consortium of fifteen partners which bought the right to mint coins in Bohemia, Moravia and Lower Austria for one year from Emperor Ferdinand II effectively devalued the currency by reducing its silver content, obtaining a handsome profit of 2 million florins in the process. But the smaller fry benefited too. The researches of Ladurie and Chaussinand-Nogaret have uncovered a plethora of Languedocian tax farmers, collectors, financiers, minor officials and small investors from the sixteenth to the eighteenth century who profited from their involvement in royal finances, for example;[129] and the numerous investors in the Dutch Republic in the first half of the seventeenth century received a steady, if unspectacular, 4–6 per cent interest on their money. As a brief from the rural communities in Lombardy pointed out, the interest charges on government loans and bonds went to a multitude of merchants, wealthy burgers, foreigners and others, 'who compared with the wretched peasantry have hardly felt the devastations of war'.[130] Here, as elsewhere, government spending in excess of taxation, in so far as it was financed by borrowing, brought about a transfer of wealth from the mass of taxpayers to a smaller elite with money to invest.

The growing number of office-holders, especially those in the tax administration, also benefited, for they found dozens of different ways, both legal and illegal, whereby public money passing through their hands could be made to stick to their fingers. In France receivers of the *taille* forwarded taxes to the king not as they came in but in fifteen 'monthly' instalments, which not only made accounting difficult but gave them the opportunity to advance the king his own money ahead of time while charging him interest on it! In addition there was the fiscal value of the office itself, which, although it fluctuated in the short term, in the longer term proved to be a solid investment. Merely to take one example, the price of a post as *conseiller* in the Paris *parlement* rose twelvefold between 1597 and 1635.[131]

Nor were the gains purely financial. Acquiring wealth through state loans, tax farming, tax collecting or army contracting was a means of rising in the world. The Pâris brothers, for example, who acquired a high social status in France in the early eighteenth century – Antoine helped to found the *Ecole Militaire* and became its first director – were sons of a humble innkeeper from the Dauphiné, who made their fortunes supplying the French armies.[132] Upward social mobility was further enhanced in those countries where the sale of honours and ennobling offices was widely practised. It was probably greatest in France: there were, after all, over 60,000 venal office-holders by Louis XIV's reign.[133] It was less significant, but far from negligible in Spain and the Austrian lands, and was of least importance in Sweden and England.[134] Clearly, the argument should not be exaggerated. The route upwards was generally only available to those who already possessed a certain level of wealth;[135] it was by no means risk-free, as we have seen; and there were other roads to social advancement. Money made in commerce, for instance, allowed a successful merchant to buy land, a grand house, horses and carriage, a title of *seigneur*, and in practice to live nobly, so that after a certain period he and his family would be accepted as such. But there is nevertheless no doubt that, if armies themselves did not serve as social escalators, indirectly warfare, by contributing to a growth in government fiscality with all that this entailed, did play an important part in extending the opportunities for upward social mobility.

Why, it might be asked, did governments countenance such extensive involvement of private financiers in the state's finances, and why did they tolerate such high levels of profit-taking by financiers, tax farmers, military contractors and officials? The answer was that they had little choice. As Richelieu noted of the financiers, they were 'prejudicial to the state, yet necessary'.[136] Necessary firstly because the underdeveloped nature of most early-modern bureaucracies rendered some privatization of state functions – farming out the collection of taxes, for example, or contracting out the supply of armies – an attractive proposition. Necessary too because governments' fixed revenues come in too slowly, and were anyway too small, to meet the immediate and heavy costs of war. By the time tax revenues had been gathered in, a state's army would have melted away or mutinied from lack of pay, or the country itself have been overrun. Hence the recourse to the sale of office, the farming out of fixed revenues, and the raising of loans, all of which brought the government much-needed cash in hand. Additionally, tax farming gave the government a regular and predictable source of income irrespective of the fluctuations in the economy which affected the yield from indirect taxes in particular; and some of the hostility to taxation could be directed towards the tax farmers and their agents. Moreover, in France particularly, financiers had developed a complex of family and business links with all those in power by the late seventeenth century, including the Crown's own venal officials, ministers and even the greatest aristocratic houses in the land who were more than happy to provide capital for the financiers' wheeling and dealing (albeit under assumed names) and share in the profits.[137] This made it impossible for the Crown to contemplate any radical structural reforms to the system: to do so would be to challenge not just the financiers but the whole social elite.

THE STATE AND WAR

'War made the state, and the state made war', noted Charles Tilly, in a pithy and beguiling aphorism, and he is merely one of the most recent of a succession of historians and others who have ascribed a central role to warfare in shaping the development of the modern state.[138] In particular, they have suggested that the unprecedented financial and administrative demands of war in the early-modern period prompted the formation of powerful, centralized bureaucratic structures; that rulers, with their standing armies, had the capacity to assert their authority over their subjects generally, and over traditional rivals for power, such as the nobility and representative institutions, in particular; and that where these processes were most developed absolute monarchy eventuated.

There is certainly no lack of evidence as to the centrality of warfare in the functions of the state. The mere fact that around one-half, or more, of its revenues were spent on warfare would support the claim of Parker and Smith that the 'early modern state was, to a large extent, a military institution'.[139] Moreover, although monarchs saw it as their duty to maintain social harmony, promote trade and industry and see to the welfare of their subjects, their chief concern was with the pursuit of *gloire* which was attained chiefly through the waging of war; while the major task of their bureaucratic and fiscal apparatus was to procure the resources of men, money and supplies, which were the essential prerequisite of this pursuit. However, while admitting the dominant role of warfare in the functions of the state, and admitting too that it was a crucial – probably indeed *the* crucial – agent of change in the development of the state, it was not the only factor leading to change, and its effects upon the growth of the state were both more complex, and more variable, than Tilly and others would allow.

The traditional view of the part played by military factors in establishing monarchical dominance over the nobility, for example, needs to be substantially modified. It has been argued that this victory was achieved first through the royal possession of heavy cannon, which allowed monarchs to demolish the fortified strongholds of the great magnates, and with them the nobles' provincial power bases; and second because the growing size and cost of armies prohibited their maintenance by even the greatest magnates, thus bringing about a concentration of military power in the hands of the king which could be used to coerce disaffected aristocrats. But it is in fact far from clear that cannon were much used in this way. It is striking that in England, where the Crown was outstandingly successful in neutralizing and demilitarizing its 'over-mighty subjects', reducing the size of their private armed retinues and causing them to abandon their fortified castles, a royal standing army did not exist, and the magnates were not tamed by the use of *force majeure*, but by the use of the legal process, fines, attainders, by the inculcation of a growing dependence on the court, and by the adoption of a more pacific lifestyle.[140]

Elsewhere in Europe rulers did begin to assert and attain a monopoly of armed force within their sovereign boundaries. But although much had been achieved by the end of the seventeenth century, the process was long drawn out and far from complete. Even at the height of royal military power in Spain under Philip II, great magnates, such as the Duke of Medina-Sidonia in the south-west, possessed formidable private arsenals and retained a capacity to call out and equip sizeable private forces. During the seventeenth century the power and military capacity of the aristocracy actually reached new heights as the defence of the realm was increasingly devolved on them. 'Power and authority is totally in the hands of the grandees', noted the Venetian ambassador in 1683.[141]

In France, too, the ability of the nobility to raise considerable private forces was clearly evidenced during the internal disturbances from the 1560s to the 1590s. Legislation passed during Henry IV's reign, ordering an inventory of hand weapons and the confiscation of heavy artillery, and under Louis XIII in 1626, which was aimed at securing the destruction of private fortresses, met with very limited success, as was demonstrated during the numerous armed noble rebellions of the 1630s and 1640s and especially by the Fronde. In many ways, however, the Fronde was the military swan-song of the nobility, and although under Louis XIV weapons, including heavy artillery, continued to be widely diffused throughout society, the independent military power of the nobility largely disappeared. Significantly however, this was not brought about so much through the use of superior force – although localized noble resistance in the Auvergne was defeated by a royal army in 1666, the *frondeurs* had not been confronted in this way – but through more subtle means: nobles were bought off with gratuities, pensions and a judicious use of patronage, for the chief advantage kings in France, and monarchs generally, had over their magnates lay not in the size of their armies but in the superior size of their patronage resources. To be sure, there was a military side to this: posts were given to the nobility inside Louis XIV's expanded military machine, and cash hand-outs from the Crown were the proceeds of higher taxes which might well have been screwed from the peasantry by the use of military force. But this is to argue that the nobility found that more was to be gained from collaborating with a regime which put itself out to recognize their interests than from opposing it as *frondeurs*. It was certainly not the growth in the military power of Louis XIV's state which ensured the quiescence of the nobility; rather, one might say, it was the co-operation of the nobility with the Crown which made possible the growth in state military power.[142]

Moreover, if under Louis XIV the Crown did succeed in establishing a monopoly of military power, the nobility finding an exclusive outlet for its martial ardour in the king's forces rather than in fronding, it was much less successful at eradicating independent noble influence in the royal army. To be sure, efforts were made to develop an officer corps with a hierarchy of ranks: the position of lieutenant-colonel, major and second lieutenant was made uniform in each regiment for example, and after 1675 promotion was supposed to be based on seniority. Additionally, civilian officials, particularly the *intendants d'armée*, were infiltrated into the army. But these reforms had only a limited effect. Except for the royal guards, the key posts of captain and colonel remained venal, the trade in companies and regiments was as lively as ever, and the influence of these officers over their units remained uncurbed until the middle of the eighteenth century. The *intendants* were tolerated when they assisted with finance and provisioning, but their interference in matters of strategy and tactics was resented and resisted. So too was interference from the secretaries of war, especially the tactless Louvois: in 1673 Marshal Bellefonds countermanded his order for a withdrawal from the Netherlands, for example, and even a direct order from Louis to the Duke of Luxembourg in 1692, that he lay siege to Charleroi, had to be issued several times before it was obeyed.[143]

If the Crown's mightiest subjects were not cowed by the use of *force majeure*, to what extent could royal armies be used as instruments of internal coercion more generally? Undeniably, rulers did see their forces as having a domestic policing role. Turenne's commission, for example, noted the need to retain

> in peace as well as in war a great number of troops, both infantry and cavalry, which will always be in good condition to act to keep our people in the obedience and respect they owe, to insure the peace and tranquillity that we have won.[144]

And Louis did indeed utilize his army in this way. Early in his reign troops were employed to overawe one of the last autonomous municipalities in France, Marseilles, which subsequently had its constitution remodelled. In the notorious *dragonnades* troops were billeted on Protestants to force them to convert. Regular soldiers suppressed revolt in the Boulonnais in 1662 and in Languedoc in 1670, when a peasant army was butchered and whole villages razed, and troops accompanied tax-collectors to protect them and enforce payment of dues. In France and Spain during the sixteenth century, too, there are examples of troops assisting in the collection of taxes, and the widespread revolt of the peasants in Germany in 1524–5 was put down by a combined army of the princes. Most striking of all was the use made of the army by the Great Elector. After 1655 it was employed to enforce payment of taxes in Brandenburg, a function subsequently extended to the ruler's other possessions.

Nevertheless, if in general terms royal armies must be regarded as adjuncts to royal power, we should not exaggerate the extent to which this was so, especially before the later seventeenth century. Sixteenth- and early-seventeenth-century rulers quite rightly had strong reservations about the use of soldiers for internal policing. The warning of Suriano, the Venetian ambassador in Paris, of 'an uprising by the lesser people against the great ones, out of revenge for the sufferings they have endured',[145] reflected a generally held fear that the grievances of the lower orders, be they peasants in revolt or rank and file in the army (foreign mercenaries excepted) might lead them to join together in a general social uprising. Even if this did not happen, the ill-paid and ill-disciplined troops were as likely to give themselves over to looting as to suppressing disorder.

Moreover, governments in this period did not maintain sufficient numbers of men to make viable their deployment on a routine basis as tax officials' assistants, and there were anyway grave disadvantages to their use in this fashion. It was expensive (the costs might well exceed the proceeds from the taxes); it worsened relations between taxpayers and the government and made future revolt and non-payment of taxes more likely; and the army would most probably keep the proceeds rather than forward them to the Crown.[146] Nor could troops easily be mustered in sufficient force to suppress a major uprising. Rulers therefore usually preferred to sit out a revolt hoping that it would burn itself out, and relied upon local magnates and worthies, united in their fear of social disorder, to control it. To intervene early with inadequate numbers of royal troops was to court the risk of defeat and a consequent loss of prestige, which was disastrous for rulers heavily dependent on preserving a façade of strength and invincibility.

During the second half of the seventeenth century, it is true, rulers were able to use the much larger forces at their disposal, if not more frequently then certainly more successfully, to repress *popular* revolts at least. The reign of Louis XIV contrasts markedly with that of his predecessors in this respect, for instance. Yet larger armies still did not give rulers unlimited potential for coercion. Low-level resistance to Crown policies – the non-payment of taxes and the murder of tax officials, for example – continued unabated and largely unchecked. Revolt and popular resistance to the payment of taxes was anyway most marked in time of war, for then the fiscal burdens were at their heaviest, but it was precisely at this time that troops would be stationed at or beyond the frontier and hence would be unavailable for domestic policing. Above all, it was crucial that the army be used selectively if its use was to be successful, in roles of which its officers approved, against opponents without widespread and especially elite social support, and generally to buttress the existing social hierarchy. In France, for example, noble army officers, as Catholics, were enthusiastic about acting against Protestants, but they were less than happy about enforcing ministerial policies of which they disapproved. In England, where the experience of the Civil War had bequeathed a powerful anti-standing-army ideology, troops could be used to assist the civil powers – arresting a few footpads, escorting prisoners, and patrolling some roads against highwaymen – and they were active in suppressing clan warfare north of the border and keeping troublesome highlanders out of the lowlands, but there was no question of the government being able to impose generally unpopular policies by force – James II's aspirations notwithstanding. In the Austrian Habsburg lands the exceptional circumstances of the war years of the 1620s had allowed Ferdinand II to crush Protestantism in Bohemia and go some way towards reducing the kingdom's independence. Yet there was subsequently no possibility of successfully using the army in this way against religious dissidents, magnates and provincial freedoms elsewhere: the army was too weak, the opposition too strong. Even in Brandenburg-Prussia, the state above all in which the ruler's position is generally perceived as resting upon the use of force, the Great Elector and his successors were careful to associate the nobility with their rule, allowing the *junkers* to extend their control over the peasants, maintaining their local authority, exempting them more completely than in most places from taxation, and providing them with lucrative posts in the army and bureaucracy.[147] Later seventeenth-century rulers (if the example of France is anything to go by) may have become more adept at buying off those social elements with power, and thus depriving popular revolts of their support, leaving the way open for the successful use of the army against such revolts. This was a far from negligible achievement, but one achieved only at the cost of making substantial concessions to the elites in society, and the limitations on the uses to which the army might be put remained considerable.[148]

If armies, even by the later seventeenth century, had only a limited value as instruments of royal coercion, to what extent did warfare contribute to the growth of princely authority by affecting constitutional procedures, in particular by precipitating a decline in the fortunes of the estates in early-modern Europe? Conventional wisdom, deriving largely from German historiography, has stressed the incompatibility of functioning estates and a ruler with a standing army. Since the estates blocked the heavy taxes which were necessary for the upkeep of a large army, it is argued, they were liable to be swept away by a ruler intent on developing his military power, the demise of the estates being a crucial step in the advance towards absolute monarchy.[149] But were matters really as straightforward as this?

It was certainly the case, as we saw earlier, that the war-induced drive for extra revenues led rulers to raise the level of taxes, adopt extraordinary fiscal measures, and generally act in a corner-cutting fashion which engendered a degree of friction with those institutions – chiefly, but not always, the estates – which had a say over the levying of taxes and a constitutional role in the business of government. Moreover, relations between rulers and their estates became particularly fraught during the seventeenth century, for the fiscal pressures of war were then at their most intense. Indeed, it is not too fanciful to suggest a generalized crisis of state finances, beginning with the Thirty Years War, and extending through the Baltic conflicts of the middle decades of the century to the wars with the Turks and with Louis XIV's France. These extended conflicts, which involved the simultaneous participation of many of the European states, were fought on an unprecedented scale and were unremitting in the demands they placed on the combatants. With the exception of Spain, sixteenth-century belligerents had enjoyed a breathing space between wars which allowed them some opportunity to pay off war debts and even to accumulate a war-chest in anticipation of the next emergency. Thus, Denmark's 1.1. million *daler* debt from the Seven Years War of the North (1563–70) was redeemed in the next twenty years; in 1584 the Venetian Senate announced that the war debt of 1570–3 was paid off and by 1609 there was a 9 million *ducats* surplus; Henry VIII's substantial debts were largely settled by his successors, and Elizabeth accumulated a fighting fund of a quarter of a million pounds in the first twenty-five years of her reign; and even in hard-pressed France Sully managed to put something aside.[150] Yet, while the anguished cry of the Danish treasurer Aksel Arenfeld in 1626 – 'God knows, there is a great shortage of money'[151] – would have been instantly familiar to all sixteenth-century administrators, the unceasing conflicts of the following century strained states' resources to the uttermost, and meant that even such limited examples of prudent good-housekeeping became rare. Accumulated war debts spilled over from one conflict to the next, the drive for extra revenues became more intense, and in these circumstances the working relationship between rulers and estates became increasingly strained.

Yet it did not follow that the estates were bound to be the losers from all this. In some instances, it is true, rulers were driven into dispensing with their estates. Thus, a fierce determination to protect Piedmont against further foreign invasion led its ruler, Emmanuel Philibert (1553–80), to summon the estates only once, in 1560, after returning to his territories following their twenty-three year occupation by the French. He employed the grant of money provided by the estates to support a mercenary army, which was then used to impose heavy and permanent taxes on the duchy's population, thus rendering further recourse to the estates unnecessary. A similar policy was pursued in his other possession, Savoy, and was continued by his successor, Charles Emmanuel. In Brandenburg-Prussia, too, the Great Elector determined that the survival of his territories, which were bordered by powerful and predatory neighbours, necessitated the establishment of a sizeable army. Opposition from the estates to the taxes which would make an army possible led to their eventual suppression in Brandenburg, while those in Cleves and Prussia were reduced to insignificance.[152]

But equally, and depending on the prevailing circumstances, the ruler's need for money might drive him into greater dependence on tax-granting bodies. This was the case in the Austrian Habsburg lands during the sixteenth century for instance, where the rulers relied heavily on the estates to raise money and troops and to organize local defence; in Denmark, Christian IV's accumulation of war debts following his unsuccessful intervention in Germany led to the Crown's freedom of action being severely circumscribed by the Council and estates; and in Saxony, where John George I (1611–56) and his successors kept a standing force which came to number 8–10,000 men, these were maintained by subsidies granted by the diet, which emerged into the eighteenth century with enhanced powers. In France, the picture with respect to the fortunes of the estates was a chequered one. If some of the twenty or so provincial assemblies came under assault from a revenue-hungry government, notably during Richelieu's period in office, when those in Normandy and the Dauphiné disappeared, others, such as the estates in Brittany and Languedoc, were able to turn the Crown's financial crises to their own advantage. They prospered during the Cardinal's ministry, subsequently becoming indispensable in the management of royal finances. Elsewhere, as in seventeenth-century Württemberg or Hesse, where after 1653 the Landgrave's forces were maintained by a mixture of foreign and domestic subsidies, the estates either proved capable of resisting the prince's demands for money, or else came to a *modus vivendi* with him.[153] Even when relations between a ruler and his estates degenerated into open conflict, as sometimes happened, it was not necessarily the former who emerged victorious: witness the success of the Catalan *cortes* against the Spanish Crown in 1640, and the triumph of the English Parliament in the Civil War.

In any event, it would be wrong to over-stress the conflictual aspect of the relationship between rulers and their estates in the early-modern period. The principle that rulers ought to consult their subjects – and the estates were a chief means of achieving this – was one which had penetrated deeply into the western political tradition, and although the provincial rights and tax immunities which estates guarded frequently proved irksome, rulers did not rush to suppress them.[154] Aside from the instance of Piedmont-Savoy, only Brandenburg-Prussia appears as a major exception to the rule that kings would not bring about far-reaching constitutional changes by force. But it is worth noting that circumstances here were uniquely favourable to the use of princely force. Because the Elector's territories were distinct and separate he could pick them off one at a time without provoking a general reaction; and the ability of his dominions to resist him had been weakened by their occupation by foreign forces during the Thirty Years War. Most importantly of all, however, the Elector was prepared to countenance the use of force in pursuit of the establishment of absolute government in a way which was not general in Europe. The first President of the Paris *parlement* who, in 1648, noted that 'The greatest advantage a sovereign can possess on earth consists in reigning always by love over his subjects...he cannot commit a graver mistake than to have himself obeyed continually through terror',[155] spoke not just for the ruled but for most rulers in the seventeenth century, few of whom wished, or were prepared, to rule in the arbitrary fashion of the Elector.

Nor were the estates consistently unsympathetic to the financial problems of the ruler and unaware of the wider problems facing the state. The case of seventeenth-century Sweden makes this clear. During the reign of Charles XI a solution to the costly defence requirements of Sweden's Baltic empire emerged in the form of the *reduktion*, a process which involved the wholesale and forced resumption by the king of former Crown lands which had been alienated, mainly to the nobility. Members of the army were allocated farms or revenues on these lands, assembling periodically in peacetime for training, this so-called allotment system providing Sweden with the means to maintain a permanent defence force which could be mobilized rapidly in time of war. However, the *reduktion* breached the fundamental laws of the kingdom, which bound the king to respect the property of his subjects, and hence it could only be carried through by what was, in effect, a constitutional revolution: Charles adopted draconian powers of legislation which enabled him to appropriate his subjects' property as he judged necessary and without consulting the estates or Council, and in practice he emerged as an absolute ruler. Yet, perhaps surprisingly, the initiative for the *reduktion* and for this constitutional revolution seems to have emanated as much from the lower orders in the *Riksdag* as from the king. In the wider interests of the Swedish state (and, to be sure, out of pique with the great nobility who had been the chief beneficiaries of the alienation of Crown lands) the *Riksdag* was prepared to connive at the eclipse of its own powers.[156]

To be fair, estates generally were not as self-sacrificing as the Swedish *Riksdag*. But, as Conrad Russell has pointed out, their opposition to requests for money was less a result of obstructive bloody-mindedness than an inability to comprehend the magnitude of the costs of war, and their attachment to a different set of priorities; for whereas kings and ministers accorded a high status to war and defence, which in time of emergency overrode constitutional niceties, the estates were more concerned to maintain local privileges and the right to consent to taxation in return for concessions and redress of grievances.[157]

Clearly, then, the apparently insatiable need of many monarchs for money to finance the rising costs of warfare was an important element conditioning the relations between them and their estates. But it did not follow from this that a major constitutional crisis was bound to develop between the two; nor that, if it did, it was the ruler who would always emerge victorious. The need for extra money might push the ruler into a greater dependence on tax-voting bodies, which thus emerged with enhanced powers; the estates might prove capable of checking the monarch's attempts to secure extra revenues; and even when relations between the two degenerated into armed conflict the ruler was not always the victor.

We need to be similarly circumspect when assessing the effects of war on bureaucratic development. Administrative expansion was certainly a feature of most states in the early-modern period, though it occurred in some more than others and at different times. But what precisely was the relationship – if any – between bureaucratization and warfare? We need to recognize at the outset that in states where venality of office was widely practised, part of this expansion was purely nominal, as rulers multiplied the number of offices in order to sell them for cash; sometimes, indeed, selling the same office to several different individuals who held it in rotation. In that the increasing cost of warfare was the major stimulant behind the drive to raise extra revenues, we may say that war, indirectly, promoted an expansion of bureaucracies. But bureaucracies also grew in 'real' terms as the amount of work undertaken by governments was extended. (Though to be sure the bureaucrats doing these 'real' jobs might be venal.) And it has been widely accepted that the bulk of this extra work was connected with the needs of the military:[158] extra administrators were required to assess, levy and collect the taxes which financed the armies; bureaucrats were needed to recruit, muster and count the troops, organize their billeting, their marches and supplies; and yet more were needed to ensure that army commanders did the bidding of their royal masters. What has been less clear is whether an efficient and developed bureaucracy was the precondition for the growth in the size and complexity of armies, especially in the later seventeenth century; or whether growth in armies stimulated growth in the bureaucratic structures of the state.

In one sense this chicken-and-egg approach rather misses the point, for, where it occurred, bureaucratic growth and the expansion of military effort tended to proceed in tandem and to be self-reinforcing. In Denmark, for example, a more efficient bureaucracy emerged after the mid-decades of the seventeenth century, divided into specialist departments, and capable of undertaking the major task of compiling a Land Register in 1688 on the basis of which recruitment and tax yields could be evaluated, all of which permitted an extension of Danish military effort. But this followed a period of conflict in the 1620s and 1630s which had revealed the inadequacy of the country's bureaucratic structures to maintain and support the level of military effort undertaken by the ruler. Similarly, in Sweden, administrative reform and military effort proceeded in a jerky, cyclical fashion. More efficient exploitation of the tax resources of the country, and its mineral resources in particular, helped to provide a base for the military campaigns of Gustavus Adolphus in Poland and Germany, which in themselves stimulated further administrative development, including the foundation of a central military authority in 1634, the College of War, to which each regiment had to submit returns of its strength, equipment and stores. The disastrous showing of the military under the Regency, and the pressing needs of defence, brought forth further administrative developments under Charles XI, including the growth of a tier of administration at county level headed by county governors (*landshövdingar*) who had wide powers over the collection of taxes and the mobilization of forces. This more developed administrative system permitted the extended military effort witnessed under Charles XII.[159]

The interdependence of the military and administrative reconstruction carried out in Brandenburg-Prussia by the Great Elector is even more striking, albeit compressed into a shorter chronological period. After 1653, and beginning with his electorate of Brandenburg, Frederick William was gradually able to establish a body of paid officials, principally the *steuerräte*, who administered the excise tax levied on the towns, the proceeds of which were directed towards the support of the army. This system was subsequently extended to his other territories, being expanded especially in times of war. A body of commissars, originally used in connection with the small number of mercenary troops maintained during the Thirty Years War, continued to supervise the military, but their range of functions and numbers were enormously extended, and this military and revenue-raising bureaucracy was fused at the highest level under the control of the *Generalkriegskommissariat*, which oversaw general as well as military administration. By 1688 the Great Elector had an elaborate and uniform network of officials established in all of his dominions to supervise the extraction of taxes, which went to maintain a permanent force of soldiers, who were used when necessary to enforce the payment of revenues. Army and administration had expanded together, and were mutually dependent.[160]

In France the process was rather more drawn out. Beginning with the Thirty Years War, the state consistently fielded numbers of men larger than it could support and administer, provoking often frenetic administrative innovations, including the use of *intendants* and *commissaires* to speed the collection of taxes, and *intendants d'armée, commissaires de guerre* and *contrôleurs* to supervise the supply of troops, their payment, discipline, billeting and movements. Each conflict generated a round of administrative developments which increased the numbers of men who could comfortably be sustained by the state, this number being exceeded in each subsequent conflict, thus leading to further administrative developments.[161]

We need, then, to reassess the mechanism whereby warfare and bureaucratization was linked. Moreover, as the preceding examples, all drawn from the 1630s onwards, suggest, there is little evidence of bureaucratic development taking place on an important scale much before the mid-seventeenth century, certainly if we exclude from consideration those venal offices which were created in the sixteenth century purely as a money-raising device rather than for the purpose of performing any genuine administrative function. It is true that in Piedmont-Savoy Emmanuel Philibert made use of an expanded administrative machine, comprising tax assessors, collectors and army inspectors for the support of his army, but the degree of bureaucratic centralization was highly unusual amongst sixteenth-century states and possible only in one of such a small size. True too that in England a Navy Board was founded in 1546 which was important in overseeing the building, supply and repair of the fleet.[162] But, overall, the number of administrators barely increased in late Tudor England, and here, as elsewhere, the administrative burden of coping with the fiscal and recruiting demands of war was either shouldered by existing administrators – such as the Lords Lieutenant – or it was delegated to private entrepreneurs.

Indeed, what is most striking about the period between *c.* 1500 and *c.* 1650 is not so much the bureaucratic centralization engendered by the demands of war, but rather the *decentralization* which they entailed. Take the provisioning of armies as

an instance. As we noted earlier,[163] the system whereby governments used their medieval rights of purveyance to allow royal
officials to requisition food supplies for the army had been
abandoned by the second half of the sixteenth century in favour
of the employment of private contractors. Not only did this
allow the Crown to economize on the salaries of some officials,
but, most importantly, the contractor extended credit to the
financially hard-pressed government by using his own money to
make the initial purchase, and he would stand the losses for any
food which went rotten. Indeed, not just food and drink but the
supply of every sort of commodity needed by the armies, from
clothing, through arms and munitions, to nails and horseshoes,
as well as their transport arrangements, was either left to the
initiative of the local commander or delegated to private
merchants and *munitionnaires*. Similarly, recruitment was
placed largely in the hands of military contractors and captains,
perhaps backed up by the authority of a local magnate; whilst
the collection of taxes was farmed out to private financiers, who
also supplied the loans which provided the monetary underpinning for the waging of war. All this suggests that we ought to
reassess not just the mechanism whereby war and bureaucratic
development was linked but also the assumption, which has
been implied in preceding examples, that there was always a
link between the two, and that the relationship was a positive
and reciprocal one: military demands produced more efficient
bureaucracies, which allowed the state subsequently to sustain a
greater military effort, and so on.

The case of Habsburg Spain, so brilliantly studied by I. A. A.
Thompson, shows not just that war and bureaucratic development did not always go hand in hand, but that warfare
might have the effect of bringing about the disintegration of
existing administrative structures. The first three decades of
Philip II's rule witnessed, in Castile at least, the development of
a large and efficient royal bureaucracy, which exercised direct
control over all aspects of the military machine. Recruits were
raised, on the direct orders of central government, by nomin-
ated royal captains, and overseen by royal officials who supervised their movement and billeting; a royal commissariat, financed by the treasury, purchased food, clothing and equipment
from producers and arranged for its supply direct to the troops,
thus cutting out the services of the *munitionnaires*; while some

items of heavy equipment, such as cannon, powder and shot, were manufactured in the king's own factories, rather than by private entrepreneurs. Yet, as Thompson clearly shows, this system of direct, centralized administration, which was favoured by the Crown, was already beginning to break down by the 1580s under the pressures of war and war finance, and five decades later it had been totally reversed. By this stage the recruitment and supply of the army, its management and the manufacture of its equipment, had been delegated to great magnates, local authorities and private contractors.[164]

To be sure, we should not ignore the fact that from the middle decades of the seventeenth century onwards the trend amongst many states in Europe was towards the development of bigger and more specialized bureaucracies, capable of mobilizing the demographic and fiscal resources of the state with an unprecedented efficiency. We have noted something of this process in relation to Denmark, Sweden, Brandenburg-Prussia and France. In the latter country a department resembling a war ministry with a staff of civilian administrators existed under Le Tellier, which by the end of the 1680s kept duplicates of all the mass of paperwork generated (a sure sign of bureaucratic development), including the twenty-five bulky sets of detailed instructions sent out on average each year to the army commanders. In Austria, too, a collective board, the *Generalkriegskommissariat*, was set up in 1650 to deal with military matters, the *Generalproviantamt* to oversee troop provisioning following shortly after, both bodies being subordinated in 1675 to a council of war, the *Hofkriegsrat*. In Piedmont-Savoy a War Council came into existence after 1592, and a War Council was formed in Portugal in 1640. In England as well, war was the great catalyst of administrative innovation from the late seventeenth century onwards. Military and fiscal departments burgeoned, so that there were over 2,500 full-time employees in the fiscal bureaucracy by 1690, 4,780 in 1708 and nearly 6,000 by 1716, a remarkable number compared to the 1,200 officials of state who served between 1649 and 1660.[165]

Yet we should not make too much of all this. If the trend was towards war-linked bureaucratization from the mid-decades of the seventeenth century, the pattern was far from uniform. Spain provides the most striking exception, but there were others, including the United Provinces, which witnessed little or no development of this kind. Moreover, when it did take place there was often less to this bureaucratic development than meets the eye. This was notably the case in the Austrian lands, for example. The *Hofskriegsrat* was grossly inefficient and imposed scarcely any centralized control over the fragmented and independent army commands, the forces from Hungary and the unruly frontier fortresses especially remaining outside central direction. In Portugal, too, the establishment of a War Council was not the prelude to a reform of, and greater central control over, the armed forces.[166] Above all, we should not assume that the increase in the number of administrators in itself necessarily provides a good guide to the efficiency of the bureaucracy and the extent of central state control. More crucial in this respect is the question of whether these officials were salaried and dismissable at will, or whether they were venal and held their office as property. It is usually reckoned that the disadvantage of venality of office to a government was the recurrent financial drain incurred by the payment of the salaries, and it was certainly true that where venality was extensive – as in France – it was impossible for the government to find the sums needed to buy back the offices, and in the long term the monies paid out in salaries far exceeded the amount gained from selling the office in the first place.[167] But in many respects the real penalty for the Crown was the loss of control over its own bureaucracy which venality of office entailed. The immovable venal bureaucrats comprised a substantial vested interest. They could block reform, refuse to implement royal directives with which they disagreed, and resist the Crown when its aims clashed with their own interests. Ironically, venality was most widespread in those bellicose countries, such as France, where the financial strains of war were most intense: the long-term disadvantages of venality were disregarded in face of the immediate need for funds. Yet these were countries whose rulers had most need of a loyal and reliable bureaucracy if they were efficiently to exploit the resources of the state.

Nor, finally, should we assume that bureaucratization necessarily meant the end of a devolved system of administration. This might, to some degree, be the case. It was in Brandenburg-Prussia where the assessment and collection of taxes, management of the royal domains and supervision of the army were placed in the hands of salaried royal officials (though for a period in the eighteenth century collection of the excise was farmed out); and it was, to an extent, in post-Restoration England, where, especially after 1688, tax farming was largely eradicated and taxes were collected by a growing body of government officials.[168] But elsewhere, the financing and management of armies remained highly decentralized. The role of the private financier in the raising of revenues remained largely undiminished: indeed in France the financial exigencies of war under Louis XIV made the services of such men ever more necessary. The supply of armies continued to be organized through private contractors, rather than by direct purchase by government officials; and recruiting, if it was taken out of the hands of military contractors, nevertheless remained the concern of captains and colonels, who continued to regard their units as pieces of private, rather than state, property.

What conclusions can be drawn with respect to war and the state? None of this discussion concerning the development of bureaucracies, nor that which preceded it on the estates, the nobility and the uses to which the army might be put, is meant to imply that the waging of war had no effect on the development of the early-modern state. Quite the contrary, for war was probably the most important single factor influencing its growth. The raising of armies and the finances to support them, the most major tasks facing early-modern rulers, created enormous strains and tensions within the body politic, more so than at any previous time, and could not fail but to have an influence on the development of state institutions. However, what is now clear is that the act of waging war did not of itself lead inevitably to a growth of state power. It might do that, by providing a ruler with the opportunity and motive to assert his authority over his subjects, by, for example, suppressing the estates, reducing the nobility, imposing higher and more uniform taxes levied via a royal bureaucracy of enhanced efficiency, and imposing his will by force of arms (though outside of Piedmont-Savoy it is hard to think of an instance where a ruler did all of these things). But on the other hand, the pressures of war could enhance the powers of estates, parliaments and the nobility, lead to a devolution of public, state functions to private individuals who raised finances, recruited troops and arranged their supplies, and generally bring about administrative decentralization. The pressures of waging war could also lead to the growth of a venal bureaucracy with the power to hamper reform and oppose royal decisions, to say nothing of the chaos, disorder and breakdown of royal authority which was engendered by the often widespread and large-scale revolts against high levels of war-induced taxation. Quite how matters would work out in a given state depended on local circumstances: the attitudes and abilities of the ruler; the nature and extent of his dominions; the timing and nature of war's demands, for example. What is certain is that if the effects of waging war on the early-modern state were undeniable, and often profound, they were nevertheless variable. As I. A. A. Thompson notes, 'war was less a stimulant than a test of the state'.[169]

If we accept that war was, above all, a test of the state, one final question needs to be posed: why did some states face up to this test better than others? There can clearly be no easy or simple answer to this. A range of factors might influence the outcome of a particular conflict: whether a state had to fight on a single or on several fronts; the degree of protection it was afforded by natural barriers; the extent of the political commitment to the struggle. But one factor, above all, tended to be decisive: the availability of resources. The long, drawn-out, attritional nature of warfare in the early-modern period, and its spiralling costs, meant that it was, as never before, as much a test of a state's financial staying power as of its purely military strength. As the sixteenth-century Spanish aphorism put it, 'Victory will go to whoever possesses the last *escudo*.'[170]

The high stakes needed to participate in warfare meant that the smaller, interstitial political units, such as the imperial cities of the Holy Roman Empire and the Italian city states, which had held their own quite adequately in the power politics of the late Middle Ages, were barely able to compete at all in the early-modern period. Nuremberg, for example, unable to sustain the military expenditure necessary to compete with the larger territorial states of the Habsburgs, Hohenzollerns and Wittelsbachs (the 1552–4 war with Margrave Albrecht had left her with a crippling debt of 4.5 million *gulden*), found it hard to sustain her autonomy and political independence after the mid-sixteenth century; Siena bankrupted itself in the effort to construct modern fortifications and fell an easy victim to Charles V in 1555; while Venetian influence on European affairs had declined irrevocably by the seventeenth century.[171] Smaller territorial princedoms also found the going difficult. Before about 1650 the rulers of Lorraine and Piedmont-Savoy had been able to retain their territorial independence, if not always their independence of action, only with great difficulty, and in the case of the latter only by the most ruthless exploitation of the state's resources, and both were effectively to become French satellites during the reign of Louis XIV.

Even medium-sized states, such as Denmark and Sweden, found it difficult to compete with the resources of the larger territorial monarchies. The latter provides the most interesting instance of a state which, for a while, was able to mask the basic lack of resources which condemned her to second-class status, and pose for a time as a first-rank power. Sweden's extraordinary military exploits during the Thirty Years War were achieved by getting others to foot the bill, not least of all through a ruthless exploitation of occupied territory in Germany, via the *kontributionssystem*. 'War', declared Gustavus Adolphus, 'must be made to pay for war.'[172] Yet ultimately, all this was sleight of hand. The Baltic empire which Sweden had acquired by 1660 was difficult and expensive to defend, even in peacetime, and cruelly exposed her want of resources; while her dependence upon foreign subsidies tied Sweden to the apron strings of her patrons. Although, as we saw earlier, Charles XI was able, through the *reduktion* of the 1680s, to provide for the defence of the empire and maintain Sweden at the level of a regional, Baltic power, she was never again to display the military predominance which, under Gustavus Adolphus, had temporarily elevated her to the level of a first-rank European power. Europe continued to consist of a plurality of states throughout the early-modern period, but by the last decades of the seventeenth century it was coming increasingly under the influence of a handful of great powers possessing the resources to enable them to wage war on a large scale.

However, if, in general terms, the size of a state's resources determined more completely than ever before its place in the European 'pecking order', resources on their own were no guarantee of dominance. Otherwise the Holy Roman Empire, with its enormous potential of money and men, would have been a major force in European politics – which it was not – and the Spanish Habsburgs of the sixteenth century and the French monarchy of the later seventeenth century, with their unequalled resources, would have achieved an unchallenged mastery within Europe, while states with much smaller resources, including the United Provinces and England under William III and Queen Anne, would not have figured amongst the great powers. Part of the answer to this puzzle lies in the fact that the two biggest power blocs of the early-modern period, the sixteenth-century Habsburg dominions and Louis XIV's France, had to expend their resources on a number of fronts and against a range of enemies who, by the late seventeenth century, were prepared to combine into loose but effective coalitions. But a more important consideration than this, and one which applies equally to all the countries under consideration, was the effectiveness with which a state was able in practice to mobilize its theoretical resources in the service of war. As an English MP put it in 1734–5, having witnessed his country's recent emergence as one of the major military powers of Europe,

> We all know, that what now makes a Nation formidable, is not the Number nor the riches of its Inhabitants, but the number of Ships of War provided with able Seaman [sic], and the number of regular and well disciplined Troops they have at their command.[173]

With the benefit of hindsight it is possible to identify two elements which were above all crucial in a state's ability to mobilize its resources.

Leaving aside *ad hoc* revenue-raising expedients such as the sale of Crown lands, currency debasement and the seizure of Church property and plate, it was taxation which underpinned a state's fiscal ability to wage war. As we noted earlier, taxes were broadly similar in most European states: governments usually eschewed direct taxes on income, and relied instead on direct taxes on land and indirect sales taxes, and there was generally little fundamental alteration in the nature of the tax system between 1500 and 1715. Nevertheless, the extractive capacity of the tax system varied considerably from one country to another. Ideally, the tax base needed to be broad, with no regional or social exemptions; and, second, taxes should be collected efficiently, with no loss to the central exchequer through corruption, tax farming or high fees paid to tax

207

officials, for instance. Nowhere were these ideal conditions met, but some states came closer to them than others.

Although the sixteenth-century Spanish Habsburgs enjoyed 'a wealth of resources that no other European power could match',[174] their tax system was singularly ill-fitted to tap them. Not only did taxes fall least heavily upon the wealthiest, privileged social groups, but important territories over which they ruled, including Catalonia, Valencia, Aragon, the Basque provinces, the Netherlands before 1566 and Portugal after 1580, enjoyed extensive regional privileges which shielded them from the full weight of the tax burden, which was shouldered pre-eminently by Castile and the Italian provinces. Ultimately, these two areas were unable to support the heavy military expenditure of their Imperial rulers, even when some of the pressure was taken off by the inflow of American treasure.

Matters were somewhat better than this in France, though Francis I's boast to the Venetian ambassador that he could tax at will throughout his dominions[175] was certainly unjustified, for here too there were enormous regional and social disparities in the king's ability to levy taxes, which, if they were to some extent eroded by the end of Louis XIV's reign, nevertheless remained very considerable: much of the country remained exempt from the basic land tax, the *taille*; indirect taxes were levied at widely differing rates throughout the kingdom, which was criss-crossed by a plethora of internal revenue barriers; while the only attempts to tax the wealth of all social classes, through the emergency wartime measures of the *capitation* (1695) and *dixième* (1710) proved only partially successful. Moreover, the tax administration remained enormously wasteful, despite the undoubted improvements made to it by ministers such as Sully, Colbert and Pontchartrain, which however stopped well short of thoroughgoing reform. Much potential revenue was lost through the practice of tax farming and revenue anticipation,[176] as well as through corruption and fraud which was an especially marked feature of venal bureaucracies, and receipt and issue of government monies remained decentralized. All this is not of course to deny that the French tax system was capable of generating enormous sums of money: the sheer extent of his resources meant that the French king would always enjoy a hefty income. In the 1620s Louis XIII got as much from the province of Normandy as Charles I obtained from all his ordinary revenues, and overall the French king drew a revenue roughly six times as large as that of his English counterpart from a population only four times as big.[177] Relative to the regime in the Habsburg Austrian lands, the French tax system was an effective one. Here, even under the more 'absolutist' rule of Ferdinand III (1637–57) and his successors, social and provincial privilege proved a yet more severe impediment than in France to the levying of taxes: proposals for an imperial excise tax which kept reappearing after 1660 always foundered on the rocks of provincialism and opposition of the social elites, for example.[178] And collection of taxes was extraordinarily slow, corrupt and decentralized. Nevertheless, this should not obscure the fact that, even in what many would regard under Louis XIV as the most absolute regime in Europe, the French tax system was wasteful, inefficient, hampered by social and provincial privilege, and capable of tapping the resources of the state with only partial success.

By contrast, the tax regime in the United Provinces was capable of much greater fiscal extraction. To be certain, in respect of their tax system the Dutch were not the model of financial probity for which they are often acclaimed. The individual provinces which made up the state exerted a jealous control of their financial machinery, and monies for the central government were often voted late and with reluctance. The taxes themselves were complex – William Temple claimed that a fish dish eaten in Holland might have paid thirty different excises before it reached the table[179] – and tax farming was common. However, some of these disadvantages were more apparent than real. Since the province of Holland footed by far the largest proportion of Dutch war costs (between 1689 and 1714 it met nearly 60 per cent of the Republic's war expenditure), provincial control of war finance was not as disastrous as it might otherwise have been. Though taxes were farmed, there was no sprawling venal bureaucracy to drain state revenues. And taxes were easy to levy in some respects, since the two richest provinces, Holland and Zeeland, were both highly urbanized, and their wealth was predominantly in the form of trade and commerce. Moreover, tax rates could be high (a contemporary estimate suggested that one-third of income in Holland went in indirect taxes),[180] without, however, provoking outright resistance, in part because the taxpayers themselves gave assent to these levels of tax via the local representative institutions, the estates, rather than having them imposed arbitrarily by princely whim.[181]

Finally, and also standing in contrast to the French situation, there was England. Before the late seventeenth and early eighteenth century, when she emerged as a major military power, England's financial weakness meant that she was able to perform only as a bit-player on the European military stage. As the French agent, Dumoulin, commented in 1627, the English 'wish to make war against heaven and earth, but they lack the means to make it against anyone.'[182] It is true that England possessed certain advantages in the fiscal sphere over her continental neighbours: there were no regional and only limited social immunities to taxation; state revenues were spared the drain resulting from a large venal bureaucracy; and her growing wealth in the seventeenth century, largely deriving from commerce, was liquid, and hence easier to tax. However, these advantages remained potential rather than actual until after the Civil War. Before then, central government lacked the overriding will and the administrative machinery to impose high levels of tax. The English Crown had no permanent land tax on which to draw, and for its ordinary revenues depended on patchy and wholly inadequate sources: the yield from Crown lands, feudal dues and the customs granted by Parliament, with, in addition, occasional parliamentary subsidies raised by means of self-assessed taxes. All this changed in the aftermath of the 'English Revolution' of 1640–60. The Church ceased to tax itself; tax farming was gradually abolished; Parliament gave the Crown permanent revenues in the form of customs, excise and land taxes; taxes were levied nationally and at uniform rates, and were collected by an expanded body of administrators under the central control of the Treasury; and, as in the case of the Dutch, tax levels could be high because they were assented to by the taxpayers' representative body, Parliament.[183] Although these changes occurred only gradually, and the tax system remained far from perfect, nevertheless it was by 1700 a more effective revenue-raising machine than anything to be found on the continent, and transformed the finances of the English state. Between 1689 and 1714 tax revenues trebled in England, outstripping their growth in Holland and Austria where they doubled, and in France, where they remained more or less stagnant, making the English one of the most heavily taxed people in Europe.[184] This growth in tax revenues was crucial in allowing England to meet the escalating costs of war and emerge as a major military power during the late seventeenth and early eighteenth centuries.

However, to focus on their tax systems is to give only a partial answer as to why some states were more effective than others in mobilizing their resources in the service of war. For nowhere were tax revenues on their own sufficient to meet the costs of waging war. The gap between revenue and expenditure was bridged, as we have seen, by a variety of devices, including currency debasement, sale of office and seizure of Church lands, but, with the exception of Prussia, it was credit which was most crucial in this respect. The *ancien régime* monarchies have commonly been condemned for their resort to borrowing, a view perhaps stemming from studies of the French Revolution which have emphasized the part played by the Crown's fiscal profligacy in bringing about its collapse, but in fact there was nothing necessarily disastrous about the resort to credit: it was the terms under which it was obtained which were crucial. Even more than taxation, state borrowing varied widely in cost and efficiency, and was closely correlated to military effectiveness.

At one end of the spectrum was late seventeenth- and early eighteenth-century Austria, which was capable of borrowing only relatively small sums. Thus, a mere 22 million florins was raised by the Treasury during fifteen years of conflict in the last two decades of the seventeenth century.[185] Foreign loans in particular were raised with great difficulty, for the monarchy was a notably poor credit risk, and although domestic borrowing was more successful, loans were contracted at ruinous terms from a small group of mainly Jewish financiers whose grip on the fiscal machinery of the state only began to be loosened with the foundation of the independently administered Vienna City Bank in 1706.

Both the French and the Spanish monarchies, on the other hand, were able to make much greater use of loans. During Henry II's reign, for example, some 6,800,000 *livres* was raised through the sale of *rentes*,[186] while the scale of the borrowing by Charles V and Philip II, which we noted earlier, has become almost legendary. However, in both countries the monarchy was obliged to contract many of its debts short-term and at high rates of interest, which nudged 49 per cent for a brief period under Charles V. The loans were commonly irredeemable, which locked the government into paying these high rates indefinitely, even when interest rates generally had fallen, a pattern which could only be broken by the Crown repudiating the debts, a manoeuvre which, however, meant that subsequently funds became even harder to raise. Moreover, although both monarchies were able to tap the resources of the wider public, by getting them to invest in government bonds, they nevertheless remained heavily dependent upon the great financiers, who extracted a heavy price for their services.

By contrast, the United Provinces were able to raise loans with an apparently consummate facility, notably in the seventeenth century, an important factor in their ability to maintain the struggle against Spain and, subsequently, the France of Louis XIV. The province of Holland alone had a debt of 153 million florins in 1651, compared with an official debt for the whole of the Netherlands of 10 million in 1565. To be sure, matters were never quite as easy as they appeared, but, unlike the credit system in France and Spain, that in the United Provinces was never in danger of collapse, war loans were always available when needed, and so secure was Dutch credit that it was possible to reduce the interest rate from 10 per cent in 1600 to 4 per cent in 1655, while still attracting sufficient funds.[187]

Standing alongside the United Provinces, at the opposite end of the spectrum to Austria, was England. Although the English credit system developed more falteringly than is often supposed during the last quarter of the seventeenth century, it nevertheless demonstrated a remarkable capacity to raise war loans from the late 1680s onwards. Between 1688 and 1713 a staggering £46 million was obtained, accounting for roughly one-third of all government expenditure, at rates of interest of about 6–8 per cent; while during the rest of the eighteenth century far larger sums were raised on even more advantageous terms. Though contemporaries expressed some anxiety at the growing size of the national debt, the credit system never faltered, and proved as consistently capable as that of the Dutch of generating long-term loans at low rates of interest, which provided the mainstay of the war effort, leading one contemporary in 1783 to observe that wars were no longer fought 'at the charge of the present generation, but at the charge of posterity'.[188]

How, then, can we explain these wide variations in the use, cost and efficiency of credit by early-modern states? In the case of the Dutch one may point to the fact that not only was theirs a prosperous country, but since much of its wealth was derived from commerce and international finance it was in liquid form, and there was thus no lack of money for investment in government loans. A poorer state, with an agrarian-based economy, such as Austria, simply could not compete in this respect. Moreover, the habit and the techniques of credit transactions were already well established across a wide social spectrum by the early sixteenth century, most notably in Holland and Zeeland, and investing in government bonds came as a natural extension to this. In England, too, the economy was expanding from the middle decades of the seventeenth century, while the techniques of public borrowing appear to have been quite consciously imported from the United Provinces during the rule of William III. Additionally, in the 1680s the English enjoyed the unusual advantage that, not having been involved in extensive warfare previously, the state was not burdened with the repayment of large accumulated debts.[189]

Important though these factors were, however, it was ultimately the confidence of investors in the soundness of their investment which explains the superior ability of the Dutch and English governments to mobilize credit. Because investors had confidence that their capital could be redeemed, and that interest would be paid regularly and in full, they were prepared to lend long-term and at low rates of interest; the government was able to attract capital not just from financiers but from a wider investing public; and it could carry indefinitely a long-term debt which was well in excess of its annual income from tax revenues. Investor confidence rested in part upon the knowledge that the superior tax systems of these two states produced not only substantial but regular revenues, which were earmarked for debt service.[190] It was also founded on the knowledge that tax funds would not be diverted, nor interest payments suspended or reduced, because these had been guaranteed by parliamentary bodies – the estates in the United Provinces and Parliament in England – which not only included amongst their numbers, and were representative of, the taxpayers and investors, but which also controlled public policy, and could therefore pledge the resources of a whole province or kingdom.[191] The state's subjects thus had a collective responsibility for the state's debts, and in this sense the debts were public ones. This had certainly not been the case in England before the Glorious Revolution of 1688. Prior to this date state debts were private, in that they were ultimately secured on the promise of the king, and hence were only as good – or as bad – as the word of the king. As a correspondent of the Duke of Buckingham complained in 1627: 'All the revenue is anticipated for the next whole year, which being so, the farmers and such like bonds are little worth, for the king may break all these assignments at his own will, and where, then, shall they be paid?'[192]

Outside of the United Provinces and England, in those major states where princely power remained relatively untrammelled, state debts always had been, and remained, guaranteed by the word of the ruler. 'Wages, pensions, huge loans and arrears on *rentes* are attached to the king', noted a French royalist pamphleteer in 1700. 'Should the monarchy totter, all this wealth would be endangered.'[193] In seeking to advance a case for rallying around the monarchy in time of national emergency, the writer inadvertently pointed to the dangers of placing money with the king. It is true that the French Crown used a hodge-podge of semi-public bodies and other institutions, such as the provincial estates, the Church, large municipalities and associations of tax farmers, to float loans and generally handle its financial operations. But none of these bodies controlled public policy, and none was capable of underwriting debts by pledging the resources of the kingdom; in the last resort, therefore, the debts remained the obligation of the king.[194] Only during one brief period did matters seem likely to change, following Colbert's foundation of a state deposit bank, the *caisse des emprunts*, in 1674. This guaranteed depositors their money on demand and paid 5 per cent interest. But it was closed after the minister's death in 1683 and loan repayments once again became, in the traditional manner, dependent on the pleasure of the king.[195] Given the financial history of the Crown, which had a long record of bankruptcies, defaults, arbitrary reduction of interest rates and creditor manipulations of all kinds, it is unsurprising that it found it difficult to borrow except under extremely disadvantageous conditions. Indeed, one might suggest that the more the king claimed absolute powers, the less likely investors were to trust him with their money, since there was nothing to prevent him breaking faith with his creditors.[196]

The instance of Spain also shows how difficult it was for a powerful monarchy to develop a long-term funded debt, because of the difficulty of inspiring investor confidence. During the reign of Philip II the so-called 'bankruptcy' decrees, of 1557, 1575 and 1594, sought to convert much of the Crown's short-term, high-interest debt into long-term annuities, or *juros*, paying 5 per cent or thereabouts, a tactic which was to be repeated by his successors. Largely by this means the state managed to increase the value of outstanding *juros* from 5 million *ducats* in 1515 to 83 million in 1600. Remarkably, there was never any suspension of interest payments on these *juros* during the sixteenth century, and the Crown appeared to be groping its way towards a permanent system of long-term funded state debt, a process which would undoubtedly have been helped had the proposal for a state bank, which would have kept borrowing within prudent limits and marshalled cheap credit for the Crown, ever come to fruition. Yet in the end nothing ever came of all this, and the major reason for this failure was the continuing doubts amongst potential investors about the reliability of the Crown. For although interest payments on *juros* were maintained in the sixteenth century, the bankruptcy decrees forcibly converted existing debts into *juros*, and investors could thus not be certain that the Crown would not unilaterally renege on its obligations to creditors in the future. Confidence in the good faith of the monarchy was wholly undermined during the reigns of Philip III and Philip IV when both monarchs defaulted on interest payments, with the result that sales of *juros*, which had achieved some popularity in the sixteenth century, virtually collapsed.[197]

To be sure, one should not overstate the contrasts between the major powers in their use of credit. If the province of Holland in the seventeenth century carried a public debt which was about twelve times as large as the annual tax revenues which sustained it, and the British debt-to-tax ratio in 1713 was of the order of 8 : 1, the Spanish Crown's debt under Philip II and his two immediate successors was equivalent to somewhere between ten and fifteen times annual revenues, while the ratio was even greater in the case of France by the end of Louis XIV's reign.[198] The real points to note, however, are that neither the Spanish nor the French monarchies could sustain this high level of debt indefinitely. Moreover, they were unable to mobilize credit in a smooth, regular fashion, by increasing borrowing on favourable terms as circumstances demanded. Instead, each bankruptcy, interest default and debt repudiation disrupted the smooth flow of funds, and the war effort suffered setbacks as a result of the shortage and erratic supply of money.

Clearly, we should not imagine that finances were the sole determinant of a country's fate in the early-modern period. Nevertheless, they were the crucial factor enabling a state to meet the 'test' of war. Given that absolute monarchies are generally viewed as emerging in response to, and best able to cope with, the demands of war, there is a certain irony in the fact that it was the constitutional states of the United Provinces and Britain, which, precisely because they had forms of parliamentary government, were better able to generate the finances needed to sustain war than the more absolutist monarchies of Spain, France and Austria.

WAR AND THE ECONOMY

If war's implications for society and the state were profound, what of its impact upon the economy? 'Warfare', wrote Hermann Kellenbenz, 'plays a crucial role in any assessment of the seventeenth-century European economy',[199] a judgement shared by other economic historians and one which would be extended to include the preceding century. However, there has been much less agreement on the nature of that role. Any effort to generalize about the impact of war on economic life must perforce begin by noting the prodigious, and unprecedented, resources of manpower, raw materials and capital which were required to fuel wars in the early-modern period. But did this demand stimulate or retard economic activity, and was this across the whole economic sector or just in a few spheres? Did warfare divert resources from 'productive' to 'unproductive' uses? And were resources found at the expense of civilian industries or by mobilizing hitherto under-used resources?

Such questions are easiest to answer with respect to the manpower demands of armies. There were occasional com-

216

plaints from manufacturers and administrators concerning labour shortages caused by military recruitment. For example, an Italian *consulta* of 1641 blamed armies for luring 'an infinite number of artisans' into service in the hope of 'an easier life and glory'.[200] Overall, however, there is little evidence of recruitment having adverse economic or demographic effects. Nor is this surprising, for the number of soldiers as a proportion of the total population, while impossible to calculate with accuracy given the unreliability of military and population statistics in the early-modern period and the difficulty of making allowance for the numbers of 'foreign' troops and those serving in militias, was certainly low. Even on the improbable assumption that French forces in the mid-sixteenth century numbered as many as 50,000, and that these were all native Frenchmen, this nevertheless represented only 0.29 per cent of the overall population of 17 million, scarcely more than the 0.25 per cent which Contamine suggests for the late fifteenth century.[201] To be sure, levels of participation rose during the seventeenth century, as military manpower demands grew and populations stagnated. A military participation ratio of 1.6 per cent may be posited for France by 1710 for example,[202] though the mean figure for most European states seems to have been rather less than 1 per cent.[203] Moreover, the regional impact of recruiting was sometimes greater than these crude overall figures would suggest. For example, a substantial proportion of the Englishmen sent to fight abroad between 1591 and 1602 were drawn from the southern counties, especially Kent, which alone furnished 6,000 recruits, representing some 4 per cent of the county's population.[204] Nevertheless, sustained recruiting on this level was unusual. Recruitment ratios generally remained low in the seventeenth century; and, most importantly, recruits continued to be drawn overwhelmingly from the economically unproductive sectors of society, such as the unemployed or semi-employed and the destitute. This, and the overcrowded state of the labour market, meant that even the greater numbers being siphoned off by the armies of the later seventeenth century did not result in any serious economic dislocation.

There were, however, a limited number of exceptions to this overall picture. In Castile the recurrent demands of the recruiting sergeant year after year during the reigns of Philip II and Philip III, coupled with emigration to the New World and the plagues of the late 1590s, appear to have played a role in the rural depopulation and shortage of agricultural labour and taxpayers which so concerned contemporaries by the early seventeenth century.[205] But most severely affected was Sweden, a tiny country of only some 1.5 million inhabitants, whose Age of Greatness was made possible only by a ruthless and ultimately unsustainable exploitation of manpower resources. A recruitment ratio of between 3 and 4 per cent in the century after 1620 may be suggested,[206] with some regions of the country being especially burdened. Thus the Grand Duchy of Finland provided some 25,000 men for Charles XII's wars against Russia, which was 6–7 per cent of its total population of 400,000 and represented one-quarter of all males between 16 and 60.[207] Few of those drafted for active service in Sweden's wars ever returned home. Losses in Poland and Germany between 1633 and 1648 have been estimated at over 100,000, and Lindegren's detailed study of the parish of Bygdeå shows just how serious sustained depopulation of this level was. The parish provided 236 recruits between 1621 and 1639, of whom 215 died while in the armies, only 6 returning home and 5 of these as cripples. Over the course of those eighteen years the population of the parish fell from around 1900 to below 1700, and its balance was altered. The number of adult males nearly halved, and, if old men and children are left out of account, women outnumbered men by 3 : 2. The number of households with a female head had increased sevenfold, and the shortage of labour on the farms was becoming acute.[208]

Rather more difficult to estimate is the effect of military demand for food and manufactured goods upon agricultural and industrial production. The best evidence that this served to stimulate output comes, not surprisingly, from the armaments industry. Orders for weapons and munitions were frequently on a huge scale. The Dutch States-General, for example, spent 1,200,000 *guilders* in re-equipping its forces with standardized firearms in 1599; and in 1648 the Austrians, by no means one of the biggest government spenders, placed orders for 4,000 bombs, 5,000 quintals of powder, 10,000 quintals of shot, 100,000 grenades, 3,000 quintals of match and 25,000 assorted swords, lances and knives.[209] Established manufacturers, such as the Pögl family in Germany, and existing manufacturing areas were the first to profit from this increased demand. The armourers of Innsbruck, Augsburg and Landshut vied with Milan in the sixteenth century, the latter producing increasing quantities of the common-service armour needed by the infantry rather than the finely chiselled suit armour on which its reputation had been founded. It could not however match Brescia and the Val Gardone as the Italian centre of gun making, which by mid-century was exporting 25,000 guns annually under licence. Production also expanded considerably in the neutral bishopric of Liège, and the small-arms industry of Vizcaya and Guipùzcoa grew by over 50 per cent in the two decades before 1590, so that by 1591 it was capable of turning out annually some 20,000 arquebuses, 3,000 muskets, and as many pikes as necessary to meet demand.[210]

New centres of production also developed. Probably because of its high phosphate content the ore mined in the Ashdown Forest produced iron of unusual strength, and cannon were being cast in considerable numbers in this area by the mid-sixteenth century, English artillery enjoying an international reputation for a time; while in 1648 an arms factory was set up at Brobyvaerk in Denmark, the backers including several noblemen as well as merchants. Not infrequently governments sought to foster the growth of a native arms industry for strategic reasons. The most conspicuously successful ruler in this respect was Gustavus Adolphus of Sweden, who encouraged the immigration of skilled artisans from Hesse, Brabant and elsewhere, and placed the overall control of the industry in the capable hands of the *Liègois* emigrant Louis de Geer. By 1627, Sweden was not only self-sufficient in arms production, but was becoming a major exporter: nearly 2,000 metric tons of cannon were sold abroad by the 1660s compared to only some 20 tons four decades previously. Nancy too flourished for a while in the sixteenth century under the benign patronage of the Dukes of Lorraine; and there were important attempts at government sponsorship, involving the importation of skilled foreign labour and the establishment of state arsenals, in seventeenth-century France, notably by Sully and Colbert. To be sure, too much government interference and regulation could serve to inhibit growth, as seems to have been the case in France for example. And the development of centres of armaments production in one part of Europe was often counterbalanced by their decline in another. Thus the Swedish arms industry grew, in part, at the expense of the Liège gun-makers; by 1700 the manufacture of small-arms and common armour had largely ceased at Milan; and the Brescian industry entered a period of decline after 1600, so that by the first half of the eighteenth century a few small enterprises were all that remained in this once thriving area.[211] Yet, if the existence of a high level of overall demand did not guarantee the survival and prosperity everywhere of an armaments industry, there can be little doubt that in general the manufacture of weapons and munitions was considerably stimulated during the early-modern period.

Nor was it the only manufacturing sector to benefit in this way. During the second half of the seventeenth century the textile industry in various countries expanded on the basis of government orders for bulk supplies of military clothing. Under Colbert the industry at Romortain in the *Orléanais* grew; the manufacturers of Jonköping, Alingses, Norköping and Stockholm expanded production, the latter being capable of turning out 6,000 ells of cloth per month under Charles XII; and in Brandenburg-Prussia military orders laid the basis for a growth in the textile industry which by the end of Frederick William I's reign employed some 18 per cent of all workers involved in manufacturing industry. Army demand provided a boost for the shoe-making industry at Northampton after 1650; and there was an increase in production by the brewing industry during the English Civil War, though it is unclear to what extent this was obtained simply by watering the original. The brick-making, quarrying and building industries benefited from the construction of fortresses, which consumed enormous quantities of raw materials. The brick works around Lille, for example, were called upon to supply some 60 million bricks for the town's citadel in the late 1660s, while a local quarry provided over three and a half million pieces of stone for the foundations. And the records of the Spanish Treasury reveal a steady outflow of money to local contractors and suppliers in the Netherlands after 1572, who, by and large, were regularly and fully paid for work they did in excavating and building a multiplicity of urban defence-works.[212]

There are, finally, some indications that agricultural production expanded to meet military needs. The dairying industry around Whitby and Stockton appears to have benefited from purchases made by Charles I's forces during the Bishops' War, for example, but a more regular source of demand was provided by garrison troops. The monthly allocation of the 20,000-man garrison at Calais in 1524 was 2,500 quarters of wheat, over £1,500 worth of bread, 5,600 quarters of beercorn and 28 thousand-weight of hops, while the requirements of the Berwick garrison were of a similar order. These amounts were not necessarily delivered in full, of course, but the level of demand was nevertheless high, and much of it was met by purchases from East Anglia. Norfolk supplied half the grain for Berwick and two-thirds of that for France, while Kent played a preponderant part in the supply of livestock. Indeed, Alan Everitt has argued that army victualling stimulated the export industry, surplus supplies being diverted for sale abroad.[213] Similarly, Frederick Corner, in his report to the Venetian Senate on the effect of the late seventeenth-century wars against the Turks in Hungary, pointed to the stimulus which agriculture outside the war zone had received, and to the profits derived by large landowners in particular. 'The charges of the present war', he wrote,

> although they appear overwhelming to many because of the weight of taxes, are nevertheless compensated by the convenience of the rivers, which are used for transporting everything needful to the army in Hungary, allowing the great lords to augment their revenues, and bringing riches and treasure to Vienna.[214]

Yet we should not make too much of all this. Agricultural production in particular was relatively inelastic in early-modern Europe – not surprisingly since it was dominated by small-holding, subsistence producers. Overall there is little evidence that military victualling needs were met through increasing output – by taking in marginal lands and using new techniques, for example. Instead, army victuallers made large-scale purchases on the open market of foodstuffs normally destined for civilian consumption, purchases which frequently disrupted the commercial life of market towns and caused local shortages. Thus in 1586 there were hunger riots in Hampshire and Gloucestershire, and in Ipswich a crowd demonstrated against the shipment of cattle to the Netherlands, in the wake of state purchases for the forces in Ireland, the Low Countries and the Channel Islands; while the mayor of Chester complained in 1595 of the local dearth and high prices which had resulted from purchases by George Beverley, a victualler for the Irish troops.[215]

Secondly, we need to bear in mind the relatively low level of demand from the military. Although precise figures will never be available, and with the important exception of munitions, it seems unlikely that military demand for clothing, footwear, building materials and food and drink was anywhere near as substantial as that provided by the expansion of overseas trade, and by the growing population of the sixteenth century, even when allowance is made for the fact that much of the demand from this burgeoning population was 'ineffective' because of its poverty. To be sure, the military–civilian balance, although still incalculable, was nevertheless clearly weighted much more heavily in favour of the former with respect to the demand for metal goods. Armies and fortresses needed not just heavy cannon of iron and bronze, muskets and arquebuses, pikes, swords and armour, but entrenching tools, hatchets, metal wheel rims and metal strappings for carts and harness. For example, the Italian ironmaster Francesco Zignone obtained a contract in 1636 for the supply to the Spanish forces in Lombardy, not just of shells and grenades, but of 6,050 axes, 7,028 shovels, and 50 metric tons of nails, together with other 'sundry hardware'.[216] But while war probably consumed a sizeable proportion of Europe's output of iron and copper and lead, an output which, if growing, was nevertheless modest – total iron production for example was only about 100,000 tons by 1600[217] – we should not overstate the proportion by exaggerating the military demand for metal. Much military hardware was durable and could be expected to last over many campaigns, the more so since sizeable quantities of arms and armour were stockpiled, and brought out only in time of emergency before being returned to the safety of a storeroom. Much hardware was anyway recycled: armour and weaponry was scavenged by soldiers from the dead, pawned, or returned at the end of a campaign to the regimental chest whence it had first come; heavy guns which had blown up or become outdated were melted down and recast; the same happened to looted church bells (technically an army's master of artillery had first claim on the bells of a town taken by assault); even cannon balls could be dug out from masonry and earthworks to be re-used. Moreover, if military demand for metal was increasing, particularly in the seventeenth century, so too was civilian demand. Lead was needed for roofing and for pipes; iron for a range of domestic utensils, from pots and pans to clocks, as well as for manufacturing machinery; while the copper currency employed at different times by Spain and Sweden consumed prodigious quantities of the metal.

It should also be noted that any additional output generated to meet military demand was produced at constant returns to scale, for there is little sign that the extra goods required proportionately less labour or raw materials, or were cheaper to produce. Military demand did not, for example, lead to inventions which reduced the costs of the manufacturing process. It is true that there were technological innovations in the early-modern period: machines for wire drawing, slitting sheets, a knitting frame invented in 1598 and a ribbon frame in 1604; while the indirect method of smelting iron ore in the blast furnace, which was more economical than the open hearth or shaft furnace, came into use early in the sixteenth century in the Valsassina region of Italy.[218] But neither this, nor any of the other innovations, was the result of any stimulus provided by war. Nor, by and large, did military demand lead to radical changes in the organization of industry, such as the establishment of large-scale manufacturing enterprises, for example, which might have improved its productiveness. Government sponsorship and control, especially of arms and munitions manufacture, occasionally seemed to point in this direction: witness the development of the gun-making industry in Sweden under Louis de Geer, Sully's efforts to concentrate the production of cannon, firearms and gunpowder in eighteen state arsenals, and the monopolistic licence granted to John Evelyn for the manufacture of gunpowder in mills around London.[219] But, with the exception of Sweden, and there only for a limited period, government intervention of this kind was ineffective and actually inhibited production, and it was generally found best to leave the manufacturing process in private hands. And this meant in multifarious hands, for whether it was the smelting of iron ore, the production of gun barrels, stocks, pike staves, swords or gunpowder, or the weaving of cloth for uniforms, the manufacturing process remained localized, artisanal and small-scale. Indeed, one of the chief features of the productive process in early-modern Europe was the small size and large number of the units of production.[220] Only with respect to the naval dockyards did war demands create large complex organizations, employing substantial numbers of workers, capable of co-ordinating many different processes and arranging the supply of a wide range of different items, to produce a single object, the warship. And even in this respect war-related demand was not a necessary prerequisite for the growth of large-scale dockyard enterprises: witness the huge Dutch shipbuilding industry, largely centred on the river Zaan, which mainly grew out of the peacetime demands of the fishing industry and the merchant fleet.[221] All this is not, of course, to deny that the supply of armies and fortresses with goods and services, and the other fiscal transactions associated with the conduct of war, allowed the accumulation of capital in the hands of financiers, money-lenders, tax farmers, arms dealers and *munitionnaires* of all sorts; but of itself war called forth no new financial techniques and no novel methods of industrial organization.

And finally, of course, against the stimulus which certain industries received from the growing demands of the military we need to set the losses engendered by the physical damage done by war and the dislocation which it caused to trade and industry. Establishing the extent of these losses is fraught with difficulties, not least of all because war's responsibility cannot easily be disentangled from other, purely economic, factors. For example, it is unclear how far the decline of Spain's textile industry was due to the general European recession of the 1590s and the 1620s and a state system of regulations, controls and dues which operated against the interests of the native trader, and how much must be ascribed to the conflict with the Dutch.[222] Similarly, Antwerp's prosperity was certainly damaged by the disastrous sack of the city in 1576, to the benefit of its rival Amsterdam, but there were clear signs of decline before this date; and who knows whether Amsterdam, which was already growing fat on the profits of banking and trade with the Baltic, the Mediterranean and the New World, might not have made yet greater economic headway had it not been obliged to cope with the strains of war.[223]

Yet even if the extent cannot be precisely determined, there is, nevertheless, a wealth of evidence that war, or the threat of it, dislocated commerce by disrupting established trade routes and trading patterns. A sheep dealer from Sherbourne, for example, complained of the widespread consternation caused by the Armada, '[which] put your Highness's subjects in so sudden a maze as your said subject could neither sell such things as he had, nor by any means borrow any money to make satisfaction according to his good-will therein'.[224] The customs dues levied at Gottorp and Rendsborg, which permit an accurate measurement of the export of cattle from the north-west coastal area of the Baltic, reveal that the trade, amounting to some 40,000 head annually in the 1620s, was seriously interrupted on subsequent occasions by outbreaks of fighting.[225] Similarly, grain exports from Danzig fluctuated violently during the sixteenth and seventeenth centuries, reflecting not just the condition of the harvest but the uncertainty caused by war. They collapsed altogether during the Polish king's siege of the city in 1577; plummeted in the 1620s as a result of the Swedish–Polish wars and the Swedish blockade of 1626–9; and were seriously reduced yet again between 1655 and 1660 during further fighting between the two powers.[226] War also disrupted the commerce in salt between France and the Baltic: shipments between 1574 and 1578 were less than one-quarter what they had been between 1562 and 1566.[227] And Dutch trade suffered considerably as a result of the Spanish embargo after 1621 – a reminder that the dislocation of commerce was not always an incidental by-product of war but was, albeit occasionally, used as a means of pursuing hostilities in its own right.[228] To be sure, trade could be redirected to avoid war-torn areas; and rival producers might step in to make good the losses. Thus Hanseatic merchants began to supply Spain with goods and services previously provided by the Dutch after the virtual cessation of commerce between the two.[229] But the re-routing of trade inevitably increased freight and insurance rates and implied a loss of competitive 'edge'; and the extent to which rivals were available or able to stand in should not be exaggerated.

With respect to the physical destruction of the means of production, agriculture was probably less severely affected by war than manufacturing enterprise. Although soldiers drove off animals, the main source of manure, the fact that peasants abandoned their land at an army's approach, sometimes leaving it untilled and fallow for many months, may, perversely, have improved its fertility. The real key to the revival of agriculture in the post-war years was capital for the purchase of new seed, livestock and tools, and when this was available agriculture picked up again remarkably quickly. With it came the revival of local towns, whose economy was often heavily dependent upon the prosperity of the countryside. Many urban figures, such as lawyers, bailiffs, tax officials, judges and clerics, drew their income from the countryside in the form of fees, seigneurial dues, rents and tithes; while the livelihood of a large section of the urban working class, who produced simple manufactured goods – pots and pans, harness, shoes, and other domestic artefacts – depended upon the purchasing power of the peasantry. Rural renewal was thus accompanied by a revival in the fortunes of local urban centres. On the other hand, the physical destruction of equipment seems to have been more damaging to the long-term prospects of manufacturing enterprises, presumably because the equipment concerned was usually more complex and expensive than that involved in agriculture. Again, one should not exaggerate the case. Recovery in the iron-producing region of Valsassina was swift following the destruction of furnaces and forges by the Duke of Rohan's French forces in 1636. But matters were not always so happily resolved. It was a severe blow to the production of paper at Essonnes when, in 1562, Huguenot troops threw the mills into the river. Similarly, textile production in Flanders and Brabant was irreparably damaged by the Dutch Revolt. The clothworks of Hondschoote were finally razed to the ground by French soldiers, having changed hands six times between 1578 and 1582, and production virtually ceased at other textiles centres, such as Dixmuide, Eecke, Menin and Poperinghe, during the 1580s. Though there was some revival in the following century these centres never fully recovered from the devastation of the 1580s. And large-scale sugar refining in Antwerp seems to have collapsed in the aftermath of the destruction of machinery during the sack of 1576.[230]

Finally, can it be argued that warfare diverted capital into unproductive uses, such as the building of fortresses, the manufacture of weapons and investment in government bonds and loans, thus tying up funds which would otherwise have gone into trade and manufacture? Overall, no. There is no doubt that a higher rate of return on capital could be obtained by investing in, say, government loans, which were floated principally to finance warfare, than in industry and commerce. But if anything was denying funds to industry it was not this, but contemporaries' lack of disposition to invest in trade and manufacture, and the alternative investment of land, which, although it offered a relatively low return of only about 4 per cent per annum, was nevertheless the most solid of securities as well as a source of prestige.[231] In fact, however, there is little evidence that early-modern industry was starved of cash: it was not, by and large, capital intensive, but rather labour intensive. Moreover, we should be sceptical of the view that money channelled into war, either indirectly through government loans or bonds, or directly, through soldiers' pay, equipment and the building of fortresses, was necessarily unproductive. After all, much of this money found its way back into the economy. Soldiers spent their pay on goods and services; quarry workers, textile producers and armaments manufacturers profited from government contracts; not inconsiderable numbers of labourers were given employment in building fortresses (there were 6,000 reported working at the site of the new fortress at Frascarolo in 1657, and this was but one of some ten forts in the state of Milan being rebuilt or newly constructed at this time);[232] and, as Sella has shown in the case of Lombardy, some of the profits made by financiers and others out of government loans, tax farming and office was reinvested in the economy, particularly in rural industry which was here the most dynamic and resilient sector of the economy.[233] Indeed, it has been argued, by Sombart for example,[234] that war, by offering opportunities for the accumulation of capital in the hands of financiers, war contractors and profiteers, served to transfer command of capital resources to men more likely than, say, peasants or landowners, to use them in wealth-producing ways. We should be sceptical about accepting such a judgement wholesale, not least of all because it understates the willingness of financiers, no less than other wealthy members of society, to put money into land and socially prestigious items of conspicuous consumption such as clothes, houses and carriages; and it understates too the preparedness of landowners, patricians, churchmen and others often classed as parasitic to invest in economic growth.[235] But it seems undeniable that war served to recycle capital resources, and that in some instances it could unlock resources which would otherwise have remained frozen, by, for example, bringing land on to the open market. Church lands plundered by

Henry VIII were later sold to pay for his French wars. Alienated Crown lands helped to finance Sweden's wars in Germany. And in Denmark the costs of defence and the growing impoverishment of the peasantry – itself a consequence of war – led to the sale of Crown estates on a massive scale after about 1650. Prior to 1675 land to the value of *c.* 7 million *rigsdaler* had been disposed of, and by 1680 over one-third of all land in the kingdom had been transferred in this way.[236]

However, there is more of a case for arguing that high levels of taxation, brought about by rulers' perpetual need for money to fight wars, did have adverse economic consequences, though the picture in this respect remains far from clear. Thus high taxation has been blamed for the parlous state of agriculture in many parts of Europe, for example Castile, where taxes and other dues might account for 50 per cent of the peasant's harvest by 1600. This not only left nothing for reinvestment but caused rural depopulation, as peasants, unable to support this heavy burden, fled. High taxes in seventeenth-century Denmark have also been held to account for a rural flight from the land, which remained derelict many years later. Similarly, an official report on the province of Cremona in 1633 blamed the burden of taxation for ruining landlords and tenants alike: tenants defaulted on their rents, land values collapsed, farms were left deserted and landlords could not afford to re-stock them.[237] Of course, it could be argued that the greater weight of taxation stimulated peasants to produce more in order to meet their fiscal obligations. This was the case urged by one tax expert in seventeenth-century Milan, who pointed out that since poor quality land was taxed whether it was left barren or not, there was an incentive to put it under crop.[238] However, this seems unlikely to have been the case generally. Smallholders – the majority of farmers – were in no position substantially to increase output to the levels needed to match the increased demands of the tax collector, as is proved by the large amounts which came to be owed as tax arrears in areas of heavy taxation.[239] On the other hand, there was a widespread agrarian depression during the seventeenth century, characterized by declining prices for foodstuffs and falling land values and rents, which stemmed principally from a stagnating level of population. And it is difficult to disentangle how far the farmer's woes were due to this, and how far to high taxation. In the case of Lombardy, Domenico Sella has argued convincingly that the crisis in agriculture was basically due to the agrarian depression, though high taxes served to compound the peasants' problems by taking a substantial bite out of an income which was anyway falling.[240] But further local studies of this type are needed to show whether this argument has a more general applicability.

With respect to manufacturing enterprise and commerce the effect of heavy taxation could be to cut the level of demand by reducing people's disposable income, erode merchants' profits, raise labour costs as the workforce demanded higher pay to meet taxes, and generally to force up the price of goods thus rendering them uncompetitive. Laments on all these counts were to be heard from merchants and others. A contemporary from the early seventeenth century bemoaned the fact that state taxes accounted for 42 per cent of the price of Venetian woollen cloths, and priced them out of the market. The Como cloth trader and manufacturer, Giovanni Tridi, in a sustained analysis of the causes of Milan's faltering economy in the same century, placed the blame firmly on high levels of state taxation:

> The cause of [our ills] lies in the scarcity of people; the scarcity of people is caused by the lack of business, and the lack of business is brought about by increased taxation; with the result that, as our commodities cannot sell within the state as cheaply as foreign commodities can, consumers buy from those countries where prices are lowest; accordingly, enterprise drifts to those countries where goods are vented, leaving our State stripped of both money and people.[241]

Even allowing for the universal tendency of merchants to blame their economic difficulties on high government taxes, there undoubtedly was some validity to all of these complaints, for high taxes assuredly could have the sorts of adverse economic consequences outlined. The real problem for the historian, however, is the lack of reliable comparative data as between one area and another on levels of taxation, profits, wage rates, transport costs and so on, which would allow a judgement to be made on whether taxes in one region were so high as to make goods produced there uncompetitive with those of a rival. Charles Wilson has given a cautious affirmative in the case of the United Provinces during the seventeenth century. It has been asserted in the case of early-modern Spain, though Sella is much more dubious in the case of Lombardy.[242] But without further comparative research any overall assessment of the problem would necessarily be premature.

Indeed any overall judgement concerning war's economic consequences has, perforce, to be so hedged about with reservations and caveats that one has sympathy with President Truman's heartfelt plea for a one-armed economist who would not reply to his questions with 'on the one hand this, on the other hand that'. Nevertheless, two points may usefully be made by way of conclusion. First, warfare clearly did not have a wholly negative impact. It undoubtedly stimulated production in certain areas, served in some circumstances to bring profit to neutrals and trading rivals, and it did help to bring into circulation some resources which would otherwise have remained frozen. However, it is difficult to resist the impression – and it can be no more than that, given our inability to quantify its effects with any precision – that such benefits were outweighed by the losses engendered by war, including the physical destruction of raw materials, crops, property and machinery, and the increased risks which it brought to commercial and manufacturing enterprises as well as to agriculture.

Second, whilst recognizing the importance of warfare in economic matters, we should not exaggerate its impact. On the whole it did not, for example, cause serious disturbances in the labour market. Nor did it have that pivotal role in bringing about fundamental change in the European economy which has sometimes been ascribed to it, by Sombart for example. It was certainly true, as John Hale has recently suggested [243] and as we noted earlier, that the enormous and unprecedented number of war-related financial transactions in the sixteenth and seventeenth centuries, ranging from tax farming and war loans, through contracts for the supply of armies with things as varied as leather jerkins, shoes, harness and pike staves, through the provision by sutlers and their agents and by civilian innkeepers and shop-owners of food, drink, fuel, fodder, bedding and utensils, to the myriad enterprises of entrepreneurial colonels and captains, all helped to disseminate a capitalistic spirit amongst society and extend the scope of capitalistic enterprise, if by capitalist we are to understand simply an awareness of the value of money and the uses to which it could be put. True, too, that war-related fiscal transactions gave opportunities for the concentration of capital in the hands of bankers, war contractors and profiteers, though war was but one factor working towards capital accumulation in the early-modern period, a trend which in any event went back into the fifteenth century and before.[244] However, we should distinguish between capital accumulation and the growth of a capitalistic spirit broadly defined, and the development of capitalism, which involves a major shift in the forms of production, implying as it does a rationalization of production methods, the creation of large-scale enterprises, and the concentration of the ownership of the means of production out of the hands of the workers into those of a few capitalist entrepreneurs. There is little evidence of any such fundamental changes in the nature of the productive processes in early-modern Europe, and, with the possible exception of the dockyards, none which can be attributed to warfare.

Indeed, one is tempted to adapt Postan's judgement on the effects of the Hundred Years War and re-apply it to the sixteenth and seventeenth centuries:

> In the machinery of economic change war was not so much the mainspring as a make-weight. Whenever its actions ran counter to the economic tendencies of the age, it was on the whole ineffective. Only at points at which changes were taking place anyhow was its influence great.[245]

Thus the growth of demand and the expansion of trade owed something to war, but much more important were factors such as the sixteenth-century population rise, the overseas discoveries and the growing taste for luxury goods. Or take the price rise of the sixteenth century as a further example. Of the 'monetary' factors which brought this about, currency debasement was certainly one, and rulers and their ministers were frequently tempted into this by the fiscal demands of war. But, with the exception of England during the 1540s and 50s, it was less important than changes in the supply of precious metals. And neither of these 'monetary' factors was as crucial in stimulating the price rise as were 'real' factors, in particular the dramatic population expansion of the sixteenth century.[246] In this way too, then, the effect of warfare was to reinforce but not to initiate economic trends.

Yet in the final analysis we must recognize that despite some

231

notable contributions to our understanding of the relationship between war and economic change, by Nef, Mathias, Parker, Sella, Jones and others, this remains, as D. C. Coleman noted, 'a region remarkably neglected by economic historians'.[247] Further research might well produce some surprises.

ATTITUDES TOWARDS WAR

Warfare had a more substantial impact upon civilian society in the sixteenth and seventeenth centuries than at any previous period, an impact which was not indeed to be exceeded until the Revolutionary and Napoleonic wars of the late eighteenth and early nineteenth centuries. The new techniques of fortification, which involved a remodelling of many medieval cities, changed the urban landscape;[248] while sieges of unprecedented frequency and extent brought about widespread civilian suffering. Wars lasted longer than in previous periods, and there were more soldiers than ever before demanding food, shelter and money, requisitioning horses and carts, and stealing what they could not otherwise obtain. Mutineers, deserters, freebooters and ex-soldiers terrorized whole areas. And civilians were confronted unavoidably with the pitiful by-products of war, the often limbless ex-soldiers who thronged the streets, pestering passers-by for charity. Even if they escaped direct contact with the soldiery, civilians could not avoid war's chief fiscal implication: higher taxes.

The printed word, that most potent bequest of the fifteenth century to succeeding ages, together with the visual arts, also contributed powerfully to expanding an awareness of the extent and reality of warfare. Governments had long since received and disseminated information using couriers and diplomats; and the larger firms of merchants also circulated letters and reports both across and between states. Increasingly, however, these sources of information, which were of necessity restricted to an elite, were supplemented and overtaken by others which were designed to reach a mass audience. Broadsheets, pamphlets, news-sheets and gazettes carrying reports of diplomatic, military and political events were produced in profusion. By 1700 the Dutch presses were turning out up to sixty different journals, gazettes and political pamphlets every month, serving a growing public appetite for news and comment.[249] Newspapers made an appearance, published erratically at first but then more regularly. Leipzig had a daily newspaper from 1660, which was making a substantial profit by the turn of the century.[250] Such local publications generally carried reports of news from farther afield, and this, together with the development in the seventeenth century of regular postal and courier systems – and they often continued to operate even between belligerent states – meant that populations well away from an area of fighting might learn in detail about military events soon after their occurrence. Readers in England, for instance, were informed within a few days of happenings in Germany during the Thirty Years War by publications such as the *Swedish Intelligencer*.[251] Nor was illiteracy necessarily a bar to learning, for pamphlets were read out in inns and public squares, not least of all by professional newspaper chanters.

For the literate and the affluent, books provided an additional source of information. Military themes were common not just in works on drill and weapons handling, in soldiers' memoirs and autobiographies, and histories such as Georg Greflinger's account of the Thirty Years War and Clarendon's *History of the Great Rebellion*, but in political works too. One-sixth of Machiavelli's *Prince*, one-fifth of the *Discourses* and large sections of the *Florentine History* dealt with warfare, for example,[252] and there is much on the same theme in Seyssel's *Monarchie de France*. Two issues which were debated with particular vigour were the value of native recruits as against foreign mercenaries,[253] and the varying military qualities to be found in soldiers of differing geographical provenance. Saulx-Tavannes argued that it was all a matter of climate: soldiers from cool areas were likely to be courageous and impetuous since the cold sent the blood towards the heart, the seat of valour; whereas in hot countries the spirits were warmed throughout the body, but especially in the head, which thereby rendered soldiers from these lands more crafty and subtle.[254] While not every author was in accord with his assessments, let alone the reason for them, debate of this type may have encouraged some national stereotyping. Military topics also occurred frequently in plays, poems and works of fiction. In 1633 Martin Opitz, one of the most celebrated of seventeenth-century German poets, published the *Trosgedichte* on the plight of Germany. The *Lament of Germany Laid Waste* by Andreas

Gryphius was a yet more telling indictment of the horrors of the Thirty Years War, which also formed the essential background to picaresque novels by Grimmelshausen.[255]

The printing press offered governments a new and powerful propaganda tool in addition to those they already possessed, perhaps the most important of which was the pulpit. As Gabriel Naudé, himself a gifted pamphleteer, noted, a prince must employ 'skilled pens, have them write clandestine pamphlets, manifestos, artfully composed apologies and declarations in order to lead [his subjects] by the nose'.[256] As a result, much that was written on the subject of war was biased, designed to convince the reader of the rightness of a ruler's cause, to portray the enemy as barbaric and to take the edge off military and political setbacks. In France, the *Gazette*, a state-sponsored journal first published in 1631, provided a sanitized version of political, military and diplomatic events on a weekly basis: its content was said to have been virtually dictated by the war minister, Louvois, between 1689 and 1691.[257] The Dutch were amongst the first to develop the techniques of 'black' propaganda, deliberately smearing the opponent through the use of lies and distortions, and thus helping to create the legend of the Spanish soldiers as uniquely cruel, acting under the orders of a pitiless ruler, a technique they sought to repeat against Louis XIV and his forces.[258] Yet, whether voluntary or propagandist, the profusion of writing on and around the subject of war served to expand public awareness of, and provoke thought about, military matters.

Scarcely less important in this respect was the contribution made by artists in the sixteenth and seventeenth centuries. Military themes had always been favoured by artistic patrons, and painters such as Titian, Van Dyck and Van der Meulen, Louis XIV's battle painter, continued to produce works of a traditional kind. Rulers, even the most unmilitary, were shown in soldierly attire and pose; while battle paintings, usually sanitized of real violence, designed to portray the grandeur and glory of war and giving pride of place to the activities of the generals and commanders, retained their popularity at the top end of the market. But at the same time artistic coverage of war took a novel turn in these two centuries. First, military subjects appeared in unprecedented numbers. It was not just that artists were pressed into service to illustrate the drill books, manuals and didactic military literature together with the propagandist pamphlet literature on war which appeared in such abundance, but that 'mass' art began to be produced for a 'mass' audience. In the Low Countries during the seventeenth century, for example, painters such as Philips Wouwerman from Haarlem, Willem Duyster, Dirck Hals, Pieter Codde, Jacob Duck and a host of others began to produce paintings, including works with military themes, in large quantities, not for a single patron but for sale at cheap prices on the open market.[259] Even more crucial in this respect, however, was the development of copper plate engraving, a technique which quickly superseded the woodcut, and which allowed large quantities of highly detailed reproductions to be made at relatively low cost. Amongst the very considerable output of highly skilled engravers such as Jacques Callot, Lukas Kilian and Ulrich Franck were a large number of works with a military theme, produced in response to the growing popular demand for material of this type. Additionally, some artist-entrepreneurs, of whom Matheus Merian would be the outstanding example, combined the printed word and the engraving to great effect. His art publishing house produced travel books, prints of cities, atlases (newly invented and important, as Hale notes,[260] in allowing readers to locate events such as military campaigns spatially) as well as military treatises and scenes of military life. His *Theatrum Europaeum*, a sort of news magazine, richly illustrated with engravings, and which eventually totalled twenty-one folio volumes, detailed political and military events in Germany and beyond.[261]

Second, there was a new realism in the visual representations of war. One aspect of this was the novel attention paid by artists to the ordinary soldier in general, and to areas of his life in particular, which had previously been neglected. He was now shown, ragged, dishevelled and with rusty armour, on the march, in camp, being recruited, taking his ease, smoking and drinking, soliciting a whore, gaming, dancing or, in the *cortegardjes* (guardroom) scenes which were a favourite of some Dutch painters, mustering, donning his armour and sleeping. A further aspect of this new realism was the exposure given to the full violence and horror of war. Civilians were depicted being killed, tortured and raped by soldiers, led off to labour at siegeworks, reduced to starving skeletons inside a besieged city, their homes and villages burned and looted; soldiers themselves were shown suffering at the hands of peasants who wreaked a savage revenge for the miseries they had endured, being cruelly punished for breaches of discipline, or, their bodies maimed and broken by the exigencies of war, ending their days as beggars. In short, soldiers were depicted as victims of war, and not simply as the perpetrators of its crimes.

Like much of the literature on war, many of these 'atrocity' paintings and engravings were partisan and propagandist in purpose. Romeyn de Hooghe, for example, catalogued the horrors committed by Louis XIV's troops against the Dutch but remained silent on the well-documented atrocities of the Dutch troops.[262] However, it has been argued that a number of early-modern artists, like Goya in a later period, produced consciously anti-war paintings which were universal in their condemnation of violence and which served to reshape public attitudes: Velazquez's tired and flabby *Mars* who sits, with his armour cast aside, contemplating the futility of his vocation; Rubens's *Peace and War* and the *Horrors of War* which, through the use of classical symbolism, show the benefits of peace and the destruction wrought by war; and Jacques Callot's series of eighteen engravings, the *Greater Miseries of War*, which were overwhelmingly concerned with the horrors which war inflicted upon soldiers and civilians alike.[263] Such an interpretation needs to be treated with caution, however. While Rubens may personally have come to detest war by 1637–8 when he completed the *Horrors of War*,[264] the painting was not apparently intended for public display, and the remainder of his work dealt with military subjects in traditional manner. Velazquez's treatment of Mars was not unusual, and was probably intended to show the god at rest rather than disenchanted with war (a painting whose message is so equivocal can anyway hardly be said to have represented a wholehearted indictment of war). Little is known with respect to Callot's personal attitude towards war, yet it is notable that he was happy to accept commissions to illustrate military manuals. Set alongside his other output of beggars, circus performers and musicians the *Miseries of War* may simply be another aspect of his fascination for depictions of the 'low-life',[265] a not unusual *vita del soldata* similar to the *Newes Soldaten-Büchlein* of Lukas Kilian. Yet if there is uncertainty as to whether Rubens, Velazquez and Callot were consciously anti-war artists, there is little doubt that their output, and that of other artists, did serve both to extend public awareness of the realities of conflict and to prompt thought and debate about the subject of war generally.

How did attitudes towards war evolve in face of this unprecedented physical, fiscal, literary and visual assault? Amongst the welter of comment and discussion on the subject it is possible to detect a shift in explanations of war and violence more generally. The older, Christian view, that war was a divinely ordained punishment for man's sin, still held some sway, especially amongst clerics of course. As one preacher told his listeners, God used many methods to chastise the unregenerate:

> Sometimes from the phials of his wrath he pours forth a pestilence upon them, that he might make them sick of their iniquity: sometimes a famine, in order to starve them out of it: but more frequently he unkennels the bloodhounds of war, to worry them into their duty, or else to hunt them to their destruction.[266]

But, increasingly, other explanations of a secular, sociological and psychological kind began to be offered, similar to those proferred by social scientists, anthropologists, ethnologists and others in the twentieth century.[267] War was a cover for governments to extend their powers; it arose because of the absence of free trade which produced envy of others' wealth, or out of the domination of society by a warrior elite; it was a product of human nature, which was naturally aggressive and brutal, or which became so when the 'Humors' and 'Temperaments' were imbalanced, thus predisposing some men to violence. As the French monk, Emeric Crucé wrote, 'Men, particularly men of war, are naturally impatient of repose.'[268] John Locke blamed religious divisions: 'the perpetual foundation of war and contention, all those flames that have made such havoc and desolation in Europe, and have not been quenched with the blood of so many millions'.[269] Out of such analyses of the causes of war were born a number of peace plans, usually based on the establishment of an international organization of states designed to eradicate inter-state competition and economic rivalry. They ranged from Guillaume Postel's hopelessly irenic vision of Christians and Muslims united under a single ruler to the most famous of all, the Abbé de Saint-Pierre's *Project de paix perpetuelle*, published in 1712.[270]

237

Above all, a more critical attitude towards war made an appearance. At one end of the spectrum were the pacifists, of the Erasmian kind on the one hand and some – though by no means all – of the Anabaptist sects on the other. The two need to be considered separately, for their pacifism was differently founded. Anabaptist pacifism, as exemplified by the Mennonites and Hutterites in the sixteenth century and the Quakers in the seventeenth, was rooted in the study of the New Testament and the conviction that Christ himself had been against the use of violence. As such it was independent of particular circumstances of time and place, and was part of a tradition of non-violence based upon religious conviction which dated back to the early Church and which had since been fitfully maintained by groups such as the Waldensians and the Taborites. By contrast, Erasmus's pacifist convictions emerged in response to the horrors of contemporary sixteenth-century warfare. Although he produced rational arguments against war – for example, that it was unnatural since animals do not make war – for him, 'it was enough to chronicle the horrors of war to condemn it'.[271]

Anabaptist sects were always condemned to a persecuted marginal existence, however; and only a relatively few people, such as Ludovicus Vives, Sebastian Franck and Gabriel Budé,[272] would have joined with the more influential Erasmus when he argued that there were no circumstances under which war could be justified (though even he equivocated when discussing war against the Turks). War was generally accepted as a fixed social institution, 'as needful and useful to the world as eating and drinking or any other work', as Luther put it.[273] Yet if necessary, it still remained an evil, and therefore to be regretted. As Thomas More suggested, via the inhabitants of his *Utopia*, warfare was inevitable, but it was also detestable and inglorious, and therefore not to be undertaken lightly.[274] Moreover, when wars were fought, they should be conducted in such a way as to minimize the shedding of blood and the physical damage to property.

A similar approach to that of the *Utopia* with respect to the conduct of war was increasingly manifested by the leading legal and theological writers on war. In the Middle Ages their concern had been predominantly, albeit not exclusively, with questions of when it was right to go to war (the *jus ad bellum*), a concern which centred around the Christian doctrine of the Just War. Yet by the sixteenth century, as definitions of what made a war just become so all-embracing as to be meaningless and as the impact of apparently unstoppable wars continued to mount, a much greater interest was shown in formulating rules to govern the conduct of war (the *jus in bello*) so as to ameliorate its effects. Both Francisco de Vitoria (1492–1546), the influential Dominican and professor of theology at Valladolid and Salamanca, and the Jesuit Francisco Suarez (1548–1617), for example, urged that wars be conducted with moderation and that in particular the safety of innocent people, including agricultural workers, women, children and clerics, should be respected. They accepted that it would be lawful to kill innocent people if their deaths were anticipated but not intended, as in the case of a besieged city which contained civilians as well as soldiers, for example. Yet both were clearly troubled by this and argued that if the numbers of casualties were expected to be high, and unless the prosecution of the siege was crucial to the outcome of the war, then it should not be undertaken.[275] A still greater concern with the conduct of war was shown by the 'father of international law', the lawyer Hugo Grotius (1583–1645). The prologue to his *De Jure Belli ac Pacis* (1625) opened with a damning indictment of the excesses in contemporary warfare:

> I observed a lack of restraint in relation to war such as even barbarous races should be ashamed of...that when arms have once been taken up there is no longer any respect for law...it is as if, in accordance with a general decree, frenzy had openly been let loose for the committing of all crimes.[276]

Accordingly, the bulk of the work was concerned with considerations of the *jus in bello*. The principle of non-combatant immunity was established (looting and other actions harmful to innocents were forbidden, for example), and the list of non-combatants was lengthy; the harming of hostages and prisoners was also forbidden; so too were some methods of waging war, including the use of poisons and terror tactics; and the rights of neutrals were defined. Grotius's legacy was to be built upon in the eighteenth century, notably by Pufendorf and Vattel, and by then the tide of thinking amongst the *philosophes* was definitely against war as a barbaric relic, unworthy of truly civilized society.

Not all of the leading intellectual figures of the early-modern period – Bossuet, Pascal and Fénelon for example – reflected particularly deeply on the subject of war. But, in so far as they thought about the matter, like Thomas More they tended to regard war without enthusiasm, as inevitable but regrettable. Yet the current was not all one way and a vigorous counter-attack was mounted against the critics of war by those seeking to justify it. Indeed, in any quantitative rather than qualitative assessment of the literary and sermonizing outpourings on the subject, the pro-war party would easily carry the day. The German, Ulrich von Hutten, advocated the indispensability of conflict if population growth were to be kept in check.[277] The Italian writer, Giovanni Botero, argued that 'military enterprises are the most effective means of keeping a people occupied....A wise prince can placate an enraged people by leading it to war against an external enemy.'[278] The sentiment was echoed by the Duke of Rohan (who knew a good deal about domestic disorder having led it himself) when he noted that war 'occupied ambitious and unquiet spirits' and 'reduced the likelihood of civil war'. Richelieu was thinking along the same lines when he wrote that war purged a state's 'bad humours'.[279] Others, arguing in a similar vein, urged that if the body politic was to remain healthy it had to rid itself of riff-raff and ne'er-do-wells, and what better way than to send them off to war?[280] At the same time, and quite contradictorily, there was a reassertion of war as a glorious undertaking and of the traditional military virtues – courage, loyalty, self-sacrifice, endurance and courtesy – even though these were notably lacking amongst the majority of soldiers with whom civilians had contact.[281]

It is true that the possible use of the sword by Christians proved disquieting for both Luther and Calvin, but this was only in the context of whether it was right for subjects actively to resist a ruler who persecuted the Protestant religion. On the wider subject of war itself Luther was typically forthright, roundly rejecting the New Testament-derived pacifism of the Anabaptists. 'When men write about war, then, and say that it is a great plague, that is all true; but they should also see how great the plague is that it prevents.' To be sure, he enjoined rulers not to go to war lightly, for, 'If men went to war on every provocation and passed by no insult, we should never be at peace and have naught but destruction besides', but subjects were duty-bound to follow their ruler in war, while the soldier's profession was not to be despised for 'it is a right office, ordained of God'. Moreover, Luther set few limits in the practice of war, since 'it is a christian act and an act of love confidently to kill, rob and pillage the enemy, and to do everything that can injure him until one has conquered him according to the methods of war.'[282] Calvin, in contrast to Luther's lengthy if haphazard approach to the subject of war, dealt with the matter in two concise sections of the *Institutes of the Christian Religion*, but he was equally dismissive of the pacifist stance. Where rulers sought to defend their subjects, 'the Holy Spirit declares such wars to be lawful by many testimonies of Scripture', he wrote, though he did go on to urge restraint in the waging of war.[283] Subsequent Protestant writers and preachers were less cautious than Calvin or Luther, and they were to provide some of the most enthusiastic and convinced defenders of war. Under the pressure of persecution Calvinism developed a doctrine justifying resistance to a ruler who oppressed the true religion.[284] Beginning with Henry Bullinger, author of the sermon 'Of War', and culminating in the writings and sermons of a large number of English divines in the 1620s and 1630s, there was a steady stream of apologists, asserting the case for an offensive war in the cause of religion. Such conflicts might be unusual, argued William Gouge, but they were the most justifiable of all, since 'they had the best warrant that could be, God's command'.[285] It was an easy step from this position – though not one taken by all holy-war apologists by any means – to suggest that holy wars should be waged without restraint: the end justified the means. As Thomas Barnes stated in the *Vox Belli, or an Alarme to Warre*:

> The stretching out of the sword to bloud, requires the putting on of a kinde of cruelty; as wee see in Samuell, who hewed Agag in pieces without any shew of compassion; as wee see in Joshua, who hanged up five heathenish kings without any compassion.[286]

Typical of this Protestant pro-war literature was Barnes's ransacking of the Old Testament, that 'book of battles of the Lord', for examples of divinely approved violence to set against the half-hinted-at pacifism of the New.

The Catholic Church has less need to rethink its position on the Christian use of the sword, having grown up with war over

241

many centuries. That it favoured peace went almost without saying, but it was not against war as such, though it urged soldiers to exercise a Christian restraint in the waging of war, and sought to set down the conditions under which the resort to war was justifiable. In practice, since Church and state lived in a condition of symbiosis it was rare – though not unknown – for Catholic theologians to condemn their ruler's resort to force,[287] the more especially so since the grounds for waging a just war had become extremely widely defined by the sixteenth century. Indeed, the age of the Reformation added yet a further cause for the just war: defence of the faith. And that could mean that a ruler was not just entitled to respond to attack from Protestants but might actively seek to suppress Protestantism outside his state's boundaries. 'Ther is no warre in the world so just or honorable be it civil or forraine, as that which is waged for Religion', proclaimed William Cardinal Allen, 'we say for the true, ancient, Catholique, Romane religion.'[288]

In the academic debate the pro-war lobby, if easily the most numerous, nevertheless often gave the impression of being on the defensive. Yet if they may be said to have lost the intellectual argument, this did not matter. Indeed, it is tempting to dismiss the whole debate as inconsequential for two reasons. First, because at the level of society at which decisions concerning war and peace were made – among kings and their largely noble advisers – there was little evidence of any shift in attitudes: little, indeed, to indicate any questioning of the rightness of war at all. If the noble lifestyle was becoming less violent during the early-modern period, and if a smaller proportion of the noble class presented itself for military service than in the past, there were few signs of an alternative to the traditional and established assumption that war was a worthwhile and glorious undertaking, and one to which the nobility was in principle committed by virtue of its estate.[289] Rulers might not go all the way with Machiavelli's dictum that 'A prince should have no other objective and no other concern, nor occupy himself with anything else except war and its methods'[290] (and they were anyway too chary about being publicly associated with the disreputable writer to concede the point openly), but they would have accepted that if war was not the *only* then it was certainly the *chief* business of kings. Rulers of course proclaimed their love of peace, but they showed little compunction in declaring war, since it remained the chief means of obtaining enduring glory. As Colbert reminded his master, kings were acclaimed by posterity for two things: the buildings they constructed and, above all, the battles they won.[291]

Nor did public opinion greatly restrict a government's freedom of action in the waging of war. It is true that matters were changing by the seventeenth century by comparison with the situation early in the sixteenth. Then, as John Hale points out, rulers had no need to woo the population to war.[292] Subsequently, however, mass communications went some way towards producing mass public opinion. War moved into the sphere of public debate, and, in a way that had not been true before, governments were obliged to take some account of public opinion. This was most notably the case, of course, in those states with some wider form of representative government, such as Holland or England. The question of whether a peace should be negotiated with Spain produced a lively controversy in the United Provinces in 1629–30 and 1646–51, for example, largely carried on via pamphleteering; and during negotiations to end the War of the Spanish Succession, Bolingbroke commented on 'The nature of our government and the character of our people, how many precautions we have to take, how many opinions we must reconcile.'[293] But it was also true in princely regimes. Both Richelieu and Olivares mounted substantial propaganda campaigns to win over public opinion before entering into war in 1635.[294] Even Louis XIV felt obliged to issue a public letter in 1709 explaining to the French people the reasons for the collapse of peace talks and seeking to rally them for a renewal of the war effort, an unusual step for a monarch who normally felt no need personally to address his subjects in this way.[295] In France, as elsewhere by the later seventeenth century, it was no longer sufficient merely to represent the decision to go to war as an emanation of the royal will (though it remained that): other arguments had to be employed. As the French propagandist Joachim Legrand noted,

It is not enough that the actions of kings be always accompanied by justice and reason. Their subjects must also be convinced of it, particularly when wars are undertaken which, although just and necessary, nearly always bring on much misery in their wake.[296]

Yet we should not overstate the power of public opinion. It is worth recalling that doubts about the waging of war *per se* were restricted to a very few. There was a general acceptance both that war was inevitable and that it was proper to wage it in the right circumstances. In so far as there was any debate, this was restricted to the rights and wrongs of a particular conflict, rather than with the issue of war in general. Here governments, with their extensive control over the pulpit, their ability to issue propaganda and, to a more limited degree, to censor opinions of which they disapproved, had enormous advantages when it came to moulding public opinion. Even when this ran counter to government policy (and it was not invariably the case that rulers favoured war and their subjects peace: occasionally the populace was more bellicose than its leaders), governments were not obliged to follow public opinion: they might choose to ignore it. As the veteran minister and diplomat, Colbert de Torcy, noted, 'Affairs of state would be very ill-administered, if the sovereign was to be guided by the public talk or to consider it as the rule of his conduct.'[297] If governments were increasingly obliged to recognize the existence of public opinion with respect to war, this was not something which, as yet, did much to hamper them.

Second, the debate may be said to have been inconsequential because there is little evidence that the practice of war was modified so as to conform to the regulations laid down by lawyers and theologians. Non-combatant status was routinely breached, as when fleeing women and children were driven back into besieged cities so as to increase pressure on food resources, and when civilians were forced to labour at the defences of a besieged fortress. The attitudes of military men towards the rights of neutrals were reflected in Gustavus Adolphus's contemptuous remark: 'Neutrality is nothing but rubbish, which the wind raises and carries away. What is neutrality anyway? I do not understand it'[298] – and this was from a professed admirer of Grotius. Equally, no practising statesman paid any serious attention whatsoever to the Abbé de Saint-Pierre's peace plan. To be sure, there were some moves to limit the excesses of war in the second half of the seventeenth century. Efforts were made to check the unrestricted plundering of civilians for example; inter-state agreements were made for the ransoming of prisoners; and in 1692 there was a Franco-German agreement to prohibit the use of poisoned projectiles.[299] But such moves resulted from an enlightened self-interest amongst military men and from the desire to improve military efficiency, rather than at the prompting of lawyers.

However, it is easy to be too negative. That war had moved into the area of public debate; that there was a more profound questioning of the rightness of war; that rules were being articulated to govern the conduct of war: these were hopeful signs. Such things scarcely amounted to a revolution, but they did perhaps represent some advance on what had gone before.

NOTES

1 INTRODUCTION

1 The English translation of volumes 1–4 of *Geschichte der Kriegs-kunst in Rahmen der Politicien Geschichte* (7 vols, Berlin, 1900–36) appeared between 1975 and 1985. Only volumes 1–4 had been the work of Delbrück himself.

2 *War in the Sixteenth Century*, p. v.

3 B. C. Hacker, 'Women and military institutions in early modern Europe: a reconnaissance', *Signs: Journal of Women in Culture and Society*, vi (1980–1), 643–71.

4 J. Jacquart, 'La fronde des princes dans la région parisienne et ses conséquences matérielles', *Revue d'histoire moderne et contemporaine*, vii (1960), 257–90 and his *La Crise rurale en Ile-de-France, 1550–1670* (Paris, 1974); M. P. Gutmann, *War and Rural Life in the Early Modern Low Countries* (Princeton, 1980); C. R. Friedrichs, *Urban Society in an Age of War: Nördlingen, 1580–1720* (Princeton, 1979).

5 *The Face of Battle: A Study of Agincourt, Waterloo and the Somme* (London, 1976).

6 C. Jones, 'New military history for old? War and society in early modern Europe', *European Studies Review*, xii (1982), 97.

7 *L'Armée française de la fin du XVIIe siècle au ministère de Choiseul: le soldat* (2 vols, Paris, 1964).

8 *The Military Revolution, 1560–1660* (Belfast, 1956), subsequently republished in a slightly revised form in *Essays in Swedish History* (London, 1967).

9 Cf., for example, G. Parker, 'The "Military Revolution, 1560–1660" – a myth?', *Journal of Modern History*, 48 (1976), 195–214; his *The Military Revolution: Military Innovation and the Rise of the West* (Cambridge, 1988); and, most recently, J. Black, *A Military Revolution? Military Change and European Society, 1550–1800* (London, 1991).

10 Parker, *The Military Revolution*, p. 45. The figure is, however, accepted by R. A. Stradling, *Europe and the Decline of Spain: A Study of the Spanish System, 1580–1720* (London, 1981), p. 62.

11 R. E. Scouller, *The Armies of Queen Anne* (Oxford, 1966), p. 80.

12 *Testament politique*, ed. L. André (Paris, 1947), p. 478. One near-contemporary estimate suggests that in 1594 Spanish companies in the northern Netherlands were at only one-quarter of their paper strength: B. H. Nickle, *The Military Reforms of Prince Maurice of Orange* (Michigan, 1984), p. 233, n. 32.

13 F. Lot, *Recherches sur les effectifs des armées françaises des guerres d'Italie aux guerres de religion, 1494–1562* (Paris, 1962), pp. 27–8. Henry IV quoted in *Les œconomies royales de Sully*, ed. D. Buisseret and B. Barbiche (Paris, 1988), ii, p. 221, n. 1.

14 On the size and permanence of French forces see J. Jacquart, *François Ier* (Paris, 1981), p. 239; J. A. Lynn, 'The growth of the French army during the seventeenth century', *Armed Forces and Society*, vi (1980), 568–77; A. Corvisier, *Louvois* (Paris, 1983), esp. pp. 79, 83, 185.

15 G. Parker, *The Army of Flanders and the Spanish Road, 1567–1659* (Cambridge, 1972), pp. 25–6, 32–3.

16 M. E. Mallett and J. R. Hale, *The Military Organization of a Renaissance State: Venice c. 1400 to 1617* (Cambridge, 1984), pp. 28ff, 476 and fig. 4, p. 477.

17 A. Åberg, 'The Swedish army, from Lützen to Narva', in M. Roberts (ed.), *Sweden's Age of Greatness, 1632–1718* (London, 1973), pp. 271–2; E. J. Feuchtwanger, *Prussia: Myth and Reality. The Role of Prussia in German History* (London, 1970), pp. 23, 48; J. A. Vann, *The Making of a State: Württemberg, 1593–1793* (Ithaca, 1984), pp. 39ff; F. L. Carsten, *Princes and Parliaments in Germany from the Fifteenth to the Eighteenth Century* (Oxford, 1959), pp. 72–123 (Württemberg), 239 (Saxony), 310–11, 314, 318–19, 324 (Jülich and Berg), 182–3 (Hesse-Cassel). On the growth of the army in Hesse-Cassel under Landgrave Charles (1654–1730) and his successors, see also H. Philippi, *Landgraf Karl von Hessen-Kassel* (Marburg, 1980) and C. W. Ingrao, *The Hessian Mercenary State: Ideas, Institutions and Reform under Frederick II, 1760–1785* (Cambridge, 1987).

18 Parker, *The Military Revolution*, pp. 24, 45; Lot, *Recherches*, p. 160; G. J. Millar, *Tudor Mercenaries and Auxiliaries, 1485–1547* (Charlottesville, 1980), p. 46. It is true that a larger number of men was assembled to meet the Armada, though estimates of 76,000 seem very high, but a majority of them were militia, poorly trained and armed to say the least, and it is doubtful if they would have been able to take the field had the Spanish landed: I. Friel, 'Rival armies', in M. J. Rodriguez-Salgado *et al.*, *Armada* (London, 1988), pp. 126–8; G. Parker, 'If the Armada had landed', *History*, lxi (1976), 358–68.

19 G. Parker, *The Thirty Years War* (London, 1987), p. 208.

20 A. Corvisier, 'Guerre et mentalité au XVIIe siècle', *XVII Siècle*, 148 (1985), 221.

21 R. Bean, 'War and the birth of the nation state', *Journal of*

Economic History, 33 (1973), 212–15 presents some interesting figures in this respect.

22 There is a succinct account of the struggles between the Habsburgs and their rivals which gives prominence to questions of resources in P. Kennedy, *The Rise and Fall of the Great Powers: Economic Change and Military Conflict from 1500 to 2000* (London, 1988), ch. 2.

23 Parker, '"Military Revolution..." – a myth?', p. 208. Cf. also Roberts, *Essays in Swedish History*, pp. 205–8.

24 G. Parker, 'Warfare', *The New Cambridge Modern History*, ed. P. Burke (Cambridge, 1979), xiii, p. 204.

25 Q. Wright, *A Study of War* (Chicago, 1965), tables 31–42, pp. 641–6; Corvisier, 'Guerre et mentalité', pp. 220–1.

26 G. Parker, 'Why did the Dutch Revolt last eighty years?', *Transactions of the Royal Historical Society*, 5th series, xxvi (1976), 53.

27 M. Roberts, *Gustavus Adolphus. A History of Sweden, 1611–1632* (2 vols, London, 1953, 1958), ii, p. 363.

28 H. G. Koenigsberger, *The Habsburgs and Europe, 1516–1660* (Ithaca, 1971), pp. 28–9, 48–9.

29 J. R. Hale, *War and Society in Renaissance Europe, 1450–1620* (London, 1985), p. 21.

30 Koenigsberger, *Habsburgs and Europe*, p. 69.

31 F. Fernandez-Armesto, *The Spanish Armada: The Experience of War in 1588* (Oxford, 1988), pp. 74–5; M. Roberts, 'The political objectives of Gustav Adolf in Germany, 1630–2', repr. in *Essays in Swedish History*, p. 84; Parker, *Thirty Years War*, pp. 121–2; G. Livet, *Guerre et paix de Machiavel à Hobbes* (Paris, 1972), p. 347.

32 Parker, 'Why did the Dutch Revolt last eighty years?', pp. 61–2.

33 H. G. Koenigsberger, 'The organization of revolutionary parties in France and the Netherlands during the sixteenth century', in *Estates and Revolutions: Essays in Early Modern History* (Ithaca, 1971), *passim*; R. M. Kingdon, 'Political resistance of the Calvinists in France and the Low Countries', *Church History*, xxvii (1958), 220–33.

34 C. J. Ekberg, *The Failure of Louis XIV's Dutch War* (Chapel Hill, 1979), pp. 5–6.

35 M. Roberts, *The Swedish Imperial Experience, 1560–1718* (Cambridge, 1979), pp. 1–42.

36 J. B. Wolf, *Louis XIV* (London, 1970), pp. 533–4.

37 V. L. Tapié, 'Louis XIV's methods in foreign policy', in R. Hatton (ed.), *Louis XIV and Europe* (London, 1976), p. 5.

38 F. J. Baumgartner, *Henry II, King of France, 1547–1559* (London, 1988), pp. 147–8.

39 K. Brandi, *The Emperor Charles V: The Growth and Destiny of a Man and of a World Empire* (London, 1939), pp. 497–8.

40 W. Roosen, 'The origins of the War of the Spanish Succession', in J. Black (ed.), *The Origins of War in Early Modern Europe* (Edinburgh, 1987), pp. 156–7.

41 Roberts, 'Political objectives', pp. 87–8, 92–7; D. Parrott, 'The causes of the Franco-Spanish War of 1635–59', in Black, *Origins of War*, pp. 96–9.

42 E. Luard, *Wars in International Society* (London, 1986), pp. 100–1, 151.

43 J. C. Rule, *Louis XIV and the Craft of Kingship* (Columbus, 1969), p. 7.

44 Roosen, 'Origins of the War of the Spanish Succession', p. 155.

45 Louis XIV to Villars, 8 January 1688, cit. in H. Méthivier, *Le Siècle de Louis XIV* (Paris, 1971), p. 63.

46 G. Zeller, 'Le principe d'équilibre dans la politique internationale avant 1789', *Revue historique*, 215 (1956), 25–7.

47 ibid., p. 28.

2   THE CHANGING ART OF WAR

1   G. Gush, *Renaissance Armies, 1480–1650* (Cambridge, 1982), p. 39.

2   Robert Monro was one of many who warned that pikemen should 'never be suffered to cut off the lengths of their pikes': *Monro, his Expedition with the Worthy Scots Regiment* (London, 1637), pt ii, p. 191. Despite his injunction there was a tendency for the length of the pike to be reduced below officially stipulated minima as pikemen sought to reduce the burden they had to carry.

3   *The Souldier's Accidence. Or an Introduction into Military Discipline* (London, 1625), p. 2.

4   G. Parker, *The Army of Flanders and the Spanish Road, 1567–1659* (Cambridge, 1972), p. 276 table *b*.

5   See the favourable comments, for example, of Sir Roger Williams, *A Brief Discourse of Warre* (1590) in J. X. Evans (ed.), *The Works of Sir Roger Williams* (Oxford, 1972), pp. 35–7.

6   The collection can still be seen in the arsenal which is now part of the Joanneum Museum.

7   D. Chandler, *The Art of Warfare in the Age of Marlborough* (London, 1976), pp. 75–9.

8   A. E. Curry, 'Military organization in Lancastrian Normandy' (Unpublished PhD thesis, 2 vols, CNAA, 1985), i, p. 98. The lighter, poplar arrow had a range of up to 250 yards.

9   *Discours politiques et militaires*, intro. by F. E. Sutcliffe (Paris, 1967, first pub. Geneva, 1587), p. 360.

10 *Monro, his Expedition*, pt ii, p. 190.

11 Cited in T. Esper, 'The replacement of the longbow by firearms in the English army', *Technology and Culture*, vi (1965), 391.

12 D. A. Parrott, 'Strategy and tactics in the Thirty Years War: the "Military Revolution"', *Militärgeschichtliche Mitteilungen*, 18 (1985), 8.

13 Parker, *Army of Flanders*, tables *a* and *b*, p. 276; M. D. Feld, 'Middle-class society and the rise of military professionalism: the

Dutch army, 1589–1609', *Armed Forces and Society*, i (1975), 426; J. B. Kist, *Jacob de Gheyn: the Exercise of Arms* (New York, 1971), p. 30.

14 Various novel deployments of pikemen and arquebusiers are discussed, for instance, in la Noue, *Discours*, pp. 369–71 and *Les Mémoires de Gaspard de Saulx-Tavannes*, in *Nouvelle Collection de mémoires pour servir à l'histoire de France*, ed. J. F. Michaud and J. J. F. Poujoulat (Paris, 1838), 1st series, viii, p. 84 (cited hereafter as *Mémoires de Saulx-Tavannes*).

15 The standard account of these developments remains W. Hahlweg, *Die Heeresreform der Oranier und die Antike* (Berlin, 1941). See also Kist, *Jacob de Gheyn*, pp. 5ff, which also has a facsimile reproduction of de Gheyn's *Wapenhandelinghe*; W. H. McNeill, *The Pursuit of Power* (Oxford, 1983), pp. 126–31; B. H. Nickle, *The Military Reforms of Prince Maurice of Orange* (Michigan, 1984), esp. pp. 145–56.

16 M. Roberts, *Essays in Swedish History* (London, 1967), p. 219 n. 11; Blaise de Monluc gives an example from an engagement in 1543: *Commentaires de Messire Blaise de Monluc*, ed. P. Courteault (Paris, 1964, first pub. Bordeaux, 1592), p. 122. Battista della Valle's handbook of 1521 enjoined men to march in step, but this probably had more application to pageantry than to war: J. R. Hale, *War and Society in Renaissance Europe, 1450–1620* (London, 1985), pp. 166–7.

17 Kist, *Jacob de Gheyn*, pp. 2–3.

18 W. Rheinhard, 'Humanismus und Militarismus. Antike-Rezeption und Kriegshandwerk in der Oranischen Heeresreform', in *Krieg und Frieden im Horizont der Renaissancehumanismus* (Wernheim, 1986), p. 195; Hahlweg, *Die Heeresreform*, pp. 51–2, 73ff.

19 On the influence of Lipsius on the Dutch reformers see G. Oestreich, *Neostoicism and the Early Modern State* (Cambridge, 1982), pp. 77–9 and *passim*.

20 Hahlweg, *Die Heeresreform*, pp. 140–90; G. Parker, *The Thirty Years War* (London, 1987), p. 206. Montgommery's *La Milice française réduite à l'ancien ordre et discipline militaire des legiōs...* (Paris, 1610) translated Maurice's words of command and detailed the key elements of Dutch drill; while de Billon's *Principes de l'art militaire* (Paris, 1622) referred frequently to the reforms of the 'great captain' Maurice.

21 Parrott, 'Strategy and tactics', pp. 11–12; Chandler, *Art of Warfare*, pp. 122–3. On the size of units see the pertinent comments in Parrott, pp. 8–10.

22 The astute Raimondo Montecuccoli blamed Tilly's rout at the battle of Breitenfeld on his failure to adopt this formation: *Sulle Battaglie*, trans. in T. M. Barker, *The Military Intellectual and Battle: Raimondo Montecuccoli and the Thirty Years War* (New York, 1975), p. 95.

23 D. Chandler, *Marlborough as Military Commander* (London, 1979), map p. 255 and pp. 252ff for the battle.

24 *Monro, his Expedition*, pt ii, p. 191; F. Redlich, *The German Military Enterpriser and his Workforce, 13th to 17th Centuries* (Wiesbaden, 1964: *Vierteljahrschrift für Sozial-und Wirthschafts-geschichte*, Beiheft, 2 vols), ii, p. 455.

25 Parrott, 'Strategy and tactics', pp. 11–12. Robert Monro advised a space of 6 feet when under cannon fire, 3 feet at other times: *Monro, his Expedition*, pt ii, 187ff; John Bingham suggested that the gap should never be less than 3 feet: *The Tactiks of Aelian* (London, 1616), pp. 153ff.

26 Details from C. H. Firth, *Cromwell's Army. A History of the Soldier during the Civil Wars, the Commonwealth and the Protectorate* (London, 1962), pp. 110–11; Parker, *Army of Flanders*, p. 11, and for what follows, p. 165; J. N. Hillgarth, *The Spanish Kingdoms, 1250–1516* (2 vols, Oxford, 1976, 1978), ii, p. 376; F. Lot, *Recherches sur les effectifs des armées françaises des guerres d'Italie aux guerres de religion, 1494–1562* (Paris, 1962), pp. 21, 53–6; M. E. Mallett and J. R. Hale, *The Military Organization of a Renaissance State: Venice c. 1400 to 1617* (Cambridge, 1984), pp. 367ff; Parker, *Thirty Years War*, p. 30; Chandler, *Art of Warfare*, and for what follows, pp. 29–31.

27 R. J. Bonney, *The King's Debts: Finance and Politics in France, 1589–1661* (Oxford, 1981), p. 173 n. 3. The Marquis of Santa-Cruz suggested a cost ratio of 1 : 2.5 in 1730: Chandler, *Art of Warfare*, p. 29. On the supply and cost of horses see ibid; J. W. Fortescue, *A History of the British Army* (13 vols, London, 1899–1930), i, p. 575; Parker, *Army of Flanders*, p. 165; R. A. Stradling, 'Spain's military failure and the supply of horses, 1600–1660', *History*, lxix (1984), 210–21.

28 Monluc, *Commentaires*, p. 95.

29 'Few horsemen wel conducted, will charge either trenches, or battailes of footmen, vnless they see a faire entrie, or the footmen begin to shake': Williams, *Discourse of Warre*, p. 40; Chandler, *Art of Warfare*, p. 104. See also la Noue, *Discours*, pp. 370–2; the comment of the Venetian, Martinegro, in Mallett and Hale, *Military Organization*, p. 370; and the remarks on Waterloo in J. Keegan, *The Face of Battle: A Study of Agincourt, Waterloo and the Somme* (London, 1976), pp. 154–60.

30 *Sulle Battaglie*, p. 92.

31 Parrott, 'Strategy and tactics', pp. 14–15.

32 Mallett and Hale, *Military Organization*, p. 370.

33 Montecuccoli, *Sulle Battaglie*, p. 106 suggested using musketeers for this purpose, but in practice it would have been difficult for the slower foot soldiers to manoeuvre with the horse.

34 See Parrott, 'Strategy and tactics' esp. pp. 15–16. I have relied heavily on the insights of this perceptive article. Accounts of the sixteenth-century battles are to be found in C. Oman, *A History of the Art of War in the Sixteenth Century* (London, 1937), though the best account of Pavia is probably still R. Thom, *Die Schlacht bei Pavia* (Berlin, 1907).

35 See the judicious comments of Monluc. At the battle of Ceresoles (1544) he observed that cannon 'often occasions more fear than it does harm': *Commentaries*, p. 158.

36 Good accounts of the development of heavy guns and gunnery are to be found in A. R. Hall, *Ballistics in the Seventeenth Century* (Cambridge, 1952); his 'Military technology', in C. Singer *et al.*, *A History of Technology* (Oxford, 1957), iii, pp. 360–9; J. F. Guilmartin, *Gunpowder and Galleys: Changing Technology and Mediterranean Warfare at Sea in the Sixteenth Century* (London, 1974); S. Pepper and N. Adams, *Firearms and Fortifications: Military Architecture and Siege Warfare in Sixteenth Century Siena* (Chicago, 1986), pp. 8–15.

37 Cited in H. C. B. Rogers, *A History of Artillery* (Secaucus, 1975), p. 36.

38 Pepper and Adams, *Firearms and Fortifications*, p. 199 n. 20.

39 Rogers, op. cit., p. 45. Though firing could not continue indefinitely or the gun overheated and burst: on some of the other dangers associated with cannon firing see W. Bourne, *The Arte of Shooting in Great Ordnaunce* (London, 1587), pp. 45–8, 62–3.

40 C. Duffy, *Siege Warfare*, (2 vols, London, 1979, 1985), i, p. 9.

41 Hillgarth, *Spanish Kingdoms*, ii, p. 376. In 1449–50 the French had captured over sixty defended sites in English-held Normandy using cannon, but here too many surrendered rather than face bombardment: A. E. Curry, 'Towns at war: relations between the towns of Normandy and their English rulers, 1417–1450', in J. A. Thomson (ed.), *Towns and Townspeople in the Fifteenth Century* (Gloucs., 1988), pp. 148–72 and conversations with the author.

42 For much of what follows see J. R. Hale, 'The early development of the bastion: an Italian chronology *c.* 1450-*c.* 1534', in J. R. Hale, J. Highfield and B. Smalley, *Europe in the Late Middle Ages* (London, 1965), pp. 466–94; Pepper and Adams, *Firearms and Fortifications*, pp. 3–6, 17–27; Duffy, *Siege Warfare*, i, pp. 25–40.

43 When the English in the mid-fifteenth century tried to defend medieval fortifications in Normandy using cannon, they found the walls and wooden floors incapable of supporting the weight and the recoil. I am grateful to Dr Curry for this information.

44 G. Dickinson (ed.), *The 'Instructions sur le faict de la Guerre' of Raymond de Beccarie de Pavie, sieur de Fourquevaux* (London, 1954), p. 85.

45 On its dissemination see Duffy, *Siege Warfare*, i, *passim*, ii, chs 1–3; Parker, *The Military Revolution: Military Innovation and the Rise of the West* (Cambridge, 1988), esp. pp. 12–13, 24–32; Q. Hughes, *Military Architecture* (London, 1974), chs 3–4.

46 Cited in Duffy, *Siege Warfare*, i, p. 45.

47 H. Langer, *The Thirty Years War* (Poole, 1982), pp. 16–17; P. Charpentrat, 'Les villes...l'exemple du Palatinat-Heidelberg et Mannheim', in P. Francastel (ed.), *L'Urbanisme de Paris et l'Europe, 1600–1680* (Paris, 1969), pp. 267–74.

48 Not until Paul Ive's *The Practice of Fortification* (London, 1589)

did any English author show much awareness of continental methods of fortification.

49 D. Stevenson, *Scottish Covenanters and Irish Confederates: Scottish-Irish Relations in the Mid-Seventeenth Century* (Belfast, 1981), p. 151.

50 Monluc, *Commentaires*, p. 303. On the importance of rate of fire in a siege, an often unappreciated point, see Pepper and Adams, *Firearms and Fortifications*, p. 14.

51 Duffy, *Siege Warfare*, i, p. 51; Bertrand de Salignac, *Le Siège de Metz*, in *Nouvelle collection de mémoires pour servir à l'histoire de France*, ed. J. F. Michaud and J. J. F. Poujoulat (Paris, 1838), 1st series, viii, p. 514; C. Vassal-Reig, *La Guerre en Roussillon sous Louis XIII, 1635-1639* (Paris, 1934), p. 54.

52 A. Corvisier, *La France de Louis XIV 1643-1715: ordre intérieur et place en Europe* (Paris, 1979), p. 95.

53 L. van der Essen, *Alexandre Farnese, Prince de Parme, Gouverneur Général des Pays-Bas, 1545-1592* (5 vols, Brussels, 1933-7), v, p. 33.

54 J. Israel, *The Dutch Republic and the Hispanic World, 1606-1661* (Oxford, 1982), pp. 96, 163, 166 table 7.

55 Piémond, cit. in M. Greengrass, 'The later wars of religion in the French Midi', in P. Clark (ed.), *The European Crisis of the 1590s: Essays in Comparative History* (London, 1985), p. 107; C. Durston, 'Reading and its county gentry, 1625-1649' (Unpublished PhD thesis, 2 vols, Reading, 1977), i, pp. 140-1.

56 There is no comprehensive listing but an idea of the volume of works is to be gained from M. J. D. Cockle, *A Bibliography of English Military Books up to 1642 and of Contemporary Foreign Works* (London, 1900); and, for England, H. J. Webb, *Elizabethan Military Science: The Books and the Practice* (London, 1965). On the importance of Venice as a centre for the printing of military books in the sixteenth century, see J. R. Hale, 'Printing and the military culture of Renaissance Venice', *Medievalia et Humanistica*, n.s., 8 (1977), repr. in *Renaissance War Studies* (London, 1983), ch. 16, esp. pp. 429-30.

57 Oestreich, *Neostoicism*, p. 78.

58 See, for example, Thomas Styward, *The Pathwaie to Martiall Discipline* (London, 1581), pp. 67-114.

59 Oestreich, *Neostoicism*, pp. 120, 124-5; H. L. Zwitzer, 'The Dutch army during the Ancien Régime', *Revue internationale d'histoire militaire*, lviii (1984), 23. The viewers at Maastricht included the young Turenne.

60 J. R. Hale, 'The military education of the officer class in early modern Europe', in C. H. Clough (ed.), *Cultural Aspects of the Italian Renaissance* (Manchester, 1976), repr. in *Renaissance War Studies*, pp. 233-4 and ch. 8 generally.

61 On the *schola militaris* see esp. ibid., pp. 227-9; his 'Military academies on the Venetian terraferma in the early seventeenth century', *Study Veneziani*, xv (1973), also repr. in *Renaissance War*

Studies, ch. 10; A. Corvisier, *Armies and Societies in Europe, 1494–1789* (Bloomington, 1979), pp. 105–9. See also his *Louvois* (Paris, 1983), pp. 337–41.

62 'A Treatise on the Art of War', in *Journal of the Society for Army Historical Research*, vi (1927), 69.

63 I. A. A. Thompson, *War and Government in Habsburg Spain, 1560–1620* (London, 1976), p. 44; Lot, *Recherches*, p. 224. In France the Artillerie Royale was formed in 1693 out of the Régiment des Fusiliers du Roi, created in 1677.

64 See, for example, Chandler, *Art of Warfare*, pts iii and iv; Nickle, *Military Reforms of Prince Maurice*, pp. 111ff; R. E. Scouller, 'Marlborough's administration in the field', *Army Quarterly*, 95–6 (1967–8), 197–208, 102–13.

65 Duffy, *Siege Warfare*, i, p. 52.

66 ibid., p. 83.

67 The sallies, ambushes and close-quarter fighting which comprised so much of the conflict at a siege are described, for example, in Salignac, *Le Siège de Metz*, esp. p. 552; Monro, *Monro, his Expedition*, pt i, p. 65 on the siege of Franckendor in 1628; J. Dorney, *A Briefe and Exact Relation of the Military Government of Gloucester* (London, 1645), in J. Washbourn (ed.), *Bibliotheca Gloucestrensis* (Gloucester, 1825), pp. 213ff on the siege of Gloucester (1643).

68 Robert Barrett, quoted in Hale, *War and Society*, p. 58.

69 A. Corvisier, 'Le moral des combattants, panique et enthousiasme: Malplaquet', *Revue historique des armées*, xii (1977), 24.

70 Details from Vassal-Reig, *La Guerre en Roussillon*, p. 59; Parrott, 'Strategy and tactics', p. 13; Monro, *Monro, his Expedition*, part ii, p. 65. In this context it is worth noting Thrasymachus' description of battle in Erasmus's *Militaria*: 'So great was the tumult and the shouting, blasts of trumpets, thunder of horns, neighing of horses, and clamour of men that I couldn't see what was going on; I scarcely knew where I myself was. What went on in my own tent I know; as to what happened in the battle, I'm completely ignorant': *The Colloquies of Erasmus*, trans. C. R. Thompson (Chicago, 1965), p. 13.

71 M. van Creveld, *Command in War* (Cambridge, Mass., 1985), p. 51.

72 Montecuccoli, *Sulle Battaglie*, p. 124.

73 ibid, p. 84.

74 Two and a half hours at Breitenfeld; six at Malplaquet: Monro, *Monro, his Expedition*, pt ii, p. 65; Corvisier, 'Le moral des combattants', p. 22. Troops under fire and unable to reply became 'discouraged', according to Montecuccoli: *Sulle Battaglie*, p. 141. In 1544, at Ceresole, Monluc's pikemen had become restive under cannon fire, although here little harm was being done, and he had difficulty in preventing them attacking forthwith: *Commentaires*, pp. 157–8.

75 'The greatest slaughter of the foe does not take place in combat but

during flight': Montecuccoli, *Sulle Battaglie*, p. 83; Monro, *Monro, his Expedition*, part ii, p. 74. In the context of the conduct of battle, it is worth noting the comments of Marshal Saxe in the mid-eighteenth century: 'When two armies arrive within a certain distance from each other, they both begin to fire and continue their approaches, till they come within about fifty or sixty paces, where, as is usually the case, either the one or the other takes to flight; and this is what is called a charge': *Reveries on the Art of War*, from G. Symcox, *War, Diplomacy and Imperialism, 1618–1763* (London, 1974), p. 187.

76 n. 69 above.

77 *The History of the Rebellion and Civil Wars in England* (7 vols, London, 1849), iv, p. 47.

78 Montecuccoli, *Sulle Battaglie*, p. 82 (quotation); pp. 127–36, 147–8 for what follows. R. Ward, *Anima'dversions of Warre* (London, 1639), bk ii, p. 6, noted: 'A generall must take away all hope of refuge from his souldiers in time of battell.'

79 Barker, *The Military Intellectual and Battle*, p. 175; Parker, *Army of Flanders*, pp. 178–9. See also Chandler, *Marlborough*, p. 145 on Blenheim.

80 Given in Symcox, *War, Diplomacy and Imperialism*, p. 139.

81 p. 78.

82 *Sulle Battaglie*, pp. 135–6. See also M. Sutcliffe, *The Practice, Proceedings and Lawes of Armes* (London, 1593), pp. 298–9.

83 *Commentaires*, p. 43. Monluc was taken prisoner but released when his captors found there was no profit to made in ransoming him.

84 Though at the siege of Tournai in 1709 even offers of money could not induce allied soldiers to enter the tunnels leading to the walls: D. McKay, *Prince Eugene of Savoy* (London, 1977), pp. 123–4. See also R. Knecht, *Francis I* (Cambridge, 1982), p. 163 for a similar sixteenth-century example.

85 Quoted by Sydnam Poyntz in 'The Relation of Syndam Poyntz, 1624–36', ed. A. T. S. Goodrick, *Camden Miscellany*, 3rd series, xiv (1908), p. 58.

86 *Sulle Battaglie*, p. 112. On the twentieth century, S. Stouffer *et al.*, *The American Soldier: Combat and its Aftermath* (Princeton, 1949).

87 On the value of veterans see Williams, *Discourse of Warre*, pp. lxxxiii, 9ff; la Noue, *Discours*, p. 715; Sutcliffe, *Lawes of Armes*, p. 86.

88 A. Du Prat, *La Vie d'Antoine Du Prat* (Paris, 1852), p. 111.

89 Duffy, *Siege Warfare*, i, pp. 70–2, 85–9, 118–21; Chandler, *Art of Warfare*, pp. 308–10 appendix 3. La Noue observed in 1587 that places which had previously required eight days to besiege now required a season: *Discours*, pp. 372–3.

90 John Cruso regretted that 'the actions of modern warres consist chiefly in sieges, assaults, sallies, skirmishes &c. and so afford but few battels': *Militarie Instructions for the Cavallrie* (Cambridge, 1632), sig. PI, cit. in Evans, *Works*, p. lxxxii.

91 J. Gillingham, 'Richard I and the science of war in the Middle Ages', in J. Gillingham and J. Holt (eds), *War and Government in the Middle Ages* (Cambridge, 1984), pp. 82–5. See also the advice of the Byzantine Emperor, Maurice, in his *Strategikon*, trans. G. Dennis (Philadelphia, 1984), maxim 28, p. 85.

92 Chandler, *Marlborough*, pp. 65, 265.

93 ibid., pp. 62–3.

94 M. van Creveld, *Supplying War: Logistics from Wallenstein to Patton* (Cambridge, 1977), p. 1.

95 Details from C. S. L. Davies, 'Provisions for armies, 1509–50; a study in the effectiveness of early Tudor government', *Economic History Review*, 2nd series, xvii (1964), 234; R. Mols, 'Population in Europe, 1500–1700' in *Fontana Economic History of Europe*, ed. C. Cipolla, (London, 1977), ii, pp. 42–3; Lot, *Recherches*, pp. 125–34; Langer, *Thirty Years War*, p. 97. See also Parker, *Army of Flanders*, pp. 87, 288–9 appendix I.

96 Wallhausen cit. in Parker, *The Military Revolution*, p. 187, n. 104; Parker, *Army of Flanders*, p. 95; Creveld, *Supplying War*, p. 250 n. 3.

97 J. Keegan and R. Holmes, *Soldiers: a History of Men in Battle* (London, 1985), p. 224; C. Barnett, *Marlborough* (London, 1974), p. 218.

98 G. Perjés, 'Army provisioning, logistics and strategy in the second half of the 17th century', *Acta Historica Academiae Scientarium Hungaricae*, 16 (1970), pp. 4–6, 14–17; Parker, *The Military Revolution*, pp. 75–6, 186 n. 96.

99 F. Redlich, 'Der Marketender', *Vierteljahrschrift für Sozial-und Wirthschaftsgeschichte*, xli (1954), pp. 227ff.

100 For what follows see F. Redlich, 'Contributions in the Thirty Years War', *Economic History Review*, xii (1959–60), 247–54; M. Ritter, 'Das Kontributionssystem Wallensteins', *Historische Zeitschrift*, lv (1903), 193–249, a rather idealized account; and L. Ekholm, *Svensk Kreigsfinansiering, 1630–1681* (Uppsala, 1974: Studia Historica Upsaliensia, lvi), pp. 35–9.

101 G. Mann, *Wallenstein* (Frankfurt, 1971), pp. 370–1.

102 Ellis Gruffydd, cit. in Davies, 'Provisions for armies', p. 244 n. 2.

103 Parker, *Army of Flanders*, pp. 88, 86–95 generally: Davies, 'Provisions for armies', p. 236; C. G. Cruickshank, *Elizabeth's Army* (Oxford, 1946), p. 53.

104 Davies, 'Provisions for armies', pp. 239, 243–5 on the failure of various expeditions in Henry VIII's reign due to transport and victualling difficulties.

105 Knecht, *Francis I*, pp. 110–1.

106 Perjés, 'Army provisioning', esp. pp. 7–11, 13ff. Dependence on local supplies was reflected in the equipment armies took with them. The Dutch army's provisioning train in 1607 included 3 prefabricated windmills, 3 water mills, 26 hand mills, 25 baker's kits and tools to build mills and handle grain: Nickle, *Military Reforms of Prince Maurice*, p. 258 n. 69.

107 Though occasionally it made sense to campaign in winter. Thus in the winter of 1630–1 Swedish forces left Stettin when 'the earth clad over with a great storme of snowe, being hard frost, wee carried along great cannons of batterie': Monro, *Monro, his Expedition*, p. ii, 14.

108 Parker, *Army of Flanders*, pp. 96–7, 280 appendix D.

109 As Captain Parker, one of those on the march, wrote, 'Surely never was such a march carried on with more order and regularity, and with less fatigue both to man and horse': D. Chandler (ed.), *The Marlborough Wars: Robert Parker and the Comte de Mérode – Westerloo* (London, 1968), p. 31.

110 Langer, *Thirty Years War*, p. 96; E. L. Petersen, 'Defence, war and finance: Christian IV and the Council of the Realm, 1596–1629', *Scandinavian Journal of History*, vii (1982), 303; McKay, *Prince Eugene*, p. 44.

111 S. Gaber, *La Lorraine meurtrie: les malheurs de la guerre de trente ans* (Nancy, 1979), pp. 91–2.

112 *Commentaires*, pp. 62–72.

113 Kist, *Jacob de Gheyn*, p. 14; S. Ellis, *Tudor Ireland: Crown, Community and the Conflict of Cultures, 1470–1603* (London, 1985), pp. 314–15 and 283ff generally. The rebels had used similar tactics in 1534: Ellis, p. 127.

114 Knecht, *Francis I*, pp. 110, 112 and 282 for the following example.

115 Vassal-Reig, *La Guerre en Roussillon*, p. 115; D. Eggenberger, *A Dictionary of Battles* (London, 1967), p. 403. Creveld, *Supplying War*, pp. 32–3 argues strongly that the Duke's objective in Bavaria was primarily military and not coercive or punitive. Of course, devastation of a territory might be designed to terrorize or punish a population and its ruler. This was the purpose of Louis XIV's destruction of the Palatinate, for example, and of the Earl of Hertford's 1544 raid into Scotland, deliberately timed to cause maximum damage: he reported that there is 'burnt a wonderful deal of corn...for they had done much of their harvest': G. J. Millar, *Tudor Mercenaries and Auxiliaries, 1485–1547* (Charlottesville, 1980), p. 150.

116 D. Underdown, *Somerset in the Civil War and Interregnum* (Newton Abbot, 1973), p. 89. On the English Civil War see Durston, 'Reading and its county gentry', i, esp. pp. 139, 165–70, 201–7; R. Hutton, *The Royalist War Effort, 1642–1646* (London, 1982), pp. 102–4; Greengrass, 'The later wars of religion', *passim*, for France; Parker, *Army of Flanders*, pp. 11–12 on the Dutch Revolt.

117 For what follows see Creveld, *Supplying War*, pp. 13–16; M. Roberts, *Gustavus Adolphus. A History of Sweden, 1611–1632* (2 vols, London, 1953, 1958), ii, pp. 439–52, 460–2, 469–83, 513–21, 531–59, ch. xi for the details of the campaigns, though the interpretation of the king's conduct does not always coincide with that advanced here.

118 Parker, *The Military Revolution*, p. 40. C. Nordmann suggests a figure of 15,000 garrison troops out of a total of 45,000 Swedish effectives after 1637: 'L'Armée suédoise au XVIIe siècle', *Revue du nord*, 54 (1972), 137.

119 Roberts, *Gustavus Adolphus*, ii, p. 494 n. 1.

120 Creveld, *Supplying War*, p. 17; Parrott, 'Strategy and tactics', pp. 20–1; though more stress is given to the political-strategic objectives of the armies in Parker, *Thirty Years War*, pp. 174–6. On what he has called the 'crisis of strategy' which resulted from the failure to overcome logistic difficulties, see Perjés, 'Army provisioning', pp. 35ff.

121 *Testament politique*, ed. L. André (Paris, 1947), p. 280.

122 D. Parrott, 'The administration of the French army during the ministry of Cardinal Richelieu' (Unpublished PhD thesis, Oxford, 1985), pp. 32, 35–7, 41–2. See B. Kroener, *Les Routes et les Etapes. Die Versorgung der Französischen Armeen in Nordostfrankreich, 1635–1661* (2 vols, Münster, 1980: Schriftenreihe der Vereinigung zur Erforschung der neuren geschichte, xi), vol. i for details of the French supply system and its failures.

123 For what follows see the fundamental work of L. André, *Michel le Tellier et l'organisation de l'armée monarchique* (Paris, 1906); his *Michel le Tellier et Louvois* (Paris 1942, repr. Geneva, 1974), chs viii–x; Corvisier, *Louvois*, pp. 87–91, 112–13, 180–1, 190–1, 351; and D. C. Baxter, *Servants of the Sword: French Intendants of the Army, 1630–1670* (Urbana, 1976), *passim*.

124 Chandler, *Art of Warfare*, pp. 16–17. An indication of the importance which Marlborough attached to questions of supply can be gained from his correspondence. See G. Murray, *The Marlborough Dispatches* (5 vols, London, 1845), the index references for Medina and bread, for example.

125 Scouller, 'Marlborough's administration in the field', pt i; Perjés is more dubious about the role of the quartermaster but admits its development: 'Army provisioning', pp. 31–4. The importance of the post is signalled in J. Turner, *Pallas Armata: Military Essayes of the Ancient Grecian, Roman and Modern Art of War* (London, 1683), p. 201.

126 H. W. Koch, *The Rise of Modern Warfare, 1618–1815* (London, 1981), pp. 93–4. See also Scouller, op. cit., pp. 203, 110, but note the cautionary remarks of J. Milot, 'Un problème opérationnel du XVIIe siècle illustré par un cas régional', *Revue du nord*, 53 (1971), 276–7.

127 A-G. Boilleau, *L'Administration militaire dans les temps modernes* (Geneva, 1980, reprint of 1879 edn), pp. 445–6.

128 Creveld, *Supplying War*, pp. 24 (quotation) and 23–5 generally.

129 *Society at War. The Experience of England and France during the 100 Years War* (Edinburgh, 1973), p. 7.

130 Gillingham, 'Richard I and the science of war in the Middle Ages', p. 80.

131 ibid., p. 85.

132 *Discorsi di Guerra* (Venice, 1567), p. 78.

133 *Essays in Swedish History*, p. 203. I owe this point to Parrott, 'Strategy and tactics', p. 20.

134 *Art of Warfare*, p. 19.

3   RECRUITMENT

1 See M. Mallet, *Mercenaries and their Masters: Warfare in Renaissance Italy* (London, 1974), esp. chs 2, 4.

2 For what follows see I. A. A. Thompson, *War and Government in Habsburg Spain, 1560–1620* (London, 1976), pp. 107ff.

3 ibid., p. 103.

4 ibid., p. 112.

5 ibid., p. 112–13.

6 This is well described in G. Parker, *The Army of Flanders and the Spanish Road, 1567–1659* (Cambridge 1972), pp. 35ff.

7 M. E. Mallet and J. R. Hale, *The Military Organization of a Renaissance State: Venice c.1400 to 1617* (Cambridge, 1984), p. 327. Five thousand *landsknechts*, contracted for service in Friuli in 1538, declined an order from their employers redirecting them to the fleet: ibid., p. 319.

8 R. Knecht, *Francis I* (Cambridge, 1982), p. 114.

9 Parker, *Army of Flanders*, p. 39; Mallett and Hale, *Military Organization*, p. 322.

10 It was the employment of German standby contractors such as Frundsberg and Eberstein which made possible the very rapid expansion of Alba's forces to meet the threat from the Dutch rebels in 1572: W. S. Maltby, *Alba: A Biography of Fernando Alvarez de Toledo, Third Duke of Alba, 1507–1582* (Berkeley, 1983), pp. 229–30.

11 See Machiavelli's views on mercenaries in *The Prince*, ed. Q. Skinner and R. Price (Cambridge, 1988), ch. xii. Similar views were held by Gonzalo de Cordoba and Lipsius: J. A. Maravell, 'The origins of the modern state', *Journal of World History*, vi (1961), 808; G. Oestreich, *Neostoicism and the Early Modern State* (Cambridge, 1982), pp. 51–2.

12 Examples are given in F. Redlich, *The German Military Enterpriser and his Workforce, 13th to 17th Centuries* (Wiesbaden, 1964: *Vierteljahrschrift für Sozial-und Wirthschaftsgeschichte*, Beiheft, 2 vols), i, pp. 173–6.

13 ibid., p. 12.

14 Thompson, *War and Government*, table 4.1 p. 104, and pp. 104–7, 116ff, 146ff.

15 ibid., p. 117 and ch. v generally.

16 G. J. Millar, *Tudor Mercenaries and Auxiliaries, 1485–1547* (Charlottesville, 1980), pp. 43–7; V. G. Kiernan, 'Foreign mercenaries and absolute monarchy', *Past and Present*, xi (1957), 73–4.

17 Mallett and Hale, *Military Organization*, pp. 319, 323.
18 C. E. Hill, *The Danish Sound Dues and Control of the Baltic* (Durham, NC, 1926), chs 3, 4; L. Jespersen, 'The *Machstaat* in seventeenth-century Denmark', *Scandinavian Journal of History*, x (1985), 275ff; G. E. Rothenberg 'Maurice of Nassau, Gustavus Adolphus, Raimondo Monecuccoli and the "Military Revolution" of the seventeenth century', in P. Paret (ed.), *Makers of Modern Strategy from Machiavelli to the Nuclear Age* (Oxford, 1986), pp. 40–1; F. Lot, *Recherches sur les effectifs des armées françaises des guerres d'Italie aux guerres de religion, 1494–1562* (Paris, 1962), p. 42; J. de Pablo, 'Contributions à l'étude de l'histoire des institutions militaires huguenotes', *Archiv für Reformationgeschichte* (1957), 204.
19 Mallett and Hale, *Military Organization*, pp. 316–8; Knecht, *Francis I*, pp. 67–8.
20 Redlich, *German Military Enterpriser*, i, pp. 32, 50.
21 M. D. Feld. 'Middle-class society and the rise of military professionalism: the Dutch army, 1589–1609', *Armed Forces and Society*, i (1975); *passim*; Oestreich, Neostoicism, p. 76. The English government did press a number of men for service with contractors, whom they helped in other ways too. For example, the loans which funded the recruitment of 6,000 men by the Marquis of Hamilton in 1630 were partly backed by the 16-year lease on the wines of Scotland given to him for this purpose by Charles I: S. J. Stearns, 'Conscription and English society in the 1620s', *Journal of British Studies*, xi (1972), 4–5; P. Dukes, 'The Leslie family in the Swedish period (1630–1635) of the Thirty Years War', *European Studies Review*, xii (1982), 412. Hamilton's expedition was not a success and left him ruined financially. On his career see H. L. Rubinstein, *Captain Luckless. James, First Duke of Hamilton 1606–1649* (Edinburgh, 1975).
22 Not surprisingly he was the largest employer of contractors: 600 compared to around 300 in Swedish service: Redlich, *German Military Enterpriser*, i, p. 206.
23 D. A. Parrott, 'Strategy and tactics in the Thirty Years War: the "Military Revolution"', *Militärgeschichtliche Mitteilungen*, 18 (1985), p. 18; his 'French military organization in the 1630s: the failure of Richelieu's ministry', *Seventeenth Century French Studies*, ix (1987), 160–3.
24 Redlich, *German Military Enterpriser*, i, pp. 170–1.
25 ibid., i, p. 219, and for the following examples pp. 295, 234.
26 ibid., pp. 228–30; G. Parker, *The Thirty Years War* (London, 1987), p. 100.
27 ibid., p. 196; Redlich, *German Military Enterpriser*, i, chs vi, vii.
28 Parker, *The Thirty Years War*, p. 100.
29 The pay of Wallenstein's colonels was some five times greater than in other armies, reflecting both the heavier initial investment they had made and the higher rate of return which they expected: J. Meyer, '"De la guerre", au XVIIe siècle', *XVIIe Siècle*, 148 (1985), p. 272–3.

30 A. Ernstberger, *Hans de Witte – Finanzmann Wallensteins* (Wiesbaden, 1954: *Vierteljahrschrift für Sozial-und Wirthschaftsgeschichte*, Beiheft 38), p. 166 and *passim*; Redlich, *German Military Enterpriser*, i, pp. 329ff.
31 W. H. McNeill, *The Pursuit of Power*, (Oxford, 1983), p. 121.
32 Redlich, *German Military Enterpriser*, ii, pp. 246ff; H. Langer, *The Thirty Years War* (Poole, 1982), pp. 129, 153–4.
33 G. Mann, *Wallenstein* (Frankfurt, 1971), *passim*; F. H. Schubert, 'Wallenstein und der Staat des 17. Jahrhunderts', *Geschichte in Wissenschaft und Unterricht*, xvi (1965), 597–611; quotation from Parker, *The Thirty Years War*, p. 139.
34 C. V. Wedgwood, *The Thirty Years War* (London, 1981, first pub. 1938), p. 366.
35 ibid., p. 386. In 1635 Oxernstierna was obliged to make a formal treaty with officers in Baner's army after its mutiny: p. 398.
36 Parker, *The Thirty Years War*, pp. 186–9.
37 Redlich, *German Military Enterpriser*, ii, pp. 8–12, 88ff. Over half of the 40,000 troops maintained in Flanders by Britain during the Spanish Succession War were contract forces; and the number of contract troops in Prince Eugene's army in 1706 – mainly paid for by the Maritime Powers – rose from 18,000 to 28,000 during the course of the year: R. E. Scouller, *The Armies of Queen Anne* (Oxford, 1966), p. 81; D. McKay, *Prince Eugene of Savoy* (London, 1977), p. 98. On the leasing of Bavarian forces, cf. P. C. Hartmann, *Karl Albrecht-Karl VII. Glucklicher Kurfürst, unglüklicher Kaiser* (Ratisbon, 1985), pp. 150ff.
38 H. W. Koch, *The Rise of Modern Warfare, 1618–1815* (London, 1981), p. 92; G. A. Craig, *The Politics of the Prussian Army, 1640–1945* (Oxford, 1964), pp. 5–6.
39 'Military organization and the organization of the state', in *The Historical Essays of Otto Hintze*, ed. F. Gilbert (New York, 1975), p. 200.
40 Scouller, *Armies of Queen Anne*, pp. 138ff; H. L. Zwitzer, 'The Dutch army during the Ancien Régime', *Revue internationale d'histoire militaire*, lviii (1984), 33; H. Rosenberg, *Bureaucracy, Aristocracy and Autocracy: the Prussian Experience, 1660–1815* (Boston, 1958), p. 79. The colonel of a regiment in the late seventeenth-century Imperial army would expect 10–12,000 *gulden* annually from the sale of commissions, promotion fees, percentage of the troops' pay and booty: McKay, *Prince Eugene*, p. 11.
41 Foreign recruiting agents were forbidden from the Palatinate and Brandenburg-Prussia in 1681, Anhalt-Dessau in 1702 and Brunswick-Wolfenbüttel in 1704, for example: Redlich, *German Military Enterpriser*, ii, p. 172 n. 5.
42 R. A. Stradling, *Europe and the Decline of Spain: A Study of the Spanish System, 1580–1720* (London, 1981), p. 181.
43 ed. M. Shugrue (London, 1966), Act III, scene i, lines 120ff.
44 A. Corvisier, *Louvois* (Paris, 1983), p. 186; Redlich, *German Military Enterpriser*, ii, p. 176.

45 Details from Stearns, 'Conscription and English society', pp. 4–5; Scouller, *Armies of Queen Anne*, pp. 114, 374–5 appendix F; W. J. Stoye, 'Soldiers and civilians', in *New Cambridge Modern History*, ed. J. S. Bromley (Cambridge, 1970), vi, p. 93; E. Léonard, *L'Armée et ses problèmes au XVIIIe siècle* (Paris, 1958), pp. 25–6.

46 Stradling, *The Decline of Spain*, p. 181; Scouller, *Armies of Queen Anne*, pp. 108, 113; H. W. Koch, *A History of Prussia* (London, 1978), pp. 49, 60.

47 Details from M. Roberts, *The Early Vasas: A History of Sweden, 1523–1611* (London, 1968), pp. 138–9; M. Roberts, *Gustavus Adolphus. A History of Sweden, 1611–1632* (2 vols, London, 1953, 1958) ii, pp. 207ff; A. Åberg, 'The Swedish army from Lützen to Narva', in M. Roberts (ed.), *Sweden's Age of Greatness, 1632–1718* (London, 1973), pp. 266ff; C. Nordmann, 'L'Armée suédoise au XVIIe siècle', *Revue du nord*, 54 (1972), pp. 133–4.

48 Details from Redlich, *German Military Enterpriser*, ii, p. 183; Mallett and Hale, *Military Organization*, pp. 350–63; C. G. Cruickshank, *Elizabeth's Army* (Oxford, 1946), pp. 5–6; L. Boynton, *The Elizabethan Militia, 1558–1638* (London, 1967), *passim*; Thompson, *War and Government*, pp. 126–31; Jespersen, 'The *Machstaat*', p. 275; Oestreich, *Neostoicism*, pp. 221–33; D. Albert, 'Staat und Gesellschaft, 1500–1745', in M. Spindler (ed.), *Handbuch der Bayerischen Geschichte* (2 vols, Munich, 1966), ii, p. 591. See also the good general study by H. Schnitter, *Volk und Landesdefension* (E. Berlin, 1977), *passim*.

49 A. Corvisier, *Armies and Societies in Europe, 1494–1789* (Bloomington, 1979), pp. 54–60; Redlich, *German Military Enterpriser*, ii, p. 184; A. de Saluces, *Histoire militaire de Piémont* (5 vols, Turin, 1817–18); i, pp. 240–3, v, pp. 18–19; Craig, *Politics of the Prussian Army*, p. 9.

50 A. Corvisier, *L'Armée française de la fin de XVIIe siècle au ministère de Choiseul: le soldat* (2 vols, Paris, 1964), tables on p. 157, and p. 249.

51 For examples of resistance and on the operation of the *milice* see the fundamental work of G. Girard, *Le Service militaire en France à la fin du règne de Louis XIV: racolage et milice* (Paris, 1922).

52 T. Wilson, 'The State of England, Anno Domini 1600', ed. F. J. Fisher, *Camden Miscellany*, 3rd series, lii (1936), p. 34.

53 Stearns, 'Conscription and English society', p. 8.

54 The Comte de St Germain in 1775, cit. in L. Ducros, *French Society in the Eighteenth Century*, trans. W. de Geijer (London, 1926), p. 294.

55 R. Chaboche, 'Les soldats français de la guerre de trente ans: une tentative d'approche', *Revue d'histoire moderne et contemporaine*, xx (1973), 20.

56 *Army of Flanders*, pp. 36–7.

57 Nordmann, 'L'Armée suédoise', p. 146.

58 J. Lindegren, *Utskrivning och utsugning. Produktion och reproduktion: Bygdeå, 1620–1640* (Uppsala, 1980: Studia Historica

Upsaliensia, cxvii), p. 159 including table 24. The average age of recruits from the nearby town of Umeå was 16: ibid.

59 *Memoirs of his own Life and Times, 1632–1670* (Edinburgh, 1829), p. 3; 'The Relation of Sydnam Poyntz, 1624–36', ed. A. T. S. Goodrick, *Camden Miscellany*, 3rd series, xiv (1908), p. 45; 'Autobiography of Thomas Raymond', ed. G. Davies, *Camden Miscellany*, 3rd series, xxviii (1917), p. 35.

60 Chaboche, 'Les soldats français', pp. 18–19.

61 Thompson, *War and Government*, p. 134.

62 J. R. Hale, *War and Society in Renaissance Europe, 1450–1620* (London, 1985), p. 107.

63 B. Riche, *A Pathway to Military Practice* (London, 1587), pp. G3f.

64 Cruickshank, *Elizabeth's Army*, p. 9; Dukes, 'The Leslie family', p. 407.

65 F. Braudel, *The Mediterranean and the Mediterranean World in the Age of Philip II*, trans. S. Reynolds (2 vols, London 1972–3), ii, p. 749; Thompson, *War and Government*, p. 117. This was no novelty: between 2 and 12 per cent of the men in the English armies 1339–61 were criminals who received a pardon at the end of their service: H. J. Hewitt, *The Organization of War under Edward III* (Manchester, 1966), pp. 29–30.

66 Hale, *War and Society*, p. 86: Oestreich, *Neostoicism*, p. 52. Thus only a handful of criminals were impressed by the Privy Council in a major recruiting drive between 1624 and 1627: Stearns, 'Conscription and English society', p. 5 and n. 17.

67 The better-off would have been included in the major categories of people exempt from the *milice royale*, for example nobles, clerics and certain urban inhabitants.

68 'The State of England', p. 20. Selection for the *milice royale* was by ballot. It was easily rigged and in practice the village's drunk or ne'er-do-well was often chosen for service.

69 S. Ellis, *Tudor Ireland: Crown, Community and the Conflict of Cultures, 1470–1603* (London, 1985), p. 144.

70 Cruickshank, *Elizabeth's Army*, p. 10.

71 Chaboche, 'Les soldats français', pp. 19–20.

72 Parker, *Army of Flanders*, pp. 28–30 including fig. 4; Millar, *Tudor Mercenaries*, pp. 44–7.

73 Redlich, *German Military Enterpriser*, i, p. 456; Parker, *Army of Flanders*, p. 29 n. 3.

74 Mallett and Hale, *Military Organization*, pp. 321–50; Nordmann, 'L'Armée suédoise', p. 136. On the substantial contingent of Scots in Swedish service, see J. Dow, *Ruthven's Army in Sweden and Esthonia* (Stockholm, 1965).

75 Corvisier, *Louvois*, pp. 96, 186, 344.

76 Quotes and details from Pablo, 'Contribution', p. 213; Millar, *Tudor Mercenaries*, p. 145; Redlich, *German Military Enterpriser*, i, p. 456; Zwitzer, 'The Dutch army', p. 33; Corvisier, *Louvois*, p. 104.

77 Dukes, 'The Leslie family', p. 404. On Irish mercenaries see esp. P.

Gouhier, 'Mercenaires irlandaises au service de la France (1635–64)', *The Irish Sword*, vii (1965–6), 58–75.

78 R. Chaboche, 'Les soldats d'origine languedocienne aux Invalides', *Actes du Congrès National des Sociétés Savantes*, 96 i Toulouse (1971), p. 29.

79 Corvisier, *Armies and Societies*, pp. 137–8; Parker, *Thirty Years War*, p. 100 table 3.

80 Chaboche, 'Les soldats français', pp. 14–16.

81 D. Underdown, *Revel, Riot and Rebellion: Popular Politics and Culture in England, 1603–1660* (Oxford, 1985), pp. 191–2, 196–8, 296 table 3.

82 G. Parker, *The Military Revolution: Military Innovation and the Rise of the West* (Cambridge, 1988), p. 53. The same was true of Brandenburg-Prussia: Koch, *Prussia*, pp. 87–8.

83 'The State of England', pp. 19–20; Riche, above n. 63. See also the doubts expressed in Hale, *War and Society*, pp. 124–5 and the cautionary remarks in A. Corvisier, 'Un problème des vocations militaires: les soldats méridionaux dans un régiment Parisien sous Louis XIV', *Actes du Congrès National des Sociétés Savantes*, 96 i Toulouse (1971), p. 11.

84 R. Gough, *The History of Myddle*, ed. D. Hey (Harmondsworth, 1981), pp. 71–2.

85 Cited in Stradling, *Decline of Spain*, p. 124.

86 Langer, *Thirty Years War*, pp. 17, 89; Corvisier, *L'Armée française*, pp. 317 and 316–30 generally; Redlich, *German Military Enterpriser*, i, p. 457.

87 C. H. Firth, *Cromwell's Army. A History of the Soldier during the Civil Wars, the Commonwealth and the Protectorate* (London, 1962), p. 2.

88 Trans. F. J. Lamport (London, 1986, 2nd edn), p. 187.

89 Langer, *Thirty Years War*, pp. 89–90; Corvisier, *Louvois*, p. 357. Almost one-third of the officers in the Elector's army were Huguenot refugees by 1688: Rosenberg, *Bureaucracy, Aristocracy and Autocracy*, p. 59. Huguenot officers were expelled from the French army and Huguenot soldiers from the *Invalides*: Chaboche, 'Les soldats d'origine languedocienne aux Invalides', p. 31.

90 Details from Thompson, *War and Government*, pp. 106–7; Mallet and Hale, *Military Organization*, pp. 495 and 494–501 for a detailed study of soldiers' pay; Wilson, 'The State of England', p. 33; Zwitzer, 'The Dutch army', p. 31.

91 Thompson, *War and Government*, p. 107; *Règlement pour le paiement des troupes cantonnées en Italie, 21 mai 1527*, in Lot, *Recherches*, pp. 196–7. See also Mallett and Hale, op. cit., pp. 497–8. It is worth noting that, since officers received higher pay and there were a fixed number per company, it was in the pecuniary interest of contractors to spread their men out and have a multiplicity of companies, albeit of small size: the smaller sized company of the sixteenth century, Maurice of Nassau's much-vaunted innovation, may in fact have owed more to this than to any revolution in tactics.

92 See Thompson, Mallet and Hale, and Zwitzer in n. 90 above. See also Scouller, *Armies of Queen Anne*, pp. 129–30.
93 Hale, *War and Society*, p. 112.
94 Scouller, *Armies of Queen Anne*, p. 110.
95 D. Chandler, 'Armies and navies', in *New Cambridge Modern History*, ed. J. S. Bromley (Cambridge, 1970), vi, p. 763.
96 Redlich, *German Military Enterpriser*, i, p. 284.
97 *Journal d'un curé de campagne au XVIIe siècle*, ed. H. Platelle (Paris, 1965), p. 24.
98 Kiernan, 'Foreign mercenaries', p. 85 n. 60; F. Redlich, *De Praeda Militari: Looting and Booty* (Wiesbaden, 1956: *Vierteljahrschrift für Sozial-und Wirthschaftsgeschichte*, Beiheft 39), p. 21 and *passim* on the subject of looting.
99 'The life of Estevanillo Gonzales, the most pleasantest and most diverting of all comical scoundrels', trans. J. S. Stevens, in *The Spanish Libertines* (London, 1707, first pub. Antwerp, 1646), p. 353. On Gonzales see R. O. Jones, 'Studies in the Spanish literature of the Golden Age', *Revue hispanique*, 77 (1929), 201–45; E. Gossart, *Les Espagnols en Flandre* (Brussels, 1914), pp. 243–97.
100 J. J. von Grimmelshausen, *Mother Courage*, trans. W. Wallich (London, 1965, first pub. 1670), p 69. See also Parker, *Army of Flanders*, p. 182.
101 Wharton to George Willingham, 13 Sept. 1642, in *Archaeologia*, 35 (1853), 322. See also the views of Jacobi von Wallhausen cited in Redlich, *De Praeda Militari*, p. 27.
102 Details and quotations from ibid., p. 55; J. Russell-Major, 'Noble income, inflation and the Wars of Religion in France', *American Historical Review*, 86i (1981), 42; 'Relation of Sydnam Poyntz', pp. 125–7; *Le Nouveau Cynée ou discours d'estat* (Paris, 1623), p. 13; 'Life', p. 313.
103 'Relation of Sydnam Poyntz', p. 45.
104 *Wallenstein's Camp*, p. 190; 'The State of England', p. 24.
105 *Commentaires de Messire Blaise de Monluc*, ed. P. Courteault (Paris, 1964, first pub. Bordeaux, 1592), p. 823.
106 P. R. Newman, 'The Royalist Officer Corps, 1642–1660: army command as a reflexion of the social structure', *Historical Journal*, xxvi (1983), 950.
107 ibid. In the 1580s and 1590s quite a number of soldiers serving in Elizabeth's military expeditions were knighted – eighty-one by Essex in 1599 alone – but this was against the wishes of the queen, and the two decades are atypical in this respect: L. Stone, *The Crisis of the Aristocracy, 1558–1641* (Oxford, 1965), pp. 72–3.
108 Examples from Åberg, 'The Swedish army', p. 273; Newman, op. cit., p. 948.
109 Chaboche, 'Les soldats français', pp. 22–3; Corvisier, 'Un problème des vocations militaires', pp. 15–17 inc. table III.
110 Gonzales, 'Life', p. 272.
111 J. J. von Grimmelshausen, *Der Abenteuerliche Simplicissimus*

Teutsch, ed. R. Tarot (Tübingen, 1967, first pub. 1669), bk I, ch. xvi.

112 Nordmann, 'L'armée suédoise', p. 142, though the high level of officer mortality in the Great Northern Wars necessitated the appointment of non-nobles, so that by 1718 the balance was in their favour by 2 : 1, ibid, p. 145. In four Prussian regiments for which figures are available in the 1690s, only 12 per cent of commissions were held by non-nobles: F. L. Carsten, *The Origins of Prussia* (Oxford, 1968), p. 271.

113 *La Monarchie de France*, ed. J. Poujol (Paris, 1961, first pub. 1515), pt. 1, chs xiii–xvi; Hale, *War and Society*, p. 91.

114 Stone, *Crisis of the Aristocracy*, p. 266 and ch. v generally; J. B. Wood, *The Nobility of the Election of Bayeux, 1436–1666* (Princeton, 1980), pp. 82–4.

115 Mallett and Hale, *Military Organization*, p. 315; Åberg, 'The Swedish army', p. 273.

116 Details from Stone, *Crisis of the Aristocracy*, pp. 456 and 455–8 generally; Duffy, *Siege Warfare*, i, p. 86; M. J. Rodriguez-Salgado et al., *Armada* (London, 1988), p. 124.

117 La Noue's views in *Discours politiques et militaires*, intro. by F. E. Sutcliffe (Paris, 1967, first pub. Geneva, 1587), pp. 210ff. Monluc cit. in A. W. Whitehead, *Gaspard de Coligny* (London, 1904), p. 334. For details of his family's poverty and early life see *Commentaires*, p. 61, and P. Courteault, *Un cadet de Gascogne au XVIe siècle, Blaise de Monluc* (Paris, 1909).

118 'Le moral des combattants', p. 10.

119 J. H. Elliott, *Europe Divided, 1559–1598* (London, 1972), p. 108.

120 Cited in J. H. M. Salmon, *Society in Crisis: France in the Sixteenth Century* (London, 1975), p. 127.

121 Elliott, op. cit., p. 98.

122 Dukes, 'The Leslie family', p. 417.

123 Mallett and Hale, *Military Organization*, p. 324.

4 LIFE AND DEATH IN THE ARMIES

1 Figures from G. Parker, *The Army of Flanders and the Spanish Road, 1567–1659*, (Cambridge, 1972), pp. 209–10; P. Landier, 'Guerre, violence et société en France de 1635 à 1659', Thèse de 3ème cycle, cit. in A. Corvisier, *La France de Louis XIV, 1643–1715: ordre intérieur et place en Europe* (Paris, 1979), p. 124; Corvisier, 'Guerre et mentalité au XVIIe siècle', *XVII Siècle*, 148 (1985), 222. E. A. Wrigley and R. S. Schofield, *The Population History of England, 1541–1871* (London, 1981), pp. 311–12, table A3 : 3, 535ff, put the median crude death rate at 2.5–3 per cent, but this, like the birth-rate, was slightly lower in England than in the rest of western Europe.

2 Sir Ralph Lane, muster-master of Ireland, cit. H. J. Webb, *Elizabethan Military Science: The Books and the Practice* (London, 1965), p. 151.

3 Cited in A. Corvisier, *La France de Louis XIV*, p. 124.
4 R. Knecht, *Francis I* (Cambridge, 1982), p. 47.
5 J. Turner, *Memoirs of his own Life and Times, 1632–1670*, (Edinburgh, 1829), p. 5.
6 A. Corvisier, 'Le moral des combattants, panique et enthousiasme: Malplaquet', *Revue historique des armées*, vii (1977), 23.
7 Corvisier, *La France de Louis XIV*, p. 123. On the large numbers of Royalist dead – around 4,000 – at Marston Moor, see C. S. Terry, *The Life and Campaigns of Alexander Leslie* (London, 1899), p. 254 n. 1.
8 R. Monro, *Monro, his Expedition with the Worthy Scots Regiment* (London, 1637), pt i, pp. 38–9, 80; pt ii, p. 35.
9 The squalid conditions characteristic of a siege meant that here too, unless the fortress was stormed, the high levels of mortality would be a result of illness rather than bullets. See, for example, the description of Charles V's camp at Metz in Bertrand de Salignac, *Le Siège de Metz*, in *Nouvelle collection de mémoires pour servir à l'histoire de France*, ed. J. F. Michaud and J. J. F. Poujoulat (Paris, 1838), 1st series, viii, pp. 555–6.
10 H. Langer, *The Thirty Years War* (Poole, 1982), p. 64.
11 Articles 44, 45. The code is reprinted in C. G. Cruickshank, *Elizabeth's Army* (Oxford, 1946), pp. 144–51. Cf. also Fourquevaux's concern with hygiene: *The 'Instructions sur le faict de la Guerre' of Raymond de Beccarie de Pavie, sieur de Fourquevaux*, ed. G. Dickinson (London, 1954), pp. 68–68v. The difficulties involved in maintaining hygiene in camps can be gauged from the fact that 2–3,000 horses would produce, in a month, some 700,000 gallons of urine and 5,000,000 pounds of manure, its removal requiring 5,000 cartloads: J. Gillingham, 'William the Bastard at war', in C. Harper-Bill *et al.* (eds), *Studies in Medieval History Presented to R. Allen Brown* (Woodbridge, 1989), p. 156.
12 Terry, *Alexander Leslie*, 24–5 n. 2; J. Lindegren, 'The Swedish "Military State", 1560–1720', *Scandinavian Journal of History*, x (1985), 317.
13 M. E. Mallett and J. R. Hale, *The Military Organization of a Renaissance State: Venice c. 1400 to 1617* (Cambridge, 1984), p. 387.
14 H. A. Lloyd, *The Rouen Campaign, 1590–1592: Politics, Warfare and the Early-Modern State* (Oxford, 1973), p. 89.
15 K. Samuelsson, *From Great Power to Welfare State: 300 Years of Swedish Social Development* (London, 1968), p. 20; A. Corvisier, *Armies and Societies in Europe, 1494–1789* (Bloomington, 1979), p. 138; P. Goubert, *L'Ancien régime* (2 vols, Paris, 1969, 1973), ii, p. 117; R. E. Scouller, *The Armies of Queen Anne* (Oxford, 1966), p. 114. (The length of a foot varied between countries.) Shortage of recruits forced Louvois to abandon the height qualification in 1685, and few recruits met new height requirements re-introduced in the eighteenth century: A. Corvisier, *Louvois* (Paris, 1983), p. 347; *L'Armée française, de la fin de XVIIe siècle au ministère de*

Choiseul: le soldat (2 vols, Paris, 1964), pp. 637–52. See too the figures in R. Mousnier, *Les Institutions de la France sous la monarchie absolue, 1598–1789* (2 vols, Paris, 1980), i, pp. 550–1.

16 *Henry IV Part I*, Act IV, scene ii.

17 G. Symcox, *War, Diplomacy and Imperialism, 1618–1763* (London, 1974), p. 145.

18 Parker, *Army of Flanders*, p. 169. On the French soldiers, who were described as 'homesick', see M. Reinhard, 'Nostalgie et service militaire pendant la révolution', *Annales historiques de la révolution française*, 150 (1958), 1–15. Cf. also J. Keegan, *The Face of Battle: A Study of Agincourt, Waterloo and the Somme* (London, 1976), pp. 334–6.

19 Langer, *Thirty Years War*, p. 189. In the eighteenth century, however, there were considerable advances in military medicine, and also medical advances achieved through the study of, and experimentation with, armies: P. Delaunay, *La Vie médicale aux XVIe, XVIIe et XVIIIe siècles* (Paris, 1955), pp. 84ff, 274ff.

20 C. Duffy, *Siege Warfare* (2 vols, London, 1979, 1985), i, p. 74. See also the preface to 'Des playes faictes par hacquebutes', book xi of Ambroise Paré's *Œuvres complètes* (Paris, 1598, 5th edn).

21 L. Delaruelle and M. Sendrail, *Textes choisis de Ambroise Paré* (Paris, 1953), pp. 27–8 and 23–44 for his life generally; J. Guillermand, *Histoire de la médicine aux armées* (2 vols, Paris, 1982), i, pp. 330–1 and *passim* for much of what follows. Paré's crucial work on gunshot wounds, the 'Des playes faictes par hacquebutes' was first published in 1545, with subsequent editions in 1552 and 1557. His collected works were first published in 1575.

22 J. J. Keevil, *Medicine and the Navy* (4 vols, London, 1957–63), i, pp. 129–37.

23 There is a graphic description of the technique of amputation, giving the number of men needed to hold the patient down, in Pierre Franeo, *Traité des hernies...et autres excéllentes parties de la chirurgerie* (Lyons, 1561), bk VI, ch lxxxii.

24 Corvisier, 'Le moral des combattants', p. 24. Monro claimed to have seen a single cannon ball take off the heads of fourteen men: *Monro, his Expedition*, pt i, pp. 65–6.

25 Delaruelle et Sendrail, *Textes choisis*, p. 27.

26 *Etat des dépenses de la campagne de Piémont, 14 mars 1538*, in F. Lot, *Recherches sur les effectifs des armées françaises des guerres d'Italie aux guerres de religion, 1494–1562* (Paris, 1962), p. 201; Webb, *Elizabethan Military Sciences*, p. 150.

27 Webb, op. cit., pp. 154–5. There is a similar comment in the *Mémoires de Saulx-Tavannes*, p. 103: 'le rasoir amy estoit plus dangereux que la balle ennemie'. Gonzales bitterly satirized the surgeons' lack of ability and their fondness for amputations. Without having examined the limb, one assumed that Gonzales needed his leg amputating and 'fell to beating up eggs and making infusions of wine': 'The Life of Estevanillo Gonzales, the most pleasantest and most diverting of all comical scoundrels', trans. J.

S. Stevens, in *The Spanish Libertines* (London, 1707, first pub. Antwerp, 1646), p. 422.

28 A. Cabanès, *Chirurgiens et blessés à travers l'histoire, des origines à la Croix-rouge* (Paris, 1912), pp. 192ff. T. Digges, *An Arithmeticall Militare Treatise Named Stratioticos* (London, 1579), p. 154. Cf. also H-A. Wauthoz, *Les Ambulances et les ambulanciers à travers les siècles* (Paris–Brussels, 1906).

29 Cited in J. des Cilleuls, 'Le Service de santé en campagne aux armées de l'ancien régime', *Revue historique de l'armée*, iii, (1953), 7 n. 1. Cf. the similar opinion of his predecessor cit. in C. Jones, 'The welfare of the French foot-soldier', *History*, 65 (1980), 194.

30 Webb, *Elizabethan Military Science*, p. 214 n. 20.

31 Parker, *Army of Flanders*, pp. 167–8; L. van Meerbeeck, 'Le Service sanitaire de l'armée espagnole des Pays-Bas à la fin du XVIe et au XVIIe siècles', *Revue internationale d'histoire militaire*, xx (1959), *passim*.

32 Jones, 'Welfare', pp. 194, 204; J. des Cilleuls, 'Chirurgiens militaires de l'ancien régime', *Revue historique de l'armée*, i (1950), 8; Guillermand, *Histoire de la médecine*, i, pp. 397–8. The establishment of effective field hospitals in Piedmont in 1551 and at the siege of Amiens in 1597 had been isolated initiatives in the sixteenth century: ibid., pp. 348–51.

33 N. Cantlie, *A History of the Army Medical Department* (2 vols, London, 1974), i, pp. 25, 32, 34.

34 R. A. Dorwart, *The Prussian Welfare State Before 1740* (Cambridge, Mass., 1971), pp. 261, 266.

35 Guillermand, *Histoire de la médecine*, i, pp. 357–60; D. McKay, *Prince Eugene of Savoy* (London, 1977), p. 64.

36 D. Stevenson, *Scottish Covenanters and Irish Confederates: Scottish–Irish Relations in the Mid-Seventeenth Century* (Belfast, 1981), p. 125. The Venetian ambassador, Nani, expressed astonishment at the state of the French army in 1664: 'lads naked or in rags, without shoes, the cavalry poorly mounted', L. André, *Michel le Tellier et Louvois* (Paris, 1942, repr. Geneva, 1974), p. 350.

37 Lloyd, *Rouen Campaign*, p. 98. See also B. H. Nickle, *The Military Reforms of Prince Maurice of Orange* (Michigan, 1984), pp. 233–4 n. 33 for a similar situation at the siege of Bergen-op-Zoom in 1589.

38 Y-M. Bercé, 'Guerre et état', *XVIIe Siècle*, 148 (1985), 260; J. Kenyon, *The Civil Wars of England* (London, 1988), pp. 126, 162; I. A. A. Thompson, *War and Government in Habsburg Spain, 1560–1620* (London, 1976), p. 74.

39 Thompson, op. cit., p. 74; F. Redlich, *The German Military Enterpriser and his Workforce, 13th to 17th Centuries* (Wiesbaden, 1964): *Vierteljahrschrift für Sozial-und Wirthschaftsgeschichte*, Beiheft, 2 vols), ii, p. 192.

40 'Life', p. 354. See also the impassioned condemnation of corrupt captains by Sir John Smythe, *Certain Discourses Military*, ed. J. Hale (Ithaca, 1964, first pub. 1590), pp. 23–4; and H. Herbert,

'Captain Henry Herbert's Narrative of his Journey through France with his Regiment, 1671 to 1673', ed. J. Childs, *Camden Miscellany*, 4th series, xxx (1990), pp. 295–6.

41 'Life', p. 461. Cf. also F. Redlich, 'Der Marketender', *Vierteljahrschrift für Sozial-und Wirthschaftsgeschichte*, xli (1954), *passim*.

42 *Monro, his Expedition*, pt ii, p. 34.

43 M. Sutcliffe, *The Practice, Proceedings and Lawes of Armes* (London, 1593), p. 132.

44 C. Vassal-Reig, *La guerre en Roussillon sous Louis XIII, 1635–1639* (Paris, 1934), p. 36.

45 Parker, *Army of Flanders*, p. 211. Similarly, soldiers, especially Italians who claimed to be particularly poorly treated, deserted from Charles V's besieging army and went into the city of Metz in 1552: Salignac, *Siège de Metz*, p. 526.

46 Thompson, *War and Government*, p. 318 n. 32: Corvisier, *Armies and Societies*, p. 70.

47 Parker, *Army of Flanders*, pp. 210, 212–13.

48 Parker, *Army of Flanders*, ch. 8; his 'Mutiny and discontent in the Spanish army of Flanders, 1572–1607', *Past and Present*, 58 (1973), *passim*. For what follows, and on mutiny generally, see also G. Wymans, 'Les mutineries militaires de 1596 à 1606', *Standen en Landen*, xxxix (1966), 105–21; J. S. Morrill, 'Mutiny and discontent in English provincial armies, 1645–1647', *Past and Present*, 56 (1972), 49–74; Nickle, *Military Reforms of Prince Maurice*, pp. 71–3.

49 *Mémoires du Maréchal Vicomte de Turenne*, in *Nouvelle collection de mémoires pour servir à l'histoire de France*, ed. J. F. Michaud and J. J. F. Poujoulat (Paris, 1838), 3rd series, iii, pp. 409–16; Parker, 'Mutiny and discontent', pp. 48–9; G. Parker, *The Thirty Years War* (London, 1987), pp. 160–1.

50 *Testament politique*, ed. L. André (Paris, 1947), pp. 475–6; L. André, *Michel le Tellier et l'organisation de l'armée monarchique* (Paris, 1906), p. 64. Cf. also the remarks of Louis XIV in des Cilleuls, 'Le Service de santé', p. 8.

51 Paré, *Œuvres*, p. 1208.

52 J. W. Wijn, *Het Krijgswezen in den Tijd vans Prins Maurits* (Utrecht, 1934), pp. 117, 120–4; J. Turner, *Pallas Armata: Military Essayes of the Ancient Grecian, Roman and Modern Art of War* (London, 1683), p. 198.

53 André, *Michel le Tellier et Louvois*, pp. 344–6: Turner, *Pallas Armata*, p. 197; Mallett and Hale, *Military Organization*, p. 385; Nickle, *Military Reforms of Prince Maurice*, pp. 183–4. The 1629 code *Michau* had sought to put musters under the control of royal *commissaires* and had raised the pay of captains and other officers by 50 per cent in an effort to obviate the necessity for them to cheat. Like much else in the code, little came of these provisions: F-A. Isambert, *Receuil général des anciennes lois françaises* (29 vols, Paris, 1822–3), xvi, esp. pp. 284–5, 287–8, 298–9.

54 In 1594 the States-General commented: 'Experience has frequently taught that, if the Colonel and Captains take the arming of the troops as their responsibility, that great shortcomings generally occur in the matter, to the loss, great disservice and cost of the Land.' Nickle, *Military Reforms of Prince Maurice*, p. 179.

55 Parker, *Army of Flanders*, pp. 162–3; *The Military Revolution: Military Innovation and the Rise of the West* (Cambridge, 1988), p. 80. See also J. Berenger, *Finances et absolutisme autrichien dans la seconde moitié du XVIIe siècle* (2 vols, Université de Lille III, 1975), ii, pp. 346–7 on contracts made by the government *proviant-verwalter* with great merchants for the provisioning of garrison troops in Austrian employ.

56 Details from M. Roberts, *Gustavus Adolphus. A History of Sweden, 1611–1632* (2 vols, London, 1953, 1958), ii, pp. 237–8; André, *Michel le Tellier et l'armée*, p. 339; *Michel le Tellier et Louvois*, p. 349; Scouller, *Armies of Queen Anne*, p. 158; Parker, *Army of Flanders*, p. 165. In the French army powder and ball were only provided free post 1727; the soldier therefore incurred a fiscal penalty every time he fired: Jones, 'Welfare', p. 198.

57 1684 recruiting warrant to constables of Guildford, 'Surrey Musters', *Surrey Record Society*, 11 (London, 1914), p. 359; McKay, *Prince Eugene*, p. 227. After 1649 troops in Hungary were given part of their wages in cloth which they were supposed to use to clothe themselves. Most, however, was re-sold: Berenger, *Finances et absolutisme*, ii, p. 339.

58 Corvisier, *Louvois*, p. 353; Vassal-Reig, *La guerre en Roussillon*, p. 57.

59 Parker, *Army of Flanders*, p. 164. A further reason was suggested by one commander in 1672 for putting troops in uniform. 'It would be harder for the men to desert if they were all dressed in the same way, since they would be more easily recognized': cit. in C. Rousset, *Histoire de Louvois* (4 vols, Paris, 1862–3), i, p. 187.

60 Corvisier, *Louvois*, p. 354.

61 Parker, *Army of Flanders*, pp. 166–7; Scouller, *Armies of Queen Anne*, pp. 165 n. 3, 166; Corvisier, *Louvois*, pp. 192, 352–3; Jones, 'Welfare', p. 201; C. Duffy, *The Army of Frederick the Great* (Newton Abbot, 1974), p. 58; P. G. M. Dickson, *Finance and Government under Maria Theresa, 1740–1780* (2 vols, Oxford, 1987), ii, pp. 19–20 on the 'Systemata' of 1748; N. Wharton, 'Letters from a Subaltern Officer', *Archaeologia*, 35 (1853), p. 236.

62 Scouller, *Armies of Queen Anne*, p. 153.

63 J. Milot, 'Un problème opérationnel du XVIIe siècle illustré par un cas régional', *Revue du nord*, 53 (1971), 273. Cf. also J. A. Houlding, *Fit for Service: the Training of the British Army, 1715–1795* (Oxford, 1981), pp. 137ff on the poor condition of British weapons post 1715.

64 Redlich, *German Military Enterpriser*, ii, p. 228. See also E. G. Léonard, *L'Armée et ses problèmes au XVIIIe siècle* (Paris, 1958),

chs 1–5; J. Childs, *The British Army of William III, 1689–1702* (Manchester, 1987), pp. 147ff; Berenger, *Finances et absolutisme*, ii, pp. 348–9, 357ff.

65 *Histoire der Nederlantscher Oorlogen* (Leuwarden, 1650), p. 324, cit. in Nickle, *Military Reforms of Prince Maurice*, pp. 90–1. Monck commented similarly, 'If a general ensures that his men are fed and clothed...if they are punctually paid...then your general can with justice punish them severely': E. M. Lloyd, *A Review of the History of Infantry* (London, 1908), p. 182.

66 C. H. Firth, *Cromwell's Army. A History of the Soldier during the Civil Wars, the Commonwealth and the Protectorate* (London, 1962), pp. 279–81; G. Oestreich, *Neostoicism and the Early Modern State* (Cambridge, 1982), p. 125; Roberts, *Gustavus Adolphus*, ii, p. 240. The *Artikelbrief* is printed in Wijn, *Krijgswezen* and (in trans.) in Nickle, *Military Reforms of Prince Maurice*, pp. 316ff. An English translation by Henry Hexham appeared in 1643. Adolphus's articles were translated by, amongst others, Ward, *Anima'dversions of Warre* (London, 1639), bk ii, pp. 42–54.

67 Reprinted in *Journal of the Society for Army Historical Research*, v (1926), 112ff.

68 Redlich, *De Praeda Militari: Looting and Booty* (Wiesbaden, 1956: *Vierteljahrschrift für Sozial-und Wirthschaftsgeschichte*, Beiheft 39), p. 11.

69 Firth, *Cromwell's Army*, p. 289.

70 Henry's and Leicester's codes are reprinted in P. L. Hughes and J. F. Larkin (eds), *Tudor Royal Proclamations* (3 vols, London, 1964), i, pp. 106–20 and Cruickshank, *Elizabeth's Army*, pp. 144–51, respectively; McKay, *Prince Eugene*, p. 228. Compare Eugene's regulation with the more elastic stipulation in the 1627 English articles that nobody go 'further than a cannon shot' from the army.

71 Redlich, *De Praeda Militari*, p. 10.

72 J. S. Fishman, *Boerenverdreit: Violence between Peasants and Soldiers in Early Modern Netherlands Art* (Ann Arbor, 1982), pp. 8–9.

73 J. Adair, 'The court martial papers of Sir William Waller's army, 1644', *Journal of the Society for Army Historical Research*, 44 (1966), 209, 211; Turner, *Pallas Armata*, pp. 205–8, 223. Details of the *prévost de la justice* and his staff used by Francis I in 1537 are given in Lot, *Recherches*, p. 198.

74 *Mémoires du Maréchal de Villars* (Société de l'histoire de France, 6 vols, Paris, 1888–1904), ii, p. 230; Redlich, *De Praeda Militari*, *passim*; Jones, 'Welfare', pp. 197–8, 202; Firth, *Cromwell's Army*, pp. 291ff.

75 Parker, *Army of Flanders*, pp. 190–1.

76 H. W. Koch, *A History of Prussia* (London, 1978), p. 59; G. Davies (ed.), 'Dundee courts martial records, 1651', *Miscellany of the Scottish History Society*, iii (1919), 35–6. Cf. also Scouller, *Armies of Queen Anne*, ch. vi.

77 A. Babeau, *La Vie militaire sous l'ancien régime* (2 vols, Paris, 1889–90), i, p. 227.

78 Roberts, *Gustavus Adolphus*, ii, p. 242; M. D. Feld, 'Middle-class society and the rise of military professionalism: the Dutch army, 1589–1609', *Armed Forces and Society*, i (1975), 438.

79 C. de Seyssel, *La Monarchie de France*, ed. J. Poujol (Paris, 1961; first pub. 1515), p. 184. The failure to establish orders for the military is the more surprising given that a number of ex-soldiers went on to found orders for other groups. Cf., for example, the careers of St John of God and Camillus of Lellis in D. H. Farmer, *The Oxford Dictionary of Saints* (Oxford, 1987), p. 234; *Diction-naire d'histoire et de géographie ecclésiastique* (Paris, 1949), xi, cols 604–5.

80 A. T. van Deursen, 'Holland's experience of war during the Revolt of the Netherlands', in A. C. Duke and C. A. Tamse (eds), *Britain and the Netherlands*, vi (The Hague, 1977), pp. 21–2; Parker, *Army of Flanders*, pp. 178–9; Babeau, *La Vie militaire*, i, pp. 228–33. Wallhausen, *L'Art militaire*, noted, 'soldat pieux, rare oiseau et bien digne Qu'accomparé il soit à un noir cygne': cit. in ibid., p. 228.

81 Seyssel, *La Monarchie de France*, p. 184.

82 Duffy, *Siege Warfare*, i, p. 74. See also W. S. Maltby, *Alba: A Biography of Fernando Alvarez de Toledo, Third Duke of Alba, 1507–1582* (Berkeley, 1983), p. 253 on atrocities at the bitter siege of Haarlem.

83 McKay, *Prince Eugene*, p. 45. See also pp. 33, 162, and Redlich, *German Military Enterpriser*, ii, p. 224. Turner wrote of seeing men killed in cold blood by the Finns 'who professe to give no quarter': *Memoirs*, pp. 5–6. Little was known of the Livonians, Finns and Scots in the Swedish army before their arrival in Germany, but they had a reputation as uncouth and savage soldiers, immune to sword and shot, and riding on reindeers. See the illustration in E. A. Beller, *Propaganda in the Thirty Years War* (Princeton, 1940), plate IX, by an artist who had clearly never set eyes on them when he made the print.

84 Stevenson, *Scottish Covenanters*, p. 106; Symcox, *War, Dip-lomacy and Imperialism*, p. 147.

85 G. d'Avenel, *Richelieu et la monarchie absolue* (4 vols, Paris, 1884–90), i, p. 316; D. Eggenberger, *A Dictionary of Battles* (London, 1967), p. 313. Cf. also R. Gough, *The History of Myddle*, ed. D. Hey (Harmondsworth, 1981), pp. 74–5.

86 T. Audley, 'A Treatise on the Art of War', in *Journal of the Society for Army Historical Research*, vi (1927), 133. See also Redlich, *De Praeda Militari*, pp. 29–30. M. Sutcliffe, *Lawes of Armes* (1593), pp. 11–12 admitted the legitimacy of executing prisoners in certain circumstances.

87 B. Donagan, 'Codes and conduct in the English Civil War', *Past and Present*, 118 (1988), 82.

88 J. L. Malcolm, *Caesar's Due: Loyalty and King Charles, 1642–1646* (London, 1983), p. 110; Donagan, 'Codes and conduct', p. 89. Fairfax commented that the finest men he had were ex-prisoners

from the Royalist army: Firth, *Cromwell's Army*, p. 37. See also the example of the fort of Lérida in Spain; two-thirds of the garrison joined up with the besiegers after its surrender in 1707: J. W. Wright, 'Sieges and customs of war at the opening of the eighteenth century', *American Historical Review*, xxxix (1934), 643.

89 C. G. Cruickshank, *Army Royal: Henry VIII's Invasion of France* (Oxford, 1969), pp. 122-3 and ch. ix generally.

90 Redlich, *De Praeda Militari*, p. 35; Van Deursen, 'Holland's experience of war', p. 37; Corvisier, *La France de Louis XIV*, pp. 105-6.

91 Act III, scene i, lines 149 ff.

92 *Army of Flanders*, p. 289 appendix I; *Thirty Years War*, p. 97.

93 Details from Corvisier, *Louvois*, pp. 354-5; Redlich, *German Military Enterpriser*, ii, pp. 208ff; H. De Watteville, *The British Soldier: his Daily Life from Tudor to Modern Times* (New York, 1954), p. 129; Mallett and Hale, *Military Organization*, pp. 385-6; Nickle, *Military Reforms of Prince Maurice*, p. 318.

94 *Sulle Battaglie*, trans. in T. M. Barker, *The Military Intellectual and Battle: Raimondo Montecuccoli and the Thirty Years War* (New York, 1975), p. 135. For the contrary opinions of Monluc see *Commentaires de Messire Blaise de Monluc*, ed. P. Corteault (Paris, 1964, first pub. Bordeaux, 1592), p. 29.

95 Vassal-Reig, *La Guerre en Roussillon*, p. 63. A capuchin claimed that the Spanish defeat resulted from the presence of large numbers of women with the army which had incurred the anger and judgement of heaven. On the theme of women as fighters, an under-researched one, see B. C. Hacker, 'Women and military institutions in early modern Europe: a reconnaissance', *Signs: Journal of Women in Culture and Society*, vi (1980-1), 658-9 and the bibliography cited there.

96 J. R. Hale, 'Armies, navies and the art of war', in *New Cambridge Modern History*, ed. R. B. Wernham (Cambridge, 1968), iii, p. 184. Seyssel acknowledged that *femmes communes et mal famées* could not be kept from the army; they had therefore to be tolerated (much as the Church was obliged to tolerate 'red light' districts in cities) and their numbers controlled: *La Monarchie de France*, p. 184.

97 Hacker, 'Women and military institutions', p. 653.

98 Symcox, *War, Diplomacy and Imperialism*, p. 146.

99 Langer, *The Thirty Years War*, pp. 95, 163.

100 F. de la Noue, *Discours politiques et militaires*, intro. by F. E. Sutcliffe (Paris, 1967, first pub. Geneva, 1587), pp. 343-5 and 341-7 generally.

101 Blaise de Vigenère, *L'Art militaire d'Onosender* (Paris, 1605), p. 149v-150, cit. in Parker, *Army of Flanders*, p. 177 n. 2; Fourquevaux, *Instructions*, cit. in la Noue, *Discours*, p. 341; Monro, *Monro, his Expedition*, pt i, pp. 10, 25.

102 *Monro, his Expedition*, pt ii, p. 89.

103 'Letters from a Subaltern Officer', pp. 313, 316,326, 328.

104 *A Warre-like Treatise of the Pike* (London, 1642), p. 14.

105 Scouller, *Armies of Queen Anne*, p. 274.
106 *Der Abentheuerlich Simplicissimus Teutsch*, ed. R. Tarot (Tübingen, 1967, first pub. 1669), bk I, ch. xvi.
107 Langer, *Thirty Years War*, p. 101; and see the incident of the magic bottle in J. J. von Grimmelshausen, *Mother Courage*, trans. W. Wallich (London, 1965, first pub. 1670), pp. 101–4.
108 Turner, *Memoirs*, pp. 6–7.
109 McKay, *Prince Eugene*, p. 229; J. Youings, *Sixteenth-century England* (London, 1984), pp. 257, 270; M. Prévost, 'L'assistance aux invalides de la guerre avant 1670', *Revue des questions historiques*, 96 (1914), *passim*. La Noue claimed that ex-soldiers in monasteries were often ill-treated and driven out by the monks: *Discours*, p. 353.
110 Details from Parker, *Army of Flanders*, p. 168; C. Nordmann, 'L'Armée suédoise au XVIIe siècle, *Revue du nord*, 54 (1972), p. 142; d'Avenel, *Richelieu*, iii, pp. 147–51; A. Solard, *Histoire de l'Hôtel Royal des Invalides depuis sa fondation jusqu'à nos jours* (Paris, 1845); Scouller, *Armies of Queen Anne*, pp. 329ff; A. de Saluces, *Historie militaire de Piémont* (5 vols, 1817–18), i, pp. 297–9, v, p. 240; Redlich, *German Military Enterpriser*, ii, pp. 259–61; *The Diary of Thomas Crosfield*, ed. F. Boas (Oxford, 1935), p. 67.
111 Parker, *Army of Flanders*, p. 182; *Thirty Years War*, p. 186.
112 P. Clark, 'A crisis contained? The condition of English towns in the 1590s', in P. Clark (ed.), *The European Crisis of the 1590s: Essays in Comparative History* (London, 1985), p. 52.
113 Scouller, *Armies of Queen Anne*, pp. 323ff; Firth, *Cromwell's Army*, pp. 273–5; Chaboche, 'Les soldats français de la guerre de trente ans: une tentative d'approche', *Revue d'histoire moderne et contemporaine*, xx (1975), p. 19, n. 5.
114 E. J. Feuchtwanger, *Prussia, Myth and Reality. The Role of Prussia in German History* (London, 1970), p. 48.
115 At sieges too there were spectators. The besiegers were unable to prevent them getting inside the city during the siege of Ostend in 1601–4: Duffy, *Siege Warfare*, i, p. 96.
116 Cited in Langer, *Thirty Years War*, pp. 64, 89.
117 J. R. Hale, *War and Society in Renaissance Europe, 1450–1620* (London, 1985), p. 129.
118 Langer, *Thirty Years War*, p. 100.
119 *Discours*, p. 211; *Memoirs*, p. 14. Note too the admission of Poyntz. 'I wandered out of my owne countrey, I knew not whither, and followed I knew not whome': 'The Relation of Sydnam Poyntz, 1624–36', ed. A. T. S. Goodrick, *Camden Miscellany*, 3rd series, xiv (1908), p. 128.
120 *Discours*, p. 211.
121 P. R. Newman, 'The royalist officer corps 1642–1660: army command as a reflexion of the social structure', *Historical Journal*, xxvi (1983), 953, though for a different point of view with respect to the officer class see Kenyon, *Civil Wars*, pp. 42–6, and below

n. 122. The real problem is to know how many professionals there were amongst the NCOs and rank and file. There is nothing to support Kenyon's assertion that 'some, perhaps many, of them returned to England in 1642' (from the continent).

122 Alexander Leslie's efforts to bring Scots veterans back from Germany to resist Charles I in 1639 had been fruitless, though more did return subsequently. One calculation suggests that amongst the Scots army of 1644 every lieutenant-colonel but four and every major but three had served in the continental wars: Terry, *Alexander Leslie*, pp. 42 n. 4, 43 n. 4.

123 J. de Pablo, 'Contribution à l'étude de l'histoire des institutions militaires huguenotes', *Archiv für Reformationgeschichte* (1957), pp. 197–8.

124 Cited in C. V. Wedgwood, *The Thirty Years War* (London, 1981, first pub. 1938), p. 386, who notes of this and other armies fighting in Germany that it exhibited 'the peculiarities of a self-conscious class'.

125 R. Chaboche, 'Les Soldats d'origine languedocienne aux Invalides', *Actes du Congrès National des Sociétés Savantes*, 96 i Toulouse (1971), p. 39. Continuous service with the same unit was not at all unusual, however. Of the French soldiers studied by Chaboche 25.5 per cent never changed unit, 19.4 per cent changed only once, and 23 per cent changed three or more times, whilst 50 per cent of the Swiss and Imperial soldiers never changed unit: 'Les Soldats français', pp. 21–2.

126 Corvisier, *L'Armée française*, p. 796.

127 *Mémoires de Saulx-Tavannes*, p. 73. Thomas Audley, 'A Treatise on the Art of War', in *Journal of the Society for Army Historical Research*, vi (1927), p. 69 suggested that a man could be trained in the use of his weapons in a mere two weeks.

128 Kenyon, *Civil Wars*, p. 229.

129 *Utopia*, ed. E. Surtz and J. H. Hexter, in *The Complete Works of St Thomas More* (15 vols, London, 1963–86), iv, p. 63.

130 Clark, 'A crisis contained?', p. 55; Langer, *Thirty Years War*, p. 99; S. Gaber, *La Lorraine meurtrie: les malheurs de la guerre de trente ans* (Nancy, 1979), p. 30. See also Corvisier, 'Guerre et mentalité', p. 229 for some French examples, and B. Kiraly, 'War and society in Western and East Central Europe in the pre-revolutionary eighteenth century', in G. E. Rothenberg *et. al.* (eds), *East Central European Society and War in the Pre-Revolutionary Eighteenth Century* (New York, 1982), p. 13 on the ex-garrison soldiers in Hungary who took to brigandage after the area's liberation from Ottoman rule late in the seventeenth century.

131 Prévost, 'L'Assistance', p. 458; Cruickshank, *Elizabeth's Army*, p. 20; Dickinson, *The 'Instructions'... of Fourquevaux*, pp. xxx-xxxi; G. Bordonove, *Les Rois qui ont fait la France: Henri IV* (Paris, 1981), p. 254.

132 Langer, *Thirty Years War*, p. 99; Dorwart, *Prussian Welfare State*, pp. 96–8.

133 Corvisier, *Louvois*, p. 213; Jones, 'Welfare', p. 200; Chaboche, 'Les soldats d'origine languedocienne', p. 43. In Brandenburg an edict of 1718 ordered the arrest of invalided and discharged soldiers and their incarceration in the fortress of Colberg: Dorwart, *Prussian Welfare State*, pp. 108–9.

5 THE IMPACT OF WAR

1 J. Turner, *Pallas Armata: Military Essayes of the Ancient Grecian, Roman and Modern Art of War* (London, 1683), p. 201.
2 A. Corvisier, *La France de Louis XIV, 1643–1715: ordre intérieur et place en Europe* (Paris, 1979), p. 108.
3 A. Dubois, *Journal d'un curé de campagne au XVIIe siècle*, ed. H. Platelle (Paris, 1965), pp. 153–6.
4 D. McKay, *Prince Eugene of Savoy* (London, 1977), p. 23.
5 A. M. Everitt, *The Community of Kent and the Great Rebellion* (Leicester, 1966), p. 186; G. Franz, *Der Dreissigjährige Krieg und das Deutsche Volk* (Stuttgart, 1961, 3rd edn), *passim*, gives a painstaking regional survey.
6 C. Durston, 'Reading and its county gentry, 1625–1649' (Unpublished PhD thesis, 2 vols, Reading, 1977), i, pp. 155, 210, and 151–210 generally; B. de Salignac, *Le Siège de Metz*, in *Nouvelle collection de mémoires pour servir à l'histoire de France*, ed. J. F. Michaud and J. J. F. Poujoulat (Paris, 1838), 1st series, viii, p. 515; H. Hasquin, *Le 'Pays de Charleroi' aux XVIIe et XVIIIe siècles* (Brussels, 1971), p. 233. See also M. Bennett, 'Leicestershire's Royalist officers and the war effort in the county, 1642–1646', *Transactions of the Leicestershire Archaeological and Historical Society*, lix (1984–5), 49, for an instance of the rival forces collecting contributions on alternate days.
7 L. S. van Doren, 'War taxation, institutional change and social conflict in provincial France – the royal taille in Dauphiné, 1494–1559', *Proceedings of the American Philosophical Society*, 121 (1977), 72. See also C. Souchon, 'Le poids de la guerre dans la vie quotidienne d'une paroisse picarde pendant la minorité de Louis XIV', *Actes du Congrès National des Sociétés Savantes* 103i, Metz/Nancy (1978), 477–93 for the damage wreaked on the 'boulevard des invasions' leading into France.
8 Corvisier, *La France de Louis XIV*, pp. 106–7.
9 Salignac, *Le Siège de Metz*, p. 517; J. Washbourn (ed.), *Bibliotheca Gloucestrensis* (Gloucester, 1825), p. clviii.
10 S. Porter, 'Property destruction in the English Civil War', *History Today*, viii (1986), 37–8 and *passim*.
11 Hasquin, *Charleroi*, p. 235.
12 Porter, 'Property destruction', p. 41.
13 J. Berenger, *Finances et absolutisme autrichien dans la seconde moitié du XVIIe siècle*(2 vols, Université de Lille, 1975), i, p. 281. See also the comment of the French commander, Grammont, on the recovery of Westphalia in the aftermath of the Thirty Years War, in

M. S. Anderson, *War and Society in Europe of the Old Regime, 1618–1789* (Leicester, 1988), p. 70.

14 G. Symcox, *War, Diplomacy and Imperialism, 1618–1763* (London, 1973) p.172; H. Langer, *The Thirty Years War* (Poole, 1982), p.124.

15 McKay, *Prince Eugene*, p. 116; P. Grouvelle and P. de Grimoard (eds), *Œuvres de Louis XIV* (6 vols, Paris, 1806), iii, p. 346; H. van Houtte, *Les Occupations étrangères en Belgique sous l'ancien régime* (2 vols, Ghent), ii, p. 23.

16 C. Vassal-Reig, *La guerre en Roussillon sous Louis XIII, 1635–1639* (Paris, 1934), pp. 102, 50; F. Lot, *Recherches sur les effectifs des armées françaises des guerres d'Italie aux guerres de religion, 1494–1562* (Paris, 1962), p. 51; B. de Monluc, *Commentaires de Messire Blaise de Monluc*, ed. P. Courteault (Paris, 1964, first pub. Bordeaux, 1592), pp. 306–7. During the siege of Bristol in 1643 women 'from ladies down to Oyster wenches' were said to have 'labour'd like pioneers in trenches': cit. in A. Fraser, *The Weaker Vessel: Woman's Lot in Seventeenth-century England* (London, 1984), p. 182.

17 E. H. Dickerman, *Bellièvre and Villeroy: Power in France under Henry III and Henry IV* (Providence, 1971), p. 86.

18 Salignac, *Le Siège de Metz*, p. 527; G. Rothrock, 'The siege of La Rochelle', *History Today*, xix (1969), 858; F. Vaux de Foletier, *Le Siège de La Rochelle* (Paris, 1931), *passim*, for the military details of the siege.

19 S. Gaber, *La Lorraine meurtrie: les malheurs de la guerre de trente ans* (Nancy, 1979), pp. 49–50, 83–4.

20 ibid., p. 64; E. Thoen, 'Warfare and the countryside: social and economic aspects of the military destruction in Flanders during the late Middle Ages and the early modern period', *Acta Historiae Neerlandicae*, xiii (1980), 28 and n. 17; Langer, *Thirty Years War*, p. 103. For one example of town–country antagonisms see D. Sella, *Crisis and Continuity: the Economy of Spanish Lombardy in the Seventeenth Century* (London, 1979), pp. 29–35.

21 G. Cabourdin, *Terre et hommes en Lorraine, 1550–1650: Toulois et comté de Vaudémont* (2 vols, Nancy, 1977), ii, p. 717, and for the following example p. 515.

22 J. Jacquart, *La Crise rurale en Ile de France, 1550–1670* (Paris, 1974), esp. pp. 213ff, 700ff; Hasquin, *Charleroi*, p. 240. See also C. Desama and A. Blaise, 'Comment les communautés villageoises avaient recours au crédit au XVIIe siècle', *Credit communal de Belgique: Bulletin Trimestriel* (1967), 55–65, as cited in Hasquin, p. 79, for the same phenomena in the duchy of Limbourg and principality of Liège. C. Viñas y Mey, *El Problema de la Tierra en la España de los siglos xvi-xvii* (Madrid, 1941), pp. 33–53 shows how heavy state taxation due to war also led to peasant indebtedness and eventual loss of land.

23 Most affected were Pomerania, Bavaria, Saxony and Mecklenburg where, in one district, the 423 peasant holdings in existence in 1618 had been reduced to 115 by 1670: Franz, *Dreissgjährige*

Krieg, p. 98 and *passim*. There were major transfers of land in Bohemia after 1621, but this was a result of deliberate expropriations by the Habsburg rulers: J. V. Polisensky, *The Thirty Years War* (London, 1974), pp. 137–50.

24 M. P. Gutmann, *War and Rural Life in the Early Modern Low Countries* (Princeton, 1980) esp. pp. 52, 109.

25 ibid., pp. 46ff; Sella, *Crisis and Continuity*, pp. 129–30; Thoen, 'Warfare', pp. 32–8; Langer, *Thirty Years War*, pp. 104–5; G. Parker, *The Thirty Years War* (London, 1987), p. 213.

26 Langer, *Thirty Years War*, pp. 106ff.

27 A. Laube, 'Precursors of the Peasant War: *Bundschuh* and *Armer Konrad*', *Journal of Peasant Studies*, iii (1975), 49–53.

28 J. S. Fishman, *Boerenverdreit: Violence between Peasants and Soldiers in Early Modern Netherlands Art* (Ann Arbor, 1982), pp. 10–11 and p. 14 for their defeat.

29 J. Chagniot, 'Guerre et société au XVIIe siècle', *XVIIe Siècle*, 148 (1985), 250; J-M. Constant, 'La troisième fronde: les gentils-hommes et les libertés nobiliares', *XVIIe Siècle*, 145 (1984), 346–8; Corvisier, *La France de Louis XIV*, p. 111.

30 D. Underdown, *Revel, Riot and Rebellion: Popular Politics and Culture in England, 1603–1660* (Oxford, 1985), p. 158. On the clubmen see also R. Hutton, *The Royalist War Effort, 1642–1646* (London, 1982), pp. 159ff and bibliography on p. 233 n. 45.

31 Dubois, *Journal*, p. 102; Corvisier, *La France de Louis XIV*, p. 121. Cf. also J. J. von Grimmelshausen, *Der Abenteuerliche Simplicissimus Teutsch*, ed. R. Tarot (Tübingen, 1967, first pub. 1669), bk I, ch. xiv.

32 D. Herlihy, *Les Toscans et leurs familles* (Paris, 1978), pp. 263–4.

33 C. R. Freidrichs, *Urban Society in an Age of War: Nördlingen, 1580–1720* (Princeton, 1979), esp. ch. 4.

34 Gaber, *Lorraine meurtrie*, pp. 58–9.

35 Dubois, *Journal*, p. 92.

36 G. Oestreich, *Neostoicism and the Early Modern State* (Cambridge, 1982), p. 79. The Venetian ambassador commented, 'I do not believe that there is any other place or country where the army observes discipline and rules as well as here': H. L. Zwitzer, 'The Dutch army during the Ancien Régime', *Revue internationale d'histoire militaire*, lviii (1984), 32.

37 Corvisier, *La France de Louis XIV*, p. 112; Gaber, *Lorraine meurtrie*, p. 29.

38 J. Meuvret, 'Les crises de subsistances et la démographie de la France d'ancien régime', *Population*, i, (1946), 643–50.

39 Parker, *Thirty Years War*, pp. 210–1; D. W. Sabeau, *Power in the Blood: Popular Culture and Village Discourse in Early Modern Germany* (Cambridge, 1984), p. 8; Franz, *Driessigjährige Krieg*, *passim* for other regional statistics.

40 P. Benedict, 'Catholics and Huguenots in sixteenth-century Rouen: the demographic effects of the religious wars', *French Historical Studies*, ix (1975), 232–3; J. Jacquart, 'La fronde des princes dans

la région parisienne et ses consequences materielles; *Revue d'histoire moderne et contemporaine* (1960), vii, pp. 283–8.

41 H. van der Wee, *The Growth of the Antwerp Market* (2 vols, The Hague, 1963), ii, pp. 250, 262.

42 J. A. van Houtte, *An Economic History of the Low Countries, 800–1800* (London, 1977), pp. 132–4.

43 ibid., p. 137; Gaber, *Lorraine meurtrie*, pp. 89–91, 98; Friedrichs, *Nördlingen*, p. 53; Parker, *Thirty Years War*, p. 211.

44 Friedrichs, *Nördlingen*, pp. 53–64; Gutmann, *War and Rural Life*, pp. 149–50. Cf. also van Houtte, *Low Countries*, p. 137 on the importance of immigration in rebuilding populations.

45 Corvisier, *La France de Louis XIV*, p. 116; Gaber, *Lorraine meurtrie*, pp. 45, 47. Cf. also J. Bouchez, *Journal de Jean Bouchez, greffier de Plappeville au XVIIe siècle* (Metz, 1868) for numerous other examples of this kind.

46 Benedict, 'Rouen', pp. 220–1.

47 D. Stevenson, *Scottish Covenanters and Irish Confederates: Scottish–Irish Relations in the Mid-Seventeenth Century* (Belfast, 1981), p. 203.

48 Cabourdin, *Lorraine*, i, pp. 102–4. The passage of Spanish troops in 1567, 1576 and 1587 also brought epidemics to Lorraine: ibid., p. 104. On the relationship between food-shortage and disease see A. B. Appleby, 'Nutrition and disease: the case of London, 1550–1750', *Journal of Interdisciplinary History*, vi, (1975), 1–22; M. Livi-Bacci, *Population and Nutrition: Antagonism and Adaptation* (Cambridge, 1989), ch. 2, summarizes much of the literature.

49 Cabourdin, *Lorraine*, i, pp. 110–1; Gutmann, *War and Rural Life*, pp. 168ff.

50 A link between soldiers and the spread of plague is put forward in J. N. Biraben, *Les Hommes et la peste en France et dans les pays européens et mediterranéens* (2 vols, Paris, 1975), i, pp. 139–47; F. Prinzing, *Epidemics Resulting from Wars* (Oxford, 1916), p. 28 and chs i–iii generally; and a link is assumed in, for example, Gaber, *Lorraine meurtrie*, pp. 55–6 and Anderson, *War and Society*, p. 65. See however the more cautious remarks in C. Cipolla, *Cristofano and the Plague: A Study in the History of Public Health in the Age of Galileo* (London, 1973), pp. 15ff; Parker, *Thirty Years War*, p. 211.

51 Friedrichs, *Nördlingen*, pp. 68–72; Gutmann, *War and Rural Life*, pp. 174–93; his 'Putting crises in perspective: the impact of war on civilian populations in the seventeenth century', *Annales de démographie historique* (1977), 122, 124–5; C. Brunel, *La Mortalité dans les campagnes: le duché de Brabant aux XVIIe et XVIIIe siècles* (2 vols, Louvain, 1977), ii, p. 465. More generally, see E. Le Roy Ladurie, 'L'histoire immobile', *Annales, E.S.C.*, xxix (1974), 673–92.

52 G. Benecke, *Germany in the Thirty Years War* (London, 1978), p. 43; Langer, *Thirty Years War*, p. 123.

53 G. Parker, 'New light on an old theme: Spain and the Netherlands,

1550–1650', *European Studies Review*, xv (1985), 226. Though Verlinden makes the point that a high level of regional mobility was anyway the norm: 'En Flandre sous Philippe II: durée de la crise économique', *Annales, E.S.C.*, vii (1952), 27.

54 Dubois, *Journal*, pp. 125, 155, 172–3.

55 Souchon, 'Le poids de la guerre', pp. 481–2.

56 ibid., p. 485.

57 Durston, 'County gentry', i, p. 97. Elsewhere the saltpetremen justified digging in church by claiming that 'the women piss in their seats which causes excellent saltpetre': C. Russell, 'Monarchies, wars and estates in England, France and Spain, c. 1580–c. 1640', *Legislative Studies Quarterly*, vii (1982), 210.

58 H. Lapeyre, *Une famille de marchands: les Ruiz* (Paris, 1955), p. 431.

59 For examples see Underdown, *Revel*, p. 211; C. Durston, *The Family in the English Revolution* (Oxford, 1989), p. 90; Fraser, *Weaker Vessel*, ch. 9.

60 Durston, 'Country gentry', i, pp. 205–6; Underdown, *Revel*, pp. 159–61.

61 Dickerman, *Bellièvre and Villeroy*, p. 86; Dubois, *Journal*, pp. 110–12, 114 for example.

62 Van der Wee, *Antwerp*, ii, p. 261 n. 130; Sabeau, *Power in the Blood*, p. 9 and n. 29.

63 Durston, *The Family*.

64 A. G. R. Smith, *The Government of Elizabethan England* (London, 1967), p. 8.

65 *Discours politiques et militaires*, intro. by F. E. Sutcliffe (Paris, 1967, first pub. Geneva, 1587), pp. 384, 386.

66 S. Pepper and N. Adams, *Firearms and Fortifications: Military Architecture and Siege Warfare in Sixteenth Century Siena* (Chicago, 1986), p. 31; E. L. Petersen, 'Defence, war and finance: Christian IV and the Council of the Realm, 1596–1629', *Scandinavian Journal of History*, vii (1982), 286; M. E. Mallett and J. R. Hale, *The Military Organization of a Renaissance State: Venice c. 1400 to 1617* (Cambridge, 1984), p. 469.

67 Parker, 'New light on an old theme', p. 225; Anderson, *War and Society*, p. 140.

68 Sella, *Crisis and Continuity*, p. 206 no. 40.

69 Smith, *Elizabethan England*, p. 8; B. H. O'Neil, *Castles and Cannon: a Study of Early Artillery Fortifications in England* (Oxford, 1960), p. 70; Parker, 'New light on an old theme', p. 225; Pepper and Adams, *Firearms and Fortifications*, pp. 26, 30.

70 Details from B. H. Nickle, *Military Reforms of Prince Maurice of Orange* (Michigan, 1984), p. 274 n. 5; Langer, *Thirty Years War*, pp. 17, 162–3. Cf. also Pepper and Adams, *Firearms and Fortifications*, pp. 11ff.

71 F. Braudel, *The Mediterranean and the Mediterranean World in the Age of Philip II*, trans. S. Reynolds (2 vols, London, 1972–3), ii, p. 842.

72 Lot, *Recherches*, p. 117; Salignac, *Le Siège de Metz*, p. 541.
73 Langer, *Thirty Years War*, p. 163; Turner, *Pallas Armata*, pp. 198–9.
74 J. Miller, *Bourbon and Stuart: Kings and Kingship in France and England in the Seventeenth Century* (London, 1987), p. 98.
75 C. Duffy, *Siege Warfare* (2 vols, London, 1979, 1985), i, p. 82.
76 H. A. Lloyd, *The Rouen Campaign, 1590–1592: Politics, Warfare and the Early-Modern State* (Oxford, 1973), pp. 93–4.
77 Petersen, 'Defence, war and finance', p. 304 table 7. 79 per cent of the 1.96 million *daler* spent on the 1611–13 war with Sweden went on recruiting costs and pay: p. 288.
78 ibid., pp. 301–2.
79 See Pepper and Adams, *Firearms and Fortifications*, pp. 30–1; Mallett and Hale, *Military Organization*, pp. 463–84, esp. pp. 467, 471 (between 1540 and c. 1600 an average of roughly 22,800 *ducats* was spent annually on fortresses, the wage bill for the standing forces coming to around 300,000 *ducats*); Petersen, 'Defence, war and finance', pp. 284–6; Duffy, *Siege Warfare*, i, p. 82.
80 G. Parker, *The Military Revolution: Military Innovation and the Rise of the West* (Cambridge, 1988), p. 61. M. Sutcliffe, *The Practice, Proceedings and Lawes of Armes described...* (London, 1593), p. 76 was one of the few to deny that costs had risen.
81 G. d'Avenel, *Richelieu et la monarchie absolue* (4 vols, Paris, 1884–90), iv, p. 728.
82 M. J. Rodriguez-Salgado *et al.*, *Armada* (London, 1988), p. 17; Nickle, *Military Reforms of Prince Maurice*, pp. 84–7.
83 A. Lovett, *Early Habsburg Spain, 1517–1598* (Oxford, 1986), pp. 232–3.
84 J. R. Hale, *War and Society in Renaissance Europe, 1450–1620* (London, 1985), p. 240; J. A. Goris, *Etude sur les colonies marchandes meridionales à Anvers* (2 vols, New York, 1971, reprint of 1925 edn), pp. 409–25.
85 R. A. Stradling, *Europe and the Decline of Spain: A Study of the Spanish System, 1580–1720* (London, 1981), p. 66.
86 Lovett, *Early Habsburg Spain*, pp. 233–4; M. Roberts, *Gustavus Adolphus: A History of Sweden, 1611–1632* (2 vols, London, 1953, 1958), ii, p. 68; McKay, *Prince Eugene*, p. 111; van Doren 'War taxation', pp. 82, 91. In France a 'new' tax, the *taillon*, was simply an adjunct to the existing *taille*.
87 P. Partner, 'Papal financial policy in the Renaissance and Counter-Reformation', *Past and Present*, 88 (1980), 19–21 and *passim*.
88 F. Braudel, 'Les Emprunts de Charles-Quint sur la place d'Anvers', *Charles-Quint et son temps* (Paris, 1959), *passim*; the magisterial study of R. Carande, *Carlos V y sus banqueros* (3 vols, Madrid, 1967); I. A. A. Thompson, *War and Government in Habsburg Spain, 1560–1620* (London, 1976), pp. 67–73; Lovett, *Early Habsburg Spain*, pp. 220ff.
89 F. C. Dietz, *English Government Finance, 1485–1558* (Illinois, 1920), pp. 147, 149, 154, 167–74; P. Williams, *The Tudor Regime*

(Oxford, 1979), pp. 59–70. Debasement of the currency also brought substantial profits to the Crown: C. E. Challis, *The Tudor Coinage* (Manchester, 1978), pp. 253–4. Only the rulers of Prussia made little use of credit, relying instead on profits from the royal demesne, taxes, subsidies and plunder to finance the military: S. E. Finer, 'State- and nation-building in Europe: the role of the military', in C. Tilly (ed.), *The Formation of National States in Western Europe* (Princeton, 1975), p. 140; W. Hubatsch, *Frederick the Great: Absolutism and Administration* (London, 1975), pp. 137–40.

90 T. Wilson, 'The State of England, Anno Domini 1600', ed. F. J. Fisher, *Camden Miscellany*, 3rd series, lii (1936), p. 33; F. C. Dietz, *English Public Finance, 1558–1661* (New York, 1932), esp. pp. 17, 26–7, 58, 62, 86–7. For subsequent reigns see R. Ashton, *The Crown and the Money Market* (Oxford, 1960).

91 R. Knecht, *Francis I* (Cambridge, 1982), p. 389; M. Wolfe, *The Fiscal System of Renaissance France* (London, 1972), esp. chs 3, 4; R. J. Bonney, *The King's Debts: Finance and Politics in France, 1589–1661* (Oxford, 1981), table VIII, p. 317; G. Parker, 'The emergence of modern finance in Europe, 1500–1730', in C. Cipolla (ed.), *The Fontana Economic History of Europe* (6 vols, London, 1977), ii, pp. 576–7; Petersen, 'Defence, war and finance', pp. 308–9. Cf. also J. B. Collins, *Fiscal Limits of Absolutism: Direct Taxation in Early Seventeenth-century France* (London, 1988), pp. 55–64.

92 For much of what follows see K. W. Swart, *The Sale of Offices in the Seventeenth Century* (The Hague, 1949).

93 Bonney, *The King's Debts*, p. 313 table VB; R. Briggs, *Early Modern France, 1560–1715* (Oxford, 1977), graph 7 p. 221.

94 F. Gilbert, *The Pope, his Banker and Venice* (Cambridge, Mass., 1980), p. 30.

95 L. Stone, *The Crisis of the Aristocracy, 1558–1641* (Oxford, 1965), p. 85; P. Goubert, *L'Ancien régime* (2 vols, Paris, 1969, 1973), i, pp. 172–3.

96 P. Burke, *Venice and Amsterdam: A Study of Seventeenth-century Elites* (London, 1974), p. 19.

97 'The State of England', p. 32.

98 M. Mann, *The Sources of Social Power: A History of Power from the Beginning to A.D. 1760* (Cambridge, 1986), pp. 457–8, 483–6 inc. fig. 14.1 and table 14.3; J. Brewer, *The Sinews of Power: War, Money and the English State, 1688–1783* (London, 1989), pp. 38–41 inc. graph and table 2.2; M. Ashley, *Financial and Commercial Policy Under the Cromwellian Protectorate* (London, 1962), p. 48; Stradling, *The Decline of Spain*, p. 65; Goubert, *L'Ancien régime*, ii, pp. 136–9; Anderson, *War and Society*, p. 143; Finer, 'State- and nation-building', p. 140.

99 A. Guéry, 'Les Finances de la monarchie française sous l'ancien régime', *Annales, E.S.C.*, 33 (1978), p. 228 graph 4.

100 Lovett, *Early Habsburg Spain*, pp. 221–2; Petersen, 'Defence, war

and finance', pp. 308–9; Williams, *Tudor Regime*, pp. 59ff.

101 Guéry, 'Finances de la monarchie', p. 230.

102 A general study of the nature and incidence of taxation in western Europe remains to be written. In the meantime, comparative material is most easily available in volumes iii–v of the *New Cambridge Modern History*. For what follows, see also M. Marion, *Dictionnaire des institutions de la France au XVIIe et XVIIIe siècles* (Paris, 1923), arts. *impots, taille, gabelle, aides, capitation*; J. H. Elliott, *Imperial Spain, 1469–1716* (Harmondsworth, 1972), pp. 199ff; R. Braun, 'Taxation, sociopolitical structure, and state-building: Great Britain and Prussia', in Tilly, *National States*, pp. 266–70; C. S. L. Davies, *Peace, Print and Protestantism, 1450–1558* (St Albans, 1977), pp. 169–70. Whether indirect taxes were regressive depended on whether they were levied on, broadly speaking, necessities (staple items of food for example) or on luxury items, which the poor could avoid buying. The *gabelle* was obviously special in this respect since purchase of salt was obligatory.

103 The literature is vast. See especially E. Le Roy Ladurie, *The French Peasantry, 1450–1660* (Aldershot, 1987), ch. v; Y-M. Bercé, *Histoire des Croquants. Etude des soulèvements populaires au XVIIe siècle dans le sud-ouest de la France* (2 vols, Geneva, 1974); R. Pillorget, *Les Mouvements insurrectionnels de Provence entre 1596 et 1715* (Paris, 1975); R. Bonney, *Political Change in France under Richelieu and Mazarin, 1642–1661* (Oxford, 1978), ch. x has an overview; L. Bernard, 'French society and popular uprisings under Louis XIV', *French Historical Studies*, iii (1964), 454–74.

104 P. Goubert, *The French Peasantry in the Seventeenth Century* (Cambridge, 1986), p. 205.

105 H. Kamen, *Spain in the Later Seventeenth Century, 1665–1700* (London, 1980), p. 213. These, and many anti-fiscal revolts elsewhere, are covered in P. Zagorin, *Rebels and Rulers, 1500–1660* (2 vols, Cambridge, 1982), *passim*. The relative absence of popular revolt in England in the sixteenth and seventeenth centuries was principally due to the lighter fiscal burdens imposed: C. S. L. Davies, 'Les Révoltes populaires en Angleterre (1500–1700)', *Annales, E.S.C.*, 24 (1969), 53–4.

106 Bercé, *Croquants*, i, p. 118 and chs 1–3 generally; Pillorget, *Mouvements insurrectionnels*, pp. 987–1009.

107 Details from Ladurie, *French Peasantry*, p. 358; Goubert, *French Peasantry*, p. 203; Sella, *Crisis and Continuity*, p. 45; A. Dominguez Ortiz, *Politica y Hacienda de Felipe IV* (Madrid, 1960), pp. 180–5; N. Salomon, *La Campagne de Nouvelle Castille à la fin du XVIe siècle* (Paris 1964), p. 234; E. Le Roy Ladurie, *Les Paysans de Languedoc* (2 vols, Paris 1966), p. 481.

108 P. Mathias and P. O'Brien, 'Taxation in England and France, 1715–1810. A comparison of the social and economic incidence of taxes collected for the central governments', *Journal of European Economic History*, v (1976), 603–11.

109 On the perception of taxes cf. J. C. Riley, *The Seven Years War and the Old Regime in France: the Economic and Financial Toll* (Princeton, 1986), ch. 2, esp. pp. 38–40.

110 See the detailed study of G. W. Bernard, *War, Taxation and Rebellion in Early Tudor England: Henry VIII, Wolsey and the Amicable Grant of 1525* (Brighton, 1986).

111 Collins, *Limits of Absolutism*, pp. 201ff stresses that the non-payment of taxes was widespread. Jacquart, *La Crise rurale*, also has multiple instances of the build-up of high arrears of tax which the government, unable to collect, was forced to renounce: see, for example, p. 701.

112 Goris, *Etude*, pp. 362ff, 394–401; Braudel, *The Mediterranean*, i, pp. 212, 444, 551 n. 66, 570; ii, p. 695.

113 Roberts, *Gustavus Adolphus*, ii, p. 82.

114 Miller, *Bourbon and Stuart*, p. 90; Wolfe, *Fiscal System*, p. 112.

115 G. Depping, 'Un banquier protestant en France au XVIIe siècle: Barthélemy Herwarth', *Revue historique* (1879), x, 285–338, xi, 63–80; Parker, 'Emergence of modern finance', p. 576. Cf. also D. W. Jones, *War and Economy in the Age of William III* (Oxford, 1988), pp. 83–90; L. Ekholm, *Svensk Kreigsfinansiering, 1630–1681* (Uppsala, 1974: Studia Historica Upsaliensia, lvi), pp. 23–4.

116 Roberts, *Gustavus Adolphus*, ii, pp. 111–20; Thompson, *War and Government*, p. 253.

117 D. Dessert and J. L. Journet, 'Le Lobby Colbert: un royaume ou une affaire de famille', *Annales, E.S.C.*, 30 (1975), pp. 1303–36; Zwitzer, 'The Dutch army', p. 32; Thompson, *War and Government*, pp. 83ff, quotation p. 87.

118 Goris, *Etude*, pp. 350–2 and pp. 375–81 on Gasparo Ducci and Cardinal Tournon, who were amongst the first to see that monarchs' financial needs could only be satisfied by tapping the funds of a wider investing public. By the 1620s the Genoese had in place an efficient system for mobilizing the resources of large numbers of private investors via the exchange fairs: J. G. da Silva and R. Romero, 'L'Histoire des changes: les foires de Bisenzone de 1600 à 1650', *Annales E.S.C.*, 17 (1962), 721. On the links between national and local financiers which facilitated the movement of funds from the provinces to Paris, see G. Chaussinand-Nogaret, *Les Financiers de Languedoc au XVIIIe siècle* (Paris, 1970), esp. pp. 11ff, 85–6 and *passim*.

119 Parker, 'Emergence of modern finance', pp. 567–71; J. D. Tracy, *A Financial Revolution in the Habsburg Netherlands: Renten and Renteniers in the County of Holland, 1515–1565* (London, 1985), chs 1, 2 and *passim*. The Banco di Sant 'Ambrogio was established in 1590 with the aim of raising money from the public for investment in government loans: Sella, *Crisis and Continuity*, p. 46.

120 C. Wilson, *The Dutch Republic and Civilization of the Seventeenth Century* (New York, 1968), p. 34. For comparative figures in

England in the eighteenth century see Brewer, *Sinews of Power*, p. 126.
121 W. Beik, *Absolutism and Society in Seventeenth-century France: State Power and Provincial Aristocracy in Languedoc* (Cambridge, 1985), p. 274; N. S. Davidson, 'Northern Italy in the '1590s' in P. Clark (ed.), *The European Crisis of the 1590s: Essays in Comparative History* (London, 1985), p. 164.
122 J. Dent, *Crisis in Finance: Crown, Financiers and Society in Seventeenth-century France* (Newton Abbot, 1973), pp. 138–41 and chs 6, 8 generally; P. Goubert and D. Roche, *Les Français et l'ancien régime* (2 vols, Paris, 1984), i, p. 305; Chaussinand-Nogaret, *Les Financiers de Languedoc*, pp. 223–33. On the Portuguese contractor, Antonio Carjaval, cf. R. Lewinsohn, *The Profits of War through the Ages* (London, 1936), p. 199; and on the London financier and contractor, Stephen Fox, cf. C. Clay, *Public Finance and Private Wealth: The Career of Sir Stephen Fox* (Oxford, 1978).
123 *L'Ancien régime*, ii, p. 145.
124 Lovett, *Early Habsburg Spain*, p. 224.
125 On the *chambres* and the Crown's treatment of financiers generally see above all Bonney, *King's Debts*, *passim*.
126 Petersen, 'Defence, war and finance', p. 308; Parker, 'Emergence of modern finance', p. 574. Similarly the Venetian ambassador noted in 1620 that 'the province of Holland alone has a debt of 40 million florins, for which it pays six and one quarter per cent interest. It could easily get rid of its debts by raising taxes, but the creditors of the state will not have it so': H. Kamen, *The Iron Century: Social Change in Europe, 1550–1660* (London, 1971), p. 107. So sound was Genoese credit that the Republic was able to borrow at rates of 1.5 per cent for some years after 1604: Parker, 'Emergence of modern finance', pp. 539–40. On Semblançay, de Witte and Foucquet see Knecht, *Francis I*, pp. 128–9, 196–8; A. Ernstberger, *Hans de Witte – Finanzmann Wallensteins* (Wiesbaden, 1954: *Vierteljahrschrift für Sozial-und Wirtschaftgeschichte*, Beiheft 38), *passim*; Bonney, *King's Debts*, pp. 251–71.
127 Carande, *Carlos V y sus banqueros*, iii, pp. 16ff; Bonney, *King's Debts*, p. 315 table VII (the effective interest rate on some tax contracts in 1651 was 42.5 per cent: p. 225); Lovett, *Early Habsburg Spain*, p. 220; Braudel, *The Mediterranean*, ii, p. 695.
128 Bonney, *King's Debts*, pp. 118–19; D. Dessert, 'Finances et société au XVIIe siècle: à propos de la chambre de justice de 1661', *Annales E.S.C.*, 29 (1974), 847–81.
129 Parker, 'New light on an old theme', p. 227; Langer, *Thirty Years War*, p. 136; Ladurie, *Paysans de Languedoc*, i, p. 484; Chaussinand-Nogaret, *Les Financiers de Languedoc*. On the share of royal taxes which found its way back into the pockets of the Languedocian elite in the form of interest payments, salaries, etc., cf. Beik, *Absolutism and Society*, esp. pp. 258–70.
130 Sella, *Crisis and Continuity*, p. 213 n. 9.

131 Miller, *Bourbon and Stuart*, p. 90; R. Mousnier, *La Vénalité des offices sous Henri IV et Louis XIII* (Paris, 1971), pp. 366 and 364–9 generally. Offices sold by the papal Dataria also proved to be sound investments in the sixteenth and seventeenth centuries: Partner, 'Papal financial policy', p. 23. In France the value of some offices may have fallen in the second half of the seventeenth century: Bonney, *Political Change*, pp. 420–1.

132 Lewinsohn, *Profits of War*, pp. 201–4.

133 D. Parker, *The Making of French Absolutism* (London, 1983), p. 147.

134 On Spain see esp. I. A. A. Thompson, 'The purchase of nobility in Castile, 1552–1700', *Journal of European Economic History*, viii (1979), 313–60; for Austria and the German lands, where the question of social mobility has yet to be fully explored, see G. Benecke, 'Ennoblement and privilege in early modern Germany', *History*, 56 (1971), 360–70. On Sweden see S. Dahlgren, 'Estates and classes', in M. Roberts (ed.), *Sweden's Age of Greatness, 1632–1718* (London, 1973), pp. 121–2, 127–8; Roberts, *Gustavus Adolphus*, ii, pp. 158–60.

135 D. Dessert stresses that capital assets were normally a prerequisite, and that those involved in state finances were often not of humble origin: *Argent, pouvoir et société au grand siècle* (Paris, 1984), pp. 98ff.

136 *Testament politique*, ed. L. André (Paris, 1947), p. 250. He went on to stress the absolute necessity of reforming the state's financial system and purging it of the financiers. Nothing was done in this respect. The fiscal demands of war prevented reform and heightened dependence on them.

137 Dessert, *Argent, pouvoir et société*, esp. chs xiv, xv. See also J-P. Labatut, *Les Ducs et pairs de France aux XVIIe siècle* (Paris, 1972) pp. 140–2 and *passim*. In his *Testament politique*, p. 251, Richelieu had noted that 'Gold and silver gives them [the financiers] alliances with the best houses in the kingdom.' Involvement in government finance was thus an important means of consolidating wealth, as well as making it.

138 *National States*, p. 42. Cf. also, for example, V. G. Kiernan, 'State and nation in western Europe', *Past and Present*, 31 (1965), 31; R. Mousnier, *Les Institutions de la France sous la monarchie absolue, 1598–1789* (2 vols, Paris, 1980), ii, pp. 7–10; S. Andreski, 'Evolution and war', *Science Journal*, vii (1971), 92. Mann, *Sources of Social Power*, p. 511, writes: 'By 1815...the "modern state" had arrived, the product of developments often called the Military Revolution.'

139 G. Parker and L. M. Smith, *The General Crisis of the Seventeenth Century* (London, 1978), p. 14. See also the essay by N. Steensgaard, 'The seventeenth-century crisis', in this volume.

140 See, for example, J. Keegan's review of Duffy, *Siege Warfare* in *The New Statesman*, 18 May 1979; J. F. C. Fuller, *The Decisive Battles of the Western World and their Influence upon History*

(3 vols, London, 1954–6), i, p. 471; H. Strachan, *European Armies and the Conduct of War* (London, 1983), p. 10. For England see Stone, *Crisis of the Aristocracy*.

141 Thompson, *War and Government*, p. 281, and 276–81 generally. For a different, though not wholly convincing, point of view with respect to the Habsburg Austrian lands,˙ see J. A. Mears, 'The Thirty Years War, the "General Crisis", and the origins of a standing professional army in the Habsburg monarchy', *Central European History*, xxi (1988), 31–2.

142 This is a recurrent theme in R. Mettam, *Power and Faction in Louis XIV's France* (Oxford, 1988). Cf. also Beik, *Absolutism and Society*, pp. 3–33. More generally see Black, *A Military Revolution? Military Change and European Society, 1550–1800* (London, 1991), pt 3.

143 Mettam, *Power and Faction*, esp. pp. 42–4, 221ff; Parker, *French Absolutism*, p. 137. See also G. Léonard, *L'Armée et ses problèmes au XVIIIe siècle* (Paris, 1958), chs 1–5.

144 J. B. Wolf, *Louis XIV* (London, 1970), p. 198. For what follows see Parker, *French Absolutism*, p. 122; Mettam, *Power and Faction*, pp. 311–12; Beik, *Absolutism and Society*, pp. 324–8; Finer, 'State- and nation-building', p. 137.

145 J. de Pablo, 'Contribution à l'étude de l'histoire des institutions militaires huguenotes', *Archiv für Reformationgeschichte* (1957), pp. 213–14.

146 Collins, *Limits of Absolutism*, p. 203.

147 For France, see Mettam, *Power and Faction*, pp. 239–40, 311–16. On p. 240 he notes, 'For the historian of the later seventeenth century the abiding impression is of how rarely the royal army was used in the internal government of the kingdom', a generalization which could be extended to many other states. Also Beik, *Absolutism and Society*, pp. 324–8 and p. 12 for his comments on the studies of Pillorget and Bercé (above, n. 103). For England see L. G. Schwoerer, *'No Standing Armies': The Anti-Army Ideology in Seventeenth Century England* (Baltimore, 1974); J. Childs, *The British Army of William III 1698–1702* (Manchester 1987), pp. 178–9; his *The Army of Charles II* (London, 1976), ch. xii; his *The Army, James II and the Glorious Revolution* (Manchester, 1980). On the more extensive but still limited use of the army in a police role in the following century, see Brewer, *Sinews of Power*, pp. 51–4; Houlding, *Fit for Service*, pp. 57–74. For the Habsburg lands see Polisensky, *Thirty Years War*, pp. 137ff; R. J. W. Evans, *The Making of the Habsburg Monarchy, 1550–1700* (Oxford, 1979), pp. 195–234 and *passim*; J. Berenger, 'The Austrian lands: Habsburg absolutism under Leopold I', in J. Miller (ed.), *Absolutism in Seventeenth-Century Europe* (London, 1990), pp. 166–72. For Brandenburg-Prussia see H. Rosenberg, *Bureaucracy, Aristocracy and Autocracy: The Prussian Experience, 1660–1815* (Boston, 1958), pp. 42ff. Note too the instance of Spain, where troops put down a revolt which, significantly, lacked elite social

support: H. Kamen, 'A forgotten insurrection of the seventeenth century: the Catalan rising of 1688', *Journal of Modern History*, 49 (1977), 210–30.

148 Beik, *Absolutism and Society*, demonstrates convincingly in the case of Languedoc that effective royal authority was not forcibly imposed on the province from above. Rather, by offering benefits and concessions to the elites in society Louis XIV was able to secure their co-operation in a system which worked largely at the expense of the lower orders. Evans, *Making of the Habsburg Monarchy*, urges that such central control as the largely un-militaristic Habsburgs gained over their heterogeneous dominions came not from the use of force, but from a set of common cultural and mental norms.

149 See, for example, J. A. Mears, 'The emergence of the standing professional army in seventeenth-century Europe', *Social Science Quarterly*, 50 (1969), 106–7; W. Näf, 'Frühformen des "Modernen Staates" im Spätmittelalter', *Historische Zeitschrift*, 171 (1951), esp. 240–1; Oestreich, *Neostoicism*, pp. 196–7. But note the revisionist views of R. G. Asch, 'Estates and princes after 1648: the consequences of the Thirty Years War', *German History*, vi (1988), 113–32.

150 Petersen, 'Defence, war and finance', pp. 308–9; Partner, 'Papal financial policy', p. 30; P. Kennedy, *The Rise and Fall of the Great Powers: Economic Change and Military Conflict from 1500 to 2000* (London, 1988), pp. 60–1; Bonney, *King's Debts*, pp. 54–65. Though war chests did not last long. As Thomas Wilson noted, 'If she [Elizabeth] spares it one yeare or two she spends it all the third, and the divel may danse in her coffers where he finds but a few crosses': 'The State of England', p. 33.

151 Petersen, op. cit., p. 304.

152 H. G. Koenigsberger, 'The Parliament of Piedmont during the Renaissance, 1460–1560', in *Estates and Revolutions* (Ithaca, 1971), pp. 72ff; his 'The Italian parliaments from their origins to the end of the eighteenth century', *Journal of Italian History*, i, (1978), 45–6; F. L. Carsten, *The Origins of Prussia* (Oxford, 1968), pp. 179–252.

153 For the Austrian lands see Oestreich, *Neostoicism*, pp. 226–8; R. J. Dillon, *King and Estates in the Bohemian Lands, 1526–64* (Brussels, 1976). On the powers and activities of the estates in the late seventeenth century, when they continued to block revenue-raising measures, Berenger, *Finances et absolutisme*, pp. 172–217, 423ff. For Denmark see L. Jespersen, 'The *Machstaat* in seventeenth-century Denmark', *Scandinavian Journal of History*, x (1985), pp. 282–3; Petersen, 'Defence, war and finance', pp. 309–10, 313. For France see Bonney, *Political Change*, ch. xv; Beik, *Absolutism and Society*, p. 277; Marion, *Dictionnaire*, 'états'. For Saxony, Württemberg and Hesse see F. L. Carsten, *Princes and Parliaments in Germany from the Fifteenth to the Eighteenth Century* (Oxford, 1959), pp. 72ff, 181ff, 228ff; M.

Fulbrook, 'Religion, revolution and absolutist rule in Germany and England', *European Studies Review*, xii (1982), 304. On the Holy Roman Empire generally, see also Tracy, *Financial Revolution in the Habsburg Netherlands*, pp. 19–21 on the assumption by the estates in several sixteenth-century principalities of the fiscal responsibilities of the state.

154 Philip II, for example, did not take the opportunity presented by the acquisition of Portugal in 1580, the Neapolitan revolt of 1585, or the Aragonese uprising of 1591 to curb the power of the local estates, although fully capable of doing so. Admittedly, when the Neapolitan Parliament protested to the Viceroy against the tax burden in 1639 and 1642 it was no longer summoned: Koenigsberger, 'The Italian parliaments', p. 35.

155 A. L. Moote, *The Revolt of the Judges: The Parlement of Paris and the Fronde* (Princeton, 1971), pp. 109–10.

156 M. Roberts, 'On aristocratic constitutionalism in Swedish history' and 'Charles XI', in *Essays in Swedish History* (London, 1967); a somewhat different interpretation is offered in A. Upton, 'The Riksdag of 1680 and the establishment of royal absolutism in Sweden', *English Historical Review*, cii (1987), 281–308.

157 'Monarchies, wars and estates', pp. 211–14.

158 J. Vicens Vives, 'The administrative structure of the state in the sixteenth and seventeenth centuries', in H. J. Cohn, *Government in Reformation Europe, 1520–1560* (London, 1971), pp. 70–1.

159 Jespersen, 'The *Machstaat*', pp. 290–5; Roberts, *Gustavus Adolphus*, ii, pp. 67ff; A. Åberg, 'The Swedish army from Lützen to Narva', in M. Roberts (ed.), *Sweden's Age of Greatness, 1632–1718* (London, 1973), pp. 267–8; J. Lindegren, 'The Swedish "Military State", 1560–1720', *Scandinavian Journal of History*, x (1985), pp. 334–5.

160 Finer, 'State- and nation-building', pp. 137–40.

161 J. A. Lynn, 'The growth of the French army during the seventeenth century', *Armed Forces and Society*, vi (1980), 581 and *passim*.

162 W. Barberis, *Le armi del Principe: la tradizione militare sabauda* (Turin, 1988), pt i; Smith, *Elizabethan England*, pp. 50, 86–9. Lloyd, *Rouen Campaign*, pp. 81–2 stresses that a judicious use was made of the Lords Lieutenant, the Privy Council insisting that each levy of men was a special occasion, arising from extraordinary circumstances. On the small number of officials – little more than 1,000 in central government – see S. T. Bindoff *et al.*, *Elizabethan Government and Society* (London, 1961), pp. 106–8. Compare with the similar number in the middle of the next century, below, p. 202.

163 See above, pp. 57–8. On the declining use of purveyance see Thompson, *War and Government*, ch. viii; C. S. L. Davies, 'Provisions for armies, 1509–50; a study in the effectiveness of early Tudor government', *Economic History Review*, 2nd series, xvii (1964), pp. 236ff.

164 *War and Government*, pp. 275–87 and *passim*.

165 Details from A. Corvisier, *Louvois* (Paris, 1983), pp. 328–30; his *Armies and Societies in Europe, 1494–1789* (Bloomington, 1979), pp. 75–6; A. de Saluces, *Histoire militaire de Piémont* (5 vols, Turin, 1859), i, p. 292; F. P. Marques, *Exército e Sociedade en Portugal. No declínio do Antigo Regime e advento do Liberalismo* (Lisbon, 1980), p. 26; Brewer, *Sinews of Power*, table 3.2 p. 66 and pp. 46ff; G. Aylmer, *The State's Servants: The Civil Service of the English Republic, 1649–60* (London, 1973), p. 169. Councils of War were also set up in Denmark in 1658 and Bavaria early in the Thirty Years War: Jespersen, 'The *Machstaat*', p. 293; Carsten, *Princes and Parliaments*, p. 407.

166 Evans, *Making of the Habsburg Monarchy*, pp. 149–50; Marques, *Exército e Sociedade en Portugal*, pp. 26ff. Cf. F. Cortés, *Guerra e pressão militar nas terras de fronteira, 1640–1668* (Lisbon, 1990).

167 Bonney, *King's Debts*, p. 281 and n. 1. Though if the original purchase price is regarded as a loan to the Crown, and the salary as the annual interest payment, then selling offices was a relatively cheap way of raising money. Cf., for example, Partner, 'Papal financial policy', pp. 23–4. The effective rate of interest on offices paid by the papacy in the sixteenth century was 5–6 per cent: the interest rates on short-term loans might be three times this.

168 Brewer, *Sinews of Power*, p. 127 and pp. 91ff generally.

169 *War and Government*, p. 287.

170 Don Bernadino de Mendoza, *Teoriá y práctica de la guerra* (Madrid, 1595), cit. in Parker, *The Military Revolution*, p. 62.

171 G. Strauss, *Nuremberg in the Sixteenth Century* (New York, 1966), esp. pp. 150–1; J. Hook, 'Fortifications and the end of the Sienese state', *History*, 62 (1977), 372–87; R. Mackenney, *The City-State, 1500–1700* (London, 1991), pp. 6, 9ff. Though, as Mackenney notes, Geneva was an exception to the general rule.

172 'Bellum se ipsum alet': M. Roberts, *Gustavus Adolphus and the Rise of Sweden* (London, 1973), p. 122. Ch. 8 has a succinct account of war finances.

173 Brewer, *Sinews of Power*, p. 24.

174 H. G. Koenigsberger, *The Habsburgs and Europe 1516–1660* (Ithaca, 1971), p. xi. A good, succinct, discussion of the Spanish Habsburgs' mobilization of resources is to be found in Kennedy, *The Great Powers*, pp. 41–55. For much of what follows on the tax systems of the different states, see P. G. M. Dickson and J. Sperling, 'War finance, 1689–1714', *The New Cambridge Modern History* (Cambridge, 1970), iv, pp. 284–315.

175 Guéry, 'Finances de la monarchie', p. 221.

176 Though one can be over-harsh about French tax farming, which carried some advantages; and in any event the government had little choice in the matter. See above, p. 187.

177 Stone, *Crisis of the Aristocracy*, p. 503; Miller, *Bourbon and Stuart*, p. 138.

178 Berenger, *Finances et absolutisme*, pp. 602ff.

179 C. Wilson, 'Taxation and the decline of empires, an unfashionable theme', in *Economic History and the Historian* (London, 1969), p. 119.

180 Berenger, *Finances et absolutisme*, p. 604.

181 It is also worth noting that there was *relative* agreement amongst the ruling elites in the Netherlands, especially after 1672, about the country's defensive needs and the foreign policy on which taxes were spent. Much the same was true in England under William III, who could therefore count on substantial sums being voted by Parliament. Contrast the more niggardly treatment of James I and Charles I by Parliament, which simply did not trust the rulers or their policies.

182 C. Russell, *Parliaments and English Politics, 1621–1629* (New York, 1979), p. 323, cit. in M. S. Kimmell, 'War, state finance and revolution: foreign policy and domestic opposition in the six-teenth and seventeenth century world economy', in P. McGowan and C. W. Kegley, *Foreign Policy and the Modern World System* (London, 1983), p. 102.

183 In addition to Dickson and Sperling, 'War finance', see above all Brewer, *Sinews of Power*, esp. parts 1 and 2, for a description of this process.

184 Dickson and Sperling, op. cit., p. 313; Mathias and O'Brien, 'Taxation in England and France', pp. 603–11. Though English revenues grew from a lower base, of course.

185 Berenger, *Finances et absolutisme*, pp. 591 and 560–91 generally; Dickson and Sperling, 'War finance', pp. 311–12. For the eigh-teenth-century improvement in Austrian finances and credit-rating, J. C. Riley, *International Government Finance and the Amsterdam Capital Market, 1740–1815* (Cambridge, 1980), chs 6, 7.

186 Tracy, *Financial Revolution in the Habsburg Netherlands*, p. 22.

187 Parker, 'Emergence of modern finance', pp. 573–4; his 'Spain, her enemies and the Revolt of the Netherlands, 1559–1648', in *Spain and the Netherlands, 1559–1659* (London, 1979), p. 21.

188 Brewer, *Sinews of Power*, pp. 114ff; Wilson, 'Taxation and the decline of empires', p. 124 (quotation); P. G. M. Dickson, *The Financial Revolution in England: A Study in the Development of Public Credit, 1688–1715* (London, 1967), is a magisterial account of the revolution in public finance. For an example of contemporary concern at the level of borrowing, see the comment of Charles Davenant cited in E. J. Hamilton, 'Origin and growth of the national debt in Western Europe', *Papers and Proceedings of the American Economic Review*, 37, no. 2 (1947), 122.

189 Brewer, *Sinews of Power*, p. 23. On the Dutch techniques of borrowing see above all Tracy, *Financial Revolution in the Habsburg Netherlands*.

190 Brewer, *Sinews of War*, pp. 88–9, makes this point forcefully.

191 'The key to the healthy public credit of the United Provinces lay in the fact that the chief investors ran the government': Parker, 'Emergence of modern finance', p. 572.

192 Lord Goring to Buckingham, cit. in Kimmell, 'War, state finance and revolution', p. 100.

193 J. Klaits, *Printed Propaganda Under Louis XIV* (Princeton, 1976), p. 265.

194 Wolfe, *Fiscal System*, pp. 92–3 stresses this point with respect to the sixteenth-century *rentes* drawn on the *hôtel de ville*.

195 Parker, 'Emergence of modern finance', pp. 575–6.

196 Tracy, *Financial Revolution in the Habsburg Netherlands*, pp. 219–20. Cf. also the conclusions of Bonney, *King's Debts*, pp. 273–6, 280–1.

197 Details from Tracey, op. cit., pp. 22–5; Parker, 'Emergence of modern finance', pp. 568–70. Cf. also the excellent description of the Spanish credit system in A. C. Pintado, 'Dette flottante et dette consolidée en Espagne de 1557 à 1600', *Annales E.S.C.*, 18 (1963), 745–59.

198 Tracy, *Financial Revolution in the Habsburg Netherlands*, p. 221 and n. 5. The British public debt was *c.* £40 million in 1713 and tax revenues were *c.* £5 million. The respective figures by the 1770s were £240 million and £12 million, giving a debt-to-tax ratio of 20 : 1: Brewer *Sinews of Power*, figure 4.1 p. 90 and figure 4.6 p. 115. Parker, 'Emergence of modern finance', pp. 570, 576.

199 H. Kellenbenz, *The Rise of the European Economy* (London, 1976), p. 197. Cf. also, for example, R. Davis, *The Rise of the Atlantic Economies* (London, 1973), pp. xii and *passim*; J. de Vries, *The Economy of Europe in an Age of Crisis, 1600–1750* (Cambridge, 1976), p. 242; and most notably W. Sombart, *Studien zur Entwicklungsgeschichte des Modernen Kapitalismus, II. Krieg und Kapitalismus* (Munich, 1913).

200 Sella, *Crisis and Continuity*, p. 76. I have relied heavily on the insights of this study.

201 P. Contamine, *War in the Middle Ages* (Oxford, 1984), p. 171 suggests forces of 20–25,000 and a population of 10 million.

202 This assumes an army of 390,000 (an over-estimate), allows 20 per cent for foreigners, and a population of 19 million: Lynn, 'Growth of the French army', figure 2 pp. 575, 577; P. Goubert, 'Recent theories and research in French population between 1500 and 1700', in D. V. Glass and D. E. C. Eversley (eds), *Population in History: Essays in Historical Demography* (London, 1965), pp. 472–3.

203 Corvisier, *Armies and Societies*, table 1, p. 113. In reality the percentage would probably have been even lower since Corvisier's figures exaggerate army size.

204 J. Youings, *Sixteenth-century England* (London, 1984), p. 152. Similarly, only about half the shires were involved in mustering for Essex's expedition in the autumn/spring of 1589–90; Lloyd, *Rouen Campaign*, p. 88. On this occasion the burden did not fall on the southern counties.

205 Thompson, *War and Government*, pp. 103ff; Stradling, *The Decline of Spain*, p. 97.

206 Based on figures for army and population size in Roberts, *Sweden's Age of Greatness*, pp. 21, 26–7, 61, 271.

207 C. Nordmann, 'L'Armée suédoise au XVIIe siècle', *Revue du nord*, 54 (1972), p. 147.

208 Parker, *Thirty Years War*, p. 193; J. Lindegren, *Utskrivning och utsugning. Produktion och reproduktion i Bygdeå, 1620–1640* (Uppsala, 1980: Studia Historica Upsaliensia, cxvii), pp. 147, 164–7, 257.

209 J. B. Kist, *Jacob de Gheyn: the Exercise of Arms* (New York, 1971), pp. 27–8; Berenger, *Finances et absolutisme*, p. 277.

210 Details from H. Kellenbenz, 'The organisation of industrial production', in *The Cambridge Economic History*, ed. E. E. Rich and C. H. Wilson (Cambridge, 1977), v, p. 501; Sella, *Crisis and Continuity*, pp. 22–3, 41; his 'Industrial production in seventeenth-century Italy: a reappraisal', *Explorations in Entrepreneurial History*, n.s., vi (1969), esp. p. 243; J. Yerneaux, *La Métallurgie Liègoise et son expansion au XVIIe siècle* (Liège, 1939); Thompson, *War and Government*, p. 241. On Liège see also C. Gaier, *Four Centuries of Liège Gunmaking* (London, 1977).

211 Details from C. Cipolla, *European Culture and Overseas Expansion* (Harmondsworth, 1970), pp. 42ff; Jespersen, 'The *Machstaat*', p. 300; Roberts, *Gustavus Adolphus*, ii, pp. 107ff; D. Sella, 'European industries, 1500–1700', in C. Cipolla (ed.), *Fontana Economic History*, ii, pp. 387–8; Kellenbenz, 'Organization of industrial production', pp. 480–3; de Vries, *Economy of Europe*, pp. 88–90; and works by Sella and Yerneaux cited in n. 210 above.

212 Details from de Vries, *Economy of Europe*, pp. 204–5; Nordmann, 'L'Armée suédoise', p. 146; H. W. Koch, *A History of Prussia* (London, 1978), p. 85; C. Duffy, *Fire and Stone: The Science of Fortress Warfare, 1660–1860* (Newton Abbot, 1975), p. 36; Parker, 'New light on an old theme', p. 225.

213 A. Everitt, 'The marketing of agricultural produce', in J. Thirsk (ed.), *The Agrarian History of England and Wales* (Cambridge, 1967), iv, pp. 524 and 519–24 for previous examples.

214 Berenger, *Finances et absolutisme* pp. 281 (quotation), 279–81 generally.

215 Everitt, 'Marketing', p. 523; B. Pearce, 'Elizabethan food policy and the armed forces', *Economic History Review*, xii (1942), 39–40, 45. On purchases by the Oppenheimers in eastern Europe, see Berenger, *Finances et absolutisme*, pp. 279–80.

216 Sella, *Crisis and Continuity*, p. 221 n. 19.

217 ibid., p. 16.

218 de Vries, *Economy of Europe*, pp. 91–2; Sella, *Crisis and Continuity*, pp. 38–9. For a different point of view see A. H. John, 'War and the English economy, 1700–1763', *Economic History Review*, 2nd series, vii (1954–5), 330–1, who argues that war, by heightening demand for metal, raising the price of wood and

making imports difficult, encouraged the use of the reverberatory furnace in England between 1688 and 1698, which used coal, rather than charcoal, for iron smelting. On the other hand, Lombard manufacturers had traditionally depended for their competitive edge on the use of advanced techniques for the production of textiles, thread and metal goods. Such techniques owed little or nothing to the demands of war; Sella, op. cit.

219 Similarly, the financier Baroncelli obtained the monopoly on gunpowder production in the Netherlands in the mid-sixteenth century: Goris, *Etude*, pp. 463–5. However, such monopolies generally meant that the holder issued licences – for a fee – to existing producers to allow them to continue production, and did not imply a rationalization of production. Government policy in sixteenth-century Spain was to give contracts for arms production to small-scale craftsmen: Thompson: *War and Government*, p. 245.

220 Sella, 'European industries', p. 405. It is true that the organization of industry was altering in the early-modern period, in that merchant capitalists gained control of production through the putting-out system. See, for example, G. H. Unwin, *Industrial Organization in the Sixteenth and Seventeenth Centuries* (London, 1963), ch. iii. But this development went back to the fourteenth century; and it was most notable in the textile industry, which overwhelmingly served civilian consumer demands. The demands of war do not, therefore, seem to have been important in stimulating the process.

221 de Vries, *Economy of Europe*, p. 93. On the English dockyards see D. A. Baugh, *British Naval Administration in the Age of Walpole* (Princeton, 1965), chs 5, 6; J. Ehrman, *The Navy in the War of William III, 1689–97* (Cambridge, 1953).

222 M. Ulloa, *La Hacienda real de Castilla en el reinado de Felipe II* (Madrid, 1977), chs 6–9; J. Casey, 'Spain: a failed transition', in Clark, *Crisis of the 1590s*, pp. 216–19.

223 M. W. Brulez, *Anvers de 1585 à 1650* (Wiesbaden, 1967: *Vierteljahrschrift für Sozial-und Wirtschaftsgeschichte*, liv), pp. 75–99; A-E. Sayous, 'Le rôle d'Amsterdam dans l'histoire du capitalisme commercial et financier', *Revue historique*, 183 (1938), 242–80.

224 Everitt, 'Marketing', p. 574.

225 K. Glamann, 'European Trade, 1500–1750', in C. Cipolla (ed.), *Fontana Economic History*, ii, p. 472.

226 K. Glamann, 'The changing patterns of trade', *Cambridge Economic History*, v, pp. 228–30.

227 J. U. Nef, 'War and economic progress, 1540–1640', *Economic History Review*, xii (1942), 29.

228 J. I. Israel, 'A conflict of empires: Spain and the Netherlands, 1618–1648', *Past and Present*, 76 (1977), esp. 44–62. On the subject of economic measures in the pursuit of hostilities see, for example, G. N. Clark, 'War trade and trade war, 1701–1713',

Economic History Review, i (1928), 262–80; C. H. Wilson, *Profit and Power. A Study of England and the Dutch Wars* (London, 1957).

229 Israel, op. cit., pp. 58–9. Cf. also G. Parker, 'War and economic change: the economic costs of the Dutch Revolt', in J. M. Winter (ed.), *War and Economic Development* (Cambridge, 1975), p. 63.

230 Details from Sella, *Crisis and Continuity,* pp. 111–12; Nef, 'War and economic progress', pp. 25, 33; Parker, 'War and economic change', pp. 51, 54.

231 Thus Leonardo Donà, one-time Doge of Venice, received about 45 per cent of his income from his landed estates and 16 per cent from government funds. For this, and a discussion of industrial funding generally, see Davidson, 'Northern Italy', pp. 163–5. Cf. also C. H. Phillips, *Ciudad Real, 1500–1750: Growth, Crisis, and Readjustment in the Spanish Economy* (Cambridge, Mass., 1979), p. 62.

232 Sella, *Crisis and Continuity,* pp. 57, 206 n. 40.

233 ibid., p. 134 and ch. vi generally.

234 *Krieg und Kapitalismus.* Sombart goes on to argue that war was decisive in bringing about the development of a fully-fledged capitalist economic system.

235 Sella, *Crisis and Continuity,* pp. 131–4.

236 Jespersen, 'The *Machstaat*', pp. 286–8 and 279–88 generally; T. Munck, *Seventeenth Century Europe. State, Conflict and the Social Order in Europe, 1598–1700* (London, 1990), p. 161. Under Philip II the Crown sold common or waste land to which it claimed ownership, the proceeds making a significant contribution to the Treasury in some years: D. E. Vassberg, *La venta de tierras baldiàs. El communitarismo agrario y la corona de Castilla durante el siglo XVI* (Madrid, 1983).

237 Salomon, *Nouvelle Castille,* p. 250; J. Lynch, *Spain under the Habsburgs* (2 vols, Oxford, 1959), ii, 156; Jespersen, 'The *Machstaat*', pp. 287–8; Sella, *Crisis and Continuity,* pp. 67–8.

238 Sella, op. cit., p. 209 no. 19.

239 Cf. Jacquart, *La Crise rurale,* p. 701, for example.

240 *Crisis and Continuity,* pp. 65–9.

241 Davidson, 'Northern Italy', p. 161; Sella, *Crisis and Continuity,* p. 71 (quotation). Cf. also the complaints from Genoese, Venetian and Milanese merchants in C. Cipolla, 'The economic decline of Italy', in B. Pullan (ed.), *Crisis and Change in the Venetian Economy in the Sixteenth and Seventeenth Centuries* (London, 1968), pp. 138–9; and Philip II's admission of the damage caused to commerce by high taxes, cit. in Parker, 'War and economic change', p. 55.

242 Wilson, 'Taxation and the decline of empires'; M. Morineau, 'Les Mancenilliers de l'Europe', in P. Deyon and J. Jacquart, *Les Hésitations de la croissance, 1580–1740* (Paris, 1978), p. 158 (though Ulloa, *La Hacienda,* chs 6–9 contains a more balanced account of most aspects of the matter); Sella, *Crisis and Continuity,* esp. ch. iv.

243 Hale, *War and Society*, p. 230 and ch. 8 generally for a discussion of war's economic impact.

244 Davis, *Atlantic Economies*, pp. 16, 18, 22. On the emergence of one financial magnate in the Middle Ages see I. Origo, *The Merchant of Prato: Francesco di Marco Datini* (London, 1937).

245 M. M. Postan, 'Some social consequences of the Hundred Years War', *Economic History Review*, xii (1942), 12.

246 See *Cambridge Economic History*, iv, ch. vii for a discussion of the issues and bibliography.

247 *What has Happened to Economic History?* (Cambridge, 1972), cit. in Winter, *War and Economic Development*, p. 3. Jones, *War and Economy*, is one of the few historians to have concentrated on the issue.

248 Parker, 'New light on an old theme', p. 225.

249 Klaits, *Printed Propaganda*, p. 58.

250 Langer, *Thirty Years War*, p. 236.

251 W. Schumacher, 'Vox populi: the Thirty Years War in English newspapers' (Unpublished PhD thesis, Princeton, 1975, microfilm), ch. vi. See also C. R. Boxer, 'Some second thoughts on the Third Anglo-Dutch War, 1672–1674', *Transactions of the Royal Historical Society*, 5th series, xix (1969), 75–6 and *passim* on the rapidity of communications. On the extensive coverage of foreign, mainly military, news in the English press, see E. S. de Beer, 'The English newspaper from 1695 to 1702', in R. Hatton and J. S. Bromley (eds), *William III and Louis XIV* (Liverpool, 1968), pp. 117–29; G. A. Cranfield, *The Development of the Provincial Newspaper, 1700–1750* (Oxford, 1962), pp. 70ff.

252 J. R. Hale, 'War and public opinion in Renaissance Italy', in E. F. Jacob (ed.), *Italian Renaissance Studies* (London, 1960), repr. in *Renaissance War Studies*, p. 381.

253 There is judicious treatment of the topic in, for example, C. de Seyssel, *La Monarchie de France*, ed. J. Poujoul (1961, first pub. 1515), pp. 169–73, and Jean Bodin, *Les six livres de la République* (Paris, 1583, first pub. 1576), bk 5, ch. v, pp. 750–63.

254 *Mémoires de Saulx-Tavannes*, pp. 71–2. Cf. also Bodin, op. cit., bk 5, ch. i.

255 Langer, *Thirty Years War*, pp. 198–200, 217. Cf. also J. R. Mulryne and M. Shewring (eds), *War, Literature and the Arts in Sixteenth-Century Europe* (London, 1989); G. Livet, *Guerre et paix de Machiavel à Hobbes* (Paris, 1972), has a good selection from writings and songs on the theme of war.

256 Klaits, *Printed Propaganda*, p. 8. On the pulpit as a possible opinion-former with respect to military matters, see J. R. Hale, 'Incitement to violence? English divines on the theme of war, 1578–1631', *Florilegium Historiale: Essays Presented to ·Wallace K. Ferguson*, ed. J. G. Rowe and W. H. Stockdale (Toronto, 1971), repr. in *Renaissance War Studies*, ch. 18. All the arts were potentially powerful propaganda vehicles, one reason why princes spent so much time and energy on their patronage and control.

257 Klaits, *Printed Propaganda*, pp. 60 and 58–68 generally. See also H. M. Solomon, *Public Welfare, Science and Propaganda in Seventeenth-Century France: The Innovations of Théophraste Renaudot* (Princeton, 1972) on the origins of the *Gazette* and its patronage by Richelieu. Dubois's *Journal* reveals the extent to which the *curé* was dependent on the *Gazette* especially for his information, and his largely uncritical attitude towards what it retailed. For other examples of the 'slanting' of news stories see Boxer, 'Second thoughts'; P. Fraser, *The Intelligence of the Secretaries of State and their Monopoly of Licenced News, 1660–1688* (Cambridge, 1956).

258 On the Dutch *spiegels* – pamphlets detailing atrocities (but only those committed by the other side) – see Fishman, *Boerenverdreit*, pp. 14, 126 n. 69. Cf. also W. S. Maltby, *The Black Legend in England* (Durham, NC, 1971), ch. iv. The extensive collection in the British Library known as the *Thomason Tracts* is composed largely of propaganda material from the English Civil War.

259 J. L. Price, *Culture and Society in the Dutch Republic During the Seventeenth Century* (London, 1974), pp. 118–23. Some examples are to be found in J. I. Watkins (ed.), *Masters of Seventeenth-Century Dutch Genre Painting* (Philadelphia Museum of Art, 1984). There appears to have been much regional typology in the art produced, the Dutch favouring sea battles and paintings which put war in an unglamorous light, the Germans in the sixteenth century having a fondness for the swaggering *landsknecht*: S. Schama, *The Embarrassment of Riches: An Interpretation of Dutch Culture in the Golden Age* (London, 1988), pp. 238ff; J. R. Hale, 'The soldier in Germanic graphic art of the Renaissance', *Journal of Interdisciplinary History*, xvii (1986), 85–114. This aspect of military/art history would surely repay more study.

260 J. R. Hale, 'Sixteenth-century explanations of war and violence', *Past and Present*, 51 (1971), 3.

261 Langer, *Thirty Years War*, pp. 232–4; A. M. Hind, *A Short History of Engraving and Etching* (London, 1923), chs ii-vii.

262 Fishman, *Boerenverdreit*, p. 76; Schama, *Embarrassment of Riches*, pp. 277–82.

263 T. K. Rabb, *The Struggle for Stability in Early Modern Europe* (New York, 1975), pp. 124–45. There are some comments on the changing depictions of Mars in Hale, 'War and public opinion in Renaissance Italy', pp. 370–3. For the view that ter Brugghen's *Sleeping Mars* was a pacifist statement see B. Nicholson, *Hendrick Terbrugghen* (London, 1958), pp. 102–3 as cited in Watkins, *Genre Painting*, p. 190.

264 The letter he wrote concerning the painting, given in R. S. Magurn, *The Letters of Peter Paul Rubens* (Cambridge, Mass., 1955), pp. 408–9 as cited in Rabb, *Struggle for Stability*, p. 131, seems conclusive. It would seem unlikely that *Peace and War* was intended as a global indictment of war, however. As Rabb himself points out, it was presented to Charles I in 1630 following

negotiations between Spain and England (conducted by Rubens) and may be taken to hint strongly at the particular advantages England would derive from peace and an alliance with Spain.

265 For reproductions of Callot's work, including the *Greater Miseries* and his illustrations for a drill manual, together with commentaries on his life and work which generally credit him with anti-war sentiments, see H. Daniel, *Callot's Etchings* (New York, 1974); D. Ternois, *L'Art de Jacques Callot* (Paris, 1962); E. de T. Bechtel, *Jacques Callot* (London, 1955). A contrary interpretation, similar to that offered here, is to be found in D. Wolfthal, 'Jacques Callot's Misères de la Guerre', *Art Bulletin*, lix (1977), 222–33. For an interpretation of Callot's *Siege of Breda* opposed to that of Rabb, see S. Zurawski, 'New sources for Jacques Callot's map of the Siege of Breda', *Art Bulletin*, lxx (1988), 621–39.

266 D. Napthine and W. A. Speck, 'Clergymen and conflict, 1600–1763', *Studies in Church History*, xx (1983), 241.

267 For a trenchant review of the latter, see T. C. W. Blanning, *The Origins of the French Revolutionary Wars* (London, 1986), ch. i.

268 M. Howard, *War and the Liberal Conscience* (London, 1978), p. 19; Hale, 'Explanations of war', *passim*.

269 Cited in Rabb, *Struggle for Stability*, p. 119. See also R. H. Cox, *Locke on War and Peace* (Oxford, 1960).

270 Livet, *Guerre et paix*, pp. 206–8; F. H. Hinsley, *Power and the Pursuit of Peace: Theory and Practice in the History of Relations between States* (Cambridge, 1963), chs 1, 2; J. A. Joyce (ed.), *Erasmus, Sully, Grotius: Three Peace Classics* (London, n.d.), pp. 10–12; M. G. de Molinari, *L'Abbé de Saint-Pierre* (Paris, 1857).

271 Howard, *Liberal Conscience*, pp. 16 (quotation) and 13–16 generally; P. Brock, *The Roots of War Resistance: Pacifism from the Early Church to Tolstoy* (Carmen Brock, Canada, 1981); J. C. Wenger, 'The Schleithem Confession of Faith', *Mennonite Quarterly Review*, xix (1945), 243–56 has a translation of the most notable statement of Anabaptist pacifism (arts. 4, 6). On Erasmus see J.-C. Margolin, *Guerre et paix dans la pensée d'Erasme* (Paris, 1973).

272 H. Bender, 'The pacifism of the sixteenth century Anabaptists', *Mennonite Quarterly Review*, xxx (1959), 5–6.

273 *Whether Soldiers Too Can Be Saved* (1526), *Works of Martin Luther* (5 vols, Philadelphia edn, 1943), v, p. 36.

274 'War, as an activity fit only for beasts, and yet practiced by no kind of beast so constantly as by man, they regard with utter loathing. Against the usage of almost all nations they count nothing so inglorious as glory sought in war': *Utopia*, ed. E. Surtz and J. H. Hexter, in *The Complete Works of Sir Thomas More* (15 vols, London, 1963–86), iv, pp. 199, 201, and 199–217 generally. Other writers who saw war as inglorious but inevitable were Rabelais and Montaigne.

275 J. T. Johnson, *Ideology, Reason and the Restraint of War: Religious and Secular Concepts* (Princeton, 1975), pt. iii; F. H.

Russell, *The Just War in the Middle Ages* (Cambridge, 1975).

276 *De Jure Belli ac Pacis Libri Tres*, in *The Classics of International Law*, ed. J. B. Scott (Oxford, 1925), p. 20, para. 28.

277 G. Bouthoul, *Les Guerres* (Paris, 1951), p. 278.

278 Hinsley, *Power*, p. 17.

279 E. Luard, *War in International Society* (London, 1986), p. 340.

280 For this reason Bodin, *Six livres de la république*, book 5, ch. v, p. 762, dubbed war 'une medicine purgative'. Thomas Barnes neatly coupled two arguments together. Since war was a punishment for sin, 'who better to taste it than the lewdest men, that most deserve it', and he urged recruiters 'to cleanse the city and rid the country as much as may be of those straggling vagrants, loytering fellowes and lewd livers...which doe so swarme amongst us': Hale, 'Incitement to violence?', p. 498.

281 The most notable author in this respect was Brantôme: *Vie des grands capitaines estrangers: Vie des grands capitaines français; Discours sur les couronnels de l'infanterie de France*, in *Oeuvres complètes de Pierre de Bourdeille, seigneur de Brantôme*, ed. L. Lalanne (11 vols, Paris, 1864–82), vols i-v.

282 *Whether Soldiers Too Can Be Saved* (1526), *Works*, v, pp. 36, 67; *The Magnificat* (1520–1), *Works*, iii, p. 175; *Secular Authority: To What Extent It Should Be Obeyed* (1523), *Works*, iii, p. 269–70.

283 *Institutes of the Christian Religion*, vols 20, 21 of the *Library of Christian Classics*, ed. J. T. McNeill (London, 1961), bk iv, ch xix, sections 11, 12.

284 Q. Skinner, *The Foundations of Modern Political Thought* (2 vols, Cambridge, 1978), ii, pt. iii.

285 Johnson, *Ideology*, pp. 119 (quotation) and 110–29 generally; Hale, 'Incitement to violence?', *passim*.

286 Johnson, *Ideology*, p. 128. Calvin urged that no restraint be shown when the honour of God was at stake: R. H. Bainton, *Christian Attitudes to War and Peace: A Historical Survey and Critical Re-evaluation* (Nashville, 1986), p. 145. But see the cautionary remarks in J. T. Johnson, *Just War Tradition and the Restraint of War* (Princeton, 1981), pp. 233–4.

287 See, for example, Vitoria's defence of the Indians and John Colet's sermon in the presence of Henry VIII against war with France: Johnson, *Ideology*, pp. 156–8; E. E. Reynolds, *Thomas More and Erasmus* (London, 1965), p. 83.

288 Johnson, *Ideology*, p. 144. See too the Jesuit, Ribadeneyra's, justification of the Armada: Elliott, *Imperial Spain*, p. 288.

289 See, for example, O. Ranum, *Paris in the Age of Absolutism* (London, 1968), pp. 132–4, 222 on the concerns of the noble leaders during the fronde. Essex spent two hours on his knees in front of Elizabeth begging for command of the French expedition: Lloyd, *Rouen Campaign*, p. 86.

290 *The Prince*, ed. Q. Skinner and R. Price (Cambridge, 1988), pp. 51–2.

291 R. W. Berger, *Versailles: The Château of Louis XIV* (Pennsylvania, 1985), p. 21.

292 'International relations in the West: diplomacy and war', *New Cambridge Modern History* (Cambridge, 1957), i, p. 261.

293 J. Israel, *The Dutch Republic and the Hispanic World, 1606–1661* (Oxford, 1982), pp. 234–6, 362–5; Klaits, *Printed Propaganda*, p. 31. Public opinion was particularly well developed in the United Provinces, in part because of the relative lack of government censorship. William Temple commented on 'The strange freedom that all men took, in boats, and inns, and all other common places, of talking openly whatever they thought upon all public affairs, both of their own state and their neighbours': Boxer, 'Second thoughts', p. 70.

294 J. H. Elliott, *Richelieu and Olivares* (Cambridge, 1984), pp. 128–9.

295 Klaits, *Printed Propaganda*, pp. 208–9.

296 ibid., p. 248.

297 ibid., p. 33.

298 E. A. Beller, 'The Thirty Years War', *The New Cambridge Modern History*, iv, p. 330.

299 Anderson, *War and Society*, p. 190.

SELECT BIBLIOGRAPHY

The literature on warfare is vast. A more extensive indication of the available reading is to be found in the notes section of this study and in the bibliographies and notes which appear in the general works below, notably those by Hale and Parker. Here I have listed only those works which I have found most useful, including some of the published sources. Volumes i to vi of the *New Cambridge Modern History* contain good chapters on armies and war by a number of authors, but in order to economize on space I have not cited them individually.

The place of publication for books in English is London and for books in French is Paris, unless otherwise indicated.

Published sources

Audley, T., 'A Treatise on the Art of War', in *Journal of the Society for Army Historical Research*, vi (1927), 65–78, 129–33.

Barker, T. M., *The Military Intellectual and Battle: Raimondo Montecuccoli and the Thirty Years War* (New York, 1975). Contains a translation of Montecuccoli's *Sulle Battaglie*.

Blackader, J., *The Life and Diary of Colonel John Blackader* (Edinburgh, 1824).

Dorney, J., *A Briefe and Exact Relation of the Military Government of Gloucester...* (1645), in J. Washbourn (ed.), *Bibliotheca Gloucestrensis* (1825).

Dubois, A., *Journal d'un curé de campagne au XVIIe siècle*, ed. H. Platelle (1965).

Gonzales, E., 'The Life of Estevanillo Gonzales, the most pleasantest and most diverting of all comical scoundrels', trans. J. S. Stevens in *The Spanish Libertines* (1707, first pub. Antwerp, 1646).

Monluc, Blaise de, *Commentaires de Messire Blaise de Monluc*, ed. P. Courteault (1964, first pub. Bordeaux, 1592).

Monro, R., *Monro, his Expedition with the Worthy Scots Regiment* (1637).

Noue, François de la, *Discours politiques et militaires*, intro. by F. E. Sutcliffe (1967, first pub. Geneva, 1587).

Salignac, Bertrand de, *Le Siège de Metz*, in *Nouvelle collection de mémoires pour servir à l'histoire de France*, ed. J. F. Michaud and J. J. F. Poujoulat (1838), 1st series, viii, 513–61.

Saulx, Gaspard de, *Les Mémoires de Gaspard de Saulx-Tavannes*, in *Nouvelle Collection de mémoires pour servir à l'histoire de France*, ed. J. F. Michaud and J. J. F. Poujoulat (Paris, 1838), 1st series, viii, 23–434.

Seyssel, Claude de, *La Monarchie de France*, ed. J. Poujol (1961, first pub. 1515).

Smythe, Sir John, *Certain Discourses Military*, ed. J. R. Hale (Ithaca, 1964, first pub. London, 1590).

Sutcliffe, M., *The Practice, Proceedings and Lawes of Armes described...* (1593).

Turner, J., *Pallas Armata: Military Essayes of the Ancient Grecian, Roman and Modern Art of War* (1683).

—— *Memoirs of his own Life and Times, 1632–1670* (Edinburgh, 1829).

Wharton, N., 'Letters from a Subaltern Officer', *Archaeologia*, 35 (1853), 310–34.

Williams, Sir Roger, *A Briefe Discourse of Warre* (1590) and *The Actions of the Lowe Countries* (1618), in J. X. Evans (ed.), *The Works of Sir Roger Williams* (Oxford, 1972).

Secondary works

Åberg, A., 'The Swedish army from Lützen to Narva', in M. Roberts (ed.), *Sweden's Age of Greatness, 1632–1718* (1973).

Anderson, M. S., *War and Society in Europe of the Old Regime, 1618–1789* (Leicester, 1988).

André, L., *Michel Le Tellier et l'organisation de l'armée monarchique* (1906).

Babeau, A., *La Vie militaire sous l'ancien régime* (2 vols, 1889–90).

Barrie-Curien, V., *Guerre et pouvoir en Europe au XVIIe siècle* (1991).

Baynard, F. and Dessert, D., 'Les finances dans l'état monarchique en guerre au XVIIe siècle', in E. Le Roy Ladurie (ed.), *Les Monarchies* (1986).

Benecke, G., *Germany in the Thirty Years War* (1978).

Benedict, P., *Rouen during the Wars of Religion* (Cambridge, 1980).

Berenger, J., *Finances et absolutisme autrichien dans la seconde moitié du XVIIe siècle* (2 vols, Université de Lille III, 1975).

Black, J. A., *A Military Revolution? Military Change and European Society, 1550–1800* (1991).

Bonney, R., *The King's Debts: Finance and Politics in France, 1589–1661* (Oxford, 1981).

Bouthoul, G., *Les Guerres* (1951).

Brewer, J., *The Sinews of Power: War, Money and the English State, 1688–1783* (1989).

Chaboche, R., 'Les soldats français de la guerre de trente ans', *Revue d'histoire moderne et contemporaine*, xx (1973), 10–24.

Chandler, D., *The Art of Warfare in the Age of Marlborough* (1976).

Corvisier, A., *L'Armée française de la fin du XVIIe siècle au ministère de Choiseul: le soldat* (2 vols, 1964).

—— *Armies and Societies in Europe, 1494–1789* (Bloomington, 1979).

—— *Louvois* (1983)

Creveld, M. van, *Supplying War: Logistics from Wallenstein to Patton* (Cambridge, 1977).

Dickson, P. G. M. and Sperling, J., 'War finance, 1689–1714', in *The New Cambridge Modern History* (Cambridge, 1970), iv, 284–315.

Duffy, C., *Siege Warfare* (2 vols, 1979, 1985).

Duke, A. C. and Tamse, C. A., *Britain and the Netherlands*, vol. vi, *War and Society: Papers delivered for the Sixth Anglo-Dutch Historical Conference* (The Hague, 1977).

Dupuy, R. E. and T. N., *The Encyclopedia of Military History: from 3500 BC to the Present* (1970).

Earle, E. M. (ed.), *Makers of Modern Strategy* (Princeton, 1944).

Ehrenberg, R., *Capital and Finance in the Age of the Renaissance* (1928).

Feld, M. D., 'Middle-class society and the rise of military professionalism: the Dutch army, 1589–1609', *Armed Forces and Society*, i (1975), 419–42.

Franz, G., *Der Dreissigjährige Krieg und das deutsche Volk* (Stuttgart, 1961).

Friedrichs, C. R., *Urban Society in an Age of War: Nördlingen, 1580–1720* (Princeton, 1979).

Goring, J., 'Social change and military decline in mid-Tudor England', *History*, 60 (1975), 185–97.

Guillermand, J., *Histoire de la médecine aux armées*, vol. i, *De l'antiquité à la révolution* (1982).

Gutmann, M. P., *War and Rural Life in the Early Modern Low Countries* (Princeton, 1980).

Hahlweg, W., *Die Heeresreform der Oranier und die Antike* (Berlin, 1941).

Hale, J. R., *Renaissance War Studies* (1983). Reprints many of his most important articles on war.

—— *War and Society in Renaissance Europe, 1450–1620* (1985).

Hughes, B. P., *Firepower Weapons' Effectiveness on the Battlefield, 1630–1850* (1974).

Hughes, Q., *Military Architecture* (1974).

Jespersen, L., 'The *Machstaat* in seventeenth-century Denmark', *Scandinavian Journal of History*, x (1985), 271–304.

Johnson, J. T., *Ideology, Reason and the Limitation of War: Religious and Secular Concepts* (Princeton, 1975).

Jones, C., 'The welfare of the French foot soldier', *History*, 65 (1980), 193–213.

Kennedy, P., *The Rise and Fall of the Great Powers: Economic Change and Military Conflict from 1500 to 2000* (1988).

Langer, H., *The Thirty Years War* (Poole, 1982).

Lindegren, J., *Utskrivning och utsugning. Produktion och reproduktion i Bygdeå, 1620–1640* (Uppsala, 1980: Studia Historica Upsaliensia, cxvii).

—— 'The Swedish "Military State", 1560–1720', *Scandinavian Journal of History*, x (1985), 305–36.

Lloyd, H. A., *The Rouen Campaign, 1590–1592: Politics, Warfare and the Early Modern State* (Oxford, 1973).

Lot, F., *Recherches sur les effectifs des armées françaises des guerres d'Italie aux guerres de religion, 1494–1562* (1962).

Mallet, M. E. and Hale, J. R., *The Military Organization of a Renaissance State: Venice c. 1400 to 1617* (Cambridge, 1984).

Nickle, B. H., *The Military Reforms of Prince Maurice of Orange* (Michigan, 1984).

Paret, P., *Makers of Modern Strategy* (1986).

Parker, G., *The Army of Flanders and the Spanish Road, 1567–1659. The Logistics of Spanish Victory and Defeat in the Low Countries* (Cambridge, 1972).

—— 'The emergence of modern finance in Europe, 1500–1730', in C. Cipolla (ed.), *The Fontana Economic History of Europe* (6 vols, 1977), ii, 527–94.

—— *The Thirty Years War* (1987)

—— *The Military Revolution: Military Innovation and the Rise of the West* (Cambridge, 1988).

Parrott, D. A., 'Strategy and tactics in the Thirty Years War: the "Military Revolution"', *Militärgeschichtliche Mitteilungen*, 18 (1985), 7–25.

—— 'The administration of the French army during the ministry of Cardinal Richelieu' (Unpublished DPhil thesis, Oxford, 1985).

Pepper, S. and Adams, N., *Firearms and Fortifications: Military Architecture and Siege Warfare in Sixteenth Century Siena* (Chicago, 1986).

Perjeés, G., 'Army provisioning, logistics and strategy in the second half of the seventeenth century', *Acta Historica Academiae Scientarium Hungaricae*, 16 (1970).

Pieri, P., 'L'evoluzione dell'arte militare nei secoli XV, XVI e XVII e la guerra del secolo XVIII', in *Nuove Questioni di Storia Moderna* (2 vols, Milan, 1966), ii, 1123–79.

Redlich, F., *The German Military Enterpriser and his Workforce, 13th to 17th Centuries* (Wiesbaden, 1964: *Vierteljahrschrift für Sozial- und Wirthschaftsgeschichte*, Beiheft, 2 vols).

Roberts, M., *Gustavus Adolphus: A History of Sweden, 1611–1632* (2 vols, 1953, 1958).

—— *Essays in Swedish History* (1967)

Russell, C., 'Monarchies, wars and estates in England, France and Spain, c. 1580–c. 1640', *Legislative Studies Quarterly*, vii (1982), 205–20.

Saluces, A. de, *Histoire militaire de Piémont* (5 vols, Turin, 1859).

Scouller, R. E., *The Armies of Queen Anne* (Oxford, 1966).

Sella, D., *Crisis and Continuity: The Economy of Spanish Lombardy in the Seventeenth Century* (1979).

Silberner, E., *La Guerre dans la pensée économique du XVIe au XVIIIe siècle* (1939)

Thoen, E. 'Warfare and the countryside: social and economic aspects of the military destruction in Flanders during the late Middle Ages and the early modern period', *Acta Historiae Neerlandicae*, xiii (1980), 25–39.

Thompson, I. A. A., *War and Government in Habsburg Spain, 1560–1620* (1976).

Tilly, C., *The Formation of National States in Western Europe* (Princeton, 1975).

Tracy, J. D., *A Financial Revolution in the Habsburg Netherlands: Renten and Renteniers in the County of Holland, 1515–1565* (1985).

XVIIe Siècle, 148 (1985) which is devoted to articles on the theme of *Présence de la guerre au XVIIe siècle*.

INDEX